Still

a House

Divided

PRINCETON STUDIES IN AMERICAN POLITICS:
HISTORICAL, INTERNATIONAL, AND COMPARATIVE PERSPECTIVES

Ira Katznelson, Martin Shefter, and Theda Skocpol,
Series Editors

A list of titles in this series appears at the back of the book

Desmond S. King & Rogers M. Smith

Still
a House
Divided

Race and Politics in Obama's America

PRINCETON UNIVERSITY PRESS • PRINCETON AND OXFORD

Library of Congress Cataloging-in-Publication Data

King, Desmond S.
Still a house divided : race and politics in Obama's America /
Desmond S. King and Rogers M. Smith.
p.   cm.—
(Princeton studies in American politics: historical, international,
and comparative perspectives)
Includes bibliographical references and index.
ISBN 978-0-691-14263-0 (hardcover : alk. paper)   1. African Americans—
Politics and government.   2. United States—Race relations—Political
aspects—History.   3. United States—Politics and government—2008–
I. Smith, Rogers M., 1953–   II. Title.
E185.615.K485 2011
323.1196'073—dc23   2011021702

British Library Cataloging-in-Publication Data is available

This book has been composed in Electra Std

Designed by Marcella Engel Roberts

Printed on acid-free paper. ∞

Printed in the United States of America

1   3   5   7   9   10   8   6   4   2

Contents

List of Figures and Tables   vii
Acknowledgments   ix

PART ONE
Obama's Inheritance

CHAPTER 1 "That They May All Be One"
America as a House Divided   3

PART TWO
The Making and Unmaking of Racial Hierarchies

CHAPTER 2 "That is the last speech he will ever make"
The Antebellum Racial Alliances   35

CHAPTER 3 "We of the North were thoroughly wrong"
How Racial Alliances Mobilized Ideas and Law   62

PART THREE
The Trajectory of Racial Alliances

CHAPTER 4 "This backdrop of entrenched inequality"
Affirmative Action in Work   93

CHAPTER 5 To "affirmatively further fair housing"
Enduring Racial Inequalities in American Homes and Mortgages   137

CHAPTER 6 "To Elect One of Their Own"
Racial Alliances and Majority-Minority Districts   168

CHAPTER 7 "Our goal is to have one classification—American"
Vouchers for Schools and the Multiracial Census   192

CHAPTER 8 "We can take the people out of the slums,
    but we cannot take the slums out of the people"
*How Today's Racial Alliances Shape Laws on
    Crime and Immigration*   215

Contents

PART FOUR
America's Inheritance

CHAPTER 9 Prospects of the House Divided   253

Notes   293
Index   349

List of Figures and Tables

FIGURES

Figure 2.1. Roll Call Votes Related to Slavery Issues in the
House of Representatives   42

Figure 2.2. Roll Call Votes Related to Slavery Issues in the
U.S. Senate   43

Figure 2.3. Regional Membership in the U.S. House of
Representatives   44

Figure 2.4. Alliances Initiating Slavery Votes in the
U.S. House of Representatives   44

Figure 2.5. Voting Consistency of U.S. House Members on
Slavery Issues during the Antebellum Period   45

TABLES

Table 2.1. Pro-slavery Alliance, 1787–1865   39

Table 2.2. Anti-slavery Alliance, 1787–1865   41

Table 3.1. Pro–Jim Crow Racial Alliance, 1896–1954   65

Table 3.2. Anti–Jim Crow Racial Alliance, 1896–1954   68

Table 4.1. Color-Blind Alliance Opposed to Affirmative
Action in Employment, 1978–2008   117

Table 4.2. Race-Conscious Alliance Supporting Affirmative
Action in Employment, 1978–2008   118

Table 5.1. Federal Government, Housing Equity, and Race,
1933–78   145

Table 5.2. Alliance for Color-Blind Housing Policies, 1978–2008   154

Table 5.3. Alliance for Race-Conscious Egalitarian Housing
Policies, 1978–2008   155

Table 5.4. Housing and Mortgage Policy Developments in the
Era of Modern Racial Alliances, 1983–2003   164

Table 6.1. Color-Blind Alliance, 1978–2008:
Anti-Majority-Minority Districts   177

Table 6.2. Race-Conscious Alliance, 1978–2008:
Pro-Majority-Minority Districts   178

Table 6.3. "Unholy Alliances" in States Creating New
Majority-Minority Districts, 1990–92   183

Figures and Tables

Table 7.1.   Color-Blind Alliance, 1978–2008: Pro-vouchers   198
Table 7.2.   Race-Conscious Alliance, 1978–2008: Anti-vouchers   200
Table 7.3.   Color-Blind Alliance, 1978–2008: Pro–Mixed Race
             Census Category (1990–2008)   209
Table 7.4.   Race-Conscious Alliance, 1978–2008: Anti–Mixed
             Race Census Category (1990–2008)   210
Table 8.1.   Color-Blind Alliance, 1978–2008: Punitive Criminal
             Justice Policies   224
Table 8.2.   Race-Conscious Alliance, 1978–2008: Preventive and
             Rehabilitative Criminal Justice Policies   225
Table 8.3.   Color-Blind / Social Conservative / Native Black "Strange
             Bedfellows": For Reducing Immigration   241
Table 8.4.   Race-Conscious / Libertarian / Economic Conservative
             "Strange Bedfellows": Against Reducing Immigration   242
Table 8.5.   Against Full Social and Civil Rights for Immigrants:
             Includes Most of Color-Blind Alliance, 1978–2008   243
Table 8.6.   For Full Social and Civil Rights for Immigrants:
             Includes Most of Race-Conscious Alliance, 1978–2008   244
Table 9.1.   Color-Blind Alliance, 1978–2008   259
Table 9.2.   Race-Conscious Alliance, 1978–2008   261
Table 9.3.   Black and Latino Legislators, National and State,
             1940–2009   270
Table 9.4.   Blacks in Selected Professions, 1940–2008   271
Table 9.5.   Percent High School Diploma or Higher, 1940–2009   272
Table 9.6.   Percent Bachelor's Degrees or Higher, 1940–2009   273
Table 9.7.   Percent High School Dropouts, 1970–2008   273
Table 9.8.   Percent Students in Predominantly Minority Schools   274
Table 9.9.   Median Income of Individuals, 1950–2009
             (Constant 2009 Dollars)   275
Table 9.10. Median Income of Households, 1970–2009
             (Constant 2009 Dollars)   276
Table 9.11. Median Net Worth of Families, 1983–2007
             (Thousands of 2007 Dollars)   277
Table 9.12. Unemployment Rates, 1980–2007   278
Table 9.13. Number of Persons under Correctional
             Supervision, 1990–2008   279

Acknowledgments

Eight years ago, we began collaborating on what became a series of articles that have now culminated in this book. We started because we found we shared dissatisfactions with the way that issues of race were addressed, or more often not addressed, in much of the political science literature on American politics and American political development. This book builds on our initial thoughts, but it also represents substantial learning and rethinking along the way. In our earlier work, we leaned heavily toward one side of the current racial policy debate. Here, without altering our motivating commitments, we are more critical of both sides. Our current positions, like those in our previous publications, emerged from so many discussions that we cannot assign individual responsibility for them. We also have each worked extensively on every chapter, so there is no need and no way to parse contributions. The order of the authors' names in all our collaborations simply reflects who initiated the project. In this case, Desmond King insisted it was time we did a book. As in his wine selections and in his constant vigilance against unneeded adverbs, he was right. Conversely, responsibility for any remaining superfluous modifiers falls to Rogers Smith. All other blame we share equally.

Our arguments have evolved in part because of the excellent and generous critical feedback we have received along the way, including the comments of the anonymous readers of this book and our previous published papers. We have presented the preceding articles and portions of this book to far too many academic audiences to detail our debts to them. They have included conference, panel, seminar and workshop participants at several annual meetings of the American Political Science Association, the Bologna Center of Johns Hopkins University, the European University Institute, Harvard University, Monmouth University, Princeton University, Sciences Po, Skidmore College, Temple University, UC Berkeley, University of Notre Dame, University of Oregon, University of Pennsylvania, UC Santa Barbara, University of Southern Denmark, Odense, Washington University, Wayne State University, and Yale University, among other venues. We are particularly indebted for often critical but always perceptive comments in these and other locales from Christopher Achen, Larry Bartels, Lawrence Bobo, Alan Brinkley, Kevin Bruyneel, Cathy Cohen, Paul Frymer, Lisa García Bedolla, Jane Gordon, Marie Gottschalk, Michael Graetz, Michael Hagen, Victoria Hattam, Jennifer Hochschild, David Hollinger, Kimberley Johnson, Richard Johnston, Ira Katznelson, Philip

Acknowledgments

Klinkner, John Lapinski, Matthew Levendusky, Robert Lieberman, Joseph Lowndes, Sidney Milkis, Naomi Murakawa, Anne Norton, Julie Novkov, Adolph Reed, Dorothy Roberts, Peter Schuck, Ronald Seyb, Ian Shapiro, Stephen Skowronek, John Skrentny, Mary Summers, Stephen Tuck, Richard Valelly, Nancy Wadsworth, Dorian Warren, Vesla Weaver, Margaret Weir, Justin Wert, Howard Winant, and Christopher Wlezien. Rogers Smith subjected students in several iterations of his undergraduate "Race, Ethnicity, and American Constitutional Law" seminar to portions of our work in progress, and the work benefited, whether or not the students did. We have also been aided by superb research assistance over the years from Willie Gin, Alexandra J. Gold, Ryan Levan, Jennifer Stepp, Stephan Stohler, Timothy Weaver, and Kahlil Williams. At Princeton University Press, we are enormously appreciative of our editor Chuck Myers for his support and comments on the project. His commitment to it has been gratifying. We are also grateful to Chuck's colleagues, including Julia Livingston, for ensuring a smooth transition into print.

We are particularly grateful to our families, who put up with our traversing the globe over a period of years so that we could rendezvous to work, without creating houses divided; and especially to Mary Summers, for tolerating several extended work sessions in Philadelphia. Our families also provided wonderful reasons to cease work from time to time.

In that spirit, Desmond King dedicates this book to Samuel King, whose young political awareness keenly observes the White House of Barack Obama. Rogers Smith dedicates the book to Reed Smith, who has grasped from an early age what it means to struggle for true equality and who displays so well the strength of heart and mind needed to succeed.

PART ONE

Obama's Inheritance

Chapter 1

"That They May All Be One"
America as a House Divided

The United Church of Christ takes as its motto John 17:21, "That They May All Be One." The UCC was created in 1957 through the union of the Congregational Christian Churches with the Evangelical and Reformed Church.[1] Its theological roots are in the Calvinism of the early New England Puritans and Congregationalists who did so much to shape American political culture. As with its Congregationalist forebears, all its local churches have autonomy in matters of doctrine and ministry, so that the UCC describes itself as a pluralistic and diverse denomination that strives to achieve "unity within its diversity."[2]

The quest for such unity amidst diversity runs deeply through American history. On the birthday of the nation, July 4, 1776, the Continental Congress authorized a committee comprising John Adams, Benjamin Franklin, and Thomas Jefferson to recommend a design for a Great Seal of the United States, then declaring their independence. The committee proposed as the seal's national motto a similar phrase: "E Pluribus Unum"—"Out of many, one."[3]

The leaders of America's founding generation knew well that of all the challenges they faced, slavery and racial equality most profoundly threatened their efforts to make the aspiration expressed in the new national motto a reality. In response, many strove mightily in ensuing years to keep those issues as remote from the national agenda as possible. But four score and two years later, an Illinois lawyer with high political aspirations, Abraham Lincoln, invoked a different biblical passage, Matthew 12:25, to argue that when it came to slavery, policies of evasion and compromise could not long endure: "a house divided against itself cannot stand."

After he did so, the American house did indeed break apart in a massive civil war. At its end, the United States purged slavery throughout the land by constitutional amendment. Still, convulsive issues of racial policy and racial equality remained. Nearly a century later, when the United Church of Christ was created, Congress was in the throes of passing the 1957 Civil Rights Act, its first major civil rights law since the Reconstruction era that followed the Civil War—thereby beginning the legislative triumphs of what some scholars call the "Second Reconstruction." Once again, Americans hoped they were at last finding the means to create unity out of their diversity, building a nation that, at least in regard to race, would no longer be a house divided.

But over a half century later, during the historic election year of 2008, when the Democratic Party appeared to be moving toward nominating a candidate who symbolized just such change, hopes for unity on matters of race within the United Church of Christ and among all Americans were disrupted by an unlikely source. At the time of the founding of the UCC, an African American teenager known as Jerry Wright Jr. was a student at predominantly white Central High, one of the most prestigious public schools in Philadelphia, the city where the Continental Congress met in 1776. Wright had grown up in Philadelphia's Germantown section, in the neighborhoods where the American anti-slavery movement had begun with the 1688 Germantown Quaker Petition Against Slavery; where the Continental Army had fought the British; and where twentieth-century Philadelphians had achieved one of the few examples of relatively sustained, successful racial integration in modern urban America.[4] Wright's father was the pastor at Grace Baptist Church in Germantown. His mother was the first African American to teach at Germantown High and the Philadelphia High School for Girls. When Jerry Wright graduated from Central High in 1959, the yearbook description read, "Always ready with a kind word, Jerry is one of the most congenial members" of the class and a "model" for younger students.[5] Wright then studied at Virginia Union University, but left to join the U.S. Marines and after two years went on to the navy, where he became a cardiopulmonary technician assigned to care for President Lyndon Johnson during his 1966 surgery. There are reports that Wright dabbled with "liquor, Islam, and black nationalism" during these years.[6] But he returned to college in Washington and to his Christian faith, graduating from Howard University, then obtaining a master's degree from the University of Chicago Divinity School, and finally earning many years later a doctor of ministry degree from the United Theological Seminary in Dayton, Ohio, where he studied with Samuel DeWitt Proctor, a mentor to Martin Luther King Jr.[7]

By then, Wright was the pastor at Trinity United Church of Christ in Chicago. When he joined the church in 1972, the congregation had only 250 members, with less than half actively involved. Under Wright's leadership, Trinity United grew to become a mega-church of over 8,000 members, the largest of the more than five thousand congregations in the United Church of Christ.[8] And there were few that Jerry Wright, now known as Dr. Jeremiah Wright Jr., touched more than another Illinois lawyer with political ambitions, one with a complex religious, national, and racial heritage and the unusual name of Barack Obama. That young man would soon make E Pluribus Unum, the nation's version of the UCC motto, the central theme of a political career that in an astonishingly short time would take him to the presidency. In his first book, Obama wrote eloquently of experiencing Reverend Wright's and Trinity Church's capacities "to hold together, if not reconcile, the conflicting strains of black experience" in support of a faith that "carried within it, nascent, incomplete, the possibility of moving beyond our narrow dreams." Those experiences led him to join the church.

Obama's subsequent political rise was, however, almost fatally punctured during the 2008 campaign by the words of Reverend Wright, a man whose life might otherwise be seen to embody all that has been good in regard to race in America. And Obama's much-praised response to that controversy, powerful though it was, nonetheless revealed the difficulties even this pathbreaking figure displays in defining a clear way forward toward racial progress in twenty-first-century America.

Although the United Church of Christ has always been largely white, Reverend Wright, in accord with the freedom the denomination provides its member churches, built its largest congregation among Chicago's black community. Wright drew on black liberation theology, modern Christian perspectives most elaborated by Union Theological Seminary professor James Hal Cone. Influenced by liberal Protestant theologian Paul Tillich's contention that theological insights always emerge from and reflect particular cultural contexts, Cone has long argued for interpreting Christianity in light of the experiences of African American oppression.[9] In explicit agreement with Cone's ideas, Wright came over time to identify himself with what he termed the "prophetic tradition of the black church." In Wright's view, that tradition traces back to Isaiah 61:1 and to the message that "the prophet is to preach the gospel to the poor and to set at liberty those who are held captive," an action that also "liberates those who are holding them captive."[10] It was precisely because Obama, who was raised by a mother and grandparents who were religious skeptics, came to be persuaded of "the power of the African American religious tradition to spur social change," instead of requiring him "to suspend critical thinking, disengage from the battle for economic and social justice," that he chose to be baptized at Trinity. He then used the text of one of Reverend Wright's sermons as the title of The Audacity of Hope, the book of political positions with which he launched his presidential campaign.[11]

But on March 13, 2008, ABC News sparked off a furor by reporting on sermons Wright gave in 2001 and 2003 that said America had supported state terrorism, so the 9/11 attacks represented America's chickens "coming home to roost," and averring that instead of singing "God Bless America," the sentiment should be "God damn America for treating our citizens as less than human."[12] Five days later, Obama responded to the controversy by delivering a speech at the National Constitution Center in Philadelphia. Entitled "A More Perfect Union," the talk was his most extended discussion of race while a presidential candidate or, thus far, as president.

In his Philadelphia speech, Obama stressed that he had "brothers, sisters, nieces, nephews, uncles and cousins, of every race and every hue, scattered across three continents" and so had "seared into my genetic makeup the idea that this nation is more than the sum of its parts—that out of many, we are truly one."[13] He also "condemned, in unequivocal terms, the statements of Reverend Wright that have caused such controversy." But Obama went on to praise Wright's record of military and social service and religious leadership. He suggested that the fact that so many white Americans were surprised to hear Reverend Wright speaking of America like a fiery Old Testament prophet denouncing the corruption of the rich and powerful confirmed the "truism," often identified with a 1963 statement of Martin Luther King that "the most segregated hour in American life occurs on Sunday morning."[14]

Obama then sought to put Wright's views in the context we examine in this book: the pervasiveness of racial "inequalities passed on from an earlier generation that suffered under the brutal legacy of slavery and Jim Crow," producing segregated schools that "were, and are, inferior schools" providing "inferior education" to blacks; legalized discrimination that long prevented blacks from owning property or obtaining loans or mortgages, or jobs in "unions, or the police force, or the fire departments," thereby creating an enduring "wealth and income gap between black and white"; a "lack of economic opportunity among black men" that "may have" been worsened by "welfare policies" and that "contributed to the erosion of black families"; and a "lack of basic services in so many urban black neighborhoods."[15] For many like Rev. Wright, Obama argued, that past and present generated an "anger and bitterness" that all too often "distracts attention from solving real problems" and "prevents the African-American community from forging the alliances it needs to bring about real change." But Obama insisted that to condemn this anger "without understanding its roots, only serves to widen the chasm of misunderstanding that exists between the races."[16]

Obama went on to express his grasp of the "similar anger" among whites who "don't feel that they have been particularly privileged by their race," an anger that "helped forge the Reagan Coalition," an anger that was often "counterproductive" but that should not be simply dismissed as "misguided or even racist." He saw the anger and distrust on both sides, and the ways that the

6

"anger is exploited by politicians," as fostering "a racial stalemate we've been stuck in for years." The way "to continue on the path of a more perfect union," Obama then argued, was for blacks to bind "our particular grievances—for better health care, and better schools, and better jobs—to the larger aspirations of all Americans," and for "the white community" to recognize that "the legacy of discrimination—and current incidents of discrimination, while less overt than in the past—are real and must be addressed" by investing in schools, by "enforcing our civil rights laws and ensuring fairness in our criminal justice system," and by providing all Americans with "ladders of opportunity."[17]

This thoughtful speech—and Obama's firm distancing of himself from Reverend Wright's views, culminating in the candidate's resignation from the Trinity congregation—lifted Obama's campaign past the uproar.[18] His interpretation of the polarization, misunderstanding, and mistrust between white and black Americans, leaving the nation "stuck" in "racial stalemate," resembles in many ways the portrait we paint here—one of a modern American house still divided between what we term rival "racial policy alliances." Yet from our perspective, Obama did not do enough, then, before, or since, to explain the conflictive, gridlocked structure of modern American racial politics or to spell out the implications of this structure for prospects of racial progress.

Obama's account stresses the understandable if often misguided popular anger and the frequently opportunistic political leadership on race among both whites and blacks in America. But by focusing on the *feelings* of blacks and whites, Obama failed to explain how modern American politics has come to be shaped by rival coalitions of political actors and institutions (each including some members of all races), whose members take opposed *policy* positions on a wide range of issues that they perceive as having racial dimensions.

One coalition contends that laws and policies should be crafted in as "colorblind" fashion as possible, treating people as individuals without reference to their racial identities. The other coalition insists that laws and policies should be made with constant, conscious concern to reduce severe racial inequalities in different arenas of American life.

Because Obama did not refer to these policy choices, much less the arguments for and against them, he left much unclear. He did not make it evident to white Americans how and why a man like Reverend Jeremiah Wright—a man who had in many ways experienced American race relations at their best, a man who had given his nation extended military service and who had gone on to extraordinary achievements and recognition in the nation's oldest, in many respects most quintessentially American, and predominantly white denomination —could see an America espousing color-blind policies as one that continues to impose obstacles to racial progress. Obama also did not explain to African Americans why many whites, in turn, perceived an anti-American and anti-white "reverse racism" in the race-conscious rhetoric of a man that many black Christians saw as carrying forward the historical social justice ministry of their religious traditions.

Most importantly, Obama's advice to what he termed the nation's African American and white communities offered few clues about how the modern philosophical and policy conflicts over race should be resolved—though his call to black Americans to link their grievances to those of "all Americans," along with his exhortation to whites to accept public investment, enforcement of civil rights laws, and fairness in the criminal justice system, leaned rhetorically toward the color-blind camp. Given the structure of contemporary American racial politics that we document in this book, probably no serious candidate for national office could be expected to do much differently, least of all one commonly identified and self-identified as black—for color-blind positions are far more popular than race-conscious ones among the nation's still predominantly white electorate. But understandable as Obama's stance was, it contained few insights into the policy challenges racial inequalities pose in modern America, and it offered few clues about the political guidance needed to move further toward their resolution.

We undertook this book in order to understand those challenges and to analyze how they might be better addressed. In this opening chapter, we first sketch the main lessons we have learned. Then we elaborate our core concept of rival racial policy alliances. Finally, we explain how the subsequent chapters use the idea of alliances to analyze the evolution of American racial politics historically, and the ways today's racial alliances shape and often distort decision making across a wide range of modern policy arenas.

Overview: The Structure of American Racial Politics and Why It Matters

The first lesson we draw is an empirical one. American racial politics has historically been structured via three evolving systems of opposed "racial policy alliances"—coalitions of leading political figures, governing institutions they have occupied, and other politically active groups—competing against each other in multiple arenas for the support of the broader political community in resolving the great "battleground" issues that have defined three eras of American racial history. From the Revolutionary era through the Civil War, the "slavery era," pro-slavery and anti-slavery alliances confronted each other, initially with the coalition favoring slavery greatly in the ascendant, but with anti-slavery support gathering over time—sufficient to spark the South's secession after Lincoln's election. The ensuing war led to the final resolution of the slavery issue by the Thirteenth Amendment in 1865. The new battleground issue then became the civic status of newly freed African Americans. After a transitional period of struggle extending through the late nineteenth century, one in which racial egalitarians at first won some major constitutional and statutory victories and white supremacists lacked a clear program, the egalitarians lost ground. A rival racial policy alliance that favored a new, thinly veiled form of institutionalized white supremacy—Jim Crow segregation and disfranchisement laws—prevailed. Battles between pro-segregation and anti-segregation racial policy alliances continued through the resulting "Jim Crow era" up to the mid-1960s, this time with anti-segregation forces gradually gaining power.

These forces gathered sufficient strength, expressed first in the 1954 *Brown v. Board of Education* decision, then the 1964 Civil Rights Act, and then the 1965 Voting Rights Act, to repudiate Jim Crow policies of segregation, discrimination, and disfranchisement definitively.[19] Yet soon, new racial issues emerged once again. Over the next decade, those issues came to center on whether policymaking should be as color-blind as possible, or whether measures should be designed and implemented with specific goals of racial equality in view. The resulting clash of rival "color-blind" and "race-conscious" racial policy alliances has produced what we term the modern "race-conscious" era in American racial politics. Many scholars and citizens might describe it as the "affirmative action" era, but we will see that quarrels over how "race-conscious" policies should be extend well beyond conflicts over affirmative action programs. Indeed, some modern civil rights activists who sharply criticize color-blind approaches and urge that we "pay careful attention to the impact of our laws, policies, and practices on racial and ethnic groups" criticize reliance on formal affirmative action programs without attention to the racial consequences of other policies.[20]

Both sides of this debate have long presented themselves as the true heirs of the preceding, triumphant civil rights movement. *Color-blind* advocates contend that they stand for judging people not on the color of their skin but on the content of their character, as the Reverend Martin Luther King Jr. called for in his 1963 "I have a dream" speech that culminated the March on Washington. *Race-conscious* proponents maintain that they stand for cashing America's "promissory note" to give the nation's racial minorities "the riches of freedom and the security of justice," as King also called for in that speech.[21] We believe that this modern rivalry between color-blind and race-conscious policy alliances emerged fully by roughly 1978, the time of the Supreme Court's *University of California Board of Regents v. Bakke* ruling on race-conscious admissions policies in higher education, which came in mutually reinforcing tandem with the anti-tax uprisings in California and other states that year, movements fueled in part by perceptions that public funds were being directed to undeserving nonwhites.[22] Contests between these two opposed racial policy alliances have had sweeping effects, some obvious, but many less apparent, on American politics ever since. It is these pervasively consequential modern policy disputes that Barack Obama failed to identify, much less discuss, in his 2008 speech on race.

Why not? Precisely because issues of racial policy have always threatened American hopes for unity, leaders seeking broad political support have long found it difficult to raise them in election campaigns. Even so, the second major lesson of our research is that the place of today's racial policy alliances in American politics is different from that of their predecessors through most of U.S. history.

Apart from the years immediately before and after the Civil War when Lincoln Republicans opposed Democrats on slavery and racial questions, the nation's two major parties have usually been too internally divided on racial policies to take strong stands against each other on those issues. The racial policy alliances have instead usually cut across party lines. There were pro-slavery and anti-slavery Federalists and Whigs, on the one hand, and pro-slavery and anti-slavery Jeffersonian Republicans and Jacksonian Democrats, on the other, even though the Jeffersonians and Jacksonians leaned more strongly toward support of slavery. Similarly, there were pro– and anti–Jim Crow Republicans and Democrats through the first two-thirds of the twentieth century, though anti–Jim Crow Democrats did not emerge as a force in American politics until after 1930. With the parties internally divided, their leaders usually sought to compromise on racial issues, with each other and with their internal factions, rather than to push for decisive resolution of the central racial questions of their day one way or the other. The result was that both slavery and Jim Crow laws persisted for many decades, until changing circumstances compelled political leaders to concede they were sustainable no more.[23]

In contrast, since the 1970s, today's racial policy alliances have become more and more fully identified with the two major parties. Every Republican Party platform since 1972 has denounced racial "quotas," and from 1980 on the party has professed commitments to color-blind policy approaches across the issue board. Every Democratic Party platform since 1972 has instead explicitly expressed support for some, often many, forms of racial "affirmative action" and other types of race-conscious policymaking, in employment, education, housing, legislative districting, criminal justice practices, and much more.[24] We will see that today's racial alliances are nonetheless not fully identical to today's political parties. They also are not fully equivalent to today's economic alignments. There are some Republicans like Colin Powell who openly support racial affirmative action, some Democrats like Senator James Webb who openly oppose it, just as there are businesses and labor unions on both sides of the issue and other modern racial controversies.[25] That is one reason why it is important to recognize the existence and impacts of today's racial policy alliances: they play a role that cannot be fully understood in terms of partisan and economic interests.

Even so, today's alliances are more fully identified with the two rival parties, and with opposing economic ideologies, than at any time in U.S. history since the Republicans championed free labor and opposed the extension of slavery into the territories, and the Democrats defended slaveholders. These reinforcing alignments on racial, partisan, and economic positions matter enormously. In the late 1850s, when the racial alliances came to be identified with the two major parties, the result was a national cataclysm. Today, more than some scholars recognize, this overlay of opposing parties, opposing economic ideologies, and opposing racial alliances has contributed to the heightened polarization that wrenches apart modern American politics.[26]

It has done so, however, with a bitter difference. When American political parties and political leaders sought to compromise and evade issues of slavery and Jim Crow racial segregation, they were seeking to avoid confronting injustices with which there should have been no compromise. Today, those past American leaders who supported concessions to proponents of racial inequality, like Senators Henry Clay and Stephen Douglas in the antebellum years, and Justices Joseph Bradley and President Woodrow Wilson in the late nineteenth and early twentieth century, are widely seen as having acted shamefully. It is the Americans who stood fast against slavery's spread like Abraham Lincoln and against segregation like Martin Luther King Jr. who are now iconic symbols of the politics of moral principle.

Yet partly as a result, today proponents of both color-blind and race-conscious policies have drawn the wrong lesson from this history. They see themselves as just such champions of principle, and they often imply that today, as in the past, compromises with their opponents would be immoral. Some on each side charge that despite the members of the rival alliance's professed allegiance to the modern civil rights movement, their positions are racist.[27] In consequence, as political scientist Jennifer Hochschild noted over a decade ago, "both supporters and opponents of affirmative action," a term she uses for much of what we call race-conscious policymaking, "are passionately committed to

11

their perspectives and concede no moral legitimacy to the other side."[28] This dogmatism holds despite the fact that "the evidence does not warrant immovable commitment on either side."[29] And the evidence is limited: the literature on color-blind and race-conscious policies displays extensive philosophical and polemical argumentation but much less rigorous empirical research.[30] Hochschild believes that this limited focus on empirical evidence in debates over racial policies is no accident. She contends that "affirmative action is more important to participants in the policy debate as a weapon with which to attack enemies . . . than as an issue in and for itself." She explains that to be "useful as a weapon, affirmative action must remain at the level of moral claims and single-dimensional outrage; the messy and complex realities that are likely to surface in careful empirical analyses do not help much."[31]

Hochschild's formulation may be overstated. We believe that most participants in the political debate over color-blind versus race-conscious policies are expressing deep, sincere, and understandable disagreements over genuinely difficult questions of how and how far persisting material racial inequalities can best be addressed. Nonetheless, the modern clash over racial issues is a political debate in which policy alliances have been built through each side presenting its preferred racial policies as the moral high road that can take America beyond its unhappy racial past, while portraying opposing racial policies as rooted in unyielding racial resentments. This framing of racial issues has produced a polarized politics of disputatious mutual disrespect, stilled only by periods of sullen silence on racial matters. We also agree with Hochschild that many of the champions of each of the opposed modern racial alliances show little interest in serious empirical inquiry into what policies or combinations of policies may work to lessen racial material gaps without harming, and often benefiting, most white Americans.

Yet the sad irony is that today, it is entirely possible—we think it likely—that only some combination of color-blind and race-conscious policy measures can really work to help Americans reduce racial inequalities in education, income and wealth, health, housing, crime and incarceration rates, political representation, and more, in ways that are both materially effective and politically sustainable. In practice, we will see, many American policymakers discreetly support such combined, compromised policies, and many American citizens accept them. But few political leaders are willing or able to make a case for combined approaches openly and honestly, out of fear of misrepresentation and denunciation by one side or the other or both.

Instead, they often rely on misleading descriptions of contorted, frequently counterproductive policy measures—as when color-blind advocates claim that providing automatic admission to state universities for the top 10 percent of all high school graduates is "race-neutral," when in fact they are departing from standard admissions criteria precisely to include more blacks and Latinos; and when race-conscious advocates claim their chief goal in providing a "plus" for racial minorities in university admissions is simply to pursue wide-ranging forms of educational "diversity," when in fact they are primarily concerned with enhancing racial inclusiveness. Whatever their other merits, both these policy rhetorics employ euphemisms and evasions that make honest assessments of the policies' efficacy in achieving educational and racial goals harder to achieve.[32]

In all the modern policy arenas we examine, including employment, housing, electoral systems, educational vouchers, census categories, immigration, and criminal justice measures, policy debates have been and continue to be distorted to varying degrees by such efforts to design measures so that they cannot be pilloried as either race-targeted or racially insensitive, even when this means crafting the policies so they do not work well. Or else leaders seek to do nothing of much substance at all.

Today's polarized politics of evasion and euphemism on racial policies matters greatly. This politics has proven unable to reduce many of the racial gaps in wealth and income, health and housing, education and political representation, and much more that continue to be massive and profoundly consequential features of modern American life. Entering 2010, blacks were more than twice as likely to be poor and nearly two times more likely to be unemployed than whites, with Latinos in the middle.[33] The median incomes of black households barely exceeded a bitterly ironic three-fifths of that of whites, and Latino households were only slightly higher.[34] Homeownership for blacks and Latinos was roughly two-thirds that of whites.[35] In terms of infant mortality, cancer, heart disease, and stroke, black health statistics were substantially worse than for whites.[36] For both blacks and Latinos, school segregation was on the rise, in fact even if not by law.[37] Perhaps most grimly, in a nation that was still roughly three-quarters white and only 12 percent black, the nation's inmate population included only slightly fewer blacks than whites, and Latinos were also greatly overrepresented.[38] In the early twenty-first century, the stark reality is that the United States remains a house divided, on race and by race.

Our analysis of American racial politics in terms of rival racial alliances has a powerful implication for the nation's political discourse. Because current racial policy stances are failing to produce progress, it is time for policymakers, party leaders, and voters to accept that some combination of color-blind and race-conscious measures is necessary to move forward. They should focus debate on what combination of policies is shown by evidence to work best to reduce the nation's persistent racial gaps, instead of wrangling over abstract racial principles. If they do so, many answers will remain unclear, and so important policy differences between racial conservatives and liberals will persist. But if Americans engage racial policy issues in this spirit, the nation's long-standing but now stalemated quest to achieve greater unity while accommodating diversity might yet be not only resumed but truly advanced.

"Manifestly a discrimination": Racial Politics as Racial Policy Alliances

Although our emphasis on the importance of racial policy alliances is far from wholly original, it is far from conventional in the scholarship on American politics, especially analyses of race in modern America. To dramatize what it means to understand American politics as shaped by the clashes of evolving racial policy alliances, we begin with a story that captures many of the dynamics we will see at work throughout U.S. history. These events took place at a kind of midpoint in America's racial history, when the nation's second racial period, the Jim Crow era, was just approaching its critical juncture, with the balance of power between the nation's pro-segregation and anti-segregation alliances starting at last to shift in favor of the anti-segregation forces. The bitter complexities of race in the United States were never more visible than on April 20, 1937.

That day, U.S. Representative Arthur W. Mitchell, the first African American Democrat ever elected to Congress, took an overnight train from his home in Chicago to Hot Springs, Arkansas, for a two-week rest. Congressman Mitchell—born to slave parents in Alabama, mentored by Booker T. Washington at the Tuskegee Institute and further educated at Columbia and Harvard, and a former Republican converted to New Deal Democrat—was smarting from the recent failure of his anti-lynching bill in the House.[39] The National Association for the Advancement of Colored People (NAACP) attacked the bill as too weak, while the Democratic administration dependent on southern senators saw it as too strong and gave it no support.[40] The defeated, weary legislator requested a bedchamber on the Chicago–Hot Springs Pullman sleeping car. None was available, so he rode in the comparable Chicago–New Orleans sleeper.

The following morning, with a space available, Mitchell had a porter transfer him to the Chicago–Hot Springs sleeper before the train stopped and split at Memphis. A short time later as the train was entering Arkansas, conductor Albert Jones came through the Pullman car to check tickets. He immediately lit upon the car's only nonwhite passenger, Representative Mitchell. Refusing to accept Mitchell's payment for his Pullman seat from Memphis, conductor

Jones instead unceremoniously forced the congressman into the "Jim Crow" carriage for black people, in compliance with Arkansas law. Bereft of wash-basins, soap, towels, running water, or air conditioning, and with a working toilet only for women passengers, the "colored" car was decidedly not of first-class quality. Congressman Mitchell reported that Jones verbally abused him while threatening him with arrest for violating the whites-only rule of the segregated train system, saying: "as long as you are a nigger you can't ride in this car."[41]

Mitchell complained about his experience to the Interstate Commerce Commission, America's first regulatory agency established in 1887. As it had so often, instead of upholding constitutional principles of equal protection against invidious discrimination, the ICC concurred in the enforcement of the segregation policies adopted by the Illinois Central and Chicago, Rock Island, and Pacific railroads to obey the Arkansas statute.[42] The racist treatment of this prominent political figure garnered wide coverage in the black press throughout the country. But Congressman Mitchell's trip to Hot Springs had already failed to provide the respite from the frustrating struggles against abuses of African Americans he had sought—or the treatment that he believed himself entitled to as a matter of right.

Yet the same complex, internally divided political system that enabled Arthur Mitchell to hold national office, but not to ride a first-class coach in Arkansas or to receive relief from a federal regulatory agency, provided him with a further institutional recourse. Mitchell sued the ICC for dismissing his complaint and took his dispute all the way to the U.S. Supreme Court. There he argued the case himself before the justices; and with the consent of FDR's attorney general, Robert Jackson, Mitchell was joined in his case *against* the United States by new U.S. Solicitor General Francis Biddle.[43] On April 28, 1941, the Court ruled unanimously that the congressman had experienced "unreasonable" discrimination and that in deferring to Arkansas law, the ICC had failed to enforce the terms of the Interstate Commerce Act guaranteeing equal treatment—a "fundamental individual right which is guaranteed against state action by the Fourteenth Amendment."[44]

Chief Justice Charles Evans Hughes, a former Republican presidential candidate, wrote of Mitchell: "He is an American citizen free to travel, and he is entitled to go by this particular route whenever he chooses to take it and in that event to have facilities for his journey without any discrimination against which the Interstate Commerce Act forbids."[45] Hughes elaborated: "Having paid a first-class fare for the entire journey from Chicago to Hot Springs, and having offered to pay the proper charge for a seat which was available in the Pullman car for the trip from Memphis to Hot Springs, he was compelled, in accordance with custom, to leave that car and ride in a second-class car and was thus denied the standard conveniences and privileges afforded to first-class passengers. This was manifestly a discrimination against him in the course of his interstate journey and admittedly that discrimination was based solely upon the fact that he was a Negro."[46]

So Mitchell won. But his case is considered only a minor legal landmark, because the Court refused Mitchell's call to rule that local segregation laws *never* applied to interstate commerce. Its judgment therefore did not alter the legal status quo holding that, if Mitchell had been provided first-class accommodations that were "separate but equal," they would have been constitutional.[47]

The Racial Alliances Framework

The distinctive elements of the framework for analyzing American racial politics we employ in the pages to come are all visible in the struggles of Congressman Arthur Mitchell. Our framework builds on but in some respects breaks with the best scholarship on race in the United States.

Our first departure is that, because we see American racial politics as recurrently structured in terms of two rival racial alliances, each in control of some governing institutions, we think for many purposes it is not useful to speak of the United States as having a "racial state" or a single "racial order," as other scholars do.[48] These authors are right to contend that despite the American state's internal divisions, in any given period it does play an aggregate role in generating a particular overall national pattern of racial identities, statuses, and policies. That is why we can speak in shorthand of the "slavery" and "Jim Crow" eras. But these periods should be understood as the eras of *struggles* over slavery and over Jim Crow laws and practices, even if these struggles usually did not take place between the leaders of the two major parties. To our ears, language suggesting a unitary character to the American state or "racial order" fails to convey that contestation with a recognizable structure has always been integral to American racial politics.

Equally important, the terminology of a "race state" fails to call attention to the reality that institutions of "the state" have always been found on *both* sides of these contests, even if in highly unequal proportions at different times. For example, in their justly influential book, *Racial Formation in the United States*, Michael Omi and Howard Winant contend that the "central elements" in American struggles over race are "the state and social movements"—a formulation that can suggest "the state" is captured and recaptured as a whole by one racially motivated social movement or another, with political parties playing relatively little role.[49] But as their ensuing discussions reveal, in fact the story of American racial contests cannot be told without recognizing that in the United States' complex governing system of federalism and separation of powers, different governing institutions have often been controlled by proponents of different racial policies, in ways bound up with, though rarely identical to, partisan politics.

Arthur Mitchell's experiences make this point clear. He was compelled to leave his first-class car by the laws of one state, Arkansas, which was supported by a national regulatory institution, the ICC. But Mitchell found an ally in another national governing institution, the Department of Justice, and he was himself a member of the U.S. Congress who took his case to the U.S. Supreme Court. His efforts also found supporters and opponents in both parties: Mitchell was a former Republican turned New Deal Democrat who was defended by the Democrats' Department of Justice, and he won in a decision written by a Republican chief justice, against the wishes of many in both parties who supported segregation, the interests of railroads, or both. Mitchell's victory is therefore not best seen as a challenge to the "racial state," so much as one success in the long struggle of a cross-party alliance of political actors that utilized some governing institutions against others held by their rivals.

In place of relying on notions of a unitary American "racial state" or "racial order," we employ our novel concept of rival "racial policy alliances." We define these alliances as coalitions of participants in social movements, civic organizations, political parties, and also officials in control of some governing institutions. Though their members often have different motives and different ultimate agendas, these alliances are united by their agreement on how the central racial policy issues of their eras—slavery, segregation, race-conscious policymaking—should be resolved. In advancing this concept, we build on recent scholarship on two topics: the role of institutions in American political development, and the role of politics in the formation of racial doctrines, identities, and statuses.

In regard to institutions, over the past generation many social scientists have concluded that political developments can rarely be explained strictly in terms of clashes of social or economic groups, classes, or political parties, as some older forms of political science sought to do.[50] Politics involves the creation of governing institutions (primarily, but not only, formal state institutions) with accepted authority to order human activities in particular spheres of life. These institutions are structured to further the aims of those who create them, and once established, they often resist change—though pressures for change do come both from external sources and from internal institutional tensions and needs. Like many southern legislatures, the Arkansas legislature that required

17

railroads operating in the state to segregate their customers by race long resisted external political pressures, including litigation, pushing for change. Torn between precedents supporting segregation and ones protecting free-flowing interstate commerce against state regulations, the Supreme Court long struggled to define authoritatively whether states could or could not adopt racial policies affecting interstate transportation.[51] The conduct of both governing institutions was typical: among other concerns, officeholders generally have interests in preserving their institutional power that can lead them to combat external pressures, as the Arkansas legislature did, or to respond to those pressures and their internal tensions by adjusting their institution's policies in ways that protect their institutional interests, as the Supreme Court sought to do.

But despite the relative autonomy they display, governing institutions must necessarily be part of what we are terming broader "policy alliances." If governing institutions are to be established and then to sustain their authority over time, they must be of some use to social and economic groups and partisan organizations that possess sufficiently extensive resources, including wealth and popular backing, to provide the institutions with supportive constituencies. In turn, no groups, movements, or parties can succeed in seeing their policies implemented on an enduring basis without control of some governing institutions. Neither the anti-segregation nor the pro-segregation alliances involved in Arthur Mitchell's case could have remained viable contenders to shape national policies for long if they did not have at least some legislatures, executives, and courts acting in their favor. That is why we stress that by "racial policy alliances" we mean not simply any coalition or social movement active on racial issues. We mean those coalitions that are in control of some governing institutions and able to order activities on those issues authoritatively to some meaningful degree.[52]

Governing institutions allied with one coalition have often been able to resist the rise of newly dominant groups, coalitions, or parties for significant amounts of time, either because they remained under the control of the original policy alliance, or because their institutional interests so dictated, or for both reasons. Southern state legislatures, courts, and the southern states' national representatives maintained support for segregation long after other governing officials throughout the country had turned against it. The Supreme Court was wary of risking its prestige by challenging segregation *tout court* in its ruling in Arthur Mitchell's case; and although it soon decided to take what many justices perceived as an institutional gamble in the first *Brown v. Board of Education* decision, it refused the entreaties of civil rights lawyers to push for aggressive enforcement in *Brown v. Board of Education II* in 1955.[53] As that example indicates, a focus on institutions helps us to grasp many of the obstacles as well as opportunities for advancing race equality.

How do we determine if a governing institution or a political group or actor belongs to one racial policy alliance or another? Admittedly, there are ambiguities. An individual institution, such as the Supreme Court, may be part of a number of policy alliances at the same time, advancing for example the interests of corporations against union strikers, of immigration exclusionists against champions of open borders, and of Jim Crow segregation against integrationists, as was true of the Court in the late nineteenth century. Since political controversies often involve more than one policy issue—Mitchell's case concerned not only segregation but also state and national regulatory authority over railroads—an institution responsive to several policy alliances may be pulled in different directions and may waver in its decisions to some degree.

Even so, generally the officials of a governing institution, along with other politically active figures or groups, push repeatedly to resolve the dominant racial issue of an era in ways that favor the position of one racial policy alliance against the other, whenever their missions lead them to engage that issue. When we have found an institution, group, or actor repeatedly active on the racial policy issues of an era and consistently on the same side, we have counted that institution, group, or actor as a member of the racial alliance whose positions they have supported.[54] These designations sometimes shift over time as the contestation between the rival policy alliances results in advances for one side over the other. At the time Arthur Mitchell brought his case, for example, the Supreme Court had long been part of the pro–Jim Crow alliance. It had routinely upheld most segregation practices since 1896. But repopulated after 1938 by a New Deal administration seeking to limit the influence of conservative southern Democrats who increasingly opposed New Deal policies, the Court had recently begun the shift to more anti-segregation positions that would culminate with the decisive repudiation of pro-segregation precedents in the *Brown v. Board of Education* decision of 1954.[55] Mitchell's suit was part of the contestation which, with that decision, finally brought the Court fully within the anti-segregation alliance.

These criteria for what constitutes membership in a racial policy alliance reveal another way in which our framework is distinctive. Unlike many analysts of race in America, our focus is not on mass beliefs or perceptions of race and different races.[56] Even though public opinion may at any given time favor one racial policy more than its main rival, in the way that Americans predominantly support color-blind policies today, we do not regard the general public as belonging to one racial policy alliance or another. We conceive of alliances as comprising those individuals, groups, and institutions that are active in advancing policies through campaigns, legislative activity, and litigation, often though not always in concert with each other. The general public is too rarely mobilized to act directly on racial policy issues to count as an alliance member. Rather, the racial alliances compete for popular support on a recurrent basis. That competition means the alliances are constrained and influenced by public opinion; but apart from occasional referenda, voters generally do not engage in direct popular decision making or governance on racial issues. Racial policy alliances therefore can be seen as elite networks, though only if the category of "elites" is seen to include "public intellectuals" like the antebellum "race" scientist Josiah Nott and social movement leaders like Martin Luther King Jr., who were active in racial policy debates and decisions.

In addition to developing the recent scholarly focus on institutions in these ways, our concept of "racial policy alliances" also seeks to make more concrete important themes in recent scholarship on race. Debates over the roles of racial categories and identities in human experience have long focused on two basic alternatives: conceptions that see those categories as efforts to discover real biological differences among subsets of humanity and to discern the consequences of any such differences, on the one hand, and views that portray racial classifications as human constructions that do not reflect biological realities, on the other. On these latter views, racial categories are thought to serve any of a wide range of economic, psychological, cultural, and political purposes. Because American racial classifications have varied and shifted so greatly in U.S. history, we are skeptical of claims that they have represented imperfect efforts to capture biological realities, so we place ourselves on the side that sees those categories as human constructions. But we also hold that racial classifications have been not just social but more specifically *political* and *legal* constructions.[57]

Changing notions of race have, to be sure, originated and continue to originate in many social settings, including scholarly treatises, popular arts, and everyday discourses, as well as political arenas. Most often racial ideas are first formulated outside of politics, though always, inescapably, within politically structured social contexts. Nonetheless, it is only because political coalitions have succeeded in writing certain racial ideas into laws and policies, in ways that have distributed status, rights, resources, and power along the racial lines thus defined, that these racial categorizations have become significant and authoritative in American life. In *Plessy v. Ferguson*, the infamous 1896 precedent for Mitchell's case in which the Supreme Court upheld the right of states to require segregation on railroads against the challenge that this violated the Fourteenth Amendment's equal protection clause, anti-segregation forces chose as their litigant Homer Plessy because he was of seven-eighths European ancestry and appeared "white," and they wished to dramatize how arbitrary racial classifications could be.[58] The Court nonetheless let Louisiana and every other state decide who was "white," "black," and who had some other racial identity, and to restrict the rights of businesses and customers on the basis of those racial categories. The categories adopted generally expressed the wishes of the locally dominant political coalition, and so they varied from state to state.

The result is that American racial identities and statuses have often been politically constructed in complex ways that not only varied in different jurisdictions but also changed over time in the same jurisdictions. Those categories have included statuses assigned to various indigenous American tribes, Chinese, Japanese, and other East Asian immigrants, South Asians, Middle Easterners, different Latino groups, and many more. But during the slavery and Jim Crow eras and, we believe, still in the modern "race-conscious" era, the politics of the nation's racial policy alliances has generally focused on the claims of those categorized as "white" and those categorized as "black," with those persons and groups not placed in either category still treated according to how closely they appeared to policymakers to resemble one or the other side of the white/black dichotomy. That is why throughout American history, many from all backgrounds have felt compelled either to win recognition as "white" or similar to "whites" or to accept considerable solidarity with "nonwhites," especially African Americans.[59] Those pressures have not ended. Because American governments so long officially structured laws and policies in unequal racial terms, privileging those deemed white over those deemed nonwhite in virtually every arena of collective life, from employment to wealth to housing to health care to education to cultural institutions to political organizations and more, today official measures affecting these arenas still have consequences for the whole range of American racial and ethnic groups, whether or not those consequences are recognized or intended.

Our approach to "race" highlights another distinctive feature of the racial alliances framework. It accords a key role to ideas. It is ideas about appropriate racial policies, inevitably including ideas about race itself, which provide the bond for racial alliances (again, even though members may embrace those policies from different motives). And all the ideas, including the racial ideas, which define the aims of governing institutions and which provide the content of the policy measures they enact, have to be understood if the political roles of those institutions are to be understood. In the chapters that follow, we will repeatedly map the groups that have formed racial alliances, the governing institutions they have controlled, and the racial ideas and policies they have advanced in order to depict the racial politics of different eras, to show how changing definitions and conceptions of race are modified and deployed

21

by the rival racial alliances to advance their goals, and to explain the nature and consequences of the alliances' conflicts.[60]

In order to delineate those consequences fully, we examine how competing racial alliances have shaped American politics at three levels: *foundational structures*; *public policies*; and the *processes of political coalition building* that ultimately govern both. First, for every era of American life, the clash of racial alliances has contributed to the formation of a distinctive set of *foundational governmental, economic, and social structures*, most shaped by the predominant alliance in that era. These foundational structures, including systems of political and juridical representation, property rights, and rights of familial relations and civil association, influence the political, economic, and social statuses available to those officially designated as having various racial identities in particular periods of U.S. history. Slavery and its wide-ranging disabilities in terms of political, economic, and familial and personal rights and liberties; Jim Crow segregation and disfranchisement laws; and the apparatus of modern civil rights laws and judicial rulings, all have shaped such foundational structures in the main epochs of American racial history.

Even so, as Arthur Mitchell's story dramatizes, like the American state as a whole, these foundational structures are rarely unitary. Just as Mitchell found both allies and opponents in the varying institutions structuring the nation's transportation systems, there were always some governing institutions that forbade slavery within their jurisdictions; some that upheld African American political, economic, and social rights against Jim Crow proponents; and today the disputes of the rival racial alliances are fundamentally contests between different political institutions and actors over how the modern structure of civil rights laws affecting foundational political, economic, and social institutions and policies should be construed and enforced. And again, racial designations themselves have long been contested elements of foundational structures that have generated contrasting, disputed, and shifting racial definitions in different states and at the national level.

The second level at which racial alliances help constitute American politics, and the means through which contestation occurs, is the level of *policy disputes* that implicate the foundational structures' stability and future. Whether slavery should be extended to the territories; who should return fugitive slaves; whether segregation in transportation is consistent with interstate commerce; whether modern civil rights laws permit prosecution of agencies whose policies have racially disparate impacts; whether some Americans should be registered as having "multiracial" identities, rather than being placed in more traditional categories—these are all examples of policy disputes with significance for the foundational structures of American society in different eras that have clearly been bound up with the clash of rival racial alliances.

But we will also see that many other policy disputes that may not first appear to be concerned with race, such as judicial interpretations of federal jurisdiction and writs of habeas corpus in the antebellum period; the structuring of power within the U.S. Senate in the Jim Crow era; and debates over the desirability of school vouchers today, all have been framed by the positions advanced by the racial alliances of their day. Indeed, the unseen impacts of racial alliance priorities toward the main alternatives considered in numerous apparently nonracial policy debates are among the most important of their historical and current consequences. It is also true that in every era, the issues featured by the racial alliances have often simply crowded out, when they have not reframed, political attention to other topics that the nation might otherwise have addressed more constructively—such as definitions of the rights of citizens in the antebellum era; the needs of agricultural and domestic workers in the Jim Crow era; and the requirements of public spending to create appropriate urban infrastructures in modern America.

But this is only so because the prevailing *political coalitions* on policy disputes in different eras, including the compositions of political parties, social movements, and interest groups, have always been affected, though far from determined, by the fact that many political actors have operated in part as members of rival racial alliances. Both individuals and groups have determined their other allegiances and chosen their political partners and issue positions partly out of concern for the goals and loyalties that their racial alliances support. We will also see that the modern conservative coalition built around Ronald Reagan drew one of its great unifying themes, the importance of public policies that reinforce and reward individual good character and penalize individual bad character, from the ideology of the color-blind racial policy alliance and its call to judge people not on the color of their skin but the content of the character. In the case of the "Reagan Revolution" and many others, the political coalitions that have driven American political development would have been different than they have been—and are—if racial alliances had not so often contributed so forcefully to their memberships and purposes.

Readers may worry, however, that to speak of "racial policy alliances" in this way is to imply more self-conscious, collaborative agency than exists among the actors involved. Although we believe the members of these alliances are broadly aware that there are many others who share their aims and with whom they may well work in concert at some point, we see racial alliances as loose political networks, not nearly so fully ordered and interconnected as a formal governmental institution.[61] But when Congressman Mitchell decided to make his Arkansas experience the basis for a legal fight against segregation, his lawsuit received massive coverage in the black press; black business associations called for boycotting the railroads involved; though Mitchell had often quarreled with the NAACP, and some of its leaders still questioned his litigation strategy, others offered assistance; and the NAACP and other civil rights organizations were also then pressing FDR's Justice Department to intervene on behalf of black civil rights, as it did in *Mitchell v. United States*. The anti-segregation policy alliance, in other words, was visibly active. Mitchell himself was led to rethink his racial policy views by this alliance, as he was persuaded to mount a somewhat broader challenge to segregation in interstate transportation in his brief to the Supreme Court than he had first stated.[62]

Arrayed against these anti-segregation forces was an equally discernible pro-segregation alliance that included attorneys for the ICC, the railroads, and Arkansas, and also a bevy of southern state executives led by Alabama governor Frank Dixon, who called a conference of southern governors to form a common strategy of response. Lawyers for ten southern states then provided amicus briefs that defended segregation.[63] In the chapters that follow, we provide similar evidence that throughout U.S. history, members of the racial alliances were conscious of and often in communication with, though not tightly coordinated with, other members whom their efforts reinforced.

That does not mean that all members of racial alliances have always agreed and acted together on every issue and strategy. It is probably wise to underline that racial alliances, like all coalitions, display significant internal diversity in regard to motivations, tactics, and ultimate goals. Many members act primarily to further their economic aims. Others do so out of ideological conviction or social anxieties, some simply as a road to power, among other motives. Some are more active on particular topics than others; all sometimes dissent; and the groups and institutions making up an alliance are themselves not monolithic. Local churches, party politicians, businesses, unions, or NAACP chapters sometimes act in ways that vary from the positions of their national organizations. Many with similar motives and aims still disagree on particular methods of pursuing them.

Nonetheless, most of the time, the members of racial alliances are united by their agreements on the basic way to resolve the fundamental racial questions of their eras: to maintain slavery or put it on the path to extinction; to maintain legal racial segregation or to abolish it; to erase racial categories from public policies or to rely on them. Frederick Douglass and William Lloyd Garrison quarreled famously over whether to invoke or condemn the Constitution. Yet on the whole, they acted more in concert than in opposition on behalf of their shared central goal, ending slavery. Justice John Marshall Harlan was long the sole voice on the Supreme Court of those Reconstruction Republicans committed to equal rights for African Americans; but he did not join those, like Massachusetts senator George F. Hoar, who extended their racial egalitarianism to Chinese immigrants. Even so, they were both sturdy opponents of the rise of the new Jim Crow system of veiled white supremacy.

Some important political actors have even felt impelled to operate in two rival racial alliances at once, such as when Booker T. Washington publicly spoke in terms favorable to segregation while he secretly funded lawsuits against it, and when President Franklin Roosevelt accepted restrictions on New Deal programs to accommodate southern Democratic segregationists but also staffed his Justice Department with officials supportive of black civil rights. Some key figures have been leaders of more "liberal" alliances in one era only to join the more "conservative" side as the nation transitioned to the next: Andrew Johnson was ardently anti-slavery but proved even more ardently white supremacist. And others have altered their allegiances during the course of their careers, sometimes with major consequences. As senators, both Missourian Harry Truman and Texan Lyndon Johnson often acted with segregationists before they led the shift of the Democratic Party to stronger anti-segregationist positions during their presidencies.[64]

Identifying these sorts of contrasts and developments within the ranks of racial alliances helps to explain why outcomes have varied on different racially tinged issues within any given era, and it clarifies how and why the balance of power between rival alliances has shifted over time, generating a succession of eras. These variations do not alter the fact, however, that in each particular period, most members of each era's racial alliances have taken the same positions, often in conscious concert, on most issues. The resulting clashes have, to be sure, represented only one of the major cleavages shaping American politics. But understanding the groups, institutions, and policies that have constituted the evolving system of racial alliances throughout U.S. history is a prerequisite for understanding the foundational structures, policy disputes, and political coalitions in American politics.

It may still seem that analyzing American racial politics in terms of evolving sets of racial alliances aligned on either side of an era's battleground issue is too crude, because there have always been many racial issues and more than two positions on each of them. Our framework may appear particularly unnuanced when extended to the kaleidoscopic racial and ethnic identities visible in twenty-first-century America. It is true that there has always been more going on in regard to race in America than the clashes of the two major racial policy alliances. We nonetheless maintain that their conflicts have been decisive. The historical evidence indicates that political actors, groups, and institutions have felt compelled over time to align themselves with one of the major alliances or the other in order to have a significant impact on American racial statuses.

Again the story of Arthur Mitchell is exemplary. Many issues with racial dimensions were evident in Mitchell's time, including efforts to combat lynching and New Deal economic programs that Mitchell vociferously championed such as the Federal Housing Administration and the Civilian Conservation Corps. Still, the inescapable, central issue of the era was legalized "Jim Crow" segregation and discrimination. The Jim Crow system was the prime obstacle to structuring New Deal programs inclusively and effectively. It was what lynching helped sustain. As a proponent of Booker T. Washington's conciliatory, gradualist, paternalistic policies who long opposed stirring up "race prejudice," who often criticized more radical civil rights activists and organizations, and who was a loyal servant of the Chicago Democratic machine that enabled him to defeat African American Republican Oscar DePriest in 1934, Mitchell personally preferred to focus on education and economic uplift programs, not desegregation. He was in many ways an improbable candidate to litigate for more rapid and radical change in segregation policies.[65] Yet he was reluctantly forced to conclude that he had to engage the battleground racial issue of his era, legal segregation, if even educated, prominent African Americans like himself were not to be in many regards second-class citizens.

The ensuing battle, ending in Mitchell's partial judicial triumph, also shows how recognizing that American racial politics has *always* involved fundamentally two-sided struggles in which both sides could deploy at least some governing institutions, along with other resources, in efforts to capture more support, is vital for understanding how racial change has occurred historically. This recognition helps us see why racial progress has been real but limited, and what the prospects are for change in the future. The circumstances that both gave Mitchell the belief he had an opportunity to push for change and that he had to do so arose as millions of blacks moved north to escape the Jim Crow South and take advantage of economic opportunities opened up by World War I, and as the Depression then gave Democrats the chance to build a massive partisan coalition. Unprecedented opportunities arose for African American groups and political aspirants to ally with northern white Democrats in support of a shared economic agenda that included at least promises of racial reform. The growing importance of northern blacks to the Democratic coalition, the growing control of the Democrats over national institutions, and the growing importance to national leaders of making the United States appear racially progressive internationally, all made it possible for Mitchell both to win a seat in Congress and, later, to gain the support of FDR's Justice Department in litigating for change. In the process, Mitchell came to see better both the necessity for larger racial transformations and the opportunities for them, bringing him more fully into the anti-segregation alliance over time and enabling him to contribute a significant success on its behalf.

But still only a partial success: as noted, the Supreme Court was not yet willing to overturn de jure segregation root and branch, for the anti–Jim Crow racial alliance was not yet so strong, even in the northern Democratic Party, to make such a decision seem feasible to the justices. Indeed, Mitchell's heightened racial activism eventually cost him his congressional seat. The white-dominated Chicago Democrat machine wanted black votes but did not think that desegregating Illinois-based railroads was a priority. Its leaders dropped Mitchell for a more reliable African American candidate, William Dawson, in 1942. Living until the age of eighty-five in 1968, Mitchell did see many of the civil rights he came to embrace realized.[66]

His elevation, then abandonment, by the Chicago machine also highlights why, though Mitchell probably would not have been elected to office or successful in his lawsuit without the support of northern Democrats, it would be wrong to identify the racial alliances during the Jim Crow era with the two major parties or with partisan allegiances. As the ruling by Republican chief justice Hughes in *Mitchell v. United States* confirms, both parties in these years still had anti-segregation and pro-segregation members, and many who were indifferent to racial issues, though in different proportions. The anti-segregation racial alliance that gained ground in the 1950s did so, moreover, in both parties, so that both adopted strong civil rights planks in their 1960 platforms. As a result, right up to the end of the Jim Crow system in the mid-1960s, struggles between supporters and opponents of segregation largely took place *within* both parties, and often *outside* the parties, rather than *between* the parties. That it is why it is one of the greatest changes from the previous U.S. history exemplified by Arthur Mitchell's story that today, this crosscutting relationship between America's parties and its racial policy alliances is no longer the case.

And though racial conflicts have almost always been intertwined with economic ones in U.S. history, as Mitchell's desire to be able to purchase a ticket for a first-class Pullman car indicates, his story is also an illustration of why the American structure of racial politics cannot be identified with or explained strictly in terms of economic alliances, interests, and ideologies. The specifics of Mitchell's case reflected the aspirations of wealthier black Americans more than those of poorer ones who could not afford such a ticket, and the congressman

found his strongest support among black businesses and more elite black political activists. Still, many poorer African Americans celebrated a victory that
did promise to limit the extent and improve the conditions of the segregation
imposed on them in public transportation systems, so Mitchell's support cut
across class lines. So did his opposition: many poor whites joined the railroads
and most other white-owned businesses in either actively defending existing
segregation policies or resting content to see them maintained. Though America's racial alliances cannot be understood without grasping the economic
motivations of many of their leaders and members, neither the coalitions nor
their goals can be accounted for by focusing only on economic classes or interests, without reference to specifically racial concerns.

One final lesson highlighted by the story of Congressman Mitchell is central to this book's overarching message concerning the consequences of clashes
between racial policy alliances. The controversy over Mitchell's train trip to
Arkansas not only impeded his own travel. It distracted the congressman from
his work for the educational and economic programs dearest to his heart. It
embroiled the railroads in unwanted litigation. And from 1937 to 1941, it
busied ICC officials, state and national attorneys, and the courts with work
that did not directly address the enormous economic and national security
challenges that the nation then confronted. Segregation was economically
inefficient but not the cause of the Depression, and an international embar-
rassment but not the cause of World War II. The time and effort spent by
all concerned on Mitchell's case could have been spent far more productively
if they had not been burdened by these struggles over Jim Crow laws and
practices.

Similarly, and in a mind-bending variety of ways, all through U.S. history,
the structure, policies, practices, and performance of American governing institutions and officials have been different and often worse than they might
have been if they had not been so pervasively shaped by struggles between the
nation's racial alliances.[67] But if this pattern can be found all through U.S.
history, the change we have noted in the relationship of racial alliances to
partisan allegiances since Arthur Mitchell's time remains distinctive as well as
momentous. By reinforcing ideological and partisan cleavages, the polarized
structure of American racial politics today, derived from the nation's violent
racial past, hinders policymakers' efforts to discuss far too extensive an array of
issues clearly and honestly, even more than in previous eras.

One recent example of this constrained public dialogue came early in President Obama's first year, when he nominated Judge Sonia Sotomayor to become the first person of Hispanic descent to sit on the U.S. Supreme Court.
Everyone understood that Sotomayor was in fact chosen because, in addition

to sterling professional credentials, she was part of an American Hispanic community not previously represented on the high bench. Even so, she drew severe criticism for having previously suggested that at least in some cases, a "wise Latina" might be able to reach better decisions than a white man.[68] The criticism of this apparent endorsement of "race-conscious" judicial decision making was not fatal. Sotomayor was confirmed. But White House press secretary Robert Gibbs sought to avoid discussing the issue, then simply said Sotomayor's "word choice" was "poor"; and President Obama himself said he thought her view needed to be "restated."[69] Probably at the advice of the White House, instead of "restating," during her confirmation hearings Sotomayor backed away from her earlier endorsement of race-conscious judging. She now contended, "I don't base my judgments on my personal experiences—or my feelings or my biases."[70] She did not attempt the steep uphill task of explaining or defending the legitimacy of decision making informed in some ways by senses of racial or ethnic identity.

Still, it is likely that most Americans in fact expect that Sotomayor's judging *will* be shaped by her perspective as a Latina. Many see some value in that quality. But most either do not think decision makers should openly acknowledge that reality, or else they are uncertain about the issue. That reluctance, uncertainty, and the often consequent disingenuousness about race and much more in American public discourse occur, we believe, because to most, neither pure color blindness nor pure race consciousness really seems right to guide America's public principles and policies. Yet the ways that racial issues are framed by today's rival racial policy alliances makes no other option seem logically or politically possible. If that is our current condition, then understanding how and why American racial politics has been and is structured in the polarized fashion that we document here is useful for considering how Americans might seek to structure their politics more productively in the future.

THE STRUCTURE OF THE BOOK

In the ensuing chapters, we begin with evidence that our racial alliances framework can indeed shed light on America's first two racial eras. We then turn to our main aim, illuminating American racial politics, problems, and possibilities today. We document how the modern racial alliances developed and the roles they play in contemporary issues, some obviously racial, some not so. Throughout, we indicate how the Obama administration appears to be responding to modern controversies, and we draw on these examples in the conclusion to characterize and assess Obama's overall approach to race. Using a variety of methods, chapters 2 and 3 examine the slavery and Jim Crow eras, respectively. We then turn to seven modern policy issues: employment in chapter 4; housing in chapter 5; voting rights in chapter 6; school vouchers and census categories in chapter 7; and criminal justice and immigration in chapter 8, before turning to our analysis of the prospects for today's racial alliances in chapter 9.

Our examination of modern policy issues begins with employment because we believe it is primarily in this labor market arena that the modern color-blind and race-conscious policy alliances first emerged. We then show in the ensuing chapters that those alliances appear, cohesively and consistently, throughout every issue we examine. We note that the coalitions nonetheless display some variations, and we analyze why those differences have arisen and what their consequences have been. In our final chapter, we show that our arguments are consistent with the data employed in major quantitative analyses of American politics—but that those analyses are in some ways misleading because they do not focus sufficiently on conflicts over racial policies.

From the plethora of policy issues we might have discussed, our selection of the seven we consider is based on two criteria. First, they are all issues involving what we term "foundational" systems of obvious importance. The controversies we consider affect the structure of the nation's economy and residences; its electoral and educational systems; its official racial categories; and its enforcement of both criminal and immigration laws. If the racial alliances are consequential for these foundational systems, they are consequential for American politics more generally.

But we could have examined any of many issues concerning these systems, or considered other systems, such as transportation, communications, environmental protection, health care, national defense, or many others. As our second criterion, after our seminal area of employment, we chose issues that appear to challenge our framework in one important way or another. Some are often seen as areas where "strange bedfellow" coalitions can be found (such as majority-minority districting and immigration policy)—alignments that can seem to contradict our contention that the major racial policy alliances are consistent across major issue arenas. Some involve groups with multiracial identities and goals that do not appear to fit into our racial alliances and that may seem to imply the inadequacy of giving special primacy to the racial categories of "white" and "black" (census classifications and immigration again). Others are issues on which many see a limited and declining role for racial concerns (housing, school vouchers, criminal justice policies).

These two criteria account for what may seem our most surprising decision, not to provide a detailed study of issues of school desegregation or affirmative action in educational admissions. Those controversies have great importance both for education and for race in America, as we note at appropriate junctures. It is also arguable that historically, the racial alliances we describe emerged roughly simultaneously in the arenas of employment and education. But school desegregation and educational affirmative action are extensively discussed topics. The scholarly literature already vividly captures the emergence of clashing color-blind and race-conscious positions.[71] We therefore discuss the role of the modern racial alliances in education by focusing on school vouchers, an issue that on its face does not appear to be about racial policy and that is indeed about much more. Even so, we show that the modern racial alliances have been major players in determining the fate of voucher proposals.

Yet though we wish to show that American politics has long displayed continuing clashes of racial alliances, our foremost goal is to indicate how and why those conflicts matter now, and what they mean for possibilities for racial progress, today and tomorrow. For many millions of Americans, hopes for that progress are now invested in President Barack Obama. We therefore note the positions Obama has taken on each issue we examine, and in our final chapter we consider his general approach to race in more detail. As suggested, we are compelled to conclude that Obama, too, has so far failed to bring out clearly the character and the harmful consequences of the ways policies have been framed by today's racial policy alliances. If his approach is to succeed, the president and his allies must make a case for combining more "universal" and more "race-conscious" measures more openly and persuasively than they have done so far. Their policies must also be seen as having some real success in reducing the material racial inequalities that remain so constitutive of American life. At the same time, we recognize that the tasks of reshaping American political and policy debates in ways conducive to racial progress cannot be met by any president or partisan alone. Only if both sides to current policy debates acknowledge the need to move beyond polarizing castigation of each other's abstract principles, and only if both sides accept the imperative to seek combinations of policies that can close inequitable racial gaps, while distributing the costs of change fairly, can the United States hope to make E Pluribus Unum not just its venerable national motto, but also its twenty-first-century achievement.

PART TWO

The Making and Unmaking
of Racial Hierarchies

Chapter 2

"That is the last speech he will ever make"
The Antebellum Racial Alliances

Nations are born in mixtures of bloodshed and violence, bitterness and idealism, intergroup rivalries and ideological struggles, hatreds and alliances. To this pungent alchemy of founding impulses, Americans added race. Beliefs about race and institutions implementing those beliefs have been elemental in American politics ever since.[1] These ideas and institutions have long spurred Americans into competing political alliances with differences over racial policies at their centers.

RACIAL ALLIANCES AND ANTEBELLUM AMERICA

Even before there was a Constitution, there were pro-slavery and anti-slavery alliances in the not-so-United States. Indeed, the Declaration of Independence, which embedded the rhetoric of human equality and inalienable rights into American political culture, still sought to justify tribal subjugation (by denouncing "merciless Indian Savages") and to avoid criticism of chattel slavery (by editing out Jefferson's language attacking the slave trade).[2] Because during the Revolution, Virginia governor Lord Dunmore offered freedom to slaves who would join His Majesty's forces, and because free blacks and white Quakers demanded that the revolutionaries live up to their proclamations of equal rights and liberties, northern states during and following the Revolution either banned slavery or adopted gradual emancipation statutes, beginning with Vermont in 1777. Middle states loosened restrictions on manumission and even taxed slave trading. The Confederation Congress also banned slavery in the Northwest Territory in 1787, with southern support.[3]

But in the South, there were many who deplored any suggestion that they should begin to move toward the end of their own reliance on slave labor. Consequently, the new nation quickly exhibited both anti-slavery and pro-slavery spokesmen, sometimes organized into groups, who controlled various governing institutions in the different states and who were represented in national assemblies. James Madison's great fear all during the summer of 1787 was that the convention in Philadelphia, called to amend the Articles of Confederation but in reality busy writing a new Constitution, would burst apart over the issue of slavery. The "great division of interest" among the states, he said repeatedly behind closed doors, was not "between the large & small states" but between "the Northern & Southern," and "principally from . . . their having or not having slaves."[4]

Madison and others sought to promote national unity, then and in the years ahead, not so much by explicitly compromising on slavery as by keeping it off the agenda, most obviously by avoiding the terms "slave" or "slavery" in the constitutional text. Even so, most framers acknowledged that the Constitution embodied a messy set of slavery-driven compromises. In return for an expansive national power to regulate interstate and foreign commerce and constitutional permission for Congress to ban the international slave trade after 1808, southerners received a guarantee in Article IV that fugitives escaped from labor would somehow be delivered up to those to whom they "owed" labor. Still more important, the South won a foundational system of political representation that gave the slave states additional members of the new House of Representatives, and so also additional members of the Electoral College that selected the president, via the three-fifths clause of Article I, Section 2. At the convention, South Carolina's Charles Cotesworth Pinckney openly stated that he was supporting the new commerce power only because of northerners' "liberal conduct" in granting these concessions to slaveholders.[5] The compromises proved not only to give pro-slavery forces power disproportionate to their shares of the population in the House and the Electoral College, as Akhil Amar has noted. In addition, slave states soon began using three-fifths clauses to apportion their own state legislatures, which in turn selected members of the U.S. Senate. This meant the Constitution's compromises over slavery worked on balance to deepen the grip of the pro-slavery alliance throughout every branch of the new national government as well as in many states.[6]

Yet if the new constitutional system began with the pro-slavery alliance in the predominant position, the rhetoric of the Revolution and more egalitarian forms of Christianity always provided antebellum anti-slavery proponents with arguments many Americans found compelling: as children of God, all human beings should be equal in basic, natural rights. And because the emergent anti-slavery alliance controlled some governing institutions in northern states, many southern slaveholders already saw themselves as threatened. After Vermont outlawed slavery in its 1777 constitution, Massachusetts's chief justice declared slavery inconsistent with his state's constitution in 1783. By 1784, Pennsylvania, Connecticut, and Rhode Island had enacted gradual emancipation statutes. And in the early years under the new Constitution, similar steps continued to be discussed in other states.[7] In one of the many less noticed impacts of contests between racial alliances, those states that had strong movements in favor of emancipation tended in this era to include clauses in their state constitutions guaranteeing that property would not be taken without "just compensation." These states often combined gradual emancipation with compensation. The southern states most opposed to ending slavery were slow to enact these "just compensation" clauses. Some never did, perhaps anxious about adopting provisions that seemed to invite emancipation laws.[8] In the wake of the Revolution with its high-flown egalitarian rhetoric championing the rights of man, many southerners feared the anti-slavery contagion might spread.

Even the most prestigious slave-master in the nation, President George Washington, felt squeezed between the rival alliances. Because the seat of the national government, including the president's residence, was initially in Philadelphia, Washington worried that his control of his slaves might be endangered by Pennsylvania's gradual emancipation act, passed in 1780. Whether or not the law affected his slaves, the slaves might believe it did, thus rendering them "insolent in a State of Slavery." Consequently, in 1791 the president ordered his secretary, Tobias Lear, to prevent his slaves from residing in Philadelphia longer than six months by sending them back to Mount Vernon periodically "under pretext." Washington said he hoped to "deceive" both his slaves "and the Public" about what he was doing.[9] As the nation's great unifying figure, he did not want his manipulations to keep his slaves to win attention. But though Washington would later provide for the emancipation of his slaves in his will, at this point in his life he wanted to keep them, and he did.[10]

Congress, too, long strove to placate pro-slavery forces quietly while avoiding public policy disputes over the issue. In February 1790 during the first Congress, Representative Thomas Fitzsimons of Philadelphia introduced a petition to the House from a Quaker congregation that urged restrictions on slave trading. It was soon reinforced by an anti-slavery memorial written by Benjamin Franklin as president of a new Society for Promoting the Abolition of Slavery. South Carolina's Thomas Tucker proclaimed that any favorable action on these petitions would mean "civil war." Though others insisted the national government had power to tax and regulate the slave trade, Congress did nothing. By 1798, southerners were able to pass a resolution stating that such petitions were for judicial, not congressional, cognizance.[11] But as those controversies showed, the antebellum period exhibited anti-slavery and pro-slavery coalitions with meaningful authority and strength right from the start, even if pro-slavery forces held by far the stronger hand in the new national institutions.

The Pro-Slavery Alliance

Table 2.1 delineates the coalition supporting slavery. Core members of the antebellum pro-slavery alliance included much of the Senate and most presidents, products of the electoral systems that overrepresented the slave states; most of the state officials in those states; and all pro-slavery Federalists, Whigs, and Jeffersonian, then Jacksonian, Democrats. The pro-slavery alliance also included politically active church and scholarly leaders who justified slavery and white rule as products of a "natural" hierarchical racial order.[12] And at its margins, the pro-slavery alliance included many who were willing in the new nation's early decades to placate slave interests, while expecting that the institution would die out in due course. As slavery instead grew entrenched with time and the invention of the cotton gin, some of these marginal coalition members began to shift sides, such as John Quincy Adams, who did little about slavery as president in the 1820s but later became a great opponent during his years in Congress.

But viewing race in the broader American canvas shows that this pro-slavery coalition, though fundamental, did not amount to the whole story. Although supporters of slavery were overwhelmingly white supremacist, all the more ardently as the antebellum era proceeded and the opposition of the rival alliances grew more intense, American racial doctrines had additional roots. Many, perhaps most, who opposed slavery nonetheless embraced white supremacy for different reasons. Discourses of racial hierarchy that exalted whites or, still more narrowly, Anglo-Saxons were elaborated in defenses of westward expansion into tribal and Mexican lands as racial "manifest destiny" and in attacks on immigration, along with pro-slavery advocacy. Political leaders consequently spread the nation's white supremacist laws and institutions into spheres that eventually extended well beyond master/slave relationships, including racial restrictions on the political, economic, and mobility rights of free blacks, Native Americans, and others deemed nonwhite.[13] Those restrictions could be found in the North, not just the South. [14] And northern white opposition to racial equality was often massive. In an 1857 Oregon constitutional referendum, 74 percent of Oregon voters rejected a proposal to permit slavery in their state, but 89 percent favored excluding all blacks.[15]

We therefore disagree with scholars who describe the origins of American racial ideologies only as rationalizations for economic interests in slavery.[16] Nor is it accurate to view American politics more generally as overwhelmingly expressing economic interests, hampered marginally by some racist "blind spots."[17] Though worker fears of cheap competitors played a large part in the Oregon voters' rejection of both free blacks and slavery, so substantial an anti-

TABLE 2.1
Pro-slavery Alliance, 1787–1865

Most Jeffersonian Republicans and Jacksonian Democrats

Most southern Federalists, Whigs (e.g., Alexander Stephens)

Most Supreme Court justices, many state courts

Slave owners and most northern textile industrialists

Many artisans and working-class European immigrants

Most white religious leaders, especially in the South

American School of Ethnology scholars

Some "civilized" Native American tribes

Source: Along with the other sources in this section, this table derives from Donald G. Nieman, *Promises to Keep: African-Americans and the Constitutional Order, 1776 to the Present* (New York: Oxford University Press, 1991), 14–17, 24–29, 44–49 (political parties, courts); Richard J. Ellis, *American Political Cultures* (New York: Oxford University Press, 1993), 96–108; John Gerring, *Party Ideologies in America, 1828–1996* (New York: Cambridge University Press, 1998), 11, 17 (political parties); William M. Wiecek, *Liberty under Law: The Supreme Court in American Life,* (Baltimore, MD: Johns Hopkins University Press, 1988), 73–81 (Supreme Court justices); John Hope Franklin and Alfred A. Moss Jr., *From Slavery to Freedom: A History of Negro Americans,* 6th ed. (New York: Alfred A. Knopf, 1988), 79–83, 96–97, 100–122 (slave owners, northern industrialists, artisans, workers, immigrants); Reginald Horsman, *Race and Manifest Destiny: The Origins of American Racial Anglo-Saxonism,* (Cambridge, MA: Harvard University Press, 1981), 125–33, 250–253 (American School of Ethnology, immigrants, parties); Sydney E. Ahlstrom, *A Religious History of the American People* (New Haven, CT: Yale University Press, 1972), 648–69 (religious leaders); Katja May, *African Americans and Native Americans in the Creek and Cherokee Nations, 1830s to 1920s: Collision and Collusion* (New York: Garland, 1996); and Rogers M. Smith, *Civic Ideals: Conflicting Visions of Citizenship in U.S. History* (New Haven, CT: Yale University Press, 1997), 284 (civilized tribes).

black vote in a state that was seeking immigrant labor reveals pervasive perceptions of nonwhites as undesirable.[18] The lopsided totals suggest that deep convictions of black inferiority, fears of racial strife, and desires to reserve power for those with whom the Oregon voters identified racially were all at work, along with economic motives.

We nonetheless concur that questions of maintaining and extending slavery formed the *central* axis of opposition on race-related issues in the antebellum years, with clashes over the extension of slavery providing the chief cause of the Civil War. It was indeed slavery's profitability both to southern slaveholders and many northern manufacturers using raw materials provided by slave labor that most propelled the accelerating elaborations of white supremacy, in ideas, laws, and customs, during the antebellum years. And it was the ensuing political and legal construction of economic, political, social, and cultural systems of racial hierarchy that made explicitly racial identities seem natural and vital to millions.[19] Those systems habituated many privileged as "white" to think of their racial status as a primary feature of their lives.[20] The nation's imposed racial inequalities gave even many white farmers and workers who did not own slaves feelings of economic dependency on the maintenance of the racial restrictions that appeared to make their lands, jobs, and wages more secure.

Those racial laws and customs also gave whites a strong sense of racial entitlement, even if in reality some benefited far more than others. That is why it is both true that slavery was central to antebellum racial issues, and that slavery contributed to attachments to white supremacist arrangements that had other sources, that exceeded its support, and that would long survive it.

The Anti-slavery Alliance

The members of the rival anti-slavery coalition built on doctrines and institutions of human rights and liberties elaborated in the course of the nation's revolutionary struggles, even though many opponents of slavery both in the Revolution and throughout the antebellum period did not support fully equal rights, and some were passionately white supremacist. Still, the nation's ideologies and senses of identity had been profoundly shaped by the American revolutionaries' rejection of monarchy and aristocracy for democratic republics, and systems of primogeniture and entail for greater individual powers over property. Early Americans professed many of their new political, economic, and cultural institutions to be dedicated to broad goals of "equal rights" and "equality before the law," defended in terms of natural rights and Christian doctrines. Those institutions did provide greater equality to European-descended men than ever before, in a whole variety of ways. In terms of its foundational systems, the new nations' courts at least promised equal justice to all; its political systems provided a comparatively broad suffrage; its market systems gave formally equal economic rights to white men; and religious groups enjoyed expansive freedom to worship in their preferred ways.[21] Even if few white men were willing to extend these doctrines fully to nonwhites or to women, many believed slavery to be incompatible with them.

The fuel to ignite those egalitarian doctrines and institutions into conflict with white supremacist ones endorsing slavery had two tapers: "free labor" economic and political interests; and the moral indignation that slavery fostered

TABLE 2.2
Anti-slavery Alliance, 1787–1865

Some Free Soil Democrats, especially in the North (e.g., David Wilmot)

Some northern Federalists, Whigs; all Liberty Party, Free Soil Party, GOP

Many northern state officials, judges, enforcing anti-slavery laws

Many small farmers, merchants, craft manufacturers, esp. in the North, border states

Some white religious groups (e.g., Quakers)

African American religious, educational, professional, and business groups

White abolitionists (e.g., American Anti-Slavery Society)

Some intellectuals, popular writers (e.g., Harriet Beecher Stowe)

Source: Along with our sources in this section, this table is derived from Franklin and Moss, *From Slavery to Freedom*, 86–95, 42–167 (African American groups, white abolitionists); Ahlstrom, *Religious History* (white religious groups); Gerring, *Party Ideologies* (political parties); and Smith, *Civic Ideals*, 246–53 (intellectuals, popular writers).

in all blacks and some whites. The two great antebellum slavery policy issues on which these passions and interests converged were the extension of slavery to the territories and the return of fugitive slaves. The first was the more decisive conflict. It was driven by "free labor" economic beliefs and interests, including white aversions to competing with either slave labor or poor blacks. But outrage against southern efforts to recapture fugitive slaves came from reformers with more racially egalitarian moral beliefs.[22] The diverse members of the anti-slavery alliance are portrayed in table 2.2.

The limited but significant governing institutions controlled by this anti-slavery alliance included the Revolutionary-era laws ending slavery in the North and promoting manumission in the South; the congressional bans on slavery in the Northwest Territory and on the international slave trade after 1808; and many of the judges and other officials charged with enforcing them. To these features the 1820 Missouri controversy added congressional contentions that free black Americans were entitled to the "privileges and immunities" provided by Article IV of the Constitution, claims upheld by some courts. Next came new statutory and procedural obstacles to the return of fugitive slaves erected by some northern legislatures and courts, prodded into action by more egalitarian white and black churches and anti-slavery organizations.[23] Even when the Northwest Ordinance–derived states began banning entry of free

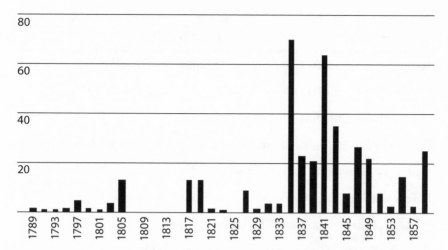

Figure 2.1: Roll Call Votes Related to Slavery Issues in the U.S. House of Representatives.

blacks as agitations over slavery and race heightened in the 1840s and 1850s, most blacks in northeastern states kept their political, educational, and economic statutory rights and used them to work for more.[24]

One imperfect measure of how these racial alliances evolved during the antebellum period is the record of congressional roll call votes on slavery and race-related issues in those years. As figures 2.1 and 2.2 demonstrate, votes related to slavery were infrequent in the House and Senate prior to the mid-1830s, spiking as Congress considered ending the international slave trade in 1807 and again in regard to the admission of Missouri as a slave state that would ban entry of free blacks in 1820.[25]

We trace this paucity of roll call votes on slavery and race issues to the desires of most of the nation's leaders to keep slavery debates out of public view, even as they provided slaveholders with much of the support they sought. But after 1830, the balance of power in the House of Representatives began to shift as faster population growth in free states led to a decline in the proportionate strength of the South (figure 2.3). In 1790, free states elected 57 members to the first House, slave states 49. By 1820 free states had 123 House members, slave states only 90, and by 1850 the numbers were 147 to 90.[26]

Not all the representatives from free states were anti-slavery. Nor were all slave state representatives active defenders of the "peculiar institution." The representation by states in the Senate meant, moreover, that the South retained more relative power in that chamber. But most southerners still saw a growing threat in these numbers, especially after the rising number of black

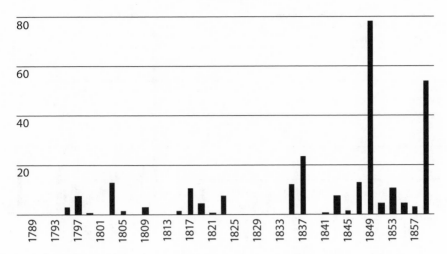

Figure 2.2: Roll Call Votes Related to Slavery Issues in the U.S. Senate.

and white abolitionists gained more visible national leadership with the formation of William Lloyd Garrison's American Anti-Slavery Society in 1833.[27]

From the mid-1830s on, Congress faced a mounting flow of anti-slavery petitions to Congress, including opposition to slavery in the District of Columbia. Northern states began adopting "personal liberty" laws that southerners correctly perceived as impediments to their efforts to recapture escaped fugitive slaves (or find substitutes among northern free blacks). And many in both the pro-slavery and anti-slavery alliances wished to end the Missouri

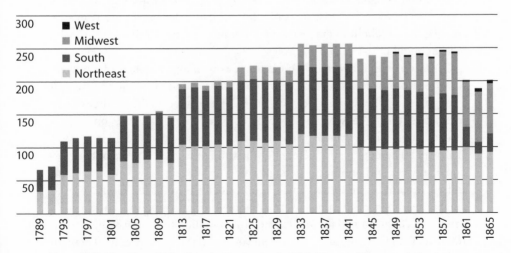

Figure 2.3: Number of Members by Region in the U.S. House of Representatives.

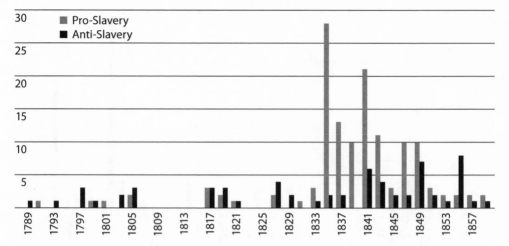

Figure 2.4: Number of Roll Call Votes on Slavery Issues Initiated by Alliances in the U.S. House of Representatives.

Compromise of forming free and slave states from the territories in equal numbers, a question that became acute with the acquisition of vast western lands as a result of the Mexican-American War in 1848.[28] In response to all these issues and more, southerners sought national action to ban the distribution of abolitionist tracts, to compel northern states to fulfill what the South saw as constitutional duties to aid in the return of fugitive slaves, to extend rights to slavery throughout the new territories, and to control or permit state controls on the rights, activities, and mobility of free blacks, among other measures.[29] As figure 2.4 shows, not only did roll call votes on slavery issues increase as the antebellum era proceeded, but pro-slavery members became the most frequent initiators of those votes.

Consistent with the racial alliances framework, many members of Congress voted repeatedly on one side or the other of slavery and race-related issues all through the antebellum period.[30] Of the 3,280 members of the House of Representatives during these years, 2,585 participated in roll call votes on slavery-related issues. A little over 24 percent of these representatives voted in support of slavery 80 percent to 100 percent of the time during their years of congressional service, and another 8 percent voted pro-slavery between 60 percent and 80 percent of the time. Hence, a bit under a third of the House proved reliable members of the pro-slavery alliance during this period. Just over 25 percent of congressional members voted in opposition to slavery 80 percent to 100 percent of the time, and 7.5 percent voted anti-slavery between 60 percent and 80 percent of the time, creating an almost identical third of the House

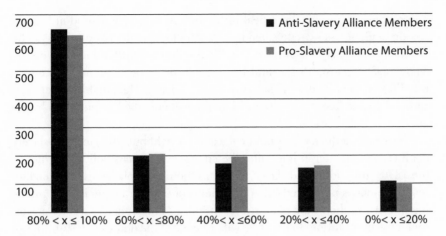

Figure 2.5: Voting Consistency of U.S. House Members on Slavery Issues during the Antebellum Period (n=2,585).

that consistently voted as an anti-slavery alliance throughout their antebellum congressional careers (figure 2.5). These numbers mean, of course, that roughly a third of the antebellum House did not vote so consistently with one alliance or the other, often seeking compromises. But the existence of these sizable, cohesive voting blocs justifies Abraham Lincoln's portrait of antebellum America as a house divided.

These numbers may indeed both understate the potency of the antebellum racial alliances and mask the shifts in their relative power during the period. Because there were few roll call votes on slavery and racial issues before 1830, even one deviation from a congressman's usual voting pattern could make him appear inconsistent, if he served only during these years. But as the numbers of free-state representatives grew during the antebellum years and slavery-related bills proliferated, more members were impelled to identify themselves consistently with pro-slavery or anti-slavery positions.

Throughout the antebellum era, pro-slavery forces retained great power, particularly in regard to the protection of slavery where it was already established. For example, in September 1850 a bill "to suspend the rules in order to introduce an act to abolish slavery in the District of Columbia" was overwhelmingly defeated in the House of Representatives (107 against the bill to 54 for, 67 not voting), with the South voting unanimously pro-slavery (56 against, 0 in favor), the Northeast decisively anti-slavery but still more divided (26 against, 42 for), and the Midwest voting 2–1 pro-slavery (24 opposed, 12 in favor). A House bill the following January "to suspend the rules and introduce a resolution calling for the repeal of the fugitive slave law passed at the last session of Congress" was defeated by 119 votes to 68 (with 42 not voting). The Northeast vote was 31 against, 47 for; the South 62 against, none in favor; the Midwest 26 against, 19 for; and the West 2 for, none opposing.[31] Even so, numbers on these scales made many southern leaders feel that if western territories became free states, Congress might well come to be controlled by the growing anti-slavery alliance.

The ways that the nation's political leaders sought but failed to avoid slavery conflicts can be seen in how, after the emergence of mass political parties in the 1830s, they addressed slavery issues in their party platforms. The Jacksonian Democrats pioneered these statements of party principle in 1840, making this one of their nine platform resolutions: "That congress has no power, under the constitution, to interfere with or control the domestic institutions of the several states . . . that all efforts by abolitionists or others, made to induce congress to interfere with questions of slavery, or to take incipient steps in relation thereto, are calculated to lead to the most alarming and dangerous consequences."[32] This language recurred with minor changes in wording in every Democratic platform thereafter through 1856, when the Democrats also promised to enforce the 1850 Fugitive Slave Act and the 1852 Kansas-Nebraska Act, in order to ensure (as they wrote in capital letters) "NON-INTERFERENCE BY CONGRESS WITH SLAVERY IN STATE AND TERRITORY, OR IN THE DISTRICT OF COLUMBIA."[33] Their rivals the Whigs began adopting platforms in 1844, but they did not seek to fight their Democratic opponents on the battleground of slavery. That year and again in 1848, they said nothing about the issue.[34] In 1852 they, too, promised enforcement of the new Fugitive Slave Law, at least "until time and experience" proved further legislation to be necessary, and they deprecated "all further agitation" of slavery issues.[35] In their last gasp in 1856, the remnant Whigs returned to silence on slavery and merely condemned "geographical parties" and "civil war."[36]

But by then, the heightening opposition of the racial alliances had generated a reconfiguring of the nation's foundational system of mass parties, with the Whigs displaced as a major party by the emergent Republicans. The Republican's first platform in 1856 defined the nation's purposes in the language of the Declaration of Independence and asserted a constitutional duty to ban slavery in the territories. As they put it:

> we hold it to be a self-evident truth, that all men are endowed with the inalienable right to life, liberty, and the pursuit of happiness, and that the primary object and ulterior design of our Federal government were to secure these rights to all persons under its exclusive jurisdiction; that, as

our Republican fathers, when they had abolished Slavery in all our Na-tional Territory, ordained that no person shall be deprived of life, liberty, or property, without due process of law, it becomes our duty to maintain this provision of the Constitution against all attempts to violate it for the purpose of establishing Slavery in the Territories of the United States by positive legislation, prohibiting its existence or extension therein.[37]

The Republicans repeated this opposition to slavery in the territories in 1860, adding criticism of the doctrine in the Supreme Court's 1857 *Dred Scott* decision that the Constitution protected slavery in the territories, and denouncing "the recent reopening of the African slave trade, under the cover of our national flag, aided by perversions of judicial power."[38] Though anti-slavery Whigs like Lincoln formed the Republican's primary base, they had broader appeal throughout the North and border states. The fact that south-erners demanded that anti-slavery white supremacists decide whether to side with more racially egalitarian actors and institutions to stop slavery's spread drove many "Free Soil" Democrats into the Republican ranks. An exemplar here is Pennsylvania Democrat David Wilmot, author of the provision that sought to ban slavery in the western territories acquired in the Mexican-American War. Representative Wilmot feared slave competition with "free white labor," con-sidered blacks inferior, and hated the prospect of sharing power with them. He wrote privately that whites should never be "ruled by men," white or black, "brought up on the milk of some damn Negro wench."[39] But faced by slavery's expansion, he became a Republican and, while urging peace with the South, sup-ported President Lincoln as a wartime senator before accepting a judgeship.

If Wilmot was by then seeking to escape the politics of slavery, the party platforms show that as their efforts to forge legislative compromises faltered, many leaders of the divided antebellum American political system instead looked to the courts to resolve slavery issues. From early on in the antebellum period, both state and federal courts engaged with the implications of a vast number of legal issues for slavery and racial statuses, including the relationship of fed-eral powers over commerce to state police powers; the location of authority over immigration; birthright citizenship; Article IV privileges and immunities of citizenship; and much more. Most were matters seen as affecting state pow-ers to deny rights to free blacks as well as slaves without facing challenges based on national or international laws.[40]

The antebellum courts divided on these issues — but they thereby gave both alliances hopes of ultimate legal victories. Especially after 1840, the federal courts found themselves pressed to decide slavery issues by asserting either that the Constitution settled those controversies on behalf of pro-slavery forces, who insisted that the Constitution sheltered slavery as a protected form of property, or anti-slavery proponents, who claimed that the Constitution only permitted state-level support of the institution while mandating national policies to put it on the path to eventual extinction. Like most of the antebellum American governing institutions prior to the Civil War, the U.S. Supreme Court at first responded with divided, compromised decisions that on the whole leaned toward slaveholders. In *Groves v. Slaughter* (1841), a majority of the justices ruled that Mississippi could not ban the importation of slaves via a state constitutional provision, without an implementing statute—but most justices indicated it could regulate the slave trade as it saw fit if it chose to do so.[41] Justice Joseph Story then ruled for the Court in *U.S. v. Schooner Amistad* (1841) that because Spanish law no longer upheld the enslavement of Africans who had mutinied aboard the Spanish slave vessel *Amistad* and escaped to Connecticut, there was no obligation for them to be returned to their putative owners.[42] That result alarmed slaveholders, despite Story's assurance to the masters that if Spanish law had still supported slavery, the Court would have ordered the mutineers' return.

Later that term, in *Prigg v. Pennsylvania* (1842), the Court struck down Pennsylvania's "personal liberty" laws establishing restrictive state processes for the "recaption" of escaped slaves.[43] Here Story ruled for the majority that only Congress could implement the fugitive slave clause—but that it had a constitutional duty to do so. Although this ruling upheld slavery as constitutionally protected, it still disturbed slaveholders by not asserting that free states had to assist in enforcing their property rights. These issues served as a backdrop for congressional struggles over the Habeas Corpus Act of 1842, intended to permit federal courts to take cases from state courts if the disputes involved agents of foreign governments claiming protection under the law of nations. Southerners feared that foreign abolitionists inciting slave revolts in their states would assert that they were acting under international treaties banning the slave trade, and so they might get their cases heard by anti-slavery federal judges.[44] They did not prevent the act's passage, but they articulated an American suspicion toward international law that has persisted.

The early antebellum judicial rulings failed to satisfy any of those who wanted the Constitution to be read as unequivocally pro- or anti-slavery. Democrats, in particular, sought to quell their internal tensions over the issue by winning more strongly pro-slavery rulings from the Supreme Court their party had largely appointed. In 1851, Jackson's former attorney general Chief Justice Roger Taney partly obliged. In *Strader v. Graham* (1851), Taney ruled that even if a slave gained freedom by residing for a sufficient period of time in a free state, as George Washington had feared would happen with his slaves, the slave states could still reimpose legal servitude if the former slave came to re-side within their bounds and the states chose to do so.[45] Slave states did not have to recognize the emancipating effects of northern pro-liberty measures. Yet this guarantee still proved insufficient, because of the South's great fears that the western territories would one day provide insurmountable majorities of anti-slavery representatives, perhaps even regarding their free black resi-dents as U.S. citizens.

Hence, with the encouragement of leading national Democrats like Pennsylvania-born president James Buchanan, the Taney Court asserted in the fateful *Dred Scott* decision (1857) that Dred Scott was unable to sue in the courts of the United States because the law of the state in which he resided, Missouri, deemed him a slave.[46] The chief justice further held that the protec-tions to property provided by the Fifth Amendment's due process clause meant that Congress had no power to ban slavery in the territories, and that the nation's racially restrictive naturalization laws and doctrines of citizenship by birth meant that no African Americans could be deemed citizens of the United States, not even those whose home states regarded them as state citizens.[47]

If these legal doctrines had prevailed, the pro-slavery alliance would have succeeded in gaining constitutional protection for slavery on most of U.S. soil, with the only remaining question being whether the free states could constitu-tionally ban slavery within their own bounds. But the new Republican Party mobilized northern opposition against the Supreme Court's interpretations as part of its assault on the Democrats' support for the extension of slavery. With the two major parties now sharply and explicitly identified with the positions of the two racial alliances for the first time in U.S. history, the nation soon ruptured so severely that four candidates ran in the 1860 election. Southern states refused to list Lincoln on their ballots. And when he was elected by a small 39 percent plurality, they seceded.

A few weeks after Lincoln's first inaugural, his erstwhile Whig ally Alexan-der H. Stephens of Georgia, now vice president of the Confederate States of America, delivered his notorious "Cornerstone Speech." The former U.S. rep-resentative contended, as Lincoln did, that Jefferson had believed that "the enslavement of the African" was "an evil" that "would be evanescent and pass away." But, Stephens maintained, that belief "rested upon the assumption of the equality of the races," a "fundamentally wrong" premise. "Our new gov-ernment," he continued, "is founded upon exactly the opposite idea: its foun-dations are laid, its cornerstone rests, upon the great truth that the negro is not equal to the white man; that slavery, subordination to the superior race, is his natural and normal condition."[48] The contrast between the pro-slavery and anti-slavery positions could not have been balder. Although Lincoln's dedication to preserving the Union was complete, he nonetheless preferred to do so via war rather than to allow slavery to be made the enduring cornerstone of what he saw as permanent parts of the United States.[49]

The Civil War's polarizations and the key military contribution of African Americans then pushed Lincoln and many others further. Believing that "as He died to make men holy," they were called to make men free, Republicans from 1865 onward passed national statutes and constitutional amendments that banned slavery and prescribed far more racially egalitarian foundational systems of economic, legal, and ultimately political rights. But they did so only amidst great contestation, first from President Andrew Johnson and from Democrats returned to Congress and then, increasingly, from many within their own ranks. After 1865, few American leaders at any level thought it feasible to seek to restore chattel slavery, though many in the South, aided by some in the North, succeeded in establishing alternative forms of forced labor.

But the biggest source of contestation was the issue of how far and in what ways free African Americans would be equal with white Americans. For roughly a dozen years, up through the election of 1876, the two major parties stood arrayed against each other on that question. Republicans then continued to support African American voting rights, the civil rights issue most important for their power, until the early 1890s. Nonetheless, from the early 1870s on, many Republicans began seeking to remove other aspects of African American civic equality off their party's agenda, for the question of how far racial equality should go split the anti-slavery alliance almost immediately after it arose in 1865. Though for a time, a coalition of strong racial egalitarians had the upper hand in the Republican Party, the Congress, and the nation, their ranks eroded. As the late nineteenth century proceeded, opponents to the racial egalitarians found new ways to craft political, economic, and social foundational systems involving "separate but equal" and politically exclusionary laws and practices. These new systems of white supremacy at best conformed to the letter, but never the spirit, of the egalitarian guarantees written into law from 1865 to 1875. By the end of the century, this emergent Jim Crow alliance had created the structures of segregation and disfranchisement that would make up America's racial battleground for the next six decades.

THE ERA OF TRANSITION, 1865–96

On April 11, 1865, a triumphant President Lincoln delivered a carefully crafted speech from the balcony of the White House. He continued to profess deference to local decisions on how the newly restored states should structure their post-slavery societies. But Lincoln advanced a new view on enfranchising African Americans. His preference was for the vote to be "now conferred on the very intelligent, and on those who serve our cause as soldiers."[50] John Wilkes Booth was in the audience and reportedly said, "That is the last speech he will ever make."[51] Booth assassinated Lincoln three days later, placing in the White House an anti-slavery former Democrat, Andrew Johnson, who had won support from strongly egalitarian Radical Republicans for his ferocious denunciations of slaveholders.

Within a few short weeks, Johnson showed that he only shared an antislavery agenda with racial egalitarians. On the central post-slavery policy issue, the status of newly freed African Americans, he was fiercely committed to white supremacy. In May 1865, he recognized a Virginia government that congressional Radicals opposed, granted amnesty to most Confederates, and promised the restoration of most confiscated lands to whites. Johnson then replaced Freedmen's Bureau officials eager to uphold black rights and redistribute land with ones who supported subjecting free blacks to coercive forms of "contract" labor.[52] Encouraged by this display of national support, southern whites in Mississippi and South Carolina passed "Black Codes" in 1865 that prevented blacks from renting land and required them to sign annual labor contracts without rights to strike, or else be arrested for vagrancy. Congress responded in 1866 with a bill authorizing the Freedmen's Bureau to purchase lands for resale to blacks and with the 1866 Civil Rights Act, outlawing the Black Codes. Johnson vetoed both bills. Radicals fell two votes short of defeating the veto of the first measure, but Republicans did override the second, as well as Johnson's subsequent veto of a bill making the Freedmen's Bureau permanent. Johnson then unsuccessfully opposed enfranchising blacks in the District of Columbia; the Fourteenth Amendment; and the Military Reconstruction Act of 1867, which appeared to put Radical Republicans in Congress in control of Reconstruction. But Democrats fared well in the 1867 elections, a signal to many Republicans that white voters lacked enthusiasm for continued efforts to secure black rights.[53]

It is impossible to judge how far national initiatives to create a racially egalitarian America might have proceeded if a president less militantly obstructionist toward radical reconstruction had succeeded Lincoln. It is indisputable that Johnson's ascension proved a major obstacle to egalitarian reform, in ways that put questions of racial equality at the center of national politics and fueled the revival of the white South and the Democratic Party. Strong commitments to racial egalitarianism also had implications for the rights of Chinese immigrants, Native Americans, and others whom many whites would deem unacceptable in the years to come. But from 1865 to 1870, the most contentious issues were whether African Americans should really have the same economic rights as whites; whether the nation should help the freedmen to obtain land; and whether blacks should have voting rights on an equal basis with whites. Radical Republicans supported all these measures. Racial conservatives in both parties opposed them. By becoming the champion of this opposition, Johnson aimed to assemble "an exclusively white coalition of southern Conservatives and northern Democrats" that would elect him president on the white supremacist basis he preferred.[54] Although at this point, neither Johnson nor other white supremacists had an agenda defining what forms postwar white supremacist institutions should take, they were passionate about rejecting the egalitarian amendments and statutes that the Radical Republicans favored.

However much they differed among themselves, most Republicans opposed Johnson's ambitions. As the historian Michael Les Benedict has shown, from the Thirty-eighth Congress that began in March 1863 through the Fortieth Congress ending in March 1869, roughly one-third of the House and the Senate, all Republicans, consistently voted for racially egalitarian Reconstruction measures; a dip in 1864–65 reflected Lincoln's advocacy of more gradual reform policies.[55] More moderate Republicans often provided enough additional votes to override vetoes of many radical measures. Yet even as Republicans managed to maintain high levels of party cohesion during these years on votes pitting their congressional program and powers against Johnson, a similarly sized bloc of Democrats and conservative Republicans voted consistently against such measures. Some Republicans then began to lose confidence in the wisdom of backing the Radicals, and many were replaced by rising numbers of Democrats in the late 1860s and early 1870s.

Meanwhile southern white vigilante violence against blacks was also on the rise, most memorably in the night raids of the new Ku Klux Klan (KKK) and other militia-style groups dedicated to destroying black communities and terrorizing African American elected officials. About a quarter of southern counties displayed Klan-style collective violence in the late 1860s.[56] This violence solidified racial divisions between predominantly white small farmers and black tenant farmers and sharecroppers. It was an informal extension of the Civil War. Under President Ulysses S. Grant, Republicans gamely responded in 1870 with the Fifteenth Amendment, enfranchising blacks nationally to shore up their electoral base. They then passed National Election bills in 1870 and 1872 and a Civil Rights bill or "Ku Klux Klan Act" in 1871 to protect black voting and black civil rights more generally.[57] But the violence did not stop: the most notorious incident occurred in the Mississippi town of Colfax on Easter Sunday, 1873. Dozens of black Americans were massacred as they struggled to control a county courthouse after a contested election. This event proved a precursor to two years of relentless violence against African Americans whose perpetrators sought to expunge any notion that the Fourteenth and Fifteenth amendments meant truly equal citizenship.[58] These conflicts seemed to benefit Democrats at the polls. Their numbers in Congress rose steadily through the 1870s, to the point where they gained control of the House in 1875 and, briefly, the Senate as well in 1879.[59]

The party platforms of those years show how these political developments affected partisan positions on racial issues. For a time, the parties remained clearly divided over the status of African Americans, though no longer over slavery. The 1868 Democratic Party platform proclaimed the slavery question "settled for all time to come"; but it also called for state regulation of the "elective franchise" and the abolition of the Freedmen's Bureau along with "all political instrumentalities designed to secure negro supremacy," even as it expressed gratitude to Andrew Johnson for his opposition to the Radicals' program.[60] The Republicans that year denounced Johnson for acting "treacherously" by resisting reconstruction, and they pledged to secure "equal civil and political rights to all." But the pledge was presented timidly—"the question of suffrage in all the loyal States properly belongs to the people of those States"—rather than promoting the franchise for blacks everywhere.[61] Their reluctance to fight over controversial racial issues was already evident.

Once the Republicans nonetheless decided they had to push through the Fifteenth Amendment, the Democrats again officially accepted the change. In 1872 they pledged to "oppose any reopening of the questions settled by the thirteenth, fourteenth and fifteenth amendments of the Constitution." But they also insisted that "local self-government, with impartial suffrage, will guard the rights of all citizens more securely than any centralized power," a states' rights rather than explicitly anti-"negro" theme that would long endure.[62] The Republicans maintained that the amendments "should be cordially sustained because they are right, not merely tolerated because they are law," and asserted that enforcement "according to their spirit" could "safely be entrusted only to the party" that sponsored them. They pledged commitment to "exact equality in the enjoyment of all civil, political, and public rights," to be achieved by "appropriate state and Federal legislation."[63] The GOP platform did not, however, propose any new concrete measures toward this end, not least because "Liberal" Republicans were breaking with the party to support white southerners' opposition to strong Reconstruction measures.

Republicans did nonetheless go on to propose a major new Civil Rights Act in 1874, inspired by the death in March of the great Radical senator Charles Sumner. But the GOP then lost ninety-six seats in the 1874 congressional elections. When the resulting lame-duck Congress ultimately passed the 1875 Civil Rights Act, it was far weaker than Sumner had envisioned. The act lacked requirements for integrated public schools, though it still banned economic discrimination in places of public accommodation in ways a Republican-dominated Supreme Court soon found unconstitutional.[64]

In 1876, the Republican platform continued to promise "vigorous exercise" of national powers to secure to every American citizen "exact equality" in all rights, and it accused the Democrats of being the "the same in character and spirit" as when they "sympathized with treason."[65] But the GOP did not overtly accuse the Democrats of opposition to the rights of black Americans, nor did they express explicit concern for the latter or propose any further measures on their behalf. Instead, in what would prove a fateful development for racially egalitarian forces, their platform called on Congress to investigate the "moral and material" effects of "the immigration and importation of Mongolians."[66] The Republicans recognized that the Democrats were capitalizing on the burgeoning uproar of western citizens over Chinese immigration to discredit racially egalitarian positions, and they felt compelled to seek compromise, not confrontation, over the issue. The Democrats were confident they had a popular cause. A week later, their platform denounced "corrupt centralism" and Republican currency policies, but it also warned vociferously against exposing "our brethren of the Pacific coast to the incursions of a race not sprung from the same great parent stock" and called for laws to prevent "immigration of the Mongolian race."[67]

These platforms signaled a realignment of political forces that proved crippling to the racial egalitarian agenda. Before the war, the South had feared that western states would oppose slavery, and after it, many in the South initially supported Chinese immigrants as alternatives to black labor, against western wishes.[68] But as western whites, who had once welcomed Chinese workers to construct the Pacific Railroad, became increasingly hostile to rising numbers of Chinese immigrants after its completion, they sought allies for national immigration restrictions. California Republican senator Aaron Sargent's 1877 report for Congress's Joint Special Committee to Investigate Chinese Immigration contended that the "Chinese race" lacked "sufficient brain capacity" to participate in the self-governing institutions of "the Aryan or European race," and San Francisco Democrat Henry George compared them in this regard to "the negroes" of the South.[69] Southern congressional Democrats responded by embracing a "political alliance of the South and the West" bonded by white supremacist commitments to oppose Chinese immigration, "Chinese citizenship and suffrage," and "negro supremacy," as Alabama senator John F. Morgan wrote in the influential *North American Review* in 1878.[70]

Some "moderate" Republicans who feared further losses from identification with full racial equality also embraced the cause of Chinese exclusion. Maine senator and later presidential candidate James G. Blaine declared in 1879 in a letter to the *New York Times* that "if as a nation we have the right to keep out infectious diseases . . . we surely have the right to exclude that immigration which reeks with impurity."[71] In the same year, President Rutherford Hayes remarked: "Our experience in dealing with the weaker races—the Negroes and Indians, for example—is not encouraging. . . . I would consider with favor any suitable measures to discourage the Chinese from coming to our shores."[72]

The positions of Blaine and Hayes bespoke growing doubts among all but the most radical Republicans about the propriety of championing authentic racial equality. The new West-South alliance in favor of white supremacist policies underscored that identification with racial egalitarianism was politically dangerous in an era of close national elections. Consequently, when in 1880 the Democrats' platform called for "No more Chinese immigration," the Republicans also promised to "limit and restrict that immigration" by "just, humane, and reasonable laws." The parties continued to clash over national efforts to protect voting rights of blacks in the South, but the Republicans no longer expressed concern for any other rights of African Americans.[73] Though Congress and ensuing presidents still struggled over how to control Chinese immigration in ways consistent with the nation's treaties with China, the first major ban on immigration of Chinese laborers became law in 1882.

In the House of Representatives, the bill was approved by 167 to 66, with 59 members not voting. The partisan and regional disaggregation is significant. The divided Republican Party contributed 60 votes in favor and 62 against; 25 Republicans abstained. Among Democrat members, only 4 opposed the legislation. Regionally, the South supported the proposed exclusion by 60 to 2, leaving 20 members from the South who did not vote. The seven western states unanimously supported the ban. In the New England states, 1 member voted in favor, 19 opposed the bill, and 2 members did not vote.[74] In the Senate, a revised version of the bill was approved by 32 to 15, with 29 senators not voting (16 of whom were in 8 party pairs of nonvoters). The opponents were all Republicans. Eleven Republicans voted for exclusion, and 13 Republicans did not vote.[75] Those patterns reveal that southerners, most other Democrats, westerners of both parties, and many Republicans, including many of the party's leaders, now endorsed policies that rested in part on the rejection of racial equality. Only a shrinking segment of old guard Republicans, led by Massachusetts senator George F. Hoar, represented the egalitarian radicalism that had held power fifteen years earlier.

The declining strength of racially egalitarian forces visible in the broad support for Chinese exclusion probably traced chiefly to the unwillingness of
most white voters throughout the country to support a sustained radical
agenda; but racially inegalitarian positions were aided by other significant developments. The ranks of racial egalitarians began splintering internally early
on. In 1866, the National Women's Rights Convention voted to join the members of the American Anti-Slavery Society in a new American Equal Rights
Association. But the organization soon came apart when most of its male
members favored language in the Fourteenth and Fifteenth amendments that
supported voting rights for black men but not any women, insisting that one
reform at a time was all that white men would accept. Angry women's movement leaders including Susan B. Anthony and Elizabeth Cady Stanton forged
an alliance with anti-black Democrats to pursue women's suffrage immediately. Both women's rights and broader equal rights efforts remained divided
by internal antagonisms for years thereafter.[76]

Then came the publication of Charles Darwin's *Descent of Man* in 1870.
Darwin declaimed that there was "no doubt that the various races . . . differ
much from each other" in both their physical and their "mental characteristics."[77] Proponents of racial inequality could claim all the more authoritatively
that they had modern science on their side when they called for the "tutelary"
subordination of less "civilized" and less "evolved" nonwhites to white governance.[78] These ideas became centerpieces of the regular science exhibitions
at America's eleven World's Fairs held between 1876 and 1916. At these exhib-
its scientists expounded the principles of race, civilization, and progress, legitimating the race hierarchies that would be elaborated by the end of the century
into the Jim Crow order.[79] Those developments were also abetted when postwar attempts at interracial labor organizing proved to compete poorly with
rival efforts to build unions around the interests of native-born white male
workers. Even the initially more inclusive, internationalist-minded Knights of
Labor became more restrictionist over the course of the late nineteenth century, and they lost out by its end to the American Federation of Labor, which
itself focused more exclusively on native white workers' interests over time.[80]

In the West, many small businessmen, a core electoral base for Republicans
of all stripes, feared competition from Chinese merchants as much as workers
feared Chinese laborers. These economic interests combined with racial concerns to generate massive white opposition to Chinese immigration, in ways that
fostered greater receptivity to white supremacist rhetoric.[81] In 1879, a referendum
in California calling for Chinese exclusion passed by a staggering 150,000 to
900.[82] In those same years, public officials like Francis Walker, briefly commissioner of Indian Affairs, later one of the nation's leading advocates of immigration

restriction, and always a "natural-born segregationist," explicitly linked Native Americans, African Americans, and Asians as races at earlier "ethnical periods" of evolutionary development who could not be treated as genuinely equal citizens at present, whether or not they might eventually achieve such status.[83] In the meantime, nonwhites should not be allowed to stand in the way of white citizens' efforts to prosper by building on western lands, including lands previously reserved to the native tribes. All these developments meant that the alliance that had supported greater racial egalitarianism prior to the abolition of slavery and at the height of Radical Reconstruction lost more and more ground in the last decades of the nineteenth century among white intellectuals, women, workers, small businesses, and Republican officeholders who wanted to continue to hold their offices.

The role of the federal courts in these years is a matter of scholarly debate. Obviously, they did not halt the mounting political opposition to strenuous pursuit of racially egalitarian reconstruction visions from prevailing in most regards. The disputes are over whether the courts should be placed on the side of those opposing such visions, either because they failed to do all they legally could to resist the rising inegalitarian tide, or because they deliberately strengthened the hand of the opponents of racial equality.[84] In decisions of the late 1860s, various federal judges did show themselves inclined to support expansive readings of the Reconstruction statutes and amendments, but that willingness ebbed after the early 1870s.[85] Representative here is Supreme Court Justice Joseph Bradley. A New Jersey commercial litigator appointed by President Grant, Bradley wrestled with his views about just what the egalitarian guarantees of the 1866 Civil Rights Act and the Fourteenth Amendment meant. Through the early 1870s, he accepted that they had created both national judicial authority to uphold robust "free labor" rights against state infringements, and national congressional power to act when states failed to protect such rights.

Bradley soon became concerned, however, about letting Congress "legislate on all subjects of legislation whatsoever." He began authoring opinions for the Supreme Court that read the postwar amendments more narrowly and found some Reconstruction statutes unconstitutional. In response to the Colfax massacre, Bradley ruled in the circuit court case of U.S. v. Cruikshank (1874) that the Thirteenth and Fifteenth amendments allowed Congress to act only on offenses against liberty and voting rights that were racially motivated, while the rights protected by the Fourteenth Amendment could be judicially enforced only against state violations, not infringements by private actors.[86] He did not find the former Confederate soldiers who had killed the blacks in the Colfax courthouse to be either state actors or racially motivated, so he ruled that Congress could not punish them. The Supreme Court soon agreed, with Bradley voting with the 8–1 majority.[87]

Then, in the landmark *Civil Rights Cases* (1883), Bradley similarly ruled that the Fourteenth Amendment allowed Congress only to legislate against state denials of equal protection.[88] And though the Thirteenth Amendment permitted Congress to ban "badges and incidents" of slavery, Bradley thought it went too far to say that this power meant that Congress could outlaw racial discrimination in the marketplace by private actors. The 1875 Civil Rights Act was therefore unconstitutional. Justice Bradley contended that its guarantees against racial discrimination in places of public accommodation made African Americans the "special favorite of the laws," in ways that placed them above the rank of "mere citizen" held by whites. Bradley, a faithful Republican who had cast the deciding vote on the electoral commission that gave the 1876 election to Rutherford B. Hayes, was probably no different from most Republican moderates in his waning enthusiasm for forceful national measures to assist African Americans. These cases did not prevent either the states or Congress from pursuing other avenues to protect African American rights. But by limiting the impact of the main statutory and constitutional provisions passed when support for racial equality was at its height, Bradley's rulings and kindred ones by the Supreme Court and many lower federal courts effectively required racial egalitarians to build a new, even stronger coalition if black rights were to be protected, at a time when the egalitarian forces were under siege and in disarray. Unsurprisingly, in these years, no such stronger alliance emerged.

Yet despite all these intellectual, economic, political, and legal developments favorable to racially inegalitarian positions by the mid-1880s, the stage was still not quite set for the rise of the Jim Crow system of segregation and disfranchisement of African Americans and often other nonwhite Americans as well. Many blacks were still voting Republican. Whatever their doubts about racial equality intellectually or socially, few GOP leaders wished to lose that electoral constituency. Every Republican platform from 1884 through 1908 endorsed protection of the franchise, often accusing southern Democrats of vote fraud, though the wording was notably muted in 1896, after the Democrats had regained power in 1892 by attacking the Republicans' 1890 National Elections bill.[89] For their part, after the adoption of the Fourteenth Amendment, the Democrats felt compelled to profess repeatedly their official commitment to "equal and exact justice to all citizens of whatever nativity, race, color, or persuasion," even as they also declaimed against the dangers of "servile races" unfit to "become citizens" and denounced federal efforts to secure black voting rights as "despotic" and a source of "the reviving of race antagonisms."[90]

All three Civil War amendments and statutes and the more egalitarian strains in American political culture they expressed stood as barriers to overt endorsement of racial discrimination directed against American citizens, even if they did not prevent racial justifications for immigrant exclusion that openly acknowledged difficulties with citizens of "weaker" or "servile" races.

Two developments completed the setting for the proliferation of Jim Crow segregation and disfranchisements laws to the point that they amounted to new foundational economic, political, educational, and social systems, with rival racial alliances arrayed for and against them. The first was the 1892 election of Grover Cleveland to the presidency he had lost to Benjamin Harrison four years before—a comeback aided substantially by the Democrats' relentless assaults on the Republican's proposed 1890 National Elections Act, which Democrats dubbed a "Force Bill." The act was motivated by expanding efforts of southern white Democrats to use fraudulent methods to disfranchise blacks, especially in Florida, Mississippi, and Tennessee, and it was supported by Republican majorities in the House and the Senate as well as the White House. It was defeated, however, by the first major southern filibuster in Senate history.[91] The Democrats' attacks on the bill then were so successful electorally that they briefly gained control of both houses of Congress as well as the White House from 1893 to 1895.

In another example of how struggles between the racial alliances have had far-reaching, often unseen impacts, Republican Speaker of the House Thomas Reed had pushed through the "Reed Rules" of 1890, many of which still structure House procedures today but which then included significant empowerment of the Speaker, in part to try to enact the 1890 National Elections bill.[92] Once they gained a majority in the House, Democrats reduced the prerogatives of the Speaker and strengthened the relative power of committees, a pattern that persisted throughout the Jim Crow era, in part because Democrats from the Solid South found they could use the clout of their seniority on committees as bulwarks against racial change.[93]

They did so aggressively. A House committee report issued during the Fifty-third Congress demanded "every trace of reconstruction measures be wiped from the books." Democrats immediately repealed the first statute passed to enforce voting rights under the Fifteenth Amendment, the 1870 Voting Rights Act. Over the next two decades, about 94 percent of the federal electoral regulatory code built up after the Civil War would be repealed. And after 1896, these repeals received substantial Republican support: though Republican Party platforms continued to profess allegiance to the cause of African American enfranchisement, the debacle of the 1892 elections finally crushed all remaining will among GOP officeholders to defend black voting rights in earnest.[94]

The new state laws and constitutional provisions to eliminate black voters then enacted without fear of federal interference made it easier for states to also adopt other new Jim Crow laws. The courts, however, had to support all these measures, despite the guarantees of the Fourteenth and Fifteenth amendments. The central constitutional strategy of racial inegalitarians relied on an 1849 opinion by the great Massachusetts chief justice, Lemuel Shaw. Shaw had ruled that the state's constitutional guarantee of equality before the law was not violated by establishing "separate but equal" schools for blacks (though Boston soon turned against school segregation).[95] In the pivotal U.S. Supreme Court case of *Plessy v. Ferguson* (1896), Justice Henry Billings Brown, a Massachusetts Republican, endorsed the claim that a state similarly did not violate equal protection when it imposed racial restrictions on who could ride on railroads or be served by other businesses, so long as citizens of different races were provided "separate but equal" facilities and services.[96] Justice Brown accepted that people had "racial instincts" prompting aversions to social and public intermixing that legislators could properly recognize and guard against. Brown also stressed that the law did not on its face endorse beliefs in black inferiority, and he refused to acknowledge that such beliefs played any part in its adoption or administration. With this decision, the nation officially entered the Jim Crow era.

Segregation was able to long endure, however, only because the Supreme Court went on to turn a blind eye to efforts to keep African Americans from voting in opposition to segregation policies. In two cases coming out of Alabama a few years later, *Giles v. Harris* (1903) and *Giles v. Teasley* (1904), another Massachusetts Republican, Oliver Wendell Holmes Jr., and an Ohio Republican, William Day, wrote for the Court upholding the state's new voter registration system against charges that it was operated fraudulently to deny black voting rights. In the first case, Holmes ruled that if so, the Court had little power to correct the fraud, because it could not hope to supervise the whole state electoral system.[97] In the second, Day endorsed the outrageous argument of the Alabama Supreme Court that if the registration system was unconstitutional, black voters had no right to be registered under it, and if it was not unconstitutional, then they had no complaint whatsoever.[98]

The justices' rulings sent a clear signal. Even with its powerful northern Republican presence, the Supreme Court was now aligned with the emergent pro–Jim Crow racial alliance. Southern states could now disfranchise as well as segregate without federal resistance. Booker T. Washington, who gave his famous Atlanta Exposition Address appearing to endorse segregation the year before the *Plessy* decision was handed down, and who thereby gave valuable legitimacy to the already powerful forces advocating Jim Crow policies, paid postal worker Jackson W. Giles's legal expenses in the cases challenging Alabama's registration laws. But Washington did so with such secrecy that Giles thought his lawyer was working pro bono.[99]

Not even the nation's most famous and widely respected African American leader felt able to openly challenge the now-dominant coalition supporting measures to establish veiled forms of white supremacy throughout most of the public and private spheres of American life. The Jim Crow alliance had formed. It would take seven decades for the balance of political power to shift enough for it to be overcome.

Chapter 3

"We of the North were thoroughly wrong"
How Racial Alliances Mobilized Ideas and Law

A TALE OF TWO ADAMS

In 1866, a former slave in Louisiana named Henry Adams joined the U.S. Army to assist in Reconstruction. He learned to read and write. He formed committees to document the brutalities blacks were suffering at the hands of Louisiana whites. He became a stump speaker for the Republican Party, and he served on a grand jury and advised fellow blacks how to seek justice in local courts. But after 1877, when the Republicans began to withdraw troops from the South in return for the election of Hayes, Adams despaired of preventing resurgent white supremacy in the South. He left his home for an ultimate fate that is not known.[1]

In 1913, another, far more prominent Republican Adams, Charles Frances Adams Jr. of Massachusetts, delivered a lecture at the University of South Carolina entitled "'Tis Sixty Years Since." His remarks showed that Henry Adams's despair had not been unfounded. This Adams compared "the ideals and actualities of the present with the ideals, anticipations and dreams" he had held as a young man enrolling at Harvard in 1853. Adams said he had then been a "youthful disciple" of a "somewhat wild-eyed school of philosophy." This philosophy believed on "scriptural" grounds that all men were "equal in the possibilities of their attributes,—physical, moral, intellectual." And so he had gone on to fight in the Union Army, leading African American soldiers and supporting their rights, during the Civil War. But subsequent experience, including the results of Reconstruction and of "more careful and intelligent ethnological study," led him to conclude that "we theorists and abstractionists of the North . . . were thoroughly wrong" when "we indulged in the curious and, as is now admitted, utterly erroneous theory that the African was, so to speak, an Anglo-Saxon, or, if you will, a Yankee 'who had never had a chance.'" Now Adams saw African Americans as "a vast alien mass which does not assimilate and which cannot be absorbed." He willingly deferred to the judgment of southern whites as to how their status should best be adjusted.[2]

Adams made a number of such speeches in the South during these years. Along with the positions on race and the Constitution of Massachusetts Republicans like Justices Brown and Holmes, these speeches made it seem clear that the egalitarian spirit of older Massachusetts Republicans like Charles Sumner and George Hoar was dead. With the Democrats even more strongly white supremacist, acceptance of renewed subordination of nonwhite Americans appeared to reign virtually uncontested in both parties and throughout the forces in control of governing institutions across the land.

The Jim Crow Racial Alliances: America's Second Racial Era

Yet in fact, diminished but determined racially egalitarian actors, groups, and institutions remained important players in American politics, and over time new ones emerged. From their own efforts, aided by changes in a range of domestic and international circumstances, they would gradually grow more powerful through the first two-thirds of the twentieth century, especially during and after World War II. As scholars have begun to stress, it is wrong to conceive of the early Jim Crow era as one in which forces seeking to elaborate local, state, and national systems of racial hierarchy went unchallenged or were always triumphant.[3] Shaped by the interactions of a wide range of groups, patterns and practices of white supremacy during the Jim Crow years varied from state to state, town to town, even neighborhood to neighborhood, and shifted over time in differing ways in all these locales, creating a far more complex tapestry of race in America than we can capture here. Yet it remains true that at the national level, major legislative, litigative, or partisan contests over racial issues were rare during the first four decades of the twentieth century. The short-term results of most of the conflicts that did occur were to reaffirm the thinly masked policies and institutions of white supremacy that most of the nation's elites had come to endorse.

The shared acceptance of those arrangements by the nation's major parties is measurable in the treatment of racial equality in the parties' platforms from 1912 through 1940. Though far from perfect predictors of what partisan officials will do in office, platforms are reliable indicators of what powerful elements within the parties wish to present publicly as their official positions. Parties often promise more in their platforms than they can deliver. But strikingly, on racial policy issues, the parties in these years did not promise very much at all. Throughout this period, and especially with the rise of Franklin D. Roosevelt's New Deal Democratic coalition after 1932, the platforms provide ample evidence that the parties represented different class interests, however much each claimed to speak for the nation as a whole. But in their platform positions, in their campaigning, and in their governing, the parties did not divide sharply over race.

Even as discriminatory Jim Crow policies became further entrenched, the Republicans' prior advocacy of national action to secure a wide range of rights for African Americans was reduced to calls for punishment of lynching from 1912 to 1928, initially through citizen action, and only later through federal measures. These calls failed. The concerns for states' rights, including their police powers, that opponents of racial equality had trumpeted since Reconstruction acted as effective obstacles to efforts to expand national authority in this realm of criminal justice policies. The GOP added vague statements of support for equal opportunity for "the Negro" in 1932 and 1936—the latter accompanied by condemnation of New Deal relief policies that threatened to "make him solely a ward of the federal government."[4] In these same years, in keeping with their efforts to avoid being identified with advocacy of full equality for all races, the Republicans also repeatedly made clear their support for the nation's racially restrictive immigration laws. Only in 1940 did the GOP call for ending discrimination against black Americans in all branches of the federal government and renew its once-frequent calls to make formal suffrage rights "effective for the Negro citizen."[5]

Content with the Jim Crow systems they had done so much to build, Democrats generally said nothing at all about African Americans in their platforms. They simply sought to prevent others from raising issues of racial justice. Democrats denounced those who stirred "discord and strife" by "arousing prejudices of a racial, religious or other nature" in 1916, and they similarly attacked "any effort to arouse religious or racial dissension" in 1924.[6] In the 1920s, they also repeatedly supported exclusion of Asian immigrants and the national origins-based immigration restrictions enacted in that decade.[7] For the Democrats, too, it was not until 1940 that they adopted a plank expressing concern for "Negroes," pledging like the Republicans to legislate "against discrimination in government service" and celebrating the participation of "Negro citizens" in New Deal "economic and social advances."[8] Similarly, the Progressive Party platforms of 1912 and 1924 said nothing about the rights of African Americans, even as they championed a variety of other democratizing reforms including nominations through primaries, direct election of senators, and the vote for women.[9]

Due to this tripartisan agreement on almost all major racial policy issues from the beginning of the century through the end of the 1930s, party competition and shifting party control of Congress and the White House did not alter the fact that the Jim Crow racial coalition enjoyed majorities in all three branches of the federal government. That alliance also included virtually all

TABLE 3.1
Pro–Jim Crow Racial Alliance, 1896–1954

Southern and conservative Democrats

Conservative Republican Party officeholders and members

Presidents of both parties, either supportive or passive

Most members of Congress, especially the Senate

Majority of the Supreme Court to late 1940s

Most federal civil service officials

Most federal court judges, many state judges

Most white businesses

Most white labor unions

Most white churches

Most academic institutions, disciplines until 1940

White supremacist groups (e.g., the KKK, the Pioneer Fund, White Citizen Councils)

Source: Because of data deficiencies and variations over time, we can state only that "most" members of these categories took the indicated positions. Table 3.1 derives chiefly from Richard Kluger, *Simple Justice: The History of* Brown v. Board of Education *and Black America's Struggle for Equality* (New York: Vintage, 1975), 66–91, 102–4, 115–23, 218–38); Harvard Sitkoff, *A New Deal for Blacks: The Emergence of Civil Rights as a National Issue: The Depression Decade* (New York: Oxford University Press, 1978), 3–33, 102–28, 169–89); Franklin and Moss, *From Slavery to Freedom*, 231–38, 301–17, 415–19; Nieman, *Promises to Keep*, 105–60; and Carol Swain, *The New White Nationalism in America: Its Challenge to Integration* (Cambridge: Cambridge University Press, 2002), 80–83, 241–42.

southern and many western officeholders, and many other local officials and police forces, as well as most private white economic, religious, and social organizations. The exceptionally powerful makeup of the Jim Crow racial alliance through the first half of the twentieth century is detailed in table 3.1.

Science and the Elaboration of Racial Hierarchies

In the modified white supremacist institutions this alliance constructed, a new confidence about the generality of race hierarchy shone through. Jim Crow proponents enacted explicit forms of racial apartheid, race-based immigration and naturalization restrictions, and exclusionary housing, educational, and employment practices, along with titularly race-neutral vagrancy laws, tenant farming rules, criminal statutes, and voter registration and jury selection systems administered to maintain white supremacy—and used also to disempower poor whites where they failed to cooperate. Though scholars sometimes treat these years as ones in which new faith in scientific expertise contributed to the development of bureaucratic agencies staffed by experts that could exercise much autonomous power, those powers were commonly used to promote segregation, disfranchisement, and other renewed forms of racial hierarchy. Bureaucratic agents acted both out of intellectual conviction of the propriety of racial inegalitarianism and in acquiescence to the power of the Jim Crow alliance.

Beginning in the early 1900s, anthropologist Franz Boas and his associates began a long campaign to discredit the biological racism dominating academic discourse in favor of more egalitarian cultural interpretations of race and ethnicity. This initiative enjoyed eventual success in most academic disciplines. However, most "popular science" writings and most popular cultural works in the first third of the twentieth century propagated evolutionary-based views of racial hierarchy, as Adams noted in South Carolina. Along with the Klan-glorifying novels of Thomas Dixon and the legendary anti-black film they inspired, *Birth of the Nation*, progressive scholars of labor, immigration, and race like Wisconsin economist John R. Commons, the discussions of race and immigration in the forty-two volumes produced by Congress's Dillingham Commission in 1910, and popular nonfiction books such as patrician Madison Grant's *The Passing of the Great Race* in 1916, all contributed to a climate shaping the conduct of officials in the Post Office, the Department of Agriculture, the Interior Department, and the Bureau of Immigration and Naturalization, among others. These bureaucracies imposed policies segregating public work forces, promoting segregation within unions, denying African Americans access to public lands, transferring tribal lands to public and private white hands, and excluding many aliens deemed "nonwhite"—especially when a southern political scientist, Woodrow Wilson, occupied the White House.[10] The new systems justified in terms of these far-ranging racial doctrines included not only anti-black measures but similar laws and practices aimed at Mexicans in the Southwest, Asians in California, and Native Americans in many western states. They also supported the racially justified imperial conquest and governance of Filipinos, Puerto Ricans, and Pacific Islanders, and eventually the systems of race-based immigration quotas enacted in the 1920s.[11]

To be sure, these other forms of racial and ethnic domination and exclusion differed in some ways from the Jim Crow system, so they can reasonably be

viewed in some respects as autonomous systems of racial hierarchy. But cru-
cially, they were created via pro-segregation alliances of western whites and
northern imperialists and immigration restrictionists with the southern architects of Jim Crow laws and practices. Much of their ideological content defined how far those they subordinated should be treated like blacks. That is
why so many groups who did not identify primarily as "white" or "black" nonetheless sought to be recognized as more like "whites," though many instead
regarded quests for such recognition as shameful and probably futile. Over
time, those who repudiated efforts to be seen as "white" or "white-like" often
proved willing to join anti-segregation alliance efforts to secure more equal
rights for all.[12]

Throughout, the new institutions of racial hierarchy were constructed in
ways that were putatively compliant with legal equality, in order to resist the
challenges that egalitarians mounted under the Reconstruction amendments
and surviving civil rights statutes. In this way, the Jim Crow era differed significantly from both the antebellum slavery era and the early Reconstruction
years, when southern whites sought to reimpose explicit systems of racial hierarchy such as the Black Codes. Yet restructured as they were, these systems of
segregation, disfranchisement, and immigrant exclusion remained white supremacist, making only formal, limited concessions to the more egalitarian
institutions and actors that opposed them. The Jim Crow racial coalition engaged in continuing coercive governmental and social measures to sustain its
rule, ranging from the violent, such as lynching and mob riots, to the institutional, such as legal limits on rights of citizenship.[13]

Even so, it produced no monolithic "racial order" or "racial state," because
again, racial segregation and exclusions never went unopposed. Just as the
Civil War egalitarians did not succeed in removing all institutional bases
for the resurgence of the white supremacists, so the architects of the new Jim
Crow system did not eradicate all the achievements or the membership of the
postwar egalitarian racial alliance (table 3.2). The Reconstruction constitutional provisions and some national and state statutes remained available for
judges willing to apply them. Often judicial dissenters and, much more rarely,
court majorities did so.[14]

Toward Equal Citizenship

This coalition contained sharp internal differences on how best to achieve
racial change—through local and state social reforms or mandatory national
legislation or litigation; through confrontational mass protests or orderly elite
negotiations; or through alliance with or repudiation of economic radicals.

TABLE 3.2
Anti–Jim Crow Racial Alliance, 1896–1954

Racially egalitarian Democrats, overwhelmingly northern, mostly after 1932

Liberal Republicans

Minority of Congress, federal bench, until 1950s

Some federal agency officials, mostly after 1932

Minority of Supreme Court (i.e., Justice Harlan)

Some lower federal court, stage judges

A few white and most black businesses

Black unions

Some liberal and socialist advocacy groups and parties

Liberal black and white religious groups

Most nonwhite advocacy groups (e.g., NAACP, Urban League)

Black fraternal organizations (e.g., Negro Fellowship League)

Liberal white-black southern reform groups (e.g., Southern Conference for Human Welfare, Committee on Interracial Cooperation, Southern Electoral Reform League)

Liberal foundations (e.g., Phelps-Stokes Foundation, Julius Rosenwald Fund)

Liberal academics, especially after 1932

Source: Along with the sources cited in the text, see Franklin and Moss, *From Slavery to Freedom*, 258–59, 286–90, 318–23, 342–59, 411–15; Richard M. Valelly, *The Two Reconstructions: The Struggle for Black Enfranchisement* (Chicago: University of Chicago Press, 2004), 61–71, 121–72; and Theda Skocpol, Ariane Liazos, and Marshall Ganz, *What a Mighty Power We Can Be: African American Fraternal Groups and the Struggle for Racial Equality* (Princeton, NJ: Princeton University Press, 2006), 174–213.

And many coalition members did not even agree on the desirability of ultimate racial integration. But they were united nonetheless in seeing Jim Crow laws as making up a system of racial hierarchy that should be dismantled in favor of enforceable equal rights, opportunities, and citizenship for all Americans regardless of origins. Their great bond was the belief that there should be no "second-class citizens" in the United States. Though such commitments had never predominated in American law and had always been contested ideologically, much in American political and religious traditions supported them, more so over time.

Organizing against Jim Crow

Even so, until its ranks were expanded by the domestic and international factors discussed later, this alliance was not powerful enough even to advance, much less to enact, new racially egalitarian national legislation. There is perhaps no better indicator of the predominance of the pro–Jim Crow racial alliance than the inability of egalitarians to win consideration in Congress for anything more substantial than legislation to prevent the vicious vigilantism of lynching—and Congress's refusal to pass laws against even this outrage. As part of white efforts to reassert dominance after the fall of Reconstruction, there were more than 100 recorded lynchings per year every year but one from 1882, the first year for which moderately reliable data exist, to 1901; and there were at least 60 per year throughout the Progressive era and World War I.[15] In 1892, when 241 black men and women were lynched, African American journalist Ida B. Wells suffered the loss of a close friend to a lynching by whites who resented his successful grocery business. She began her visible and flinty international anti-lynching campaign.[16] Wells's activism became part of an efflorescence of African American reform efforts during the 1890s and early 1900s that included New York editor Thomas Fortune's Afro-American League and then Council, begun in 1890; Boston editor William Monroe Trotter's New England Suffrage League, organized in 1903; the Niagara Movement founded by W.E.B. Du Bois and Trotter in 1905; and the Negro Fellowship League created in 1910 by Wells (then Ida Wells-Barnett), along with other groups, many short-lived.[17]

The most enduring political organization was the National Association for the Advancement of Colored People (NAACP). It was organized in 1909 by prominent African American leaders including Du Bois, Trotter, and a somewhat reluctant Wells-Barnett, in conjunction with leading white reformers such as radical journalists Oswald Garrison Villard and William English Walling, social worker Jane Addams, socialist Charles Edward Russell, and leading Massachusetts lawyers Moorfield Storey, once Charles Sumner's personal secretary, and Albert Pillsbury, the author of an anti-lynching statute. Responding in part to a vicious race riot in Lincoln's hometown of Springfield, Illinois, in 1908, Villard issued his famous "Lincoln's Birthday Call" in 1909, the one hundredth anniversary of Lincoln's birth, initiating the new organization, which formally founded itself in Springfield and soon began an anti-lynching campaign.[18] In 1918, the NAACP found an ally in Republican congressman

Leonidas Dyer, elected from a heavily African American district in St. Louis since 1911. Dyer introduced a bill to make lynching a federal crime. He had no immediate success, but prospects appeared promising in the Sixty-seventh Congress in 1921. Republicans had captured large majorities in the House and the Senate as well as the White House, and new president Warren Harding endorsed Dyer's proposal.

But taking a position with implications that went well beyond racial policies, states' rights proponents insisted there was no federal "police power" under the Constitution to combat what was essentially the crime of murder. Southerners also denounced the bill as a means "to encourage rape" of white women by black men.[19] The Dyer bill nonetheless passed the House of Representatives in January 1922 by 231 votes to 119, with 4 members voting present and 74 not voting. The voting fell largely along party lines, with only 17 Republicans openly opposing the bill and only 8 Democrats, all from northern and border states, voting for it.

Still, most Republicans were lukewarm even toward this modest effort to protect the very right to life of black Americans. Senate Majority Leader Henry Cabot Lodge did not bring the measure to the Senate floor until late November, and on December 2, the Republican Senate Caucus voted to withdraw the bill and move to other business, promising but failing to return to it in 1923. One of the NAACP's most prominent black leaders, James Johnson, who had worked closely with Dyer, wrote in fury to President Harding: "If the Republicans had been in actual collusion with the Democrats to have the latter pull their chestnuts out of the fire, the appearances could not have been worse."[20]

The following year, most Republicans were in open collusion with Democrats in support of a measure the NAACP also vigorously opposed, the 1924 Johnson-Reed Immigration Act that modified and institutionalized the race-based national origins quota system for immigration Congress had tentatively initiated in 1921. The House version, championed by Washington State Republican congressman Albert Johnson, sought to base quotas on the percentage of the U.S. population different national groups had in 1890, before the peak of southern and eastern European immigration. His bill passed the House 322–71. The Senate version, advanced by Republican senator David Reed of Pennsylvania, used a different system for calculating quotas, but one that Madison Grant assured Johnson would reserve 84 percent of immigration slots for northern and western Europeans. The Senate enacted it 62–6, with 28 abstentions. A compromise quota system closer to the Senate bill was soon adopted. In each chamber, members of both parties from the West and South gave race-based immigration restrictions strong support. Only the Northeast was divided between its conservative nativists and some liberals who had immigrant constituents and who sometimes still identified with the now-faded Sumner-Hoar Radical Republican legacy. The law both expressed and reinforced derogatory stances toward southern and eastern Europeans, including those whom Johnson termed "the Hebrew race."[21] It thereby strengthened barriers to American willingness to assist Europeans and especially European Jews as their circumstances became dire before and during World War II.[22]

THE BOUNDARIES OF ROUTINE JIM CROWISM

The race-based limits on immigration proved effective, abetted after 1929 by the Depression. But even with such broad bipartisan agreement on most racial issues, the threat of federal action on lynching prompted some white southerners to undertake state and local reforms to curb the abusive practice. Occurrences declined sharply from 1922 to 1930. The change was difficult. Violence toward African Americans was a pillar of the segregationist racial order. But the Association of Southern Women for the Prevention of Lynching argued against the myth portraying vigilante killings as chivalrous actions to stop black men from violating white women, with some effect. Male reformers publicized objective data about the scale and horror of lynching to shift attitudes among the bulk of white southerners. Political scientist Kimberley Johnson argues that these efforts, coordinated by southern liberals on the Commission on Interracial Cooperation, did make open support of lynching by local law officials less common during the 1920s and 1930s. Cumulatively, these efforts "sent an important signal about the new limits" of the Jim Crow system.[23]

Even so, lynching rates rose again in the Depression years of the 1930s. With the Democrats now in control of all three branches of the national government and far more northern liberal Democrats than ever before — and with Republican Dyer among those defeated in 1932 — it was two Democratic senators, Robert Wagner of New York and Edward Costigan of Colorado, who proposed a new anti-lynching bill in 1934. But though it garnered support across party lines, it succumbed to a southern filibuster on an issue upon which southern Democrats felt able to defy Roosevelt. Fearing resistance to other parts of his program, the president showed no enthusiasm for the anti-lynching law. Efforts to revive the legislation through the remainder of the 1930s fared no better. The bills were repeatedly defeated by southern filibusters increasingly explicit in their inflammatory racist rhetoric.[24]

For opponents of Jim Crow, the fate of anti-lynching bills was emblematic of many disappointments they experienced in the 1930s. To be sure, their alliance was gaining strength. The contrast was stark with the early 1920s, when the failure of the Dyer bill and the adoption of more elaborate race-based immigration restrictions dashed any hopes that the return of the Republicans to power would mean a renewed national civil rights agenda. In those years, hundreds of thousands of alienated African Americans supported Marcus Garvey's separatist Universal Negro Improvement Association, which rejected white supremacy, yet at times made common cause with segregationists.[25] If, in creating a network of black vocational schools, Garvey's hero Booker T. Washington tried to operate in both racial orders at once, Garvey strove instead to create a third, black institutional order. Both men inspired millions of African Americans. Still, their public acceptance of racial separatism helped legitimate the Jim Crow system. W.E.B. Du Bois concluded that they were on balance aiding white supremacy.[26] On a racial alliances analysis, it is hard to dissent from his view.

But by the 1930s, accumulating changes gave many African American leaders and their allies in the anti-segregation alliance renewed confidence that pressuring the political system could produce results. The First World War and industrialization had created new demands for black workers. The ensuing migration of more than a third of a million blacks to northern industrial cities as well as to western states made them a potentially important voting bloc.[27] The growth of black communities in the North also generated still more, and still more activist, African American organizations, including the National Urban League, which adopted that name in 1920; the American Negro Labor Congress and A. Philip Randolph's Brotherhood of Sleeping Car Porters, organized in 1925; and when founded in 1932, the Congress of Industrial Organization engaged in some interracial union organizing.[28] Momentously, northern Democrats, a minority within their party's congressional membership until 1932, became a majority thereafter. Many were liberals who sought to win rather than suppress black votes.[29]

Republicans, who elected Oscar DePriest to Congress in 1928, nonetheless alienated many African Americans in that year by seeking to replace black party leaders in the South with white ones in order to build support in the region, a choice that increased the chances for northern Democrats to win black votes.[30] The seniority of southern Democrats empowered them to command veto power in both chambers for years to come, but not without facing increasingly serious challenges from opponents. In the early 1930s, the Communist Party also launched efforts to win rights for, and support from, black Americans, and it sought to ally African American and white workers in various industries. Both the Communists and left-leaning CIO unions participated in the National Negro Congress, initiated in 1935, with Philip Randolph as its president. It sought to consolidate a united and often militant front against Jim Crow racism at home, as well as fascism abroad.[31]

All these developments strengthened anti-segregation forces.[32] Many New Dealers in the Congress, the new executive agencies, on courts, and in northern state and local governments wished to include black Americans in the economic restructuring they were pursuing. Major New Deal federal agencies such as the National Youth Administration, the Public Works Administration, and later the Fair Employment Practices Committee included liberal whites who aimed to get some emergency funding to African Americans in the South and to stop the monies being supplied exclusively to whites. Within the South a new generation of university academics and administrators, funded by northern liberal foundations, pressed cautiously for the rights of citizenship, notably voting, for African Americans. Underlying these southern developments and mostly invisible in national institutions were the efforts of what Kimberley Johnson calls "Jim Crow reformers." These were academics, policy experts, university administrators, foundation directors and activist men and women, African American and white, often racial moderates like Congressman Arthur Mitchell, who rejected radical activism against the prevailing social systems, but who nonetheless chipped away at aspects of the entrenched Jim Crow order—chippings that had cumulative effects, even if only of a modest order.[33]

PUBLIC POLICY FOR JIM CROW

The national picture, however, remained resolutely in support of Jim Crow. A number of scholars have shown how the major reforms represented by the Social Security Act and unemployment insurance enacted in the mid-1930s were seared through with race hierarchy, as Jim Crow coalition members in Congress used the legislative process to drain out clauses beneficial to African Americans.[34] Some scholars explain these partialities by noting parallel exclusions of domestic and agricultural workers in some social legislation in other parts of the world during these years. But as Ira Katznelson has argued, the legislative history of the passage of these measures leaves no room for doubt that in the United States, the exclusionary provisions were crafted so that the federal government would not threaten the way white southerners addressed what Virginia senator Harry Byrd termed "the Negro question."[35] He and other senior white supremacist representatives of the one-party Democratic South not only held many key congressional posts; they were also strongly represented in FDR's executive branch and the courts, especially during his first two terms. Equally important, they dominated many of the state and local governments that implemented most New Deal programs, thereby tempering the ameliorative potential of these innovations.[36]

Over and over again, proponents of Jim Crow won exclusionary concessions from Roosevelt and racially liberal New Deal policymakers in the design or administration of programs for old age insurance, unemployment compensation, housing aid, the Civilian Conservation Corps, federal housing mortgage support, and new labor laws. The final package of measures enacted in the Social Security Act of 1935 is illustrative of this influence. The bill's roll call figures in Congress (372 for and 33 against in the House on April 19, 1935, and 77–6 in the Senate on June 19) convey overwhelming support for this innovative national social protection enacted in the midst of nationwide economic hardship and poverty. But the law advanced racial exclusion over inclusion and entrenched instead of loosening segregation. This distortion is apparent in the dilution of the recommendations presented by President Roosevelt's Committee on Economic Security, the committee charged to produce the basis for a draft bill, and the legislation signed off by the House Committee on Ways and Means and Senate Finance Committee.[37] The Committee on Economic Security's ambitious plans would have created contributory-based, inclusive, and nationally administered old age pensions, unemployment insurance, and child support. Southern members of Congress eyed the prospective fiscal support as welcome assistance for overstretched state coffers.

But the potential erosion of segregation terrified these bastions of the Jim Crow alliance. Nine out of fifteen Democrats on the twenty-one-member Finance Committee were from southern or border states, as were eight of eighteen Democrats on the twenty-five-member Ways and Means Committee. The disproportionate longevity of service enjoyed by southerners because of guaranteed reelection provided seniority power to the pro-segregation alliance. [38] Redrafting the bill, both chambers' committees quickly abandoned the Committee on Economic Security's intention that all workers should be eligible for the new old age and unemployment insurance schemes. Instead they excluded agricultural and domestic laborers. This elimination of over five million workers—halving the working population of African Americans covered, while excluding only one-fifth of white workers—had an obvious purpose, as the *Pittsburgh Courier* intoned: "This has been done to satisfy reactionary elements in the South who cannot bear the thought of Negroes getting pensions and compensations."[39] As political scientist Robert Lieberman observes, "The racial structure affected the political possibilities for policymaking, forcing the administration to purchase a national policy at the cost of less than universal inclusion."[40] This racial structure had significant northern spokes. African Americans were hired disproportionately more in the excluded occupations in the midwestern and northeastern industrial states, as well as in the South.[41]

The exclusions also exacerbated the racially damaging effects of the national unemployment insurance scheme included in the 1935 Social Security

Act. Since the predominantly African American farm and domestic workers did not pay into the unemployment insurance fund (nor did casual workers), they received no coverage when laid off. A national scheme with no occupational exclusions and open to currently unemployed workers would have avoided these racially unequal institutional patterns and would have been more widely beneficial as well. National Urban League and NAACP leaders protested this structural bias, unsuccessfully. The Aid to Dependent Children title of the Social Security Act (later AFDC and now replaced by TANF— Temporary Assistance for Needy Families) became particularly contentious, because the Committee on Economic Security wanted federal standards to define eligibility, a deliberate means of reducing discriminatory state racism. In his maiden speech to the House as the Democrats' first African American member, Congressman Arthur Mitchell denounced state administration of ADC, advocating federal responsibility. The Ways and Means Committee overrode these objections and gave the federal government authority to approve state public assistance plans, but not to inspect their implementation.

Such concessions meant that these new institutions not only propped up the white supremacist order. They exacerbated its inegalitarian consequences in multiple ways, as many poorer, working-class, and middle-class white Americans received new forms of housing, employment, education, health, and retirement assistance that most black Americans did not receive. As Ira Katznelson has argued, the impacts of those inequities have endured ever since.[42] These developments embittered activists like Randolph, who concluded that whites should never provide movement leadership.[43] To be sure, African Americans did benefit from many New Deal programs over time (especially from programs administered nationally with reduced state discretionary powers), and through some of his appointments to administrative agencies and, particularly, to the judiciary, FDR made the nation's conflicting racial alliances less unequal in power. But he shaped American political development most with regard to the nation's economic and federalist structures, not its racial ones.[44]

Along with electoral fears and concerns about southern leaders' power in Congress, especially the Senate, a central reason that Roosevelt shied away from attacking the Jim Crow system was the broad persistence among whites of values and attitudes exalting race hierarchy. Though Franz Boas, his student Ruth Benedict, their ally in psychology Otto Kleinberg, and others began to convince many more scholars that older doctrines of biological racism were misguided during the 1930s, so that the American Anthropological Association unanimously adopted a resolution against racism in 1938, presumptions of the superiority of whites and their cultures still retained many eminent intellectuals' support. Like their Progressive predecessors, many white southern moderates cited social science studies to show how New Deal economic and political reforms could be achieved while retaining segregation. Many of the white politicians supporting poll tax reform in this era, for example, argued in terms of redeeming white democracy, not enfranchising blacks.[45] As his conduct in World War II would prove, Roosevelt himself conceived of Japanese as a different race, and even as the views of many national elites began to shift during that war, he remained concerned to design postwar immigration policies that would produce an appropriate "racial" mix.[46]

With Congress, the executive branch, and much of the national leadership in both parties unwilling to act even against lawless racial violence, much less institutionalized Jim Crow systems of racial discrimination, and with New Deal programs sometimes exacerbating rather than reducing the impact of Jim Crow policies, the NAACP and other members of the anti-segregation racial alliance often turned to the courts. Although the Reconstruction amendments and surviving statutes obviously were far from self-enforcing, they represented the greatest institutionalized foundational resources for racial reformers. As black protest organizations burgeoned in the first third of the twentieth century, the rhetoric and tactics of many activists focused on winning court decisions that could realize the egalitarian principles proclaimed in these legal documents and in what they took to be the nation's founding statement of its values, the "self-evident" truths of equal and inalienable human rights proclaimed in the Declaration of Independence. Advocates for other racial and ethnic minorities, such as Chinese immigrants, made similar efforts.

American judges usually treat the Declaration with reverence, but most do not regard it as legally binding. Up through the eve of World War II, many justices continued to read constitutional and statutory protections for the rights of nonwhites narrowly. As far back as *U.S. v. Wong Kim Ark* (1898), the Court did find that the children of Chinese immigrants, unlike children of the members of native tribes, could claim birthright citizenship under the Fourteenth Amendment.[47] The majority suggested that otherwise the citizenship of children of European immigrants might be challenged. But in Progressive era cases, the Court generally supported deference to administrative judgments that persons of Chinese descent were deportable, even in cases of those with credible claims to U.S. citizenship.[48] The Court also had little difficulty upholding imperial rule over the Asian, Pacific Islander, and Latino colonies acquired in the Spanish-American War era, sometimes invoking racial grounds for denying their inhabitants equal rights.[49]

In light of the clear command of the equal protection clause of the Fourteenth Amendment, the Court was always willing to strike down some overt forms of racial discrimination toward African Americans, such as blatant jury exclusions. But for many decades, it ignored pervasive practices of covert discrimination.[50] After initial resistance, in the Progressive years the Court did uphold efforts to enforce an 1867 anti-peonage law and the Thirteenth Amendment against various new means of imposing forced labor on blacks. But because the Court refused to acknowledge that these measures were parts of a new system of white supremacy, its rulings had only limited impact on what some scholars term "the new slavery" of the Jim Crow years.[51] Aided by briefs submitted by NAACP founding member Moorfield Storey, the Court also struck down Oklahoma's contrived "grandfather clause" in 1915. This pernicious rule exempted descendants of former voters (all, of course, white) from literacy tests. The case initiated a long history of NAACP involvement in civil rights litigation.[52] But most forms of black disfranchisement continued untrammeled. The Court invalidated Texas's egregious 1923 law confining participation in party primaries to whites only, but it initially acquiesced when the Texas Democratic Party, whose primary determined the results in the state's official election, itself made its primary "whites-only." That pro-segregation ruling in *Grovey v. Townsend* (1935) stood until the balance of power between the racial alliances began to shift in World War II.[53]

Well before then, Storey and the NAACP persuaded the Supreme Court to strike down Louisville's ordinance that prevented a white man from selling property in a predominantly white neighborhood to a black man in *Buchanan v. Warley* (1917).[54] But white supremacists then resorted to private "restrictive covenants" banning resales to persons of a different race, and the Supreme Court upheld those contracts in *Corrigan v. Buckley* (1926).[55] Racial residential segregation mounted thereafter, especially in northern cities.[56]

Beginning in the 1920s and especially in the 1930s, the NAACP and the International Labor Defense organization, founded by the Communist Party, did begin to win legal victories for African Americans subjected to virulently unfair local and state criminal justice procedures, though they rarely did so cooperatively. Both acted as members of the anti-segregation racial alliance and their legal efforts generated precedents on which both could draw, but they did not act in concert. The most famous of these cases were those involving the "Scottsboro boys," black teenagers in Alabama accused of raping two white girls while riding a freight train. All but one of the teenagers had been speedily sentenced to death by an all-white local jury despite lack of corroborating medical evidence and clearly inadequate representation by an intimidated, alcoholic attorney.

On appeal, the Supreme Court found their trials faulty and sent them back for new proceedings. But though these cases exhibited substantial judicial commitments to due process guarantees, it is doubtful that they would have been taken all the way to the Supreme Court if domestic and international Communists, seeking to discredit the world's richest capitalist nation, had not trumpeted them throughout the globe. And despite their victories on procedural grounds, most of the Scottsboro defendants ultimately ended up convicted and imprisoned, their lives ruined. While the vindications for the rights of accused persons in these and related cases of the era did benefit African Americans, other nonwhite defendants, and indigent defendants generally, they curbed the abuses of the Jim Crow system only at the margins, leaving its foundations intact.[57]

As Arthur Mitchell learned, attacking those foundations required attacking racial segregation itself. In the 1930s, the NAACP, led now by Charles Houston and his mentee Thurgood Marshall, began to do so in a series of education cases in which they were often able to prove that public "separate but equal" education was anything but equal. Early victories came in cases in which states funded all-white law schools and offered no real alternatives to black applicants.[58] But much more would have to change before these litigative efforts could bear greater fruit. Even then, segregation would be buried in law but remain alive in everyday American life.

BREAKING THE JIM CROW WALL

While the NAACP stressed litigative strategies, many other sorts of pressures for change, both domestic and international, were accumulating. These included intensifying African American reform efforts of all sorts; growing numbers of northern political leaders who saw the potential to gain the expanding black urban vote; and the small but influential intellectual critics of doctrines of racial superiority, whose credibility was reinforced both by the denunciations of the Jim Crow system that proponents of Soviet Communism advanced and by the repellent examples of the racist new Nazi and Fascist regimes in Europe that emerged during the Depression years. As historian Carl Degler has written, the "impact of Nazi practices" on "American scholarly thinking" can "hardly be overestimated" in explaining why academic endorsements of racial hierarchy declined in the 1930s and 1940s.[59] Still, the stranglehold that southern Democrats in Congress held on all national policies affecting race, and the unabashed endorsement of doctrines of Nordic or Aryan superiority that many Americans were still willing to provide publicly, meant that these factors alone were not enough to break the hold of the Jim Crow racial alliance.

The works of many scholars find that it was during World War II and its cold war aftermath that power decisively tilted toward the anti-segregation coalition in America. From the late 1930s on, the need first to prepare for the possibility of war, then to sustain massive military operations, gave enormous new impetus to efforts to utilize African Americans for economic production and military service. Desires to reply to Communist criticisms and to repudiate Nazis' abuses strengthened the appeal of interpreting American principles as committed to democracy and human rights instead of white rule. [60] The impact of these pressures can be seen during the quarter century from 1940 to 1965 in the shift toward ever stronger endorsements of equal rights in party platforms, and in executive actions, judicial rulings, and finally national legislation supporting civil rights.

In 1940, the Republicans still "firmly opposed" involving the United States in a "foreign war," but their platform assailed the Roosevelt administration for leaving the national government "unprepared to defend our country, its institutions, and our individual liberties in a war that threatens to engulf the whole world." It was in this context that the party added a plank urging that "American citizens of Negro descent" be given "a square deal in the economic and political life of this nation." This "square deal" should include an end to discrimination "in the civil service, the army, navy, and all other branches of the Government" and effective suffrage rights.[61] A month later, the Democrats declared that the war "raging in Europe, Asia and Africa, shall not come to America," while promising to make the United States "so strong that no possible combination of powers would dare to attack us." Stressing that the nation's "Negro citizens" had "participated actively" in the New Deal's labor, social security, health, work relief, housing, education, and farm programs, they too promised "legislative safeguards against discrimination in government service and benefits, and in the national defense forces."[62]

And when, after the German conquest of Poland had provoked World War II, the nation's leaders instituted a draft and began spending billions on rearmament in 1940, African American leaders realized they had the opportunity to push the national government on civil rights much harder than ever before. Most dramatically, in January 1941, A. Philip Randolph threatened to organize a March on Washington to compel the administration to desegregate the armed forces, to equalize job opportunities, and to secure fair pay for African Americans working in defense industries. In June on the eve of the march, President Roosevelt responded by creating a temporary Fair Employment Practices Committee (FEPC) to investigate and redress complaints of employment discrimination. Encouraged by this partial success, many black leaders pushed throughout the war for a "Double V" campaign, pursuing victories against racism at home as well as abroad. The war years saw passage of a bill eliminating the poll tax for soldiers overseas, and though an effort to abolish the poll tax generally succumbed to another southern filibuster in 1942, the fact that the House passed the military bill overwhelmingly suggested that power was shifting at last. Even so, when southerners protested the FEPC's work against racial discrimination, the White House downgraded its status; and FDR refused to desegregate the military.[63]

Momentum for Reform

Yet political pressures to do so were building. In 1944, the Republicans went much further than they had four years before, calling for an investigation and corrective legislation for "segregation and discrimination" in the armed forces; a new Fair Employment Practice Commission; a constitutional amendment to ban poll taxes in federal elections; and, for the first time since 1928, they explicitly urged anti-lynching legislation.[64] The Democratic platform, brief overall, simply stated "racial and religious minorities have the right to live, develop and vote equally with all citizens." It added that Congress "should exert its full constitutional powers" to ensure that all shared the rights guaranteed by the Constitution.[65] The war years had strengthened anti–Jim Crow forces sufficiently to put racial equality on the agenda of both parties—not in sharp opposition to each other, but with the GOP a bit more outspoken in its calls for racial change. As Republicans campaigned to dislodge FDR's domination of American politics, they strove to recapture their former status as the champion of the citizenship rights of African Americans. Even so, the balance of power between the alliances had yet to shift decisively. Neither party stated opposition to segregation outside the context of the armed forces and other government services.

THE COURT MOVES

But under the influence of FDR and his Justice Department, another key American governing institution, the Supreme Court, slowly began to do so. In his first two terms, Franklin Roosevelt sought to maintain the support of southern Democrats, including the nomination of two to the Supreme Court. Despite these efforts, many southerners still feared the growing numbers of northern racial liberals in the party and the potential of New Deal programs to give African Americans economic resources and opportunities to break free of their peonage in southern agricultural and domestic work. By the late 1930s, southern conservatives were breaking more and more with New Deal nationalism; and after FDR tried but failed to purge the party of such states' rights conservatives in the 1938 campaign, he began to appoint more liberal justices who supported national action on civil rights—five between 1939 and 1943, including Frank Murphy, the attorney general who had created a Civil Rights

Section in the Justice Department in 1939, and Robert Jackson, the attorney general who had ordered support for Arthur Mitchell in 1941. Only one segregationist southerner, FDR's old friend and congressional supporter James Byrnes of South Carolina, broke the pattern, and he served on the Court only a year before moving to administrative posts in the executive branch during World War II.[66]

It soon became clear that, at least in regard to the rights of African Americans, the Roosevelt Justice Department, the repopulated Supreme Court, and many similarly staffed lower federal courts were moving gradually and unsteadily, but nonetheless discernibly, toward the positions of the anti-segregation alliance. These positions were commonly presented by the lawyers of the NAACP and, after 1937, the NAACP Legal Defense Fund. With the Justice Department's aid, Congressman Mitchell won his partial victory against segregation in interstate transportation in 1941. That same year, the Court held that the federal right to vote applied to primaries; and three years later, it struck down the Texas Democratic Party's white primary for effectively nullifying black voting rights in *Smith v. Allwright* (1944).[67] To be sure, the Court went on to hand down one of its most notorious decisions, upholding internment of all Japanese-descended persons on the West Coast, in *Korematsu v. United States* (1944). But even there, the Roosevelt justices insisted, "legal restrictions which curtail the civil rights of a single racial group are immediately suspect."[68]

After the war, civil rights victories began coming more rapidly. *Morgan v. Virginia* (1946) held at last that state segregation laws could not be imposed on interstate transportation without unconstitutionally burdening interstate commerce. Even more strikingly, *Shelley v. Kraemer* (1948) ruled that courts could not enforce racial and religious "restrictive covenants" in real estate transactions.[69] The election year of 1948, in the early stages of the cold war, represented a major turning point in many ways. In their party platform that year, the Republicans called again for anti-lynching legislation, for abolition of the poll tax, and for an end to segregation in the armed services. For the first time they added endorsement of any federal legislation "as may be necessary" to secure the "right of equal opportunity to work" regardless of "race, religion, color, or country of origin."[70]

Truman's Education

Portentously, the Democrats finally split apart over civil rights, with the national platform applauding President Harry Truman for his "courageous stand" on racial issues; contending that the Democratic Party had achieved "great civil rights gains in recent years" in eliminating racial discrimination;

and pledging to continue those efforts so that "racial and religious minorities" would have rights to live, work, vote, and receive legal protection on an equal basis with all citizens. The Democrats also opposed "race and religious" restrictions on admission of persons displaced from their homes by the war.[71]

The emergence of Harry Truman as a champion of civil rights was hardly inevitable. Indeed it was improbable. Truman had generally voted as a moderate racial liberal as a senator, but only, he told southerners, because he, like Leonidas Dyer before him, represented black voters in St. Louis. Yet on assuming the presidency after Franklin Roosevelt's death on April 12, 1945, Truman's stance shifted toward more full-fledged racial liberalism. Personally appalled at reports of vicious white assaults on returning black servicemen who sought to assert their rights, and counseled by his Secretary of State Dean Acheson that domestic racial discrimination was harming the United States internationally in the changing postwar and increasingly postcolonial world, Truman chose to risk alienating southern Democrats and to gain greater white liberal and black support by establishing a President's Committee on Civil Rights in 1946 and supporting a permanent FEPC.[72]

His committee's report, *To Secure These Rights*, advocated a sweeping federal civil rights agenda and also condemned the internment of Japanese Americans. Its example spurred supportive efforts by a broad range of civil rights organizations and helped persuade some, like the predominantly white Federal Council of Churches, to join the fight against segregation for the first time. Truman's Justice Department also began giving still more consistent support to the NAACP LDF in civil rights litigation—all the more so after Truman's upset victory in 1948 indicated that opposition to Jim Crow no longer meant political suicide in American national elections.[73]

That victory was all the more surprising because southern Democrats walked out of the 1948 Democratic Convention when it adopted its civil rights provisions. The dissidents formed a rival "Dixiecrat" or States' Rights Democratic Party that ran South Carolina governor Strom Thurmond for president. The new party's platform denounced the "totalitarian, centralized bureaucratic government and the police nation called for by the platforms adopted by the Democratic and Republican Conventions" and pledged support for "the segregation of the races and the racial integrity of each race." The Dixiecrats further denounced the Democratic Convention for sponsoring "a civil rights program calling for the elimination of segregation, social equality by Federal fiat, regulations of private employment practices, voting, and local law enforcement."[74] With these developments, the control of the Jim Crow alliance over both major parties was effectively lost, though it remained powerful in many other governing institutions, especially the United States Senate.

Even so, the major parties themselves were still not sharply opposed on civil rights. Both had simply shifted to support gradual reform measures. Hints of different trajectories to come appeared in 1952, when the Republican plank on "civil rights" called for federal action against lynching, poll taxes, discriminatory employment practices, and also segregation in the District of Columbia. But sounding like the Democratic platforms of the early twentieth century, the same document upheld "the primary responsibility of each State to order and control its own domestic institutions" and criticized those who would "mislead, exploit or attempt to confuse minority groups for political purposes."[75] The Democrats, in contrast, made their civil rights plank the climax of their platform. They celebrated the role of the Department of Justice in "successfully arguing in the courts" for elimination of discrimination in "rights to own and use real property, to engage in gainful occupations and to enroll in publicly supported higher educational institutions." The Democrat platform promised that the party would go on to do more, including enacting federal legislation to secure equal opportunity in employment, personal physical security, and "full and equal participation in the Nation's political life"— rhetorically, at least, a more sweeping agenda.[76]

Even so, it was Truman's Republican successor, former Allied Supreme Commander Dwight D. Eisenhower, who finally implemented the desegregation of the armed forces in the early 1950s. And though FDR's judicial appointees played crucial roles, it was the former Republican governor of California whom Eisenhower made chief justice of the United States, Earl Warren, who wrote the decision that finally declared most Jim Crow segregation unconstitutional. The way had been further prepared by *Sweatt v. Painter* (1950). In this judgment the Supreme Court ruled that a recently created black law school in Texas could not provide an education constitutionally equal to that of the all-white University of Texas Law School because it lacked "intangibles" that made for "greatness" in legal education.[77] While *Sweatt v. Painter* did not formally overrule any precedents, it broadened the range of circumstances that could show "separate" public institutions not to be adequately "equal." That innovation helped set the stage for *Brown v. Board of Education* (1954).[78] Though his reasoning was and remains controversial, Chief Justice Warren's opinion for a unanimous Court in that landmark case plainly signaled that henceforth, the American judiciary would reject all white efforts to impose segregated institutions on African Americans as violations of the Fourteenth Amendment's equal protection clause.

The *Brown* ruling was historic. But neither *Brown* nor any of the Court's rulings on civil rights were ever enough to eradicate in practice the pervasive systems of discrimination and exclusion in public and private employment, housing, voting rights, access to public education and to political offices, immigration, and much more that the Jim Crow alliance entrenched over the eight decades since Reconstruction. In fact, federal judicial rulings helped spur significant white opposition to change. Most congressmen from southern states signed a "Southern Manifesto" in 1956 denouncing court-ordered desegregation as unconstitutional.[79] Ambitious southern politicians with prior histories of racial moderation, including George Wallace of Alabama and Orval Faubus of Arkansas, found they could win elections by presenting themselves as ardent champions of segregation.[80] To begin to modify everyday American practices, federal executive actions and new legislation would be needed.

In 1956, the Republicans appeared inclined to act, as their platform boasted of their appointments of "Negroes" to "high public position," the ending of segregation in the armed forces and in the District of Columbia's public facilities, the curbing of discrimination in federal employment, and progress in ending discrimination by those with whom the federal government contracted. The GOP also promised to enforce *Brown v. Board of Education* through the federal district courts. And for the first time, their platform called for an immigration policy free "from implications of discrimination between racial, nationality, and religious groups."[81] The Democrats nonetheless accused the Republicans of delaying elimination of the national origins quota system. In their concluding civil rights plank, the Republicans elaborated their 1952 pledges to include efforts to eliminate discrimination in all public educational institutions, as well as in rights to vote, to gain employment, and to enjoy personal physical security. The Democrats, too, called for national support to implement judicial decisions terminating school segregation.[82]

Drivers of Reform

These shifts of the courts and the national parties toward greater action to secure civil rights in the 1950s were propelled by international concerns, changing political and economic interests and normative beliefs, and the dramatic efforts of many civil rights protestors, including now-fabled names like Rosa Parks, Martin Luther King Jr., Ralph Abernathy and Ella Baker of the Southern Christian Leadership Conference; James Farmer and Bayard Rustin of the

Congress on Racial Equality; Marion Barry and John Lewis of the Student Nonviolent Coordinating Committee; Whitney Young of the Urban League; Roy Wilkins of the NAACP; Dorothy Height of the National Council of Negro Women, and many more. In addition to organizing boycotts, sit-ins, freedom marches, and other forms of protest during the 1950s and early 1960s, many of these groups also sought to strengthen African Americans' electoral clout. Black voter registration in the South soared from less than ten thousand in 1940, drawn from a potential pool of fifteen million black voters, to over one million by 1956.[83]

Since that number still represented only a small fraction of eligible African Americans, these groups supported racial liberals in both parties in passing a new Civil Rights Act in 1957, the first major civil rights bill since the end of Reconstruction. The act created a Commission on Civil Rights, upgraded the Justice Department's Civil Rights Section to a division, and gave it some additional powers to protect voting rights. Their efforts were only reinforced by continuing efforts of leaders of Communist nations to deflect their own countries' problems through lambasting the violence and inequality endured by African Americans. The act's supporters stressed its value in winning what Republican senator Jacob Javits of New York called "the great contest between freedom and communism" by gaining the allegiance of "the approximately 1.2 billion largely Negro and Oriental population who occupy the underdeveloped areas of the Far East, the Middle East, and Africa."[84]

Former governor Strom Thurmond, now a Democratic senator from South Carolina, staged the longest one-man filibuster in history trying to prevent the bill's passage; but his need to do so only displayed the declining influence of the pro–Jim Crow alliance. The bill passed the House of Representatives by a margin of 279 to 97, and, after Thurmond's obstructionism finally ended, the Senate approved it 60 to 15. Virtually all the opposition came from southern Democrats and a few conservative Republicans. But this broad support was won only by reducing the commission and Civil Rights Division powers proposed in the initial bill.

Many civil rights leaders saw the result as a sham. Only two hundred thousand additional blacks were registered by 1960.[85] A further civil rights act aimed at protecting voting rights passed that year despite a filibuster by three teams of eighteen southern Democrats. Again the new law gave only limited additional powers to oppose those who prevented voter registration or voting. Robust legislation to protect the suffrage would not come until the Voting Rights Act of 1965. But even though African American voting percentages rose only slightly between 1957 and 1965, black votes did help John F. Kennedy win the very close 1960 election.[86]

Kennedy's victory also came because in 1960, it was the Republicans who had their convention rent apart by dissension over racial issues, as burgeoning numbers of states' rights conservatives sought to oppose calls for federal interventions. Still, at this point the anti–Jim Crow elements of the party prevailed decisively. With the support of their candidate, Vice President Richard Nixon, the Republicans enacted a platform that included the longest discussion of civil rights in the party's history, boasting of the 1957 and 1960 civil rights laws that Republicans had championed while complaining that Democrats in Congress had "watered them down." The GOP also promised further action on voting rights, desegregation of schools, transportation, and public facilities, equal opportunity employment, and federally subsidized housing. Their platform explicitly defended the "constitutional right to peaceable assembly to protest" of civil rights activists. They supported doubling immigration, with admissions based on "individual merit."[87]

The Democrats, noting that it was Americans' "faith in human dignity that distinguishes our open free society from the closed totalitarian society of the Communists," similarly applauded the "peaceful demonstrations for first-class citizenship" undertaken by civil rights protestors. They endorsed a lengthy list of desegregation and anti-discrimination measures, including a permanent federal Fair Employment Practices Commission and a Commission on Civil Rights. They denounced the national origins quota system as a Republican policy "inconsistent with our beliefs in the rights of man."[88]

These platforms showed that both parties were now officially taking stands against the Jim Crow system and its formally equal racial separations and exclusions defended on the basis of alleged inherent racial differences. Even so, President Kennedy remained reluctant to push hard for civil rights until protestors further heightened foreign policy pressures for change, aided by the intransigent behavior and truculent statements of ardent members of the pro–Jim Crow racial alliance, such as Birmingham, Alabama's, notorious public safety commissioner, Eugene "Bull" Connor. Connor was willing in the spring of 1963 to subject civil rights demonstrators, including schoolchildren, to fire hoses, aggressive dogs, and clubs, with cameras rolling. That August, Philip Randolph, Bayard Rustin, and Dorothy Height organized, and Martin Luther King galvanized, nearly a quarter of a million civil rights supporters at the long-awaited March on Washington.[89]

Johnson's Education

Then on November 22, 1963, Kennedy's assassination placed the former Senate majority leader and Texan Lyndon Johnson in the White House. Johnson was determined to win his place in history by becoming the president who oversaw enactment of the statutes that would give the federal government the tools to end the Jim Crow system in practice as well as in constitutional law. In his first speech after assuming the presidency, Johnson told the nation that "no memorial oration or eulogy could more eloquently honor" the late president "than the earliest possible passage of the civil rights bill for which he fought so long," a bill that would strengthen the nation "at home and abroad."[90]

Though once again eighteen southern senators conducted a lengthy filibuster against the bill Johnson sent to Congress, the Senate for the first time ever voted for cloture to end a racial filibuster in June 1964, and brought to the floor an only mildly compromised version of Johnson's proposals. Republicans in the House supported the initial version of the Civil Rights Act 138–34, the compromise final version 136–35. House Democrats were only somewhat more divided, supporting the first bill 152–96, the final one 153–91. Republicans in the Senate supported the Senate's bill 27–6, Senate Democrats 46–21. The opposition was plainly regional, not partisan, because by now only the white South retained substantial support for Jim Crow policies. In the House, representatives from the eleven states of the old Confederacy voted 7–97 against the original bill, including eighty-seven Democrats and all ten southern Republicans, while Democrats outside the South voted for it 145–9, Republicans 138–24. In the Senate, twenty southern Democrats and one southern Republican voted against the bill, with only one southern Democrat in favor, while Democrats from other regions voted for it 45–1, Republicans 27–5.[91]

The Republicans' presidential candidate in 1964, Senator Barry Goldwater of Arizona, who had voted for the 1957 and 1960 Civil Rights acts, was one of the few Republicans who opposed the 1964 bill, chiefly because he objected to Title II of the act. Title II banned racial discrimination in private businesses operating in interstate commerce.[92] For Goldwater, this ban went too far in the direction of national regulation of a free market economy—though he was also far from unaware that by opposing this bill, he might be able to add to his economic libertarian conservative base greater support from racial conservatives, particularly in the South, a strategy he had advocated since 1961. But at this point in American history, with the anti-segregation alliance in ascendancy and Jim Crow discredited, not even Goldwater's own party was prepared to repudiate the moral authority of the Civil Rights Act. In their 1964 platforms, the Republicans as well as the Democrats pledged to enforce the recently passed act, just as both parties after 1870 had pledged to uphold the Reconstruction amendments. Goldwater went on to carry five southern states, plus his home state of Arizona, but to lose the rest of the nation overwhelmingly to President Lyndon Johnson in the November election.[93] No major

American politician has since dared to openly attack the moral or constitutional legitimacy of the 1964 Civil Rights Act.[94]

Toward the Modern Racial Alliances

But in time, the two modern racial alliances would interpret the act's principles very differently. Already in 1964, the parties' platforms revealed some of the racial issues that would feature in the ensuing period of transition. Instead of praising civil rights protestors, the Republicans now accused the Democrats of failing to give "Negro citizens" the opportunities afford by "Republican-initiated retraining programs" and therefore of instead exploiting "interracial tensions by extravagant campaign promises" and "divisive political proposals" that encouraged "disorderly and lawless elements." The GOP opposed "Federally-sponsored 'inverse discrimination,' whether by the shifting of jobs, or the abandonment of neighborhood schools, for reasons of race."[95] The Democrats claimed credit for the 1964 Civil Rights Act, "the greatest civil rights measure in the history of the American people." The party called for civil rights reforms to continue—though they also firmly rejected "any policy of quotas or 'discrimination in reverse.'"[96]

The platforms demonstrate that, moved by common national security and foreign policy concerns, domestic civil rights protests, electoral and economic calculations, and those American traditions that had long championed genuinely equal rights, both parties moved from heightened concern about racial inequities on the eve of World War II to strong support for the elimination of Jim Crow practices twenty-five years later. Each experienced severe internal dissension on the journey, but they reached common resolutions. Neither party would ever again speak out in favor of racial segregation or race-based immigration restrictions.

Yet the issues of how to continue civil rights progress and what proved to be their diverging stances on "reverse discrimination" would soon render the parties more divided on racial issues than at any time since the late nineteenth century. Those divisions are the subject of the remainder of this book.

The Fate of Two Adams

For now, we observe that by passing the historic 1964 Civil Rights Act, which had much the same purposes as the long-invalidated 1875 Civil Rights Act, the repealed Reconstruction national election statutes, and other long-abandoned

Reconstruction-era civil rights laws, the nation did something that seemed almost unimaginable in 1913. It officially repudiated the judgment of the grand patrician Charles Francis Adams Jr. in favor of the views of the more humbly born African American Henry Adams. Except for a declining minority of old guard segregationists, Americans decided that it was not when they constitutionally established the equal protection of the laws, but rather when they abandoned the cause of equal civil rights, that they had been "thoroughly wrong."

PART THREE

The Trajectory of Racial Alliances

"This backdrop of entrenched inequality"
Affirmative Action in Work

Even after Americans agreed that systems of Jim Crow segregation should finally be laid to rest, great policy questions remained.[1] How might all the persisting racial gaps displaying the damage Jim Crow laws and practices wreaked on the nation somehow be overcome? Since the mid-1960s, Americans have struggled to climb out of the quagmire of racial inequalities that government policies did so much to create. Americans continue to struggle today—by wrestling over choices now defined by the modern racial alliances, in ways that can block concerted quests for paths to progress.

Those realities were dramatized when just weeks before Justice Sonia Sotomayor was confirmed by the Senate Judiciary Committee to be a member of the U.S. Supreme Court in July 2009, the Court issued a major ruling on government involvement in race and employment patterns, *Ricci v. DeStefano*.[2] The City of New Haven, Connecticut, led by Mayor John DeStefano, had used a largely multiple choice, 60 percent written, 40 percent oral test in 2003 as its primary method of selecting municipal firefighters for promotion to lieutenant and captain positions. Though some African American candidates scored high enough to pass the bar for promotion, their scores were too far below those of one Latino and nineteen white candidates for them to have any chance of receiving one of the few officer posts available. Believing that there were African American firefighters possessing the requisite skills to be officers, New Haven officials worried that the results might violate the ban on selection methods with avoidable racially "disparate impacts" that Congress had adopted in 1991 as an amendment to Title VII of the 1964 Civil Rights Act. They decided not to certify the test results, and to start anew.

Firefighter Frank Ricci, who had overcome a learning disability to score well through rigorous study, joined with the other high-scoring candidates and sued the city for refusing to use their test scores in its promotion decisions. They deemed the city's action to be "disparate treatment" of employees on the basis of race, a violation of federal law ever since Title VII was first adopted.

The Second Circuit Court of Appeals, on which then judge Sotomayor served, dismissed their claims. Its short opinion held that setting aside the test results affected all firefighters who had taken it and so was not "disparate treatment." The appeals court found the city's priority to avoid a "disparate impact" lawsuit reasonable. The firefighters appealed, and the case landed in the Supreme Court in the summer of 2009. The Justice Department of new president Barack Obama filed a brief on behalf of New Haven that was, as we shall see, representative of Obama's general approach to racial issues. It endorsed the use of employment tests that were "race-neutral." But the Obama Justice Department also argued that if one race-neutral test that identified merit as well as or better than another was likely to produce more racially inclusive promotions, it was permissible for New Haven to shift to that more inclusive test, especially since failure to do so might indeed leave the city vulnerable to a "disparate impact" claim.[3]

The Supreme Court's 5–4 *Ricci* ruling instead upheld the white firefighters' complaint, agreeing that it was New Haven's "express, race-based decision making" that had violated Title VII.[4] Although the city had not adopted any racial quota or formal "affirmative action" promotion system, the fact that it decided not to use the test it had administered due to its racial consequences still represented a form of "race-conscious" policymaking that the Court saw as requiring heightened judicial scrutiny. To evaluate the city's contention that it might lose a disparate impact case, Justice Anthony Kennedy, writing for the majority, imported from equal protection litigation a standard that had not previously been applied to Title VII claims: the "strong basis in evidence" test.

Since 1986, the Court has held that the equal protection clause prevents a public agency from adopting race-based policies in hiring, school admissions, school attendance, and other areas in order to remedy past discrimination, unless the agency can provide a "strong basis in evidence" for concluding that there has been official racial discrimination against the parties who would benefit from such remedies.[5] Similarly, Kennedy ruled, a city could not adopt a new employment test on racial grounds unless it had a "strong basis in evidence" that otherwise it would lose a disparate impact lawsuit. Kennedy thought that New Haven had used a reasonable, merit-focused test, and so he did not think that it had shown it was in sufficient legal danger to justify a race-based alteration. As a result, whites were eventually promoted. Public employers were also put on notice that they might instead be in legal jeopardy if they deliberately changed their existing tests for hiring and promotion to make them more racially inclusive, even if they had not previously been careful to see that they were using promotion criteria that identified merit without adversely impacting racial and ethnic minorities.

In dissent, Justice Ruth Bader Ginsburg noted the unavoidable historical context for such cases: a "backdrop of entrenched inequality."[6] She maintained that the new, heavier burden of proof the majority was imposing on those who wished to shift to more racially inclusive employment tests might well undermine voluntary efforts to alter selection methods for hiring in order to combat "pre-existing racial hierarchies." She thought this all the more true because New Haven long failed to consider alternatives to written tests, particularly "performance assessments" of responses to simulated emergencies, that many experts felt assessed merit more accurately than written exams, while producing more racially inclusive results. Ginsburg found the majority's judgment that the city's neglect was insufficient to produce any serious legal vulnerability to a disparate impact suit to be a disturbingly weak reading of Title VII's demands in that regard. To Ginsburg and the Obama Justice Department, it was legally appropriate, if not mandatory, for cities to use "race-neutral" tests that focused on merit, but also to look, in unavoidably "race-conscious" fashion, for tests that could identify the merits of long-excluded groups, as well as whites, better than past alternatives. To the majority, such race-conscious selection between putatively race-neutral tests threatened constitutional commitments to judge applicants in color-blind fashion.

This clash of views illustrates vividly the conflicting approaches advanced by today's racial alliances on issues of race equality in the workplace, as on so many other topics—conflicts that include disagreements not only over formal affirmative action programs but also over the legitimacy of race-conscious policymaking of any sort. In *Ricci* these disputes divided the Supreme Court by a razor thin margin. But the division was still not even: here as in most other areas, the majority moved legal requirements further in the direction of absolute color blindness.

It is no accident when these issues emerge with particular intensity in employment policy. No area of American life is more central to the quest to eradicate unjust material racial inequalities. That is why members of the anti–Jim Crow racial coalition always made labor market reform a priority during their struggles throughout the first two-thirds of the twentieth century. They sought the end of segregation in large part in order to open up equality of opportunity in job hirings and promotions. That is also why, when the Second World War tightened the labor supply and gave civil rights reformers more leverage with the Roosevelt administration, they pushed hardest for employment measures, including creation of the Fair Employment Practices Committee.[7] It is why the March on Washington in 1963 that culminated in Martin Luther King Jr.'s "I have a dream" speech was officially a campaign for "Jobs and Freedom."[8] And it is why, after the 1964 Civil Rights Act enacted Title VII's historic ban on discrimination by employers on the basis of race, color, religion, sex, or national origin, it was over employment discrimination policies and principles that the clashing coalitions that make up today's racial alliances first formed. In the late 1960s, administrators at the Equal Employment Opportunity Commission (EEOC), created by and authorized to enforce Title VII, and the Office of Federal Contract Compliance (OFCC), a descendant of Roosevelt's FEPC that was placed in the Department of Labor by an executive order from Lyndon Johnson, began requiring employers doing business with the government to demonstrate that they had integrated their workforces and subcontractors. The Small Business Administration (SBA) also began directing federal contracts to minority-owned firms. The results were "race-conscious" hiring, promotion, and subcontracting practices that many veterans of the civil rights movement hailed as necessary, but color-blind proponents assailed as new forms of unjust racial discrimination. Contestation over these policies became the central "battleground" around which modern racial policy coalitions formed.

"Race-conscious" or "color-blind": these are the competing mantras of America's contemporary racial alliances.

THE ENDURING BACKDROP

Despite profound disagreements on appropriate policies, few would deny what Justice Ginsburg stressed: that most American labor markets continue to display intractable patterns of racial inequality that are descended in some way from the "racial hierarchies" that the nation's laws enforced for so long. For instance, in 2000, at the end of a decade of exceptional job creation, the unemployment rates for white, African American, and Latino males were 3.3 percent, 7.3 percent, and 5.7 percent, respectively. For females the percentages were 2.6 percent for whites, 6.5 percent for African Americans, and 5.6 percent for Latinos.[9] In April 2010, after the worst economic recession since the 1930s, the figures were far higher but the patterns remained the same. Unemployment for white men twenty years and over was 9.2 percent; for African American men in that age group, it was 18.4 percent. For white women twenty years or older it was 7.2 percent, for black women, 12.9 percent.[10]

As these figures show, the almost two-to-one differential ratio in unemployment rates between African Americans and white Americans, particularly for men, is a long-standing contrast, observable whether the labor market is expanding or contracting. And this differential has continued despite substantial educational gains by African Americans joining the labor market. The differential between Hispanics and whites is slightly lower but not much, in part because African American and Hispanic unemployed workers have longer periods of joblessness than whites. This fact was underlined in the wake of the crisis in manufacturing employment in the United States in the 1970s and 1980s, when many jobs in the steel, auto, and durable goods industries vanished. All blue-collar workers suffered, but African American men's unemployment rate shot up to 20 percent in 1983. And during the 1980s and 1990s, while from roughly 67 percent to 76.4 percent of displaced white men were reemployed after a year, the figures for African American and Latino men ranged from 46.4 percent to 66.6 percent and 55.7 percent to 64.9 percent, respectively.[11]

These trends persist in the twenty-first century despite marked improvements in two periods after World War II: first, the substantial entry of African Americans into mainstream industries during the war years (only after vigorous pressure from civil rights reformers to open these opportunities) paid dividends in the late 1940s and 1950s. Many of these workers moved into comparable peacetime occupations. And second, after the passage of civil rights legislation in the 1960s combined with, in the 1970s, expanded federal enforcement of nondiscrimination and affirmative action measures—the subject of this chapter—wage and working hour differentials between white workers and African American workers declined. Still, sociologist Douglas Massey notes that even after adjusting "for the influence of such variables as education, veteran and marital status, region, urban residence, number of children, and hours worked, a significant racial gap [in wage levels] of 20 percent persists."[12]

These patterns are not in dispute. But because members of the modern racial alliances explain today's inequalities in very different ways, there is no agreement on appropriate racial policies to remedy the gaps. Many Americans, especially white Americans, believe that job opportunities are available to African Americans and Latinos on a reasonably fair basis, if indeed nonwhites are not unfairly advantaged by affirmative action programs and other types of race-conscious hiring practices. They interpret persisting labor inequalities as evidence that, perhaps due to pathologies generated by a long history of mistreatment but sustained today by bad choices, blacks and Latinos are not taking advantage of the educational and economic opportunities available to them. Many other Americans think instead that explicit and implicit forms of discrimination against blacks and Latinos, especially, persist in labor markets, through practices such as the designation of residential areas populated by these groups as unsuitable sources for potential employees.[13] They cite, among other evidence, "audit" studies involving comparable black and white job applicants, which by the mid-2000s found that "the employment prospects of black job-seekers are roughly half those of equally qualified whites," with the differentials, remarkably, increasing when African American job seekers possess higher skill levels.[14] Experimental audit studies also suggest that the severe negative effects of a criminal record for job seekers are 40 percent greater for African Americans compared with whites (a trend that expanded employer access to databases collating criminal records may exacerbate).[15] White ex-offenders sometimes receive callbacks to job openings before African American applicants with no criminal record.[16] Still, many Americans believe that modern patterns of black criminality, whatever their source, make these judgments by employers understandable, indeed reasonable.

These differing interpretations form part of the battles over the desirability of affirmative action and, more generally, race-conscious policymaking in employment and other areas that make up the rival positions of today's racial alliances. We will see that although these alliances differ on how to respond to the persistent interlacing of race and economic status in America, their memberships still cannot be defined simply in economic or, for that matter, racial terms. Though their numbers are often overstated, some Latinos and Asian Americans as well as some predominantly white unions oppose affirmative action, for example, while many large businesses, along with many unions and Latino and Asian American advocacy groups, instead favor race-conscious "diversity" hires.[17]

Today's racial coalitions are unified most of all by their ideological positions on how, in the wake of the civil rights laws and judicial rulings of the 1950s and 1960s, race should or should not figure in employment and other policies, positions that emerged in the transitional decade following the great triumphs of the anti-segregation coalition. Understanding how the modern alliances developed is crucial for understanding the structure of racial politics in America today.

The Rise of Affirmative Action in Employment

During much of the Jim Crow era, labor markets and employment opportunities were segregated, sometimes by law and still more often through common practice. For decades most southern Democrats and some Republican conservatives, along with most white business and union leaders and white supremacist groups, joined to fend off the efforts of African Americans, with some white liberal allies, to prod the federal government to combat employment discrimination. Only the advent of World War II, and the threat raised by the March on Washington movement of mass protests when workers were needed for the war, compelled the executive branch to take the first steps toward fair employment. President Roosevelt issued his historic Executive Order 8802 on June 25 1941, establishing the temporary Fair Employment Practices Committee (FEPC). The five-member agency (expanded to seven in 1943) reviewed complaints about inequities, held hearings around the country, and monitored anti-discrimination and hiring efforts among contractors with federal grants. Still, it was bereft of tough powers to enforce compliance. Its portfolio was soon extended to include unions, but it had little success in delving into this segregated sector of the political economy.[18]

Even though it lacked enforcement clout, the FEPC's mandate threatened southern Democrats and allied economic and social conservatives.[19] Consequently, it faced heavy congressional pressure. Delegates at the Democrat Party convention in 1944 fought over a platform plank recommending a permanent FEPC, foreshadowing the Dixiecrat rupture four years later. As part of President Harry Truman's decision to align with northern liberals on racial issues, he supported new FEPC bills in 1945. Southern Democrats on the House of Representatives Committees on Rules and on Appropriations blocked the legislation. The cause was kept burning by the National Council for a Permanent FEPC and by NAACP activists, who convened a two-day conference in Washington D.C. entitled the "National Emergency Civil Rights Mobilization."[20] When Truman again tried in 1949 to make the FEPC permanent, the opponents included Texas's new senator, Lyndon Johnson, a pivotal figure who at this point still served the South-based Jim Crow alliance.[21] Because the segregationist coalition was so impregnable, the FEPC never lost its temporary status.

Still, sociologist Anthony Chen believes that resistance to a permanent FEPC had an unintended but hugely consequential effect.[22] After strong civil rights laws were finally passed, Chen suggests, the long preceding era of enduring opposition by Jim Crow supporters to all efforts to address entrenched labor market racial discrimination made some sort of race-conscious compensatory employment programs virtually unavoidable, both politically and as a matter of achieving effective policies. Jim Crow employment practices left the nation with pervasive economic inequalities that generated passionate commitments for change in the leaders of the anti-segregation alliance and many of those they strove to represent. The struggles against economic discrimination were widespread and took place at many levels of American politics. Along with advocating for a permanent FEPC, members of the anti-segregationist coalition focused on getting state legislatures to create state employment practices committees to root out discriminatory hiring and promotion practices.[23]

In this effort they had modest success. Some state legislatures outside the South created such agencies in the 1950s and early 1960s, following a precedent set by New York in 1945.[24] Despite significant opposition from segregationists and some business and union interest groups, by 1963 twenty-five states had enacted FEP laws and agencies. Progress accelerated as both parties moved toward strong civil rights positions: eleven of the states passed legislation between 1959 and 1963, in many cases after numerous earlier bills failed. One state—Illinois—was among the 1961 group to enact, a relative lateness not unnoticed by segregationist critics of FEPC laws. When one of several bills failed to pass in Illinois in 1959, the southern *Shreveport Times* editorialized that "it is not the south alone that realizes that the racial problem cannot be solved by punitive legislation."[25] California passed an FEP law in 1959. But eleven years before, the state's voters had crushed Proposition 11, proposing a similar measure, by 2–1 (1,632,646 against, 675,697 in favor). Racial opposition then appeared to be a principal factor, because the proposition's supporters framed it as a measure to help African Americans. California Republican voters rejected it even more strongly than Democrats.[26] Business groups who feared FEP regulation abetted opponents in many states, though their stance would change after the 1964 Civil Rights Act.

At the federal level, although only minor changes came until the 1960s, they still laid the groundwork for more substantial subsequent actions. In 1948, two years after the FEPC ended, a Fair Employment Board was established in the U.S. Civil Service Commission to monitor hiring practices. Eisenhower replaced it from 1955 to 1961 with a President's Committee on Government Employment Policy. Both agencies lacked enforcement power. But agencies' survey-based reports demonstrated that racially skewed employment patterns in federal agencies and private industries persisted. When the anti-segregation alliance finally captured Congress and the executive branch in the early 1960s, this evidence supported legislation to end employment discrimination. And under Kennedy, the President's Committee (renamed the Committee on Equal Employment Opportunity) was chaired by then vice president Lyndon Johnson, a role that gave him the knowledge to push for stronger enforcement powers when he became president. Under Executive Order 10925 creating the Employment Opportunity Committee, issued on March 6, 1961, President Kennedy ordered employers with federal contracts to "take affirmative action" to ensure equal employment opportunity and treatment in work. That exhortation had a future, although just what the phrase meant was far from clear.[27]

Title VII

All these developments prepared the way, but Title VII of the 1964 Civil Rights Act and its creation of the EEOC were far more substantial steps (even though the EEOC's formal establishment was postponed for a year to give firms time to begin to address their discriminatory practices).[28] Despite the fact that the act represented a major increase in national economic regulation, the political power and the moral authority of the anti-segregation alliance were so great by 1964 that the business community was divided and largely inactive on the legislation.[29] Even so, to get the act through the southern filibuster in the Senate, the EEOC had to be weakened at birth. As part of the compromise needed to win conservative Republican votes for cloture, the EEOC's intended powers to issue "cease and desist" orders to firms engaging in discriminatory practices were curtailed. Enforcement was to come only through the courts. The administration's initial ambition to make the EEOC independent of the Justice Department, like the National Labor Relations Board, was also eviscerated. Finally, the Senate sponsors of the bill revised it to require proof of intentional discrimination by an employer before sanctions could occur, a deliberate curtailing of regulatory teeth. Mere statistical discrimination—for example, the fact that a firm hired a far smaller number of African Americans than proportionate to its catchment residential area—would not alone be grounds for action.[30] Demonstrating intentional racially "disparate treatment" was anticipated to be, and has since proven to be, a difficult task.

After these compromises, reformers looked to the Johnson administration's staffing and operation of the EEOC, as well as the president's September 1965 order transferring the Office of Federal Contract Compliance to the Department of Labor, to achieve enforcement efficacy in practice. The burden that federal administrators felt to achieve results proved weighty. Congress expanded the anti-discrimination provisions of Title VII to smaller employers in 1967, and further augmented EEOC enforcement powers in 1972, because early assessments of the EEOC's tepid impact were scathing.[31]

ENFORCEMENT

Although many criticisms had force, the challenges faced by federal officials charged with curbing employment discrimination in the late 1960s and 1970s were undeniably complex. With Jim Crow practices finally proscribed, the nation entered a dyspeptic transitional era. Even as they came to take pride in the ending of formal segregation, many white Americans worried about the widespread racial transformations that were beginning and, especially, the riots and violence that broke out in U.S. cities in 1967 and 1968, as some African Americans grew frustrated with the slow pace of change. With radical groups such as the Black Panthers achieving prominence, mainstream civil rights groups concluded that the nation needed stronger mechanisms to promote material racial equality. Some Republicans still hoped to win black voter support for their party, and they were willing to support further measures to achieve racial equity. But many white voters turned instead to those who said changes had gone too far. Alabama governor George Wallace, who had ardently championed segregation in the early 1960s, split the Democrats again with his third-party campaign in 1968. Then Richard Nixon, presenting himself as a pragmatic Republican alternative to the riven Democrats, narrowly won the presidency, aware of the power of civil rights forces in Congress but also attuned to white dissatisfactions with racial reforms.[32] Although Nixon had supported the strong 1960 GOP civil rights platform, by the late 1960s he was keen to try to win white union members and disgruntled southern Democrats over to the Republicans.

It was this combination of policy and political circumstances that soon led to the new focus on, and to new controversies over, race-conscious regulations, starting with administrative actions on employment. Modern critics of these policies are right to say that many, though by no means all, of the proponents of the 1964 Civil Rights Act not only failed to anticipate, they robustly repudiated racial preferences. Alert to conservative opposition in the congressional debates that led to the eventual passage of the act, one of the Senate's leading civil rights liberals, Hubert Humphrey, had in fact insisted that such preferences were not part of the law, saying, "I will eat my hat if anyone can find any language which provides that an employer will have to hire on the basis of percentage or quota related to color, race, religion or national origin."[33] Then as we have noted, the 1964 Democratic platform opposed "quotas" and "preferential practices," while the Republicans rejected "inverse discrimination" in jobs "for reasons of race."

Despite this apparent agreement, the GOP also accused the Democrats of offering "divisive political proposals" on civil rights and employment instead of applying "Republican-initiated retraining programs" to "afford new economic opportunities to Negro citizens."[34] Sociologist John David Skrentny exaggerates only slightly when he says that at this point, advocacy of racial preferences was a "third rail" in American politics: "Touch it and you die."[35] Because the great unifying idea of the anti-segregation coalition had been opposition to all forms of "second class citizenship" and support for opening up opportunities on an equal basis, and because racial classifications had long been used to impose subordinations and exclusions, when the Jim Crow era came to an end, there was no significant coalition urging race-conscious public policies in opposition to advocates of color blindness.

But soon, the newly authorized EEOC and OFCC administrators began monitoring discriminatory hiring and promotion practices amidst demands by civil rights activists for tangible progress. Top officials applied political pressures on the staffs of these agencies to achieve results that might quiet black urban unrest. Some more liberal business executives, along with more prag-matic ones keen to avoid lawsuits under Title VII, also sought to achieve inte-grated workforces. As a result, both public and private employers began to use various sorts of race-conscious employment standards.[36]

Johnson's Executive Order

These developments could claim important authorization from President Johnson. Three months after LBJ's seminal commencement speech at How-ard University in June 1965, in which he acknowledged the need for policies designed to translate legal civil rights into material progress, his Executive Order 11246, issued on September 24, 1965, established a general principle of affirmative action to address the effects of past employment discrimination toward blacks and other minorities. What this principle would imply in prac-tice was unspecified, but the tone of the order was proactive.[37] It mandated all government agencies to instruct every contractor "to take affirmative action to ensure that applicants are employed, and that employees are treated during employment, without regard to their race, color, religion, sex or national ori-gin."[38] The order gave responsibility for enforcement to the OFCC, which had to ensure that all employers receiving federal government contracts exercised "good faith" so that workforces carrying out federally funded tasks would include minority employees. Firms found noncompliant could not apply for future federal contracts, and they could be suspended from existing contracts. As part of the deci-sion to rely on the judiciary for enforcement of the 1964 law, Section 706(g) of Title VII gave the courts authority to order that firms found guilty of "intentional" discrimination undertake "affirmative action responses."[39] Administered by civil servants seeking results, Title VII and Johnson's executive order nudged private hiring toward quantifiable employment goals, although initially EEOC and OFCC staff members had great trepidation about pushing employers too hard to comply. Still, to receive federal contracts, employers discovered they needed to show the OFCC that they were employing African Americans.

The EEOC also soon proved willing to bring employment discrimination charges against employers who did not hire certain percentages of qualified blacks. The EEOC's staff numbers were small, but the agency found support for its work among lawyers based in the NAACP Legal Defense Fund and other civil rights organizations. Indeed, as political scientist Sean Farhang has argued, even though it was conservative Republicans who made private law-suits "the dominant mode of Title VII enforcement," they thereby created "an engine that would, in the years to come, produce levels of private enforcement litigation beyond their imagining."[40] They also spurred the creation of first many new liberal, then many conservative "public interest" litigation organizations, expanding the two rival racial policy alliances in the process. The burgeoning private enforcement litigation had yet another unanticipated consequence. Business leaders disliked these lawsuits, but few sought openly to oppose the legislation or the executive order that authorized them. Instead, in the late 1960s, the National Alliance of Businessmen, first brought together by President Johnson, worked to foster race-conscious hiring in many sectors.[41]

In contrast, by the late 1960s many unions began to complain both about being the targets of EEOC investigations and about their lack of influence within the agency.[42] These complaints encouraged many of the former defenders of segregation in Congress to believe that they could discredit the new employment initiatives and agencies and undermine their impact. Skrentny underlines the hostile national context in which these two agencies consequently worked: the EEOC's annual budget requests were invariably reduced substantially, and irate Congress members filled the budget hearings with sharp criticisms raising doubts about the agency's purpose and legitimacy.[43]

As the number of filings designed to lead to lawsuits mounted, the harms caused by EEOC underfunding mounted. The agency was unable to avoid huge backlogs of complaints and quickly found itself unable to process complaints within the statutory sixty days.[44] By 1976, the backlog of unresolved cases, either pending investigation or begun but not yet concluded, was a staggering 125,000.[45] In these circumstances, EEOC supporters and advocates of race equity continued to seek to devise and implement new, stronger, and often blunter mechanisms with which the economic promises of the recent civil rights bills could be made effective, including the collection of employment data by race in firms falling under federal regulation. Such compilation enabled accurate profiling of present employee demographics and helped to establish reasonable targets toward which employers should aim. But these were, of course, numerical racial targets for hiring and promotion, of the sort that appeared to require Senator Humphrey to begin dining at his haberdashery.

In addition to the EEOC and the FEPC, a third federal agency contributed to the rise of race-conscious employment policies: the Small Business Administration (SBA). Created in 1953, the SBA had a program, Section 8(a), through which it acted as an intermediary to help small businesses win federal contracts. Aided by a 1968 executive order, President Lyndon Johnson's appointee to head the SBA, Howard Samuels, used the 8(a) program to provide contracts to companies comprising "socially or economically disadvantaged persons." Over time those persons came to be specified to include "black Americans, American Indians, Spanish Americans, oriental Americans, Eskimos and Aleuts." Significantly for debates over the purposes and duration of race-conscious measures, the Johnson administration justified this initiative in terms of expanding opportunities, not as redress for specific forms of past discrimination against these groups. It quietly set precedents for directing federal funds on the basis of racial and ethnic identities, perhaps on an indefinitely continuing basis.[46]

As public and private employers began to develop formal affirmative action programs and other race-conscious employment policies, this emerging trend received some unexpected reinforcement. In 1967, the OFCC had announced a plan to pursue roughly proportional representation of minorities in the local workforce in projects receiving federal funds in Philadelphia. Business interests protested, and the Labor Department ended the initiative after Nixon's election.[47] But Nixon's secretary of labor, economist George Schultz, was eager to promote integrated federal workforces. Nixon himself reportedly recognized that he might be able to divide white and black workers, while alienating only some businesses, by requiring racial "goals and timetables" for federal contractors, as in the Philadelphia Plan.[48]

Similar plans were devised and implemented for Cleveland, St. Louis, and San Francisco, but the Philadelphia Plan became the key experiment for racial targets. Overseen by the OFCC, authorized by Arthur Fletcher, the assistant secretary of labor who was the Nixon administration's highest-ranking African American, and reinforced by the direct participation of Secretary Schultz, the scheme gave construction craft firms (ironworkers, steamfitters, sheet metal workers, electricians, and plumbers and pipe fitters) holding federal contracts four years in which to achieve a percentage of African American workers roughly consistent with the percentage of black residents in the metropolitan area.[49] This scheme most challenged unions. Though some locals, including many in Philadelphia, had begun desegregating, racial exclusions remained blatant in others. Efforts to desegregate the Labor Department's funded apprenticeship programs, for example, had little success because unions controlled them to maintain racially exclusionary practices.[50]

The Nixon administration advocated Philadelphia-style hiring plans only for areas where it claimed to find evidence of serious labor shortages. The initiatives nonetheless represented an interventionist race-conscious strategy to use federal resources for substantial labor market desegregation. Recognizing that segregated and racist unions remained bulwarks against reducing employment inequities, Labor Assistant Secretary Fletcher explained that "targets were essential if we are to measure results in terms of increased minority employment."[51] Thus, the plan specified the percentages of African American employees a contractor needed to hire, and under the "good faith" clause, failure to meet those targets had to be explained as arising from factors other than discrimination. Insufficient reason for missing hiring targets generated penalties, including potentially abrogation of the contract. But the Labor Department termed these targets "goals," not quotas, since both the 1964 Civil Rights Act and Johnson's executive order had explicitly forsworn quotas.

Employer and union organizations dissented immediately from this interpretation, as did their political allies in Congress. In congressional hearings on the new policy in 1969, these dissents produced one of the earliest direct clashes between government officials over the legitimacy of race-conscious as opposed to color-blind policymaking. Senator Sam Ervin of North Carolina upbraided Labor Secretary Schultz in a heated exchange: "Your affirmative step is to do exactly opposite of what the Executive order says, and that is not to hire people without regard to race, but to hire them on the basis of race." Dismissing Schultz's demurral, the senator restated his proposition: "In other words, an affirmative action program within the purview of the Philadelphia Plan is that in order to achieve hiring without regard to matters of race, a contractor must take into consideration matters of race in hiring." Schultz insisted that the plan only required race-conscious development of a broad pool of potential employees, not decisions "between A and B on the basis of race."[52] But to Ervin and many others, that was a distinction without a difference. Once race became a factor in any way in the design of hiring systems, it meant that in practice some applicants' race would be used against them. Ervin insisted that policy violated Johnson's executive order, Title VII, and the Constitution.

Whatever its legality or merits as public policy, the plan also served in practice a key partisan purpose for the Nixon White House. It inflamed tensions in the Democratic Party coalition between liberal politicians such as Californian Augustus Hawkins and conservative southerners, along with anti–affirmative action union leaders. Though it is impossible to know, many suspected that these political consequences were really the source of the plan's appeal in Nixon's eyes. Indeed, the NAACP's chief Washington lobbyist, Clarence Mitchell, called the plan a "calculated attempt coming right from the President's desk to break up the coalition between Negroes and labor unions."[53] Intentionally or not, the Republicans' early support for such affirmative action proved a politically deft Trojan horse whose role in imploding the Democratic coalition lasted for decades, consolidated by the Reagan administration's successful wooing of blue-collar white workers. The GOP first helped place racial affirmative action programs more squarely on the nation's agenda. Later, when rival racial policy coalitions began to form in opposition and support for them, it allied with the opponents of race-conscious hiring.

In this early phase, the lower courts upheld the Philadelphia Plan. Under the Labor Department's Order No. 4, the Nixon administration went on to establish similar requirements for other federal contractors.[54] In 1969, Nixon also issued Executive Order 11458, creating the Office of Minority Business Enterprise. In 1970, he added Executive Order 11518, directing the SBA particularly to consider aid to "minority-owned small business concerns" and to minorities seeking to enter the business community. The latter order ensured that the Section 8(a) program would continue to focus on minorities. Together these initiatives enabled the Nixon administration to assert, in undeniably race-conscious fashion, that it was sincere in trying to promote material racial progress by fostering "black capitalism."

But as a means to increase the number of African Americans in federally funded construction jobs, the Philadelphia Plan accomplished little, foundering on union intransigence and the OFCC's failure to make much use of the sanctions laid out in Executive Order 1146. Nixon soon switched his support to alternative plans featuring apprenticeships for blacks in separate training centers—plans that, again, traditional unions favored but that rarely led to union membership for nonwhites. Arthur Fletcher also lost his job at the Labor Department. (He would go on to a long career in other forms of public service and be eulogized at his 2005 funeral by the Reverend Jeremiah Wright.)[55] By 1974, the initiatives spearheaded by the Philadelphia Plan had faded. The U.S. Commission on Civil Rights declared the OFCC's enforcement actions "virtually" nonexistent.[56]

Many more civil rights proponents were coming to feel that extensive and explicit race-targeted initiatives were a prerequisite if the nation's massive racial inequalities were to be alleviated, especially as the economy went into recession. But at the same time other Americans, predominantly white, became more aware of and more upset over the federal bureaucracy's increased prodding to achieve integrated workforces and public institutions. The character and structure of the modern racial alliances were now solidifying.

The Judiciary and the Consolidation of the Modern Racial Coalitions

Before these two alliances emerged, however, the courts provided important and evolving rulings on the civil rights laws and administrative programs initiated in the Great Society years and perpetuated in varied ways by the Nixon administration. Those cases supplied striking examples, conceptual frames and language that contributed to the processes of racial policy realignment, in part by presenting positions on the propriety or impropriety of race-conscious policies as matters of high constitutional principle. At first, they did so in ways that reinforced the increasing embrace by civil rights advocates of stronger race-conscious measures. That development occurred in part because the additional demands the new civil rights laws placed on the federal judiciary required an expansion of its size. The number of federal judges staffing federal courts of appeals grew significantly in the 1960s and 1970s.[57] Most of the judges appointed in these years were racial liberals who interpreted the civil rights laws of the 1960s, including Title VII, in ways that loosened some of the restrictions conservatives had imposed on the goals and powers authorized in the bills at their passage.[58]

Most notable was the Supreme Court's decision in *Griggs v. Duke Power Co.* (1971), which not incidentally strengthened the willingness of many businesses to embrace race-conscious measures.[59] There, black employees backed by the EEOC successfully sued the power company under Title VII. Despite legislative history documenting that the 1964 Civil Rights Act was concerned only with intentional racial discrimination, not unintended but disparate racial impacts, the employees contended that the company's use of intelligence test scores in hiring was illegal discrimination. They argued that the tests did not measure qualities needed for the jobs in question, and they had a disproportionately adverse impact on African Americans. Later cases extended the ruling to other forms of employment tests with discriminatory effects on African American employees. The U.S. Chamber of Commerce filed a brief for the employer, but the Nixon administration and the United Steelworkers of America backed the black employees.[60] Chief Justice Warren Burger, a Nixon appointee, wrote for a unanimous court, agreeing with the EEOC's view that job requirements that had a disparate impact on blacks and that were not reasonably related to job performance were banned by the statute.[61]

In the wake of *Griggs*, Title VII lawsuits increased from the hundreds to over five thousand a year. As political scientist Paul Frymer notes, the Court soon held that employees could pursue disputes against employers both under Title VII and under the National Labor Relations Act, thereby providing additional channels through which victims of racial discrimination might seek redress.[62] Although civil rights groups continued to push for the EEOC to obtain cease-and-desist powers, they also began to feel that private litigation, rather than NLRB-style administrative empowerment, might actually be the best way to generate effective enforcement.[63] Under the pressure of this mounting litigation, many more employers resolved that they needed affirmative action programs to forestall lawsuits. As legal scholar Peter Schuck notes, firms came to see "affirmative action as a safe harbor sheltering them from Title VII claims."[64]

By the late 1970s, anti-discrimination offices in many large corporations had become proponents of race-conscious measures to promote "diversity," understood as enabling companies to design and market products better because their workforces included more varied skills and backgrounds.[65] This stance has endured. In 2003, when a more conservative Court sustained the affirmative action program of the University of Michigan Law School in *Grutter v. Bollinger* (while striking down the university's undergraduate affirmative action program in *Gratz v. Bollinger*), amicus curiae briefs filed by sixty-five Fortune 500 companies, including American Express, American Airlines, Coca-Cola, Chrysler, Dow Chemical, Kodak, Eli Lilly, General Electric, Hewlett-Packard, Intel, Kellogg, Kraft, Lockheed Martin, Mitsubishi, Nike, Reebok, and Sara Lee Corporation, helped build the case in defense of race-conscious admission policies.[66]

But if big business, along with many civil rights groups and liberal Democrats, moved into the emerging alliance of those committed to race-conscious employment policies after *Griggs*, many more political actors were moving in the other direction. In 1972, the Democrats adopted rules to ensure that long underrepresented groups would have greater, ideally proportional, presence at their convention and in their decisions, and they nominated the very liberal George McGovern.[67] Their platform called for more "affirmative action" efforts to achieve "proportional representation to 'previously discriminated against groups'" within the party; urged support for "the cultural identity and pride of black people" and "Ethnic Studies"; and they also called for "affirmative action to end discrimination" in the armed forces, "affirmative programs in universities and colleges for recruitments of minorities," and "an affirmative action program to train and to hire bilingual-bicultural Spanish-speaking persons." Specifically in regard to employment, the Democrats urged the "full enforcement of all equal employment opportunity laws, including federal contract compliance and federally regulated industries and giving the Equal Employment Opportunity Commission adequate staff and resources and power to issue cease and desist orders promptly."[68]

Recognizing his opportunity, Nixon insisted in contrast that while he had always opposed segregation, he also had always opposed racial "quotas." He launched his 1972 convention acceptance speech by denouncing the Democrats for "dividing Americans into quotas," contending, "the way to end discrimination against some is not to begin to discriminate against others."[69] The Republican platform condemned "the imposition of arbitrary quotas in the hiring of faculties or the enrollment of students," though it also promised "efforts to remedy the ancient neglect of disadvantaged groups" and to "search out new employment opportunities for minorities," without "displacing those already at work." The GOP also boasted of Nixon's creation of the Office of Minority Business Enterprise.[70]

That contrasting language made clear that the Democrats were becoming the party that openly endorsed "affirmative action," including various types of numerically defined proportional representation, while the Republicans defined themselves even more resolutely as anti-quotas. Still, the GOP was not opposed to all race-conscious policymaking: it supported efforts to promote minority employment and businesses. The alignment of the parties with firmly opposed color-blind and race-conscious policy alliances was not yet complete. But in ensuing years, neoconservative academics and burgeoning numbers of conservative think tanks, advocacy groups, and media commentators began to criticize all kinds of race-conscious policies as "affirmative action" programs that were morally equivalent to, if they did not in practice entail, unjust "racial quotas" subjecting whites to unconscionable "reverse discrimination." Frequently such opponents used the slogans of the civil rights movement they had in many cases resisted to argue against this new racial equality agenda.[71]

The Broader Language of Affirmative Action

In the course of these developments, the meaning of "affirmative action" began to shift in ways that have become fundamental to the modern structure of American racial politics and racial policymaking. Not only the growing number of critics, but also many proponents of affirmative action increasingly blurred any distinction between what historian Hugh Davis Graham called "hard" affirmative action, strict numerical quotas and targets, and "soft" affirmative action, race-conscious measures that sought to expand outreach to minorities without rigid racial preferences.[72] Many members of both the emerging alliances came to present all concerns to design or to justify policies in race-conscious terms—as choice-worthy primarily because the policies would promote racial inclusiveness or reduce material racial inequalities—as in sharp contradiction to treating people strictly as individuals, without regard for their race or ethnicity, in fully color-blind fashion. As a result, increasingly much American political discourse came to treat all forms of race-conscious policymaking as either equally acceptable or equally unacceptable. In practice, as throughout most of America's past, American legislators, executive officials, and judges nonetheless often sought, as many continue to seek today, to blend various color-blind and race-conscious measures within policies that they believe can be effective. But from the mid-1970s on, few American political leaders thought it politic to argue explicitly for the desirability of combinations of race-neutral and race-conscious measures. Even those who held race-neutral policies to be more beneficial in the long run often resisted efforts to judge alternative policies explicitly by their empirical consequences for racial equality, because those tests seemed unduly race-conscious.

There are several reasons for this move to treating the choice between "race-neutral" and "race-conscious" as all-or-none. The first is philosophical: it is simply true that there is a sharp dichotomy between either giving great weight to probable impacts on material racial inequalities in policymaking, or instead giving little weight to probable impacts on material racial inequalities. Not just "hard" affirmative action measures, but most sorts of race-conscious policies, are on the "give great weight" side of that divide. But by itself, this logical distinction does not explain why American policymakers could not in practice use both color-blind and race-conscious measures, whenever one sort or the other seemed most efficacious.

The second reason for disparaging that approach came from experiences of the practicalities of effective administration in the late 1960s and early 1970s. The burgeoning of bureaucratically sponsored affirmative action measures during those years showed that administrative logistics often meant that policies that were presented simply as "soft" efforts to combat invidious discrimination and, at most, prompt expansions in the pool of beneficiaries, as the EEOC, OFCC, and Philadelphia Plan measures all were, often ended up resulting in "hard" numerical targets and quotas. Once policies are set to achieve racial purposes or at least justified as likely to reduce racial disparities, it is hard for officials to avoid some form of counting to see if those purposes are being achieved. And once officials start counting, it is hard for those they regulate to resist adopting policies with quantitative targets. Peter Schuck has summarized this tendency well: even to engage in "soft" efforts to expand employment pools, "one must expend additional resources, targeting them on some groups and not on others and . . . increasing the probability that members of the target group will win the prize . . .we are now on a slippery slope that could move us toward preferences of a more robust sort."[73]

Nonetheless, by itself the tendency to use numbers did not prevent policymakers from seeking to combine various race-neutral policies, many "soft" race-conscious measures, and some "hard" affirmative action programs in ways that minimized the "hardness" and still produced results. The final factor at work that did the most to make these efforts publicly almost indefensible, pressuring officials to resort to disingenuous characterizations of them, was politics.

Opponents of race-conscious efforts to reduce material racial inequalities had and still have many motives. Some doubt that affirmative action programs can work. Some are conservative libertarians or proponents of individualistic conceptions of human dignity who see race-based policies as profound affronts to individual rights. Some are primarily believers in states' rights who hold

111

that national institutions should not compel states and municipalities to adopt policies local majorities oppose. Some are strongly attached for various reasons to the racial status quo. Some are simply seeking political power by any means feasible, including attacking policies that make many voters uneasy. But whatever their motives, most have found over time that they can credibly claim to occupy the moral and constitutional high ground by insisting that color-blind policies represent the principles of civic equality that the anti-segregation movement championed and that the Constitution embodies. Race-conscious decision making, they maintain, is always at bottom invidious racism.

From the mid-1970s on, many aspiring political leaders realized the value of mobilizing mass political support by attacking all race-conscious policy-making as violations of constitutional and moral principles. The approval their arguments received primarily from white Americans encouraged them to issue such condemnations more and more forcefully. In response, although proponents of stronger governmental measures to achieve material racial inequality were and are often divided over the desirability and sometimes over the appropriate beneficiaries of affirmative action and other race-conscious policies, many soon concluded that they could not afford nuanced positions. Often it seemed politically necessary to attack pure "color blindness" as a veiled but intentional effort to sustain existing racial inequalities; to defend race-conscious policymaking in most of its varieties; and to work in alliance with other race-conscious proponents, at least on most issues, most of the time. As a result, the two modern racial alliances emerged, producing highly polarized modern policy debates over race in America in which frequently, each side dismisses most of the measures suggested by the other as unprincipled efforts to gain or maintain unjust racial advantages.

THE PARTIES POLARIZE IN PRINCIPLE AND PARTLY IN PRACTICE

The politics generating this polarization over racial policies grew all the more institutionalized and intense as the two major parties aligned on an enduring basis with the proponents of the opposing philosophies of racial policies—even though the actual policies of officials of each party have still often remained mixes of both approaches. There are, again, philosophical, logistical, and political reasons why the move of the parties to these ideological polar positions has never been nearly as complete in practice as it has been in political rhetoric.

Philosophically, it is at best paradoxical to claim to treat all persons equally as unique individuals, but to disregard the claims of those who contend that their individual identities and aspirations require recognition of their racially shaped experiences, affiliations, and aspirations. Most American political leaders in the modern era have professed to value the diverse cultural heritages with which Americans identify; and it does not seem consistent either to disregard racial heritages or to value some racial identities but not others. Yet it is also paradoxical to claim to treat all persons equally as unique individuals, while explicitly lessening the opportunities for some to pursue their aspirations because of racial identities they did not create or choose and may not embrace. These contrasting paradoxes make it difficult for policymakers to sustain fully color-blind or race-conscious courses without appearing to many to be disingenuous, even hypocritical. While rhetorically leaning one way or another, then, they often adopt a fuzzy combination of measures designed more to reduce criticisms than to implement principles or solve policy problems.

Logistically, color-blind advocates also face difficulties because their principles support efforts to combat invidious racial discrimination, at least by public agencies, and often by private bodies receiving federal funds. Yet those anti-discrimination efforts cannot be conducted without some focus on racial motives and consequences. In practice they generally have to involve compiling racial statistics to be effective. And again, once government agencies collect such data, many officials can feel pressured to make sure the results display inclusiveness, so race-conscious decisions result. The corresponding logistical challenge for race-conscious advocates is that few of them want to assert that race should be the sole or, usually, even the primary factor in decision making. They only urge that racial inequalities and exclusions be lessened as much as possible as other policy goals are pursued. Yet in some contexts, racially egalitarian and inclusive aspirations appear attainable only if numerous decisions turn strictly on racial consequences, to a degree that can prompt many advocates to back away from their insistence on race-conscious approaches. So they, in turn, may not adhere to the assiduous concerns to promote racial equity they promise. Again, political officials aligned with both camps often find themselves pursuing not very well considered or defined middle paths.

Finally, part of the political power and appeal of principles of both color blindness and race consciousness comes from their claims that their commitments carry forward the values and purposes of the civil rights movement. To keep those claims politically credible, proponents of color blindness often seek to show that they are genuinely concerned with the well-being of America's

113

racial minorities and that their policies benefit them. As political scientist Steven Teles has noted, even leading critics of race-conscious policies like Clint Bolick, cofounder of the libertarian Institute for Justice, have generally accepted that "policies need to be justified in terms of their impact on less privileged groups."[74] Doing so, however, means keeping policy discourse partly on the terrain of race-conscious decision making. Proponents of race-conscious measures, in turn, feel compelled to show that they are finding ways to move the nation beyond racial antagonisms, toward the vision of civic friendship and community King painted at the end of his March on Washington address. Doing so often means announcing that treating people as individuals without regard to race is the ultimate goal and striving to make race-conscious policies as "soft," as temporary, and as beneficial for whites as possible, even if this means making them less effective in combating racial inequalities.

So in practice the modern Republican Party has not adhered rigorously to color-blind policies, nor has the modern Democratic Party always vigorously pursued affirmative action and other race-conscious policies. Nonetheless, the GOP trajectory over time toward a stronger and stronger rhetorical and legal embrace of color blindness as the proper racial principle is undeniable. Here the symmetry between the parties ends—because the Republicans have the policy position more popular with much of the electorate, and so they have stressed their support for it. Democrats in contrast have concluded that they cannot afford either to abandon affirmative action measures, alienating the race-conscious alliance that otherwise supports them almost unanimously, or to trumpet their support for race-conscious measures in ways that will drive away white voters (though many individual Democrats have been tempted by each of these alternatives). The result is that the Republicans have become more vociferous proponents of color-blind policies in principle and to some degree in practice since 1972, while the Democrats have become more muted advocates of affirmative action and other forms of race-conscious policymaking—without, again, ever renouncing those racial policy positions.

The party platforms exhibit these developing patterns in the party's official positions clearly. In 1976, the Republicans' platform once more insisted there must be no "quota system." They added an attack on "forced busing" to achieve racial integration, even though they endorsed efforts to expand educational opportunities for "minority citizens" in other ways, as well as "loans to minority businesses"; and they encouraged all Americans to take pride in their ancestral "cultural heritage" and "cultural diversity."[75] Undaunted by McGovern's massive defeat in 1972, the Democrats instead promised "full and vigorous enforcement of all equal opportunities laws and affirmative action," and urged not only "loans" but also "federal contract and procurement opportunities" for "minority" businesses. They also urged "vigorous federal programs and policies of compensatory opportunity to remedy for many Americans the generations of injustice and deprivation." And though they suggested a variety of measures to improve educational quality and achieve school integration in terms of both "race and economic class," they also stated that mandatory "transportation of students beyond their neighborhoods for the purpose of desegregation remains a judicial tool of the last resort for the purpose of achieving school desegregation."[76]

By 1980, when the Republicans nominated Ronald Reagan, the contrast was even greater. To the Republicans, the most threatening foes of "equal opportunity" now were "bureaucratic regulations and decisions which rely on quotas, ratios, and numerical requirements to exclude some individuals in favor of others." They repeated their condemnation of "forced busing," and they called only for "enforcement of laws to assure equal treatment in job recruitment, hiring, promotion, pay, credit, mortgage access, and housing," abandoning any reference to programs designed to aid minorities in these regards. Instead, they proposed only "color-blind" economic policies, saying, "Our fundamental answer to the economic problems of black Americans is the same answer we make to all Americans—full employment without inflation through economic growth."[77]

The Democrats held to different, race-conscious answers. Their platform called on "the public and private sectors to live up to and enforce civil rights laws and regulations, i.e., Equal Employment Opportunity Programs, Title VI and Title VII of the Civil Rights Act, the Fair Housing Laws, and affirmative action requirements."[78] It devoted a long section to "Minority Business" that celebrated the Democrats' strengthening of the Small Business Administration's Section 8(a) programs and expanded loans to minority businesses, while promising that the party would "implement vigorously all set-aside provisions for minority business." The Democrats defined such businesses expansively, as including "Black, Hispanic, Asian/Pacific Americans, Native Americans, and other minorities." Their platform also endorsed "affirmative action goals to overturn patterns of discrimination in education and employment," including "special efforts in recruitment, training, and promotion to aid minority Americans," and it reiterated support for school desegregation, including mandatory transportation "as a last resort."[79]

Those basic contrasts have endured: every subsequent Republican Party platform has explicitly denounced quotas and racial preferences. Every subsequent Democratic platform has explicitly endorsed "affirmative action," even though in 1996 the Democrats endorsed President Bill Clinton's promise to "mend it, don't end it," and later platforms have not often displayed the overt enthusiasm for it expressed by the Democratic Party of the 1970s.[80]

THE MODERN RACIAL ALLIANCES

Partly as a result of the sharpened contrast between the parties in their 1980 platforms, we designate 1978 as roughly the completion of the transition from the end of the Jim Crow era and the start of the modern era, defined by opposition between the modern color-blind and race-conscious alliances. Nineteen seventy-eight is significant for another reason: it is also the year when the modern anti-tax movement scored its first dramatic victory, the passage in California of Proposition 13, imposing state limits on property taxes.[81] The chief proponent of that proposition, Howard Jarvis, used a rhetoric that denounced bureaucrats and politicians, not racial minorities. He did, however, put in charge of the measure's media and advertising campaign Roland Vincent, who had managed George Wallace's 1976 presidential bid in California, and it is probable that whites and blacks saw the consequences of the proposal in very different terms: whites were three times more likely to support it.[82] The coalition of the California-based Ronald Reagan, soon to win his historic 1980 victory, was similarly built in part by blending economic ideologies championing self-help rather than government spending programs with calls for color-blind policies focused on rewarding individual merit, not racial identities. It is not hard to see why and how opposition to governmental taxing and spending and opposition to race-conscious measures have often buttressed each other. Still, support or opposition to color-blind policies has never simply mirrored economic interests or ideologies. Tables 4.1 and 4.2 display the memberships of the modern color-blind alliance and the modern race-conscious alliance on employment issues. As we will show, these contrasting coalitions have since remained largely though not perfectly intact on virtually all other issues with racial dimensions.

These tabular depictions of the modern alliances inevitably gloss over many nuances. Officials of both parties have deviated at times from the racial positions to which their platforms pledged them; there has been some variance in the beliefs and actions of different members of the groups we place in one alliance or the other; and in particular there are many local and state variations within national groups, such as federated labor unions. Many group positions evolve over time as well.

Yet while there is great value in documenting and assessing these variations, in aggregate the evidence shows that pressures to maintain political allies and

Affirmative Action in Work

Table 4.1

Color-Blind Alliance Opposed to Affirmative Action in Employment, 1978–2008

Most Republican Party officeholders and members after 1976

Presidents, 1981–93, 2001–9

Some conservative, neoconservative Democrats

Majority of Supreme Court after 1980

Most lower federal court judges, many state judges after 1980

Some predominantly white-owned businesses and business lobbyists (e.g., Equal Employment Advisory Council)

Some labor unions, particularly union locals

Conservative media (e.g., Rush Limbaugh, Charles Krauthammer)

Conservative think tanks / advocacy groups (e.g., Center for Individual Rights, Cato Institute)

Fringe white supremacist groups

Christian Right groups (e.g., Family Research Council)

Conservative foundations (e.g., Lynde and Harry Bradley Foundation)

Source: Data in this table derived from: American Presidency Project, http://www.presidency.ucsb.edu/platforms.php (Republican Platforms); Democratic Leadership Council, The Hyde Park Declaration: A Statement of Principles and a Policy Agenda for the 21st Century, http://www.dlc.org/ndol_ci.cfm?kaid=128subid=174contentid=1926; Barbara Reskin, *The Realities of Affirmative Action in Employment* (Washington, DC: American Sociological Association, 1998), 78–79; Marie Gryphon, "The Affirmative Action Myth" *Policy Analysis* 540, April 13, 2005), http://www.cato.org/pub_display.php?pub_id=377; Linda Faye Williams, *The Constraint of Race Legacies of White Skin Privilege in America* (University Park: Pennsylvania State University Press, 2003), 286–91, 300–312; "Affirmative Action Bites Democrats," *Rush Limbaugh Show* (transcript), August 19, 2008, http://www.rushlimbaugh.com/home/daily/site_081908/content/01125117.guest.html (Rush Limbaugh); "Charles Krauthammer: Prize Writer," Mitchell Bard.com, http://www.mitchellbard.com/articles/kraut.html (noting that Krauthammer originally supported affirmative action); Swain, *New White Nationalism*, 77–81; Family Research Council, "Policy Areas: Other Issues, Affirmative Action," www.frc.org/get.cfm?c=RESEARCH; and Lynde and Harry Bradley Foundation, 2007 Bradley Prize Recipients, www.bradleyfdn.org/bradley_prizes.asp (Bradley Prize to Stephen and Abigail Thernstrom).

Chapter 4

T A B L E 4.2
Race-Conscious Alliance Supporting Affirmative Action in Employment, 1978–2008

Most Democratic Party officeholders and members

President (mixed support), 1993–2001

Some liberal, pro-corporate Republicans

Some federal, state judges

Many civil service members of executive agencies

Many large businesses, minority-owned businesses

Most labor unions

Military leadership

Liberal media (e.g., *New York Times*)

Liberal advocacy groups (e.g. ACLU)

Most nonwhite advocacy groups (e.g., NAACP, National Council of La Raza, Asian American Legal Defense Fund)

Liberal religious groups (e.g., National Council of Churches)

Liberal foundations (e.g., Soros Foundation, Ford Foundation)

Source: American Presidency Project, http://www.presidency.ucsb.edu/platforms.php (Democratic platforms); Williams, *Constraint of Race*, 292-301; Reskin, *Realities of Affirmative Action*, 97–98; Frank Dobbin and John R. Sutton, "The Strength of a Weak State The Employment Rights Revolution and the Rise of Human Resources Management Divisions," *American Journal of Sociolgy* 104 (1998)"; George Stephanopoulos and Christopher Edley, *Affirmative Action Review: Report to the President,* 1995," sec. 7, http://clinton2.nara.gov/WH/EOP/OP/html/aa/aa07 .html; David Bacon, "Peace and Justice: California Labor Prepares to Defend Affirmative Action," 1995, http://dbacon.igc.org/PJust/01LabDef.html; "Affirmative Action in Play," *New York Times,* November 6, 1997, http://www.nytimes.com/1997/11/06/opinion/affirmative-action-in-play.html ?scp=1&sq=affirmative+action+employment&st=nyt; The Leadership Conference, "Coalition Members of the Leadership Conference on Civil and Human Rights," http://www.civilrights .org/aymt/the_leadership_conference/coalitionmembers, and http://www.civilrights.org.equal opportunity/about/; Open Society Institute, ISU form: Defending and Protecting Opportunity— Affirmative Action and Beyond, http://www.soros.org/initiatives/usprograms/focus/equality/events/ affirmative_20050620 and *"Peace and Social Justice: Human Rights,"* Ford Foundation Annual Report 2006 http://www.fordfoundation.org/pdfs/library/ar2006.pdf, 76.

remain politically salient mean that when push has come to shove on policies with racial dimensions, most of the actors in both alliances have lined up on the sides we identify most of the time, urging color-blind or race-conscious measures. One indication of that pattern is the fact that, as Hugh Davis Graham noted, throughout the modern era most civil rights groups have worked with the influential umbrella lobby, the Leadership Conference for Civil Rights, including unions, religious groups, and feminist organizations, as well as a wide range of nonwhite advocacy associations.[83] But from the late 1970s through the election of Barack Obama in 2008, it was the color-blind alliance that most grew in adherents, in institutions under its control, and in its influence on public policies. Even so, the already institutionalized agencies and programs of the race-conscious alliance, and its always substantial size and power, mean that the contestation between the two alliances has continued, in employment and in other areas, though with contextual differences that produce a range of outcomes.

Set-Aside Employment

In employment, perhaps the most important development, coming at the end of the transitional era, was the success of race-conscious forces in getting Congress to adopt the first explicitly race-based national legislation in the twentieth century, the "minority set-aside" provision of the Public Works Employment Act of 1977. The act required that at least 10 percent of the $4 billion appropriated for federally funded public works contracts should go to business enterprises with at least 50 percent minority ownership (MBEs). The act defined minorities as "Negroes, Spanish-speaking, Orientals, Indians, Eskimos, and Aleuts," designations drawn from the Small Business Administration's program to aid minority contractors.[84] The sponsor of the provision was Democratic representative Parren Mitchell, the first African American to be elected to Congress from Maryland; cofounder and then chair of the Congressional Black Caucus; and (though he was no relation to former Congressman Arthur Mitchell) he was also the brother of the NAACP's Washington lobbyist, Clarence Mitchell.

Some scholars identify Clarence as "a lifelong champion of constitutional color-blindness."[85] Whether or not that was so, it was clearly not true of Parren. Perhaps aware of the political dangers of holding hearings on his proposal, he offered it as an amendment on the House floor on February 23, 1977. He cited the SBA's Section 8(a) program as a legitimating precedent, noting that MBEs received only 1 percent of federal contracts even though minorities made up 15 percent to 18 percent of the population. The House adopted Mitchell's amendment with little discussion by a vote of 295–85.[86] The Senate's only African American member, Republican Edward Brooke of Massachusetts, introduced a similar amendment to the Senate's bill, which passed 74–11 without debate. The House then ratified the conference report consolidating the two bills by 335–77, the Senate by 71–14.[87] Both parties' 1976 platforms had, after all, promised to aid minority businesses, though the bill ventured into the area of numerical racial quotas that the Republicans officially disavowed.

Democratic president Jimmy Carter, a southern liberal elected after the Watergate scandal disgraced the Republicans, promptly signed the legislation, and his administration eagerly promoted its minority set-aside program. With the administration's support, Congress in 1978 gave statutory authorization for the first time to the SBA's Section 8(a) program via the Small Business Investment Act, again sponsored by Mitchell and passed by voice vote in both chambers.[88] With Mitchell's continuing advocacy, Congress went on to adopt set-aside provisions in the Highway Improvement Act of 1982 and the Foreign Assistance Act of 1983, providing not simply bureaucratic but clear national legislative authority for race-conscious measures.[89]

Alliances in Amicus Briefs

Proponents of such policies were able to argue confidently in part because the Supreme Court continued to give them its imprimatur of constitutionality. The amicus briefs in the decisions upholding affirmative action in these years and later ones are highly significant for our analysis. They provide illuminating indicators of the coalescence and makeup of the modern racial alliances as they have battled to control this key national institution.

Notably, in *Steelworkers v. Weber* (1979), a 5–2 majority ruled in favor of a plan resulting from a collective bargaining agreement between the United Steelworkers of America and Kaiser Aluminum that reserved 50 percent of the positions in an in-plant training program for blacks.[90] The company conceded that its percentage of African American employees was miniscule compared with the African American population in its area, leaving it vulnerable to litigation if it did not agree to change. The American Civil Liberties Union (ACLU), NAACP, NAACP Legal Defense Fund, Asian American Legal Defense Fund, the Lawyers' Committee for Civil Rights Under Law headed by LBJ's attorney general Nicholas Katzenbach, the National Puerto Rican Coalition, the National Union of Hospital and Health Care Employees, the Women's Caucus of the United Steelworkers of America, and the AFL-CIO all filed briefs on behalf of this union-and-business-created program.[91] The coalition in favor of race-conscious policies thus included predominantly white liberal public interest advocacy groups, African American, Latino, and Asian American civil rights organizations, women's groups, and major unions, along with the large corporation involved in the case.

In contrast, the Government Contract Employers' Association, California Correctional Officers' Association, conservative litigation groups including the Pacific Legal Foundation, the Southeastern Legal Foundation, and the Washington Legal Foundation, the Polish American Congress, the Equal Employment Advisory Council (an employers' association), the National Coordinating Committee for Trade Union Action and Democracy, and the United Electrical Workers, among others, urged its overturning.[92] The three legal foundations were among many conservative legal advocacy organizations, regional and national, that emerged in the 1970s and 1980s, beginning with the Pacific Legal Foundation in 1973. All were devoted to litigating to achieve "color-blind justice," among other conservative causes.[93] They would prove key members of the modern color-blind alliance. And although the United Steelworkers and the AFL-CIO were on the other side, one major union, the United Electrical Workers, and the Correctional Officers' Association filed with the new conservative legal foundations. So did two employer groups, including one, the Equal Employment Advisory Council, which had been created in 1976 in part to assist businesses in designing "diversity" programs that could shield them against litigation—but it has primarily filed amicus briefs in opposition to government-imposed affirmative action programs.[94] The filings by unions and employer associations on both sides of the case showed the cross-class divisions in labor and business ranks over affirmative action.

Yet while opponents of race-conscious measures included important established groups and energetic new ones, at this point the developing color-blind alliance had not yet captured the Supreme Court. One of the Court's leading racial liberals, Justice William Brennan, ruled for the majority that Title VII did not forbid "private employers and unions from voluntarily agreeing upon bona fide affirmative action plans that accord racial preferences" as provided in the collective bargaining agreement.[95] The privately negotiated but publicly fostered affirmative action program was upheld.

Then in *Fullilove v. Klutznick* (1980), the Supreme Court voted 6–3 to sustain the 10 percent set-aside minority business enterprise provision of the federal Public Works Employment Act of 1977.[96] By this time, many unions were organizing women and workers of color. Reversing historical stances, most of those unions embraced affirmative action and other race-conscious employment measures, tilting America's unions predominantly into the race-conscious alliance.[97] In *Fullilove*, there were no union briefs opposing the program, though the Equal Employment Advisory Council and the Pacific

Chapter 4

Legal Foundation urged its invalidation.[98] The ACLU, Asian American LDF, Lawyers' Committee for Civil Rights Under Law, NAACP, NAACP LDF, Mexican American/Hispanic Contractors and Truckers Association, Minority Contractors Assistance Project, the National Bar Association, and the American Savings and Loan League all filed on behalf of the set-aside requirement.[99]

These amicus alignments exhibit wide support for race-conscious measures from a range of minority advocacy groups, a growing number of unions, minority owned businesses, and some larger businesses, though various employer associations, including many primarily representing small businesses, remained then and have remained since more often in opposition. Despite the breadth of this coalition, *Fullilove* was the last major Supreme Court decision strongly favorable to affirmative action in employment. Over time, Ronald Reagan's triumph in 1980 produced an extensive though not total capture of the executive branch by color-blind proponents and led to courts repopulated with conservative judges hostile to race-conscious measures. The Reagan presidency, particularly after Reagan's reelection in 1984, proved the turning point in favor of the predominance of the color-blind alliance in modern American politics and, to a lesser degree, policymaking, though the race-conscious alliances still retained control of many American governing institutions and policies throughout those years.

The Reagan Effect

Reagan's historic victory and the substantial political success of the ensuing "Reagan Revolution" had many sources. But as his speechwriter, Peggy Noonan, has argued, a great part of his appeal came from the perception that, unlike morally lax liberals, Reagan was a man of strong and good character whose positions reflected and reinforced policies that promoted good character.[100] That was an appeal suitably general to bring a great variety of perspectives under the Republican umbrella. The conservative coalition Reagan's candidacy knit together succeeded in large part because it united partisans of diverse conceptions of "good character"—including Goldwater-style economic libertarians who saw liberal social welfare policies as breeding dependency and slothful repudiation of the work ethic; religious and cultural conservatives who believed liberal permissiveness undermined good and pious moral character; military and foreign policy conservatives who contended that liberals' emphasis on diplomacy in dealing with Communists and militant Islamic radicals eroded the martial virtues needed to protect the nation; and some communitarians who thought that liberal individualism worked against the development of civic spirit and willingness to sacrifice for the common good.[101]

For Reagan and most conservatives in all these groups, in principle promoting "good character" required not only cutting taxes and government spending programs that burdened hard workers and rewarded the lazy. It also meant the adoption of color-blind policies. The charismatic president and his advisers recognized that for many Americans, championing color blindness instead of racially discriminatory preferences seemed more clearly virtuous than simply advocating conservative economic policies that could be portrayed as harsh toward the disadvantaged. Consequently, Reagan made his support for color blindness a central feature of his 1980 campaign, in which he contended, "We must not allow the noble concept of equal opportunity to be distorted into federal guidelines or quotas which require race, ethnicity, or sex—rather than ability and qualifications—to be the principal factor in hiring or education."[102] Again, the Republican platform on which Reagan ran in that year stressed that its "fundamental answer to the economic problems of black Americans" was the "same answer we make to all Americans—full employment without inflation through economic growth. First and foremost, we are committed to a policy of economic expansion through tax-rate reductions, spending restraint, regulatory reform, and other incentives." For Reagan and his GOP, civil rights enforcement meant primarily ensuring in color-blind fashion "that the federal government follows a nondiscriminatory system of appointments up and down the line," though still "with a careful eye for qualified minority aspirants."[103]

As that caveat indicated, the Reagan administration was careful to present its racial policies as the fulfillment, not the rejection, of the principles of the modern civil rights movement. When Reagan signed a bill in 1983 making Martin Luther King Jr.'s birthday a national holiday, the president explicitly praised King for awakening the "sense that true justice must be colorblind." He interpreted the Civil Rights Act of 1964 as conferring "the right to compete for employment on the sole basis of individual merit," and in his eyes affirmative action wrongly judged people on the color of their skin, not the content of their character.[104] Reagan's attorney general, Edwin Meese, along with several cabinet secretaries, therefore urged the new president to change the executive orders authorizing various kinds of race-conscious employment measures. Reagan's EEOC chairman, future Supreme Court Justice Clarence Thomas, correspondingly focused the commission's work only on cases of intentional individual discrimination, abandoning "disparate impact" lawsuits entirely, and often deciding against individuals claiming to have experienced intentional racial discrimination.[105]

But the desire to show that the administration had not rejected the goals of the civil rights movement still created pressures on those executive branch officials with immediate responsibilities for employment not to abandon all race-conscious policies. Reagan's labor secretaries, Raymond Donovan and then in 1985 William Brock, supported the OFCC's programs, as did others in the Reagan cabinet. And though small business interests represented by the U.S. Chamber of Commerce and the Association of General Contractors supported Meese, big business, represented by the National Association of Manufacturers (NAM), was now committed to its "diversity" programs.[106] It regularly expressed support for many (but not all) kinds of race-conscious programs. Consequently, although the Reagan administration sharply cut the OFCC budget, sought to appoint anti–affirmative action judges, and litigated in court against race-conscious measures, hoping the courts would do the politically charged work of eliminating affirmative action for it, the Reagan White House did not in the end rescind most existing race-conscious policies in employment and in other policy arenas.[107] Nor was it able to stifle the rise of private civil rights litigation.[108]

Narrowing Affirmative Action at the Workplace

The Reagan administration's actions nonetheless had a major long-term impact, much as Franklin D. Roosevelt's transformation of the federal judiciary did. During the 1980s, Reagan appointed three justices and elevated William Rehnquist to chief justice. The Supreme Court gravitated further toward membership in the color-blind alliance, and the conservative-staffed Justice Department began to win important legal victories.[109] In *General Building Contractors Association v. Pennsylvania* (1982), blacks seeking to work as operating engineers in the construction industry sued the contractors' association under various civil rights statutes because the association's members had signed contracts with the International Union of Operating Engineers to hire only operating engineers referred by the union. The district court had found the union guilty under Title VII and also found the contractors' association to be in violation of 42 U.S.C. §1981, a provision derived from the 1866 Civil Rights Act and the 1870 Enforcement Act, which the lower court interpreted as banning actions with racially disparate impacts.

With Justices Marshall and Brennan in dissent, then-Associate Justice Rehnquist ruled instead that §1981, like the equal protection clause, must be read in color-blind fashion as banning only intentional racial discrimination. He concluded the record provided no evidence that the contractors' association had endorsed or even known about the union's discriminatory practices.[110] Here the Court concurred with briefs filed by the Equal Employment Advisory Council and the conservative Washington Legal Foundation, rejecting the NAACP's brief on behalf of the African American litigants.[111]

The next year in *Guardians Association v. Civil Service Commission of the City of New York* (1983), the Court accepted that discriminatory intent did not have to be shown to prove a violation of Title VI of the 1964 Civil Rights Act, which bans discrimination by any program receiving federal financial assistance; but it also limited the extent of the relief for which victims of discrimination were eligible, absent a showing that the discrimination was intentional.[112] The case involved New York blacks and Latinos who had passed tests to become police officers. Because they were hired in order of their test scores and so had less seniority than higher-scoring whites, they were the first to be laid off when cuts had to be made. Against briefs filed by the NAACP, the ACLU, and the Asian American Legal Defense Fund, and in accord with an Equal Employment Advisory Council brief, the Court decided that the racially disparate impact of the New York Civil Service Commission's hiring and layoff procedures did not justify granting the minority police officers retroactive seniority.[113]

In 1984, Reagan ran for reelection on a platform arguing, "Americans demand a civil rights policy premised on the letter of the Civil Rights Act of 1964. That law requires equal rights; and it is our policy to end discrimination on account of sex, race, color, creed, or national origin. We have vigorously enforced civil rights statutes. The Equal Employment Opportunity Commission has recovered record amounts of back pay and other compensation for victims of employment discrimination." But the GOP continued, "Just as we must guarantee opportunity, we oppose attempts to dictate results. We will resist efforts to replace equal rights with discriminatory quota systems and preferential treatment. Quotas are the most insidious form of discrimination: reverse discrimination against the innocent. We must always remember that, in a free society, different individual goals will yield different results."[114]

The Democrats charged in turn that the Reagan Republicans not only opposed affirmative action, they were reluctant to enforce the Civil Rights Acts' employment provisions at all. "In the first year after the Reagan Administration assumed office," their 1984 platform contended, "the number of cases involving charges of employment discrimination filed in court by the EEOC dropped by more than 70 percent . . . the Reagan Justice Department has sought to destroy effective affirmative action remedies, and even to undermine private plans to reduce discrimination in employment. The actions of the Reagan administration serve only to delay the day when fairness is achieved and such remedial measures are, therefore, no longer needed."[115]

Whether or not that was so, Republican efforts to limit race-conscious employment measures intensified, especially via litigation, and with mounting successes. Most significant was *Wards Cove Packing Co. v. Atonio* (1989), where the Supreme Court ruled 5–4 that Title VII did not prevent an Alaskan salmon cannery from hiring mostly whites for skilled jobs and mostly non-whites for unskilled jobs, because the Court accepted that there was a dearth of skilled nonwhites for reasons that were not the cannery's fault.[116] In an apparent reversal of the understandings that had prevailed since *Griggs v. Duke Power*, the majority held that, since there did not seem to be large numbers of skilled nonwhites available, employees bore the burden of showing that the racially disparate impact hiring pattern was not the result of legitimate business reasons. Until they did so, the employer did not need to provide any further evidence for the validity of its hiring practices, and even then, that evidence did not have to show the practices were "essential" or "indispensable," only useful. The Reagan Justice Department, the U.S. Chamber of Commerce, the Equal Employment Advisory Council, the American Society for Personnel Administration, and an important new conservative litigation group, the anti–affirmative action Center for Individual Rights, all filed briefs on behalf of the company. The ACLU, the NAACP and the NAACP LDF, and the Lawyers' Committee for Civil Rights Under Law filed for the workers. After their defeat, they turned from the Court to their Democratic allies in Congress.[117]

That same year, color-blind forces won another landmark victory in *Richmond v. J.A. Croson Co.* (1989). There the Supreme Court found the Richmond City Council's Minority Business Utilization Plan unconstitutional. It required white contractors who received city contracts to employ minority subcontractors for at least 30 percent of the total dollar amount of each contract. The city modeled the plan on the program upheld in *Fullilove*, but the court ruled 6–3 that Richmond lacked Congress's equal protection enforcement powers. It also saw no evidence that Richmond had discriminated against all the groups, including Eskimos and Aleuts, eligible for the program.[118]

A number of primarily Democratic state attorneys general, along with the ACLU, the NAACP LDF, the Lawyers' Committee for Civil Rights Under Law, the Maryland Legislative Black Caucus, the Minority Business Enterprise LDF, and the National League of Cities, an advocacy group for municipal governments, all unsuccessfully filed briefs in support of Richmond's plan. The Reagan administration, the Associated Specialty Contractors, the Equal Employment Advisory Council, the Pacific Legal Foundation, the Washington Legal Foundation, and two newer conservative litigation groups, the Mountain States Legal Foundation and the Southeastern Legal Foundation, all helped defeat the program.[119] Overall the memberships of the racial policy alliances remained fairly constant—but the Court had now been added to the color-blind side.

AFTER REAGAN

By the end of the 1980s, the color-blind alliance and the Republican Party were also ascendant in American politics more generally. Still, they were hardly unchallenged. Democrats had never lost control of the House under Reagan, and they regained control of the Senate after 1985. House Democrats in particular challenged what they saw as the inadequate civil rights enforcement policies of the EEOC throughout the Reagan years.[120] Though most of the public, particularly white Americans, firmly agreed with the GOP attacks on rigid racial quotas and preferences, many whites continued to support "soft" race-conscious outreach measures. And as a consequence of the ending of the race-based national origins quota system for immigrants in 1965, there were growing numbers of nonwhite voters, many of whom supported affirmative action.[121] The consolidation of both alliances also meant that more and more Democrats and unions continued to shift into the race-conscious ranks, joined by the burgeoning numbers of Latino, Asian American, and Native American advocacy groups.[122] As congressional testimony, litigation briefs, and referendum results over the past three decades show, politically active Latinos and Asian Americans, including advocacy groups such as the Mexican American Legal Defense and Educational Fund (MALDEF) and the Asian American Justice Center, have consistently backed race-conscious employment measures, from which they and their constituents often benefit.[123] Asian Americans are not always included in affirmative action programs in areas with large, established Asian American communities, such as California, and some in these groups oppose race-conscious policies; but not a majority. Native American advocacy organizations also support affirmative action, though their constituents have had only limited benefits from such programs.[124] They do wish for their distinctive ethnic, cultural, and political identities to be recognized in a variety of public policies, so race-conscious approaches to public policy are congenial to them.

And as a legacy of Truman's initiatives to integrate the armed forces, many in the modern military have also been affirmative action supporters. None has been more conspicuous than Colin Powell, chairman of the Joint Chiefs of Staff from 1989 to 1993; but many military veterans and some military associations have advanced similar views. Perhaps most strikingly, a large number of

127

military leaders including Persian Gulf War hero Norman Schwartzkopf and prominent generals John Shalikashvili and Anthony Zinni signed a brief submitted on behalf of the University of Michigan's affirmative action admissions program in *Grutter v. Bollinger* (2003), arguing that a racially inclusive educated citizenry was necessary for national security.[125]

Yet as the Reagan years showed, among the ranks of those working to sustain race-conscious employment measures against a rising color-blind tide, few have been politically more significant than large businesses with affirmative action or diversity officers and written equal employment plans that guide their hiring practices and promotion reviews.[126] It is true that sometimes these businesses have sought only to preserve their own freedom to adopt whatever employment policies they wish to have, so they have not supported public regulations requiring affirmative action. And from 1940 to 1972, employers testifying before Congress on civil rights measures split evenly in support and opposition, with predominant support emerging only after those laws were passed.[127] Consequently, sociologist Frank Dobbin has suggested that the support for race-conscious measures large businesses do express is a contingent adaptation to modern anti-discrimination laws, powered by networks of personnel managers concerned with preventing costly lawsuits who have now sometimes changed their titles to "equal opportunity consultants."[128] Still, corporate human resources managers, many now racial minorities themselves, often defend their equal opportunity programs as aids to productivity, not as affirmative action measures.[129] Perhaps if anti-discrimination laws were ended, more big businesses might join smaller white-owned ones in opposing race-conscious employment policies. Perhaps the pro-diversity personnel now in place would prevent such a shift.[130]

Civil Rights Act 1991

Whichever we speculate may be the case, the reality is that, with these measures in place, many large businesses have remained members of the race-conscious alliance in the years since *Wards Cove* was handed down. Their role was significant when Ronald Reagan turned the White House over to his vice president, George H. W. Bush. Bush had opposed the 1964 Civil Rights Act when running for Congress in Texas, but he had since been a racial moderate on most policy issues, in keeping with his northeastern GOP roots (though his presidential campaign was willing to countenance negative race images, such as the controversial Willie Horton ad launched against Democratic candidate Michael Dukakis).[131] These circumstances explain how Democrats in Congress managed to effectively repeal the *Wards Cove* decision by passing the Civil Rights Act of 1991 as an amendment to Title VII.

The previous year, Senator Edward Kennedy had introduced a bill to make it easier for Title VII plaintiffs to win disparate impact lawsuits. Among other things, the proposal would have lowered the requirement for plaintiffs to show that specific practices were racially discriminatory, while raising the standard for what businesses must show to justify measures with disparate racial impacts. The Leadership Conference on Civil Rights formed a drafting committee to prepare the legislation that included numerous members of the race-conscious alliance, such as the NAACP and the NAACP LDF, the Lawyers' Committee for Civil Rights Under Law, the Mexican-American Legal Defense Fund, the National Urban League, the American Civil Liberties Union, the Women's Legal Defense Fund, the National Women's Law Center, and People for the American Way. They now rejected the once-favored idea of including cease-and-desist powers for the EEOC, suspicious of how conservative officials might implement them and preferring to continue to rely on their own crafting of private enforcement litigation.[132] Because it restored the potential for extensive "disparate impact" litigation, many congressional Republicans opposed their bill as likely to foster quotas, and they voted against it at a rate of 80 percent—while Democrats voted in favor at a rate of 92 percent during the bill's stages of consideration.[133] In tune with his party, President Bush vetoed the 1990 law, calling it a "quota bill," while insisting he supported civil rights. But the strong Democratic majorities combined with some Republican and some big business support meant that Congress came within a vote of overriding his veto.

Then as congressional attention turned toward the 1992 election and Republicans faced the embarrassments of the race- and sex-charged Supreme Court confirmation hearings of Clarence Thomas, along with the unnerving rise to prominence in the Louisiana Republican Party of former Klansman David Duke, many Republicans became more reluctant to appear to oppose civil rights.[134] Very large majorities of both parties voted for the only slightly different 1991 Civil Rights Act, which President Bush signed. Bush insisted the act did not do what most of its supporters said it did—ban most hiring practices with racially disparate impacts.[135] The vote for the bill was 381 to 38 in the House, with 13 not voting, the opposition coming from 33 Republicans and 5 Democrats. The Senate voted 93 in favor, 5 against, all Republicans, with 2 not voting.[136] Those totals were probably sufficient to discourage another veto. Bush's gloss on the law, however, contributed to the ambiguities about Title VII's "disparate impact" and "disparate treatment" mandates that the Court continued to wrestle with in the *Ricci* decision. Still, the law was followed by dramatic increases in job discrimination lawsuits, which rose from less than ten thousand in 1991 to over twenty-two thousand by 1995, and in charges filed with the EEOC, which increased by 58 percent.[137]

The alignment of the race-conscious alliance, including some big businesses, unions, and military leaders, and above all the control of Congress by Democrats firmly in that alliance, thus enabled race-conscious proponents to win a major legislative victory, even though the nation was eleven years into the "Reagan Revolution." A moderate Democrat, Bill Clinton, then won the presidency in 1992. But the color-blind alliance grew more assertive in its turn after the Republicans captured both chambers of Congress in 1994. The GOP "Contract with America" that featured prominently in congressional campaigns that year did not mention affirmative action; and although the new GOP Speaker of the House, Newt Gingrich, relished delivering his party's now-traditional denunciations of racial quotas and set-asides and endorsed color blindness, he was wary of appearing too hostile to civil rights.[138] He also faced the threat of vetoes from Clinton. So after gaining control of Congress, Gingrich's Republicans did not launch any major new legislative initiatives to eradicate race-conscious policies.

AGAINST AFFIRMATIVE ACTION

But Republicans outside of Congress did. Ward Connerly, an African American businessman and former California GOP treasurer, began in the mid-1990s to promote repeal of affirmative action in employment and education via state initiative and referendum processes. Connerly and his allies won major victories, ranging from 54 percent to 58 percent of the vote, beginning with California in 1996, where Proposition 209 ended the use of racial classifications in education and employment, and including the adoption of similar referenda in Washington in 1998, Michigan in 2006, and Nevada in 2008, though a similar measure failed narrowly in Colorado.[139] In Michigan, the victory came despite opposition to the ban from black and Latino voters, the gubernatorial candidates of both parties, and a coalition of religious, business, labor, and civic groups, though with the aid of conservative groups, most other Republicans, and ultimately most white voters.[140] After 2008, Connerly stated he might cease his personal work on state referenda, but his organization, the American Civil Rights Institute, still champions them.[141]

Even so, from the early 1990s to the present, the main strategy of anti–affirmative action efforts in employment has been to win favorable rulings from the Supreme Court. Like proponents of slavery in the nineteenth century and opponents of Jim Crow segregation in the twentieth, color-blind advocates have consistently pursued litigation in the hope that the Court will invalidate more and more race-conscious policies and eventually insist on thoroughgoing color blindness. The Court's rulings on labor market affirmative action, in particular, encourage this strategy by providing the color-blind alliance with ever more positive decisions. By a 5–4 vote in *Adarand Constructors Inc. v. Pena* (1995), the Court ruled that not even Congress could authorize a 1990 highway program that awarded bonuses to public contractors who gave at least 10 percent of their subcontracts to "disadvantaged business enterprises," unless the contracting government unit had demonstrably discriminated against the groups benefited by the program. The Associated General Contractors of America, the Pacific Legal Foundation, the Atlantic Legal Foundation, the Washington Legal Foundation, and the Ohio State chapter of the Federalist Society filed briefs against the program. Fifteen largely Democratic state attorneys general, the Coalition for Economic Equity, the Congressional Asian Pacific American Caucus, the Congressional Black Caucus, the Equality in Enterprise Opportunities, the Lawyers' Committee for Civil Rights Under Law, the Minority Business Enterprise LDF, the Minority Media and Telecommunications Council, Latin American Management Association, the NAACP and the NAACP LDF, the National Bar Association, and the National Coalition of Minority Businesses filed on its behalf, without success.[142] Writing for the majority in *Adarand*, Justice Sandra Day O'Connor also rejected what she rightly termed the "surprising" decision in *Metro Broadcasting, Inc. v. FCC* (1990). In this decision Justice Brennan managed to persuade a majority to support an opinion indicating that "benign" federal racial classifications only had to pass intermediate, not strict, scrutiny. O'Connor emphatically insisted on the strict scrutiny standard. She did not believe the program in *Adarand* survived it.[143]

Because of this ruling and others like it, many states modified or abandoned affirmative action programs in public employment in the late 1990s. In direct response to the *Adarand* ruling, the Clinton White House commissioned a review of affirmative action programs that sought to "mend, not end" any that it judged as fostering quotas. The Clinton administration did eliminate at least seventeen programs and cut funding for more.[144] Still, even in *Adarand*, O'Connor stated that "we wish to dispel the notion that strict scrutiny" of racial classifications "is strict in theory but fatal in practice."[145] Support from many government officials, civil rights groups, military leaders, and businesses continued to persuade a bare majority of the justices that in exceptional circumstances, race-conscious employment measures were defensible. The Court has since adhered to that stance, but it continues to narrow the circumstances when race can be considered in employment, as in the *Ricci v. DeStefano* decision.

OBAMA AND RACE-CONSCIOUS EMPLOYMENT

The question that looms large in the aftermath of the *Ricci* ruling is what the consequences of the 2008 election of Barack Obama will be for race-conscious employment policies and for the clash of the two modern racial alliances more generally. Obama's writings, his strategy as a presidential candidate, and his actions early in his administration all show that he understands both the political and the policy challenges that the modern structure of partisan-allied racial alliances poses for him. On the one hand, in the still predominantly white national electorate, most voters favor color-blind principles, and any candidate strongly identified with race-conscious measures will lose. On the other, a Democratic president like Obama cannot hope to satisfy the substantial portion of his constituents who adhere to the race-conscious alliance if he openly repudiates all race-targeted measures. And as a policy matter, it is unlikely that he can be confident of making progress toward alleviating material racial inequalities if he entirely forswears all race-targeted measures. He certainly has to consider the racial consequences of any facially "race-neutral" programs he advocates. Aided by exceptional circumstances, Obama negotiated adroitly the electoral challenges the structure of modern racial politics posed for him in his run for the presidency. But it remains to be seen whether he can also navigate the policy challenges generated by the modern racial alliances.

Indeed, the campaign strategies of both the major parties in 2008 represent an often-unnoticed impact of the modern racial alliances, for the rhetorical appeals of Republican nominee John McCain and Obama each showed awareness of the political constraints as well as the opportunities these alliances created for them.[146] Senator McCain, the candidate of the color-blind alliance's party, knew he could not openly comment on the race of his opponent: after all, the ideology of his coalition was that race should be treated as politically irrelevant. At the same time, because Barack Obama appears black to most Americans and accepts identification as African American, his candidacy raised worries among many in the color-blind order that a President Obama would expand pro-black racial preferences in many ways.[147] But unless Obama openly urged such policies, which he was careful not to do, the McCain campaign had the challenge of making those concerns salient to voters without explicitly speaking of race. This may account for the McCain ads asking, "Who is the real Barack Obama?" and saying that McCain was in contrast "the American President Americans have been waiting for."[148] These appeals were efforts to stir fears about Obama, and for at least some of those who favored color-blind policies, those fears must have included concerns that he would champion racial preferences.[149]

Obama faced still greater strategic challenges when campaigning for the presidency as an African American to win the support of an electorate that predominantly favors color-blind policies. Press coverage based on interviews with white working-class voters suggest that it would have been immensely difficult for him to speak at length about race and racial issues without exacerbating concerns that he would indeed support more expansive race-targeted programs, fears that might well have sealed his defeat.[150] At the same time, his racial identity and his background as a civil rights lawyer meant that many proponents of race-conscious measures were willing to presume he would be far more sympathetic to their positions than his opponent, without Obama having to articulate a specifically racial agenda. But Obama would have alienated important segments of his core supporters if he had unequivocally repudiated race-conscious programs and policies. Hence, his best option was to campaign in ways that were largely "race-neutral" in the policies he foregrounded, while retaining in the background indications of constrained but continuing support for race-conscious measures like affirmative action in employment and education.

Obama showed in his book of policy positions, *The Audacity of Hope*, that he did indeed favor this strategy, for these reasons. In his chapter entitled "Race," Obama offered "a word of caution" about whether "we have arrived at a 'postracial' politics" or "already live in a color-blind society."[151] He invoked the stark statistics on persisting material racial inequalities, and his own personal experiences of racism. Obama then argued, in accord with race-conscious proponents, that "affirmative action programs, when properly structured, can open up opportunities otherwise closed to qualified minorities without diminishing opportunities for white students," and he added that "where there's strong evidence of prolonged and systematic discrimination by large corporations, trade unions, or branches of municipal government, goals and timetables for minority hiring may be the only meaningful remedy available"—a clear acceptance of some forms of race-conscious employment policies.[152] But Obama also stressed his understanding of the arguments of those who favor color-blind measures. He advocated an "emphasis on universal, as opposed to race-specific programs" as not only "good policy" but also as "good politics."[153] His discussion suggested that in fact his preference for race-neutral approaches was driven more by the "good politics" than the "good policy" considerations. Obama concluded that "proposals that solely benefit minorities and dissect Americans into 'us' and 'them' may generate a few short-term concessions when the costs to whites aren't too high, but they can't serve as the basis for the kinds of sustained, broad-based political coalitions needed to transform America."[154]

In so arguing, Obama in his book and campaign suggested the possibility of a racial alliance based on a unifying compromise: one that joined those Americans who predominantly favored color-blind policies, but who did want to see material racial progress and so could tolerate some race-conscious measures if their costs were not chiefly imposed on less advantaged white Americans, with those who thought substantial race-conscious measures were needed, but who were willing to minimize them if progress was being achieved through other means. The only viable alliance that might stand in opposition to this "mixed-strategy" coalition seemingly had to consist primarily of those openly opposed to further progress toward material racial equality altogether—a group that Obama could reasonably expect to be small in twenty-first-century America. He pursued this strategy, for the most part, simply by not talking about race and by minimizing its likely impact on the election. Even when he felt compelled to discuss race explicitly during the Jeremiah Wright contretemps, he avoided any analysis of racial policy issues. He thereby allowed both color-blind and race-conscious advocates to hear his rhetorical emphases on unity and change in terms congenial to them. Though he did not eliminate the impact of racial resentments, it is probable that he reduced them.

In dealing with race in these ways, Obama skillfully pursued what we have suggested to be the central theme of his campaign, indeed of his whole political career: America must strive to achieve the promise of E Pluribus Unum, "that out of many, we are truly one."[155] He also benefited, however, from the sorts of extraordinary pressures for change that have abetted racial progress in the past. Obama was the candidate of the "out" party at a time when the nation was drained by warfare in two countries and wracked by the most severe economic collapse since the Great Depression—circumstances that many political scientists believe should have made for a Democratic landslide.[156] The Republicans ran a strategically dubious campaign, with McCain's choice of an undeniably inexperienced vice presidential candidate, Sarah Palin, undercutting his argument that Obama was not ready for the presidency. Obama's deft presentation of his theme of shared commitments to fellow Americans, rather than race-consciousness, reinforced by this remarkable conjunction of favorable external circumstances, helped him overcome the factors that long made it seem impossible for a black candidate to be elected president of the United States.

Beyond the Racial Alliances?

But if Obama's strategy for dealing with racial issues, largely by avoiding any prominent discussion of them, worked politically during the campaign, what about his approach to racial policies? Can his theme of finding common grounds of unity and mutual service, even while respecting diversity, and the attendant strategy of stressing universalistic measures while not rejecting all race-conscious ones, also enable Obama to end America's third racial era of contestation over color-blind versus race-conscious policies, at least in employment policies, and perhaps more generally? We will return to this question after canvassing the political and policy landscapes shaped by the clashes of the modern racial alliances in other policy arenas. For now, we note that the strategy of stressing color-blind or race-neutral approaches without rejecting all race-conscious policies puts Obama on a tightrope from which it is easy to fall. The Supreme Court rejected the approach of choosing among "race-neutral" hiring criteria with a "race-conscious" eye to consequences that his Justice Department recommended in the *Ricci* case. And as we have seen, his administration was also buffeted by controversies over the race-conscious remarks of his Supreme Court nominee, Sonia Sotomayor.[157]

Even so, Sotomayor was confirmed. If municipalities henceforth choose to avoid *Ricci*-style litigation by adopting in advance of any actual testing the sorts of observational "assessment center" examinations for promotion that New Haven failed to consider, tests which are indeed likely to produce more racially diverse outcomes, the general strategy preferred by the Obama administration, race-neutral means chosen on race-conscious grounds, may prove more acceptable as a quietly routine practice than it was when held up to judicial and political scrutiny. Though Obama's approach to racial issues may sometimes embroil him and his coalition in the sorts of controversies that he wishes to avoid, it is possible that the strategy may still form part of endeavors that on balance succeed both politically and as policy.

But for such success to occur, Obama's approach to race, and his more general strategy of seeking "E Pluribus Unum" solutions, must sooner or later produce measurable progress in reducing the nation's material racial inequalities. Almost certainly it also must do so without placing the costs of change on the great mass of less prosperous white Americans. As Obama recognizes, as long as severe racial disparities persist in most spheres of life, it is a virtual certainty that racial divisions will be salient in American politics as well. From the mid-1960s to the present, members of the race-conscious alliance have concluded, in many cases reluctantly, that racial employment inequalities and the huge economic disparities they spawn cannot be altered without some version of the same mechanisms that did so much to create them—race-conscious public policies. Past experience indicates that race-neutral assistance policies may aid all less advantaged Americans to some extent, but they often leave racial gaps intact or even increase them. Yet as long as race-conscious measures are seen as chiefly burdening white working- and middle-class Americans like Frank Ricci, it is hard to see how political support for them can be sustained. Unless either material improvements or political defeats persuade modern race-conscious proponents to abandon their positions, or unless many of those who now support color-blind principles come to accept that, at least to some limited extent, race-conscious measures are needed and can be structured so that they do not pose major obstacles to the mobility of less advantaged whites, it is not likely that the clash of racial alliances that has done so much to structure public policies in this area, as in many others, will be overcome.

Chapter 5

To "affirmatively further fair housing"
Enduring Racial Inequalities in
American Homes and Mortgages

Even as America's first black president moved into the White House, controversies over race and housing abounded in what many wished to be a "postracial" country.[1] In August 2009, one of the nation's most affluent counties, Westchester, New York, acceded to a housing agreement with a nonprofit advocacy group, the Anti-Discrimination Center of Metro New York, brokered by Obama officials in the Department of Housing and Urban Development and the Justice Department. In February 2009, U.S. District Court judge Denise Cote, a Clinton appointee, had ruled in favor of the center's claim that the county had violated the federal False Claims Act. Westchester had repeatedly submitted certifications that it would use the more than $52 million in federal Community Development Block Grant (CDBG) funding it obtained between 2000 and 2006 to meet statutory and agency requirements to "affirmatively further fair housing." Cote ruled that, although the county knew that its residential patterns displayed severe racial segregation, it in fact made no effort to analyze the complaints of racial discrimination it received or to consider how its efforts to provide affordable housing might reduce race as well as class segregation.[2]

After first objecting to the ruling, the county agreed six months later to develop a plan to spend $51.6 million over seven years to build or acquire 750 housing units, with at least 630 in towns and villages where African Americans made up 3 percent or less of the population and Latino residents made up less than 7 percent. Though the units were to be available to any families earning up to $53,000 for renters and $75,000 for homeowners, without racial quotas, the county agreed to market them aggressively to black and Latino residents of the New York metropolitan area. Obama's deputy secretary of Housing and Urban Development, Ronald Sims, announced that the settlement was "consistent with the president's desire to see a fully integrated society."[3] Sims promised the administration would apply its principles to the other twelve hundred jurisdictions around the country that receive block grants.[4] Wade Henderson, director of the Leadership Conference for Civil Rights, a lynchpin of the modern race-conscious alliance, called the agreement "only the first step in resolving a persistent problem of housing segregation" nationwide.[5]

For that reason among others, proponents of color-blind policies found the agreement appalling. Howard Husock, vice president for policy research at the Manhattan Institute, contended that when income was taken into account, blacks were only "slightly underrepresented" in affluent areas of Westchester, and that in any case, moving blacks into such areas would not help their economic, educational, or health statuses.[6] One of the county's Republican leaders, Jim Russell went further, calling the settlement a terrible precedent for the nation. The decision allowed "radical bureaucrats" to reconfigure residential neighborhoods, Russell contended, adding, "It's the worst kind of affirmative action."[7] In February 2010, James E. Johnson, the monitor appointed by the district court to determine if the county was meeting the terms of Judge Cote's ruling, rejected the county's efforts thus far, saying it still lacked substantial plans to develop or market the promised affordable housing.[8] At this writing, the controversy continues.

While the more affluent residents of Westchester wrestled with the requirements of the 1960s civil rights laws and the enforcement policies of the new Obama administration, Americans as a whole were struggling with the devastating economic consequences of a sharp decline in housing values linked to the spread, especially in the last decade, of "subprime" mortgages. These are mortgage products with frequently adjustable rates. Subprime mortgages became appealing to lenders in recent years partly because of the development of innovative ways to assess and then to "securitize" these debts by "bundling" them with other, more predictable investments. Because these subprime mortgages could then be resold profitably, lenders were willing to offer them to borrowers whose credit would otherwise not permit them to purchase homes, on terms that were initially affordable. But adjustable rates are often adjusted upward over time; so subprime loans generally prove more costly to borrowers than once-conventional fixed rate mortgages. In the housing crisis, the novel securities into which they were bundled, then resold, often proved incapable of sustaining their value as subprime borrowers began to default — creating pressures for banks to foreclose on others, further dropping the value of mortgage-based bonds, and leading in the end to a precipitous collapse of housing financing and prices in 2007.[9]

By 2009, no one denied that African Americans and Latinos were suffering financial hardships from subprime mortgages to a greater degree than white Americans and were likely to suffer more. One group urging race-conscious policies, United for a Fair Economy, contended that the distribution of sub-prime loans among racial and ethnic groups in 2004 was whites, 53.9 percent; blacks, 20.1 percent; Latinos, 21.3 percent.[10] Compared with white Americans, blacks and Latinos were disproportionately higher holders of subprime mortgages: 54.7 percent of the loans held by African Americans were sub-prime, compared with just 17.2 percent for whites.[11] Though other sources calculated somewhat differently, none challenged the general picture of ra-cially skewed impacts. The debate has been over how these statistics came to be.

The nation's most venerable civil rights group and a core member of the modern race-conscious alliance, the NAACP, believed the answer was "sys-tematic, institutionalized racism" on the part of various lenders seeking Afri-can American customers. In 2007 the NAACP filed the first of several lawsuits in a federal district court in Los Angeles, claiming some California lenders had violated the 1968 Fair Housing Act, the 1964 Civil Rights Act, and other federal laws. In March 2009, the NAACP added lawsuits against Wells Fargo Bank and Wells Fargo Home Mortgage, Inc., and two HSBC Holdings subsid-iaries (HSBC Mortgage Corp USA and HSBC Bank USA), charging them with purposefully and unfairly steering African American borrowers into costly subprime loans.[12] In Memphis, former Wells Fargo loan officers supplied af-fidavits for that city's suit against the company for directing them to focus on African American neighborhoods and to sell blacks more expensive mortgages even when they qualified for prime loans.[13] The Illinois attorney general and the city of Baltimore filed similar suits against Wells Fargo, which, like other mortgage companies, has denied all charges. The NAACP lawsuits seek to have records made public to show wrongdoing, rather than to recover finan-cial compensation.[14] It was not only members of the race-conscious alliance who raised these concerns. The Federal Reserve Bank of San Francisco con-cluded in a study of the subprime implosion that "race has an independent effect on foreclosure even after controlling for borrower income and credit score."[15] One nonprofit organization calculated the loss to African American household wealth achieved by subprime foreclosures to be immense, between $71 and $92 billion from 2000 to 2008.[16]

Even so, without denying that subprime loans have been "particularly con-centrated in neighborhoods with a high concentration of black and Hispanic residents," a 2009 staff report by the Federal Reserve Bank of New York exam-ined seventy-five thousand subprime mortgages and concluded tentatively that there was "no evidence of adverse pricing by race, ethnicity or sex of the borrower in either the initial rate or the reset margin" of these loans. Instead if "any pricing differential exists, minority borrowers" and "borrowers in Zip Codes with a higher percentage of black or Hispanic residents" pay "slightly lower mortgage rates."[17] Members of the color-blind alliance seized on such arguments to contend that rather than predatory lender discrimination, it was misguided race-conscious efforts to assist minorities that generated the subprime crisis and its racially disparate consequences. For example, Republican representative and Tea Partier Michele Bachmann of Minnesota argued to the House Committee on Financial Services in 2008 that the Clinton administration had used the Community Reinvestment Act of 1977 to pressure the main government-sponsored home credit enterprises, Fannie Mae and Freddie Mac, to make loans "on the basis of race and often on little else."[18] In an interview on the Larry King show, the congresswoman explained her position:

> If you look at the housing crisis, government has to take its share of the blame. After all, government was goading these mortgage lenders, saying you're redlining. You're being discriminatory. If you don't give loans out to marginally credit worthy people, we're going to come after you. In fact, Chairman Barney Frank has made comments like that as well. The Democrat-controlled Congress wants to have these mortgage lenders make loans to people with marginal credit.
>
> Well guess what? If you aren't making money lending, this is not a shock when you have loans that aren't paid back. And now the American people have to come in and step in and pay for these bad loans when people have zero equity or negative equity.[19]

Another Minnesota representative and a member of the Congressional Black Caucus, Keith Ellison, responded that Bachmann's comments fit a narrative implying "poor blacks caused this" crisis.[20] Though Bachmann might be more charitably interpreted as simply blaming the government, conservative media commentators did appear to apportion at least equal blame to both liberals in government and those they aided. Fox News's Neil Cavuto, host of *Your World*, suggested on September 18, 2008, that Congress should have realized that "[l]oaning to minorities and risky folks is a disaster."[21] Conservative columnist Charles Krauthammer made a similar claim in more sophisticated fashion:

> For decades, starting with Jimmy Carter's Community Reinvestment Act of 1977, there has been bipartisan agreement to use government power to expand homeownership to people who had been shut out for economic reasons or, sometimes, because of racial and ethnic discrimination. What could be a more worthy cause? But it led to tremendous pressure on Fannie Mae and Freddie Mac—which in turn pressured banks and other lenders—to extend mortgages to people who were borrowing

over their heads. That's called subprime lending. It lies at the root of our current calamity.[22]

The conservative media provocateur Ann Coulter took a similar stance in a piece entitled "They Gave Your Mortgage to a Less Qualified Minority":

Under Clinton, the entire federal government put massive pressure on banks to grant more mortgages to the poor and minorities. Clinton's secretary of Housing and Urban Development, Andrew Cuomo, investigated Fannie Mae for racial discrimination and proposed that 50 percent of Fannie Mae's and Freddie Mac's portfolio be made up of loans to low- to moderate-income borrowers by the year 2001.[23]

She went on to insist that "[a] decade later, the housing bubble burst and, as predicted, food-stamp-backed mortgages collapsed. Democrats set an affirmative action time-bomb and now it's gone off."[24]

Most analysts in academia and government argue instead that the Community Reinvestment Act requirements affected "only a very small share of the high-priced loans that have been a key driver of the crisis," perhaps 6 percent, and that most of the growth of subprime lending came in the years after 2000, after Clinton's presidency. In January 2010, HUD's Office of Policy Development found the roots of the crisis in laws beginning in 1980 that liberalized the permissible features of loan products. These new policies, followed by technological advances in credit risk analysis, facilitated the creation of many new, riskier types of mortgages in the 1990s that subprime lenders marketed aggressively. Federal regulators failed to adapt.[25] Other analysts concur that inadequate regulation, especially of Fannie Mae and Freddie Mac, contributed greatly to the housing and financial crises, leading many liberals to conclude that the anti-government free market conservatism of the second Bush administration and the broader patterns of the era of the Reagan Revolution laid the seeds of wild investments and risky loans that finally reaped the whirlwind.[26]

But did the aggressive mortgage marketing in recent years produce disproportionate percentages of African American and Latino subprime purchasers because those communities simply had disproportionate numbers of members who were poor credit risks, perhaps due to past and continuing practices of racial discrimination, but perhaps due to their own failings? Or did lenders with adverse, perhaps unconscious racial stereotypes sell subprime mortgages even to nonwhite borrowers who were qualified for less risky fixed rate mortgages? Did some instead consciously and callously regard these customers as easy prey for their profitable products? Or were many lenders in fact eager to sell to nonwhites who were credit risks out of a misguided sense of social conscience, even if that sensibility did not come from the Community Reinvestment Act? Insufficient research to date precludes decisive answers to these questions. But at a minimum, the mortgage crisis shows how hard it is to disentangle judgments of persons' economic characteristics from their racial identities in a nation that long structured housing and other economic rights and opportunities along racial lines. It is often difficult for economic decision makers and anti-discrimination law enforcers alike to determine whether actions putatively based on economic grounds are truly "color-blind," whether or not they should be. But the politics of the modern racial alliances prompts partisans of each side to minimize these complexities, to explain events in terms of their preferred frameworks, to accuse the other side of supporting unjust racial discrimination, and to shape their policy and legal positions accordingly.

The Westchester controversy may be yet more revealing about the issues posed by the structure of American racial politics today. Westchester officials acted on the assumption that the main aim of affordable housing was and should be to address class, not racial inequalities. More than four decades after the end of the Jim Crow era, the county testified in the lawsuit that it saw "discrimination in terms of income, rather than in terms of race," as the great problem it faced. Its officials have presumed that if they provided more affordable housing, less affluent nonwhites would benefit along with less affluent whites.[27] They have been and remain reluctant to order controversial race-conscious efforts to promote racial integration. But in the evidence of past and present racial discrimination in employment discussed in the last chapter, in similar evidence on real estate practices, and in the racial disparities in the mortgage crisis, the Obama Justice Department, the Anti-Discrimination Center of Metro New York, and many others see proof that today as in the past, efforts to expand housing opportunities must be designed to offset race as well as class discrimination by explicitly pursuing both racial and economic residential integration.

Even so, here as in the *Ricci* employment case, the Obama administration has sought a characteristically mixed, middle-ground strategy. Its officials urged an agreement that contained no racial criteria for eligibility, much less formal quotas. But more than any administration in decades, it also pushed for race-conscious placing of new units and race-conscious marketing in pursuit of more racially integrated housing. Because housing choices profoundly affect people's personal lives and yet also have enormous public consequences for the structure of the nation as a whole, these concerns to make sure that America's housing systems are not systems of racial inequality are understandable.

But the fact that housing is so central to their personal lives is also a major reason why Americans have long been more resistant to efforts to end de facto segregation in this area than in any other, except the related one of public schools. Here they remain profoundly divided even on the desirability of strong enforcement of anti-discrimination policies aimed at making residential racial integration not only an attractive ideal but an everyday reality.

The Roots of Racial Inequality in Housing

Yet if major controversies over race and housing persist and may again grow, there is much in this area that is no longer in dispute. First, no one denies that the United States is marked by massive racial residential segregation, especially in urban and suburban areas, and by severe racial inequalities in home-ownership. Second, no one denies that these patterns became entrenched during the era of Jim Crow segregation, when residential racial segregation was broadly embraced as both public and private policy. Third, few deny that these patterns were historically compounded by racial discrimination against blacks in employment and eligibility for public and private loans and other forms of assistance. Before examining the political clashes over housing of the modern racial alliances, it is worth reviewing these points of agreement.

The first is that racial segregation persists even though the residential isolation of African Americans from whites declined slightly in some, mostly newer cities and suburbs in between the 1990 and 2000 census. As sociologist Douglas Massey has shown, in 2000 almost 60 percent of African Americans still resided in older urban areas that remained segregated by race. Forty-one percent lived in what Massey called "hypersegregation," defined as a group having high scores (60+) on five different dimensions of geographical segregation. He also found that in hypersegregated areas, declines in black-white housing segregation over the preceding two decades had been modest, a mere 8 percent.[28] Other scholars report that, though Latinos and Asians were generally less segregated from non-Latino whites than were blacks, their levels of segregation rose slightly, from an index of 50.8 for Latinos/whites in 1980 to 51.5 in 2000 (on a scale of 1 to 100 running from full integration to full segregation). Asian/white segregation increased marginally from in 1980 to 42.1 in 2000.[29] Data from the 2010 Census are not yet available, but most see few signs of major changes in these patterns of severe residential segregation.

As in the Jim Crow era, residential segregation remains tied to deep material inequalities. For most Americans, homeownership is their chief financial asset, and so also the mainstay of their capacity to transmit wealth to future generations. Homeownership remains racially skewed. According to U.S. Census data, in the years from 1996 to 2007, just as the housing collapse began, non-Hispanic white homeownership went from 71.7 percent of all such households to 75.2 percent; Asian or Pacific Islander went from 50.8 percent to 60 percent; but Hispanic home owning went from 42.8 percent to only 49.7 percent, and black homeowners went from 44.1 percent of all black households to 47.2 percent.[30] As Americans of all demographics have lost homes in the foreclosure crisis, their wealth has declined: the Economic Policy Institute found that in December 2009, median white wealth had dipped 34 percent since the recession began, to $94,600; but median black wealth had dropped an extraordinary 77 percent, to $2,100, little more than 2 percent that of whites.[31] The ravages wrought by the foreclosure crisis deepen at this writing. But because nonwhites have disproportionately held subprime mortgages and so have disproportionately defaulted, it seems certain that not only will these percentages be lower for the foreseeable future for all groups, the racial inequalities will increase.

Historically, these patterns hardly arose as random products of an open U.S. market and consumer choices, however much such choices may be factors today. Like job discrimination, racial residential segregation was a foundational system of the "separate but equal" Jim Crow America created in the 1880s, judicially legitimated in the 1890s, and sustained de jure until 1954, with consequences that, to some disputed degree, endure. Though the Supreme Court invalidated public laws imposing residential segregation in *Buchanan v. Warley* (1917), its subsequent validation of racially restrictive covenants in *Corrigan v. Buckley* (1926) permitted public enforcement of pervasive private discrimination in housing markets.[32] During the Jim Crow years, those discriminatory acts included violent resistance to pioneering African Americans seeking to purchase or rent in white neighborhoods in northern cities; landlords and private realtors who refused to sell or rent to blacks; and bankers unwilling to lend mortgages to African Americans. These private actors had important governmental allies. Segregationist federal housing agencies, complicit city authorities, and public policies of urban redevelopment that used federal funds to promote residential racial homogeneity all conferred legitimacy and often provided guidance to the businesses involved.[33]

Because segregation is frequently seen as primarily southern and local, it is especially important to stress how fundamental the federal government was in creating residential segregation in northern and western cities from the 1930s onward. The major developments leading up to the emergence of the modern racial alliance are summarized in table 5.1.

144

TABLE 5.1
Federal Government, Housing Equity, and Race, 1933–78

Year	Initiative
1933	Congress creates Home Owners' Loan Corporation (HOLC).
1934	National Housing Act creates Federal Housing Authority (FHA).
1937	Wagner-Steagall / National Housing Act: FHA starts to construct public housing.
1948	Supreme Court bans enforcement of racial covenants; FHA is slow to ensure federal funds are not used on covenant sales.
1949	Taft-Ellender-Wagner Housing Act makes "decent" housing a national goal, allocating millions of dollars for new public housing construction.
1954	Omnibus Housing Act of 1954 creates Urban Renewal Administration, origins of "urban renewal" program.
1955	Beginning of slum clearance under urban renewal.
1961	Housing Act of 1961 passed, focused on homes for low- and moderate-income families.
1961	U.S. Civil Rights Commission issues major report focused on housing discrimination, especially racial.
1962	EO 11063 issued by President Kennedy prohibits racial discrimination in housing built, purchased, or financed with federal assistance (3 percent of nation's units); creates President's Committee on Equal Opportunity in Housing.
1963	Omnibus Housing Act of 1964 authorizes Fannie Mae to pool its mortgages, sell interests to private investors.
1965	Department of Housing and Urban Development (HUD) created.
1968	Fair Housing Act (Title VIII of the 1968 Civil Rights Act) proscribes racial discrimination in public and private housing.
1968	President Johnson's Commission on Urban Housing issues the Kaiser Report, focusing mainly on housing quality.
1968	Housing and Urban Development Act of 1968 expands aid to low- and moderate-income home buyers

(continued)

TABLE 5.1 *(continued)*

Year	Initiative
1970	Freddie Mac created to establish market for mortgage securities.
1971	President Nixon interprets 1968 Fair Housing Act to require nondiscrimination but not integration in America's suburbs.
1973	Nixon imposes moratorium on federal housing programs, seeks to end Federal Housing Authority.
1974	Housing and Community Development Act passes, creating Community Development Block Grant program (CDBG) and Section 8 Housing Assistance Payments program.
1977	Community Reinvestment Act passes.

Source: Desmond S. King, *Separate and Unequal: African Americans and the U.S. Federal Government* (New York: Oxford University Press, 2007); National Association of Home Builders, "A Century of Progress: America's Housing, 1900–2000," April 2003, http://www.ewcupdate.com/fckeditor/userfiles/baec_net/A%20Century%20of%20Progress(1).pdf.

The federal role began in 1932. President Herbert Hoover and the Congress created the Federal Home Loan Bank Board to aid home buyers in acquiring mortgages, as endorsed in the GOP platform of that year.[34] Then in 1933, the New Deal Democrats added the Home Owners' Loan Corporation (HOLC), primarily to refinance urban mortgages threatened with default. Unfortunately, HOLC gave the national government's imprimatur and a formal structure to practices of exclusionary "redlining." It created a system that ranked neighborhoods into four color-coded categories, with "A" (green) and "B" (blue) more desirable, and "C" (yellow) and "D" (red) progressively more risky—assessments based in part on how racially "homogeneous" as well as how prosperous the areas were.[35] African American neighborhoods were generally ranked in the lowest category and "redlined" as presumptively ineligible for loans, as were blacks seeking to move into white areas.[36] Thereafter, both the federal home loan bank system and the Veterans Administration used the same system in their housing programs.[37]

In 1934, the National Housing Act creating the Federal Housing Authority (FHA) as the government's prime lending agency and regulator of housing, and it employed the same grading system. The FHA's *Underwriting Manual* gave guidance for decisions governing mortgage lending that baldly stated its presumption of segregation as a maxim of government policy. The 1938 manual advised: "If a neighborhood is to retain stability, it is necessary that properties shall continue to be occupied by the same social and racial classes. A change in social or racial occupancy generally contributes to instability and a decline in values."[38] Even though the 1940 Democratic platform boasted that "Our Negro citizens" had participated in New Deal programs to provide "decent housing," the FHA did not change this recommendation until 1950, two years after the Supreme Court ruled restrictive covenants unenforceable in *Shelley v. Kraemer.*[39]

Until that decision, locally formed neighborhood improvement associations also helped maintain legal segregation by encouraging members to write restrictive covenants about who could buy properties in their neighborhood. These covenants guaranteed a homogeneous community, that is, a white community. Historian Thomas Sugrue reports that 80 percent of housing in Detroit in the 1940s had restrictive covenants stipulating that future sale of a property could be to "Caucasians only."[40] Even after *Shelley* in 1948, the pattern of entrenched segregated residential housing endured through a combination of private realtors' selling practices, white householders' preferences, and the modified but persisting federal mortgage A–D grading schema. On occasions, white homeowners resorted to violence to block any inroads into segregated residential housing. Because racially restrictive covenants were still not technically illegal, simply not judicially enforceable, advocates of the ascendant anti-segregation alliance in the 1950s and 1960s called for federal laws to proscribe discrimination by real estate agents or vendors. In the strong civil rights planks both parties adopted in 1960, before they moved to sharp opposition on racial issues, the Republicans claimed credit for "initial steps toward the elimination of segregation in federally-aided housing," while the Democrats called for actions "to end discrimination in Federal housing programs, including Federally assisted housing," and to combat "problems of discrimination in housing . . . in general."[41]

As those passages indicate, by this time issues of housing segregation involved not only racially discriminatory real estate and lending practices but also the consequences of public housing programs. The 1937 Wagner-Steagall Act initiated these programs. Both parties supported their expansion after World War II, when returning members of the armed services faced housing shortages. But as the FHA's "Racial Relations Adviser" Joseph Ray explained in the 1950s, "From its inception, the public housing program accepted the 'separate-but-equal' doctrine and, through its racial equity policy, undertook to insist upon uniform enforcement of the 'equal' while allowing local communities to decide upon the 'separate.'"[42] Then in 1954, the first of a series of six Omnibus Housing acts created the Urban Renewal Administration, charged with leading the pursuit of long-standing goals of "slum clearance."[43]

However noble its intentions may have been, the act had harmful consequences. It fostered urban development and highway construction programs that often destroyed black neighborhoods and concentrated African Americans in public housing high-rises. Local governments and private developers, generally supported by white voters and community groups, saw to it that public housing was never located in suburbs.[44]

Within many cities divisions arose between liberal reformers, including civil rights activists in the NAACP keen to use federal funds to expand public housing and to integrate housing, and primarily white working-class and middle-class homeowners, opposed to both integrated housing and increased public housing. When the latter groups were able to organize effectively as part of what some termed the "Homeowners Movement" and built alliances with key local and federal officials, they put up many barriers to more racially egalitarian housing policies. The contestation was intense: African American inner-city residents, urban planners, and, at times, organized labor supported the pro-integration public housing advocates. But, in part because many residents of nonwhite neighborhoods did not actually wish to move, however much they wanted the rights and resources to move, when local political opposition to integration was too strong, the pro-public housing coalition sometimes settled simply on building public housing and made desegregation a secondary aim.[45] And in some cities, private developers coalesced into pro-growth supporters of federally funded public housing, embracing the business opportunity without regard for integrationist goals, and sometimes without regard for quality housing.[46] In Chicago, Cleveland, Philadelphia, Baltimore, Gary, Columbus, Detroit, New York, and St. Louis, among others, post-1949 public housing proved staples in maintaining segregated residential housing, too often of inferior quality.

Believing that breaking up residential segregation was crucial to achieving social equity and greater material well-being for African Americans, Martin Luther King Jr. and other leaders of the civil rights movement repeatedly targeted segregated public and private housing, particularly its persistence in northern cities, especially after passage of the 1964 Civil Rights Act. In 1966 King led open housing marches in Chicago demanding anti-discrimination legislation and desegregation of housing. As had been true after each of the world wars, the fate of Vietnam War veterans underlined the salience of racial discrimination. Many of those from poor African American and Latino families could not buy or rent houses in segregated suburbs or cities.[47] King joined with the GI Forum, the NAACP, and the National Committee Against Discrimination in Housing to lobby Congress to pass fair housing legislation. But as we have seen, after 1965, concerns that civil rights reforms were going too

148

far began to mount. Pushing people to accept neighbors they did not want courted controversy, and until April 4, 1968, numerous efforts to get fair housing bills through Congress failed.[48]

That evening Martin Luther King Jr. was assassinated. Fearful of urban rioting, Congress finally heeded the reports of numerous special civil rights commissions, including President Lyndon Johnson's Commission on Urban Housing (also known as the Kaiser Report) and the Kerner Commission Report on civil disorders, which had concluded that the United States was becoming two societies, black and white, "separate and unequal." Following House action, the Senate passed the Fair Housing Act as the major provision of the 1968 Civil Rights Act without debate seven days after King's assassination, enabling the president to sign it speedily.[49] The bill banned a wide range of types of housing discrimination, not just racial acts. HUD then created a Title VIII Field Operations Handbook setting out regulations to implement those restrictions.[50]

These federal regulations represent the last major legislative victory of the anti-segregation alliance, with America's transition to a new racial era already under way.

A new era of racial divisions over this issue like so many others proved inescapable. Historic as it was, passage of the 1968 law did not generate massive housing desegregation or terminate racial discrimination in public and private housing. Not even King's death could displace anxieties raised by the resurgent disquiet at strong federal efforts to foster material racial equality. The law therefore had important limits. As a result of a compromise brokered by Republican Senate leader Everett Dirksen, it applied to more than 80 percent of the nation's housing stock, but it did not cover single-family homes sold or rented directly by their owners and small apartment buildings with resident owners, and it again did not provide any federal agency with authority to issue cease-and-desist orders. It only empowered HUD to investigate housing complaints and negotiate voluntary agreements. The Department of Justice and individual victims could then bring lawsuits.[51] In their platform adopted later that summer for the 1968 presidential election, the Democrats promised to follow the Kerner Commission's recommendations on housing and urban renewal, but they made no pledges to strengthen HUD's powers to implement the Fair Housing Act.[52]

Given this reliance on the judiciary for ultimate enforcement, it was important that the Supreme Court quickly signaled its receptivity to federal power to end housing discrimination. Not long after the law was passed, the justices voted 7–2 in *Jones v. Alfred Mayer Co.* (1968) to give new life to provisions in the Civil Rights Act of 1866 banning racial discrimination in the rights of citizens to "inherit, purchase, lease, sell, hold, and convey real and personal property."[53] Supported by briefs by the ACLU, the American Federation of Teachers, the National Committee against Discrimination in Housing, and Catholic, liberal Protestant, and Jewish groups, along with various state attorneys general, Justice Potter Stewart ruled that the Thirteenth amendment gave Congress the power to ban private racial discrimination that it saw as perpetuating "badges and incidents of slavery."[54] Stewart stressed that the Court's revival of the 1866 act did not "in any way" diminish the significance of the recently passed Fair Housing Act, since that law banned more types of discrimination and provided more avenues for enforcement. But as the dissenters noted, his opinion meant that federal anti-discrimination laws applied to *all* real estate transactions, despite the exemptions provided to resident owners in the 1968 law.[55] The Supreme Court and a number of lower federal courts then went on during the 1970s to interpret both standing to sue under the Fair Housing Act and the practices it prohibited broadly. This strategy strengthened the practical enforceability of the new statute.[56] Many observers sought forceful actions in response. In their searing book, *American Apartheid*, Douglas Massey and Nancy Denton report that "in the three decades after 1940, black-white segregation remained high and virtually constant," so that by 1970, "at least 70% of blacks would have had to move to achieve an even residential configuration in most cities, and in many places the figure was closer to 90%."[57] Those circumstances provided ample bases for the litigation the courts encouraged.

Nixon and the Transition to the Modern Racial Alliances

But if the Supreme Court and many civil rights advocates supported muscular national action to curb racial discrimination and segregation in housing at this time, the Nixon administration that presided over most of the initial enforcement of the Fair Housing Act was far less enthusiastic. President Richard Nixon had long felt that talk of "open housing is pursuing a will-o'-the wisp."[58] Amidst the heightening tensions of the late 1960s, Nixon and his political advisers saw no advantage and considerable risk in seeking to impose low-income housing on American suburbs or promoting racial residential integration. When Nixon's HUD secretary George Romney formulated bold plans to pursue both economic and racial housing integration aggressively, he soon met stiff resistance from the White House.[59] As a result, HUD moved slowly to develop regulations to enforce the 1968 act; the Justice Department brought only an average of thirty-five lawsuits per year under it from 1971 through

1974; and taking the lead on housing away from Romney in April 1971, Nixon told his aides to prepare a policy directive that "waffles" on open housing.[60]

The result, issued on June 14, 1971, promised to "eliminate racial discrimination in housing"; but the directive also vowed the administration would "not seek to impose economic integration upon an existing local jurisdiction" by mandating affordable housing in suburbs, since an "open society does not have to be homogeneous, or even fully integrated." The existence of "Italian or Irish or Negro or Norwegian neighborhoods" bound by "group pride" was "natural and right." What mattered was "mobility," the right and the ability to move to congenial environs.[61] Nixon later contrasted ending discrimination to mandating integration. He argued, "For the Federal Government to go further than the law, to force integration in the suburbs, I think is unrealistic. I think it will be counter-productive and not in the interest of better race relations."[62]

Many Americans strongly agreed. Yet legal and political commitments to overcome Jim Crow residential racial segregation also remained potent. Nixon's 1971 policy statement added that the Fair Housing Act's mandate for "affirmative action" meant that proposals for federal housing funds should be judged, among other criteria, by the extent to which proposed projects "will in fact open up new, nonsegregated housing opportunities."[63] It therefore did not entirely eschew race-conscious decision making. Sociologist Chris Bonastia argues that Nixon, like many politicians, was more concerned with avoiding political blame for racial issues from either the right or the left than he was with establishing unambiguous new racial policies.[64]

Still, the direction the Republicans were taking was clear: their 1972 platform promised much action on housing but proclaimed, "We strongly oppose the use of housing or community development programs to impose arbitrary housing patterns on unwilling communities."[65] The Democrats, in contrast, stressed their aim to promote "the right of all families, regardless of race, color, religion, or income, to choose among a wide range of homes and neighborhoods in urban, suburban and rural areas—through the greater use of grants to individuals for housing, the development of new communities offering diversified housing and neighborhood options and the enforcement of fair housing laws."[66] After Nixon's massive reelection victory in 1972, he took advantage of scandals involving misuse of FHA funds to announce a freeze on a number of federal housing programs from 1973 to 1974. This action finally laid to rest the Romney-initiated efforts to promote suburban integration. When Nixon's own scandals then forced him to resign amidst an economic downturn and political turmoil, Congress passed the Housing and Community Development Act of 1974. It cut funding for all but direct "Section 8" grants to rental tenants, a program not structured to have great impact on residential racial segregation.[67]

Despite the disgrace of Watergate, Nixon's White House years marked a significant turning point for America's racial coalitions. His opposition to active pursuit of racially integrated housing, like his heightened denunciations of quotas in employment and education and busing to achieve school integration, helped spur the coalescence of the modern racial alliances. So, too, did the justices Nixon nominated for the Supreme Court. They began shifting the law in a more color-blind direction in housing as in other areas. Nixon appointee Justice Lewis Powell's opinion for the Court in *Arlington Heights v. Metropolitan Housing Development Corporation* (1977) was significant.[68] A Chicago-area nonprofit organization sought to obtain land in the village of Arlington Heights to create multifamily housing units with the aid of federal housing funds. In accordance with the federal requirements for such assistance, this housing was to be marketed to promote racial integration, just as in the recent Westchester case. Arlington Heights's zoning laws had, however, long permitted only single-family housing in the area, and the village refused to rezone to permit the development.

Justice Powell ruled that although the village's decision might well have a "racially disproportionate impact," the Constitution's equal protection clause banned only "racially discriminatory intent or purpose." Because Arlington Heights was sustaining its long-standing single-family housing policy, no such intent or purpose on its part had been shown. Powell, who would later formulate the demanding "strong basis in evidence" standard for proof of the need for race-conscious remedies of intentional equal protection violations, underlined that, despite what he acknowledged to be "some contrary indications" in previous cases, it was now the settled view of the Court that the Constitution banned only intentional racially disparate treatment, not unintended racially disparate impacts.[69]

But because the preceding Court of Appeals had not addressed the question of whether the Fair Housing Act and other civil rights laws banned the racially disparate impact of the village's decision, Powell remanded the case for further consideration of the statutory issues. The Court of Appeals then ruled that since the goal of the Fair Housing Act was to promote racial integration, the village's decision perpetuating segregation was indeed illegal, even if not unconstitutional. This ruling was allowed to stand.[70] Then in several cases decided over the next five years, the Supreme Court confirmed the legitimacy of most legislative measures "promoting stable, racially integrated housing," and it upheld the standing to sue of "testers" or "auditors" who found evidence of illegal "racial steering" by realtors.[71] As a result, while the Supreme Court had clearly indicated that the Constitution did not mandate racially integrated housing, it was permissible for legislators and municipalities to pursue, even require, the race-conscious goal of housing integration if they so chose.

The Racial Policy Alliances in Housing

Whether or not to pursue racial housing integration became a chief dividing line between the emerging modern racial policy alliances. But just as in the case of public housing in the 1950s and 1960s, here many race-conscious proponents put as much or more stress on reducing racial inequalities in home-ownership and housing quality as on reducing residential racial segregation, especially as the color-blind alliance grew in influence. As on other racial issues, during the 1970s the two major parties' platforms diverged visibly on these questions, in ways aligned with their contrasting stances on federal economic regulation and assistance generally. Even as both parties reiterated their opposition to public and private racial discrimination, the Republicans proclaimed their goals of "reducing the degree of direct federal involvement in housing" (1976), providing housing assistance "without federal subsidies" or via "decentralized block grants" (1980), and developing a "voucher system" to return "public housing to the free market" (1984). The GOP repeatedly rejected the "distortion" of "fair housing laws" into housing "quotas and controls" (1984, 1988).[72]

The Democrats, in contrast, called for "direct federal subsidies" and "strong fair housing enforcement" to achieve "racial and economic integration" in 1976, and advocated strengthening the Fair Housing Act to give HUD "cease and desist authority" in 1980.[73] Their overt demands for racial integration then did subside in the wake of Reagan's success, giving way to support for upgrading and replenishing "housing in minority communities" while vigorously addressing "persistent discrimination in the housing market for buyers and renters" in 1984, followed by a vaguer promise of "assuring equal access" to "housing" in 1988.[74] But despite this Democratic hunkering down in the face of adverse political winds, from the late 1970s on, the racial alliances on housing policy as delineated in tables 5.2 and 5.3 closely resembled those on employment policy.

These alliances are virtually identical to those supporting either color-blind or race-conscious employment policies—though unsurprisingly, both businesses and advocacy groups focused on housing are distinctively active here, while some groups more concerned with employment issues, like many employers and unions, are less so. It is true that there have always been divisions

TABLE 5.2

Alliance for Color-Blind Housing Policies, 1978–2008

Most Republican officeholders after 1976

Presidents, 1981–93, 2001–9

Some conservative, neoconservative Democrats

Majority of Supreme Court after 1980

Most lower federal court judges, many state judges after 1980

Some senior bureaucrats in Freddie Mac and Fannie Mae after 1980

Some white-owned businesses, officially supportive of color blindness but resistant to strong enforcement of anti-discrimination laws

National Association of Realtors, American Advertising Council, American Society of Appraisers, Independent Insurance Agents of America, National Association of Insurance Commissioners

Conservative think tanks / lobbyists (e.g., Manhattan Institute, Cato Institute)

Conservative media (e.g., Charles Krauthammer, Ann Coulter)

Conservative foundations (e.g., Heritage Foundation)

Source: In addition to the sources cited for this chapter's text, especially Douglas S. Massey and Nancy A. Denton, *American Apartheid: Segregation and the Making of the Underclass* (Cambridge, MA: Harvard University Press, 1993); Thomas J. Sugrue, *Sweet Land of Liberty: The Forgotten Struggle for Civil Rights in the North* (New York: Random House, 2008); King, *Separate and Unequal*; Brown et al., *Whitewashing Race: The Myth of a Color-Blind Society* (Berkeley: University of California Press, 2003); and Charles M. Lamb, *Housing Segregation in Suburban America since 1960: Presidential and Judicial Politics* (New York: Cambridge University Press, 2005), this table is based on Edward H. Crane, "The Government Habit," *Cato Policy Report*, November/December 1995, Cato Institute, www.cato.org/pubs/policy_report/pr-nd-ec.html; Cato Institute, *Cato Handbook for Congress:* Civil Liberties, www.cato.org/pubs/handbook.html; National Association of Realtors, http://www.realtor.org/law_and_policy; Nina Siodryanskaya, "Smoking Gun of the Housing Crisis" *The Foundry* (blog) Heritage Foundation, July 8, 2009, http://blog.heritage.org/2009/07/08/smoking-gun-of-the-housing-crisis (Heritage Foundation). The National Association of Realtors' website and online magazine provides regular updates and warnings to members about what fair housing compliance requires and warns members that testers appear regularly disguised as members of the public or as government officials.

TABLE 5.3
Alliance for Race-Conscious Egalitarian Housing Policies, 1978–2008

Most Democratic officeholders, including municipal level

President 1993–2001

Executive bureaucrats in HUD, Federal Housing Agency

Some liberal Republicans (e.g., Hamilton Fish)

Liberal think tanks (e.g., Urban Institute)

Liberal advocacy groups (e.g., ACLU, League of Women Voters)

Nonwhite advocacy groups (e.g., NAACP, National Council of La Raza, Leadership Conference on Civil Rights)

Housing advocacy groups (e.g., National Fair Housing Alliance, Housing Advocates, Inc.)

Most labor unions (e.g., AFT, NEA, AFL-CIO)

Liberal media (e.g., *New York Times*)

Liberal religious groups (e.g., National Catholic Conference for Interracial Justice, National Council of Churches)

Liberal foundations (e.g., Ford Foundation, Mott Foundation)

Source: In addition to sources cited for table 5.2 and in this chapter's text, this table is based on Margery Austin Turner and Karina Fortuny, "Residential Segregation and Low-Income Working Families" (discussion paper, Urban Institute, Washington, DC, February 2009) (Urban Institute); ACLU, "Promoting Opportunity and Racial Equality in America: A Guide for Federal, State and Local Governments," Washington, DC, ACLU, July 22, 2009; ACLU letter to the HUD on the Rule to Deconcentrate Poverty and Promote Integration in Public Housing, June 1, 2000; http://www.achi.org/racial-justice_prisoners-rights_drug-law-reform_immigrants-rights/letter-department-housing-urban-de; NAACP, "Building on a Dream Report: A Joint Housing Report by the NAACP and the National Association of Home Builders," Washington, DC, NAACP, August 2006; National Council of La Raza, Janet Murguia, "Fair Housing Issues in the Gulf Coast in the Aftermath of Hurricane Katrina and Rita," February 2006, http://www.ncl.org/images/uploads/publications/37396_file_katrina_test.pdf; "Housing Integration Loses, and Wins," *New York Times*, November 12, 1988, http://www.nytimes.com/1988/11/12/opinion/housing-integration-loses-and-wins.html?scp=1&sq=integrated%20housing&st=Search; National Council of Churches, General Assembly, "A Social Creed for the 21st Century," November 7, 2007; Susan V. Berresford, "We Need Affirmative Action," March 27, 2003, Ford Foundation, http://www.fordfound.org/newsroom/speeches/123 (Ford Foundation); G. William Domhoff, "The Ford Foundation in the Inner City: Forging an Alliance with Neighborhood Activists," September 2005, Who Rules America? http://sociology.ucsc.edu/whorulesamerica/local/ford_foundation.html (Ford Foundation, Mott Foundation, other liberal foundations).

in these ranks, for in housing, the ideological and political tensions internal to efforts to advocate either color-blind or race-conscious policies have been acute. But those tensions internal to each alliance have largely been over whether activism should focus on economic or racial themes in particular disputes, not over whether in principle government efforts should or should not actively assist racial housing integration. For members of the race-conscious alliance, that has usually been a desirable goal, even if decidedly secondary for many. For members of the color-blind coalition, it has been a pernicious one.

Most advocates of color blindness nonetheless support federal laws banning racial discrimination in housing. But many have long been concerned that vigorous enforcement of such laws is likely to generate various sorts of mandatory racial quotas, as in employment, and that enforcement will be costly, ineffective, and a burden on the efficient operation of markets. Others who are also economic and social conservatives, keen to protect both individual economic rights and the character of traditional communities, consider anti-discrimination as a principle that should bind the government and those receiving many forms of federal support, but not private individuals and groups. Conversely, many modern proponents of race-conscious policies have not wished to push mandates for racial integration so far as to endanger the maintenance of primarily nonwhite neighborhoods which they value as much as traditionalist conservatives value their homogeneous communities. Many also continue to believe that, in face of daunting obstacles to any progress, the goals of improving housing quality and homeownership for minorities should take priority over reducing residential racial segregation.

Still, it would be erroneous to permit these internal differences on housing goals to obscure the larger picture. Since the late 1970s, we can discern color-blind and race-conscious alliances on housing issues that generally hold together, in opposition to each other, in legislative contests, court cases, agency regulatory hearings, and policy debates. For while their reasons differ, most if not all members of the color-blind alliance agree that anti-discrimination laws are good in principle, but that the federal government should not devote major resources to enforcing them stringently. Most if not all members of the race-conscious alliance believe instead that vigorous efforts to combat racial discrimination, sometimes including pursuit of residential racial integration, are needed. Time and again in the modern era, the alliances have therefore clashed over the extent and content of anti-discrimination enforcement measures, despite their common espousal of anti-discrimination as a settled constitutional principle.

Many race-conscious proponents insist on aggressive enforcement all the more firmly because, especially in housing, they suspect that many who profess support for color blindness are not speaking in good faith. The history of housing and employment discrimination against nonwhites, and blacks in particular, makes it difficult to discern whether realtors, sellers, renters, or loan officers view persons as good or bad potential customers on "purely" economic grounds, or on economic judgments informed by presumptions about racial probabilities concerning capacities to pay, effects on property values, and intrinsic desirability. Those complexities obviously provide openings for individuals to defend what is really racially motivated conduct as strictly color-blind economic decisions. Advocates of racially integrated housing, such as the National Fair Housing Alliance, a consortium of over two hundred local organizations founded in 1988, are therefore angered when they continue to find evidence that realtors deliberately steer African American and white home buyers into neighborhoods in which their race is dominant, even when potential buyers ask to see homes in areas where they would be in the racial minority.[75] In 2005, the alliance estimated an annual average of 3.7 million instances of housing discrimination perpetrated against African Americans, Latinos, Asian Americans, and Pacific Islanders.[76] But often realtors couched such steering in terms of school preferences, again an example of how hard it is to separate legitimate "color-blind" concerns from the illegal promotion of racial segregation.[77]

This complexity has made it difficult both in law and in scholarship to definitively prove or disprove claims of unlawful racial steering. To be sure, a great deal of pertinent evidence exists. From the mid-1970s, a wide range of organizations, including HUD in the Reagan years, have sponsored "audit" studies to see if racial steering and other forms of discrimination in housing have persisted, with color-blind advocates often hoping for evidence of sharp declines. Most studies have instead shown at least some such discrimination, causing debates to shift to methodological validity, the significance of the magnitude of the results, and the underlying question of whether racial prejudices or reasonable economic considerations and consumer preferences are driving these results. For example, a 2000 HUD report based on forty-six hundred paired tests in twenty-three metropolitan areas found that sellers preferred comparable white home buyers over African Americans in 17 percent of paired tested, and by 21.6 percent in rental. These numbers had declined since 1989, but steering of buyers to racially kindred neighborhoods had risen.[78]

Though the positions of top officials have shifted with different administrations, most members of federal regulatory agencies have leaned toward the less benign interpretations of such data. HUD Assistant Secretary Kim Kendrick told Congress in 2008 that "discrimination persists. HUD studies show that African Americans, Hispanics, Asian Americans and Native Americans receive consistently unfavorable treatment at least 20 percent of the time when they seek to purchase or rent a home."[79] African American borrowers were also "more likely than whites" to be charged at a higher rate for mortgages and to receive less favorable terms for homeowners' insurance, even when they held similar credit ratings and income levels.[80] According to Kendrick, "whites were treated better than minorities when inquiring about loans. The discrimination found in the studies was usually subtle. In other words, the minority testers almost never realized that they had received inferior treatment compared to the white testers."[81] Yet to many color-blind proponents, statistical patterns are not enough to prove that what Assistant Secretary Kendrick judged to be "very subtle" racial discrimination was intentional prejudicial conduct. They believe the economic and social costs of seeking more decisive evidence and prosecuting offenders outweigh any benefits.[82]

Similarly, as the *Arlington Heights* case makes clear, zoning laws predictably operate to preclude affordable housing in areas experiencing rapid growth, and it can be hard to tell if decision makers are unintentionally (even if knowingly) perpetuating residential segregation, and so acting in ways arguably consistent with color blindness, or if the maintenance of racial segregation is deliberate. The same is true of many other governmental decisions that concentrate subsidized housing in a limited number of areas, that rely on local property taxes for public schools, and that provide transportation, infrastructure, and other forms of support that aid the movement of businesses to new locations outside city centers and farther away from predominantly nonwhite housing areas. For race-conscious advocates, the abundant evidence of continuing inequalities suggests that many of those who do not support extensive federal efforts to combat residential discrimination do not really believe in color blindness; they prefer the status quo of racially separate and unequal housing. But to color-blind proponents, governmental efforts to compel people to live next door to unwanted and perhaps irresponsible neighbors who depend on federal subsidies for their housing are unjust, expensive, and destructive for the lives of all concerned. In this area as much or more than any other, many members of the rival racial alliances therefore regard their opponents with righteous indignation and deep suspicion about their true intentions and moral integrity.

Under these circumstances, it is understandable that the battles over housing policy since the emergence of the modern racial alliances have centered first on the extent and funding of federal anti-discrimination efforts, second on how far the government should seek to combat racial inequalities in housing that are not demonstrably the result of intentional racial discrimination, and only lastly on how far achieving residential racial integration should be a goal. When Watergate helped catapult Jimmy Carter to the presidency in 1976, many liberals in Congress hoped to reinvigorate fair housing and public housing initiatives. But they were able only to win the modest Community Reinvestment Act of 1977. This act was designed to spur banks to make housing loans in urban areas by requiring federal regulators to consider whether banks had served the geographical areas in which they were chartered when they applied for new charters or approval of relocations, mergers, or acquisition. Sponsors of the act hoped to combat discriminatory redlining. But to forestall opposition from proponents of color blindness, their bill included no explicitly racial targets or standards.[83]

The Carter administration and its allies in Congress did try to strengthen the enforcement provisions of the Fair Housing Act, and they were making slow progress when the election of Ronald Reagan in November 1980 derailed their efforts. The genesis of their 1980 bill began a decade earlier as members of Congress uncovered evidence through committee hearings about the inadequacies of the 1968 law as a framework to achieve fair housing.[84] In 1979 the House Judiciary Committee promulgated proposals to enhance federal anti-discrimination powers, giving authority to HUD-appointed judges to impose fines on firms engaged in discriminatory practices. The Carter White House and Justice Department supported the tougher measures. So did key elements of the pro-housing race-conscious coalition, including the NAACP, the AFL-CIO, the League of Women Voters, and the ACLU. Opposition to the bill came from many members of the modern color-blind racial alliance, including most Republicans and some conservative Democrats, along with the National Association of Realtors, and the Society of Real Estate Appraisers.[85]

Even so, Republicans did not wish to appear pro-discrimination, and in the House the bill—HR 5200—eventually passed on June 12, 1980, by a substantial 310–95 margin. But the previous day, an amendment protecting the enforcement powers had passed by only 205–204. Of the 204 who voted against that measure, 128 were Republicans and 76 were Democrats. Among this set of Democrat opponents, two-thirds were from the South.[86] In the final 305–95 vote, a narrow majority of Republicans supported the bill (87–67), while 28 Democrats stayed with the opposing side, 21 of whom were from southern states.

From Reagan to George W. Bush

Then in November, Reagan won the White House and the Republicans captured the Senate. Consequently, the next month in the lame-duck Senate's last session, the battle to dilute or exclude housing enforcement powers became more intense, with conservative Republicans led by Orrin Hatch and Strom

Thurmond especially pressing for the law to require proof of intentional discrimination by real estate dealers, not simply racially disparate outcomes. Liberal Democrat senators such as Edward Kennedy, along with the former segregationist majority leader Robert Byrd, fought the "intent only" amendment. But they failed to muster enough votes to invoke a motion of cloture against the coalition of conservative, primarily southern Democrats and Republicans, and the entire bill failed. [87]

After Reagan's inauguration, the number of complaints of housing discrimination filed with HUD continued to rise; but the Justice Department's willingness to file fair housing suits almost vanished. In the eight years of the Reagan administration, the *total* number of cases filed was roughly the same as the number filed *per year* under Carter.[88] Reagan officials also modified an agreement between HUD and the National Association of Realtors to relieve its members from having to promise to enforce the Fair Housing Act in order to receive HUD approval for federal funds. The Reagan Office of Management and Budget sought to restrict HUD's gathering of data on the race of participants in housing programs.[89] At the same time, the Reagan White House and its Republican allies in Congress began deregulating FHA mortgage rates and housing financing more generally, and the FHA started to insure adjustable rate mortgages.[90] They also "de-funded" housing subsidy programs, like other forms of federal assistance. From 1981 to 1992, the end of the administration of Reagan's successor, his vice president George H. W. Bush, the Republicans cut federal aid to cities by 60 percent and appropriations for HUD-subsidized housing programs by over 80 percent.[91]

Led by the Ford Foundation, liberal private foundations responded to what they saw as adverse developments in the Reagan era by expanding their housing initiatives. Then after the Democrats regained control of both houses of Congress in 1987, while the Reagan administration was burdened by the Iran-Contra scandal, race-conscious proponents successfully revived their 1980 bill as the Fair Housing Amendments Act of 1988.[92] The late historian Hugh Davis Graham noted that proponents of these amendments studiously avoided the unpopular language of affirmative action, and he speculated plausibly that this strategy contributed to what he recognized as a "surprising" success against the currents of the Reagan era.[93] But advocates of the 1980 bill had used similar rhetoric, so Democratic control of Congress; the mobilization of still-potent race-conscious forces angered at the Reagan administration's policies; and the political vulnerability of the Republicans as the 1988 election loomed were probably the decisive factors.

In the House a bill emerged from the Judiciary Committee on April 27, 1987, garnering 26 votes in support, 9 opposing. This victory came only after numerous Republican committee members introduced multiple amendments, mostly minor variations on previous ones already rejected, in order to stall passage of the bill.[94] When it reached the House floor, the Reagan White House strongly supported the Republican position that judicial review of alleged discriminations should be held in courtrooms with local juries, not before federal administrative judges. However, many on the White House political team, and particularly the likely GOP presidential nominee, Vice President Bush, wanted Congress to enact some law. This would liberate the Republicans of any taint of appearing unsupportive of racial justice—especially since Bush saw himself and wished to be seen as a racial moderate.

Hence, most of the GOP accepted a compromise brokered by the liberal Republican Hamilton Fish, ranking minority member of the House Judiciary Committee, and the Leadership Conference on Civil Rights. Firms or individuals accused of discrimination could opt either to appear before a HUD administrative judge and be liable to a maximum fine of $50,000, or to take their cases to jury trials in federal courts, with the prospect of facing potentially higher legal costs and larger remedies if convicted. The compromise bill passed the House by 376–23 and the Senate by 94–3, huge majorities that included some of those most hostile to the 1980 legislative effort, such as Senators Hatch and Thurmond—although Thurmond's support came only after he won an amendment permitting landlords to decline renting to anyone with a narcotics conviction, a measure that had racial significance due to the racially skewed patterns of drug law enforcement.[95]

Once elected, the first President Bush took some steps to strengthen enforcement of fair housing laws and to promote homeownership, largely via tax credits. He then ran for reelection on a GOP platform that stressed the latter policies and again forswore "quotas and controls" in pursuit of "open housing."[96] The Democrats did not explicitly promise much more, but after his election in 1992, President Bill Clinton escalated fair housing efforts.[97] In 1993 Clinton launched a "fair lending" initiative. It greatly expanded HUD's grants to private groups to test and litigate discrimination in real estate practices; established fair lending divisions in all ten HUD regional offices; instructed federal regulatory officials to ensure that lenders were equally accommodating to applicants from all racial groups; and shifted HUD's strategy from contesting public housing suits alleging discrimination in HUD programs to seeking instead to work out consent decrees as bases for settlements.[98]

At the same time, the new president issued an "Interagency Policy Statement on Credit Availability." This policy gave lenders more discretionary power to make "character loans" to those they trusted who might not otherwise appear creditworthy—the sort of discretion long used against nonwhites, but now urged as a means to assist promising but disadvantaged applicants, including minority applicants. The next year, Clinton proposed and Congress enacted a Community Development and Financial Institutions Act to increase investment in poorer urban areas. Fannie Mae committed $1 trillion for mortgage lending targeted to the poor, minorities, immigrants, and inner-city residents.[99] Clinton also created a Fair Housing Council to coordinate concern for anti-discrimination in housing initiatives, including revisions of regulations issued under the Community Reinvestment Act to require, among other goals, greater disclosure about the extent of banks' community development loans.[100] These were the initiatives that some color-blind proponents would later attack as the "affirmative action" basis of the subprime mortgage crisis.

In a climate hostile to race-conscious measures, the 1996 Democratic platform did not mention these fair housing programs. Instead the party stressed tax credits and vouchers to improve home owning and conditions for public housing residents, much like the Republicans. Nonetheless, the GOP repeated its rejection of "quotas or controls." The party condemned the Clinton administration's "abuse of fair housing laws to harass citizens," while also calling for the elimination of HUD.[101] Faced with a Republican Congress and preoccupied by his own scandal, Clinton did less on housing in his second term. Presenting himself as a "compassionate conservative," George W. Bush then won the presidency on a platform that stressed tax measures to promote affordable housing. And while the GOP repeated its standard condemnation of "quotas or controls," it now added praise for "the proactive efforts by the realty and housing industries to assure access for everyone."[102] Bush was less hostile to race-conscious goals than many in his party, but he also did not wish to alienate the color-blind alliance, including economic libertarians, who formed so much of the Republican base. The platform's phrasing neatly combined endorsement of fair housing goals with confidence in the capacity of the private sector to meet them. The Democrats stressed similar strategies but also included the need to eliminate "community redlining."[103]

Once in office, Bush announced a mildly race-conscious housing initiative. Entitled "A Home of Your Own: Expanding Opportunities for All Americans," the program did not involve racial preferences, but it still explicitly sought to raise the number of minority homeowners. The initiative set a goal of at least 5.5 million more by the end of the decade, to be achieved via tax credits, an "American Dream Downpayment Fund," and grants to housing organizations, among other means.[104] The Republicans celebrated this race-conscious initiative in their 2004 platform, even forgoing their usual disparagement of housing "quotas or controls," perhaps because of Bush's numerical target for increases in minority homeownership, perhaps because it had now been many years since any Democrat could credibly be accused of advocating housing quotas.[105] The Democratic platform that year once more urged only "vigorous federal enforcement of our civil rights laws" to achieve "fair housing."[106]

Yet enforcement remained an issue over which the parties, and the racial alliances, did indeed have major differences. In accordance with color-blind principles, the Bush administration announced in 2003 that it would hence-forth prosecute only housing cases involving intentional racial discrimination, not "disparate impact" lawsuits, even though the courts continued to read the Fair Housing Act as authorizing both types of litigation.[107] Critics including the U.S. Civil Rights Commission complained that the Bush administration did not support adequate funding for its own proposals, nor Section 8 or voucher programs, and that it rarely initiated discrimination suits of any sort despite growing complaints, leaving enforcement to private litigation.[108]

After the end of the second Bush term, a U.S. Government Accountability Office (GAO) investigation reported "a significant drop in the enforcement of several major anti-discrimination laws" in the Bush years in comparison with the Clinton administration, notably in employment and voting rights. Bush's housing discrimination enforcement efforts focused heavily on cases involving disability, not race.[109] Obama officials traced these declines in enforcement to the fact that, even as discrimination complaints almost doubled from 2002 to 2007, federal resources provided for processing complaints about housing dis-crimination were cut significantly, leading to the closure of some local organi-zations funded under the Fair Housing Assistance Program through which most complaints were filed.[110] Table 5.4 summarizes these policy develop-ments from Reagan through the second Bush administration.

Expanding Fair Housing Enforcement: The Obama Era

In 2008, Barack Obama won the presidency on a platform that called for ag-gressive federal action to combat the subprime mortgage and housing crisis, noting: "Minorities have been hit particularly hard—in 2006, more than 40 percent of the home loans made to Hispanic borrowers were subprime, while more than half of those made to African Americans were subprime." The Democrats promised to "restore cuts to public housing operating subsidies" and to "restore vigorous enforcement of civil rights laws," including efforts "to end housing discrimination."[111] Obama's campaign materials stressed those points, including criticisms of the Bush Justice Department for abandoning "dispa-rate impact cases involving housing discrimination" and for appointing Civil

Chapter 5

TABLE 5.4
Housing and Mortgage Policy Developments in the Era of Modern
Racial Alliances, 1983–2003

1983	FHA mortgage rates deregulated; FHA begins insuring adjustable rate mortgages (ARMs).
1986	Low Income Housing Tax Credit created to encourage private sector development of affordable housing.
1988	Fair Housing Amendments Act of 1988 increases enforcement powers.
1989	Freddie Mac begins trading publicly, with shareholder-elected board members; Financial Institutions Reform, Recovery, and Enforcement Act bails out, restructures thrift industry.
1990	Cranston-Gonzalez National Affordable Housing Act provides funds to states and homeowners to build, rehabilitate affordable housing.
1993	President Bill Clinton issues Interagency Policy Statement on Credit Availability to free up financing for housing.
1994	Community Development and Financial Institutions Act of 1994; Fannie Mae commits $1 trillion for mortgage lending targeted to minorities, inner cities, people below median income, immigrants; Clinton creates Fair Housing Council to coordinate efforts.
2002	President George W. Bush announces initiative to promote minority homeownership.
2003	Bush DOJ announces it will not pursue disparate impact housing suits.

Source: Michael S. Barr, "Credit Where it Counts: The Community Reinvestment Act and Its Critics," *New York University Law Review* 80(2005), 527–33; Anthony D. Taibi, "Racial Justice in the Age of the Global Economy: Community Empowerment and Global Strategy," *Duke Law Journal* 44 (1995); National Fair Housing Alliance, "Dr. King's Dream Denied Forty Years of Failed Federal Enforcement," 2008 Fair Housing Trends Report, April 8, 2008; National Association of Home Builders, "A Century of Progress."

Rights Division lawyers who had cut their teeth "either by defending employers against discrimination lawsuits or by fighting against race-conscious policies." Obama promised to "reverse" these trends.[112]

The Republicans were far more muted on these topics. Even though they did not again denounce housing "quotas," their platform was in many respects more "color-blind" than ever. It promised only to "support timely and carefully targeted aid to those hurt by the housing crisis so that affected individuals can have a chance to trade a burdensome mortgage for a manageable loan that reflects their home's market value." It made no explicit reference to the disproportionate housing hardships of minorities. Instead the platform's authors observed, "At the same time, government action must not implicitly encourage anyone to borrow more than they can afford to repay," an apparent invocation of the "affirmative action" explanation for the housing crisis. And rather than endorsing heightened enforcement of anti-discrimination laws, the GOP explained that "Republican policy aims to make owning a home more accessible through enforcement of open housing laws, voucher programs, urban homesteading and—what is most important—a strong economy with low interest rates."[113] Late in his struggling campaign, GOP presidential candidate John McCain then denounced Obama as a proponent of subprime lending, without noting Obama's contention that the idea had been abused. Unlike other conservatives, however, McCain did not accuse Obama of supporting them to help minority homebuyers.[114]

The positions of both parties, then, continued to reflect the analyses of housing issues of the two modern racial alliances. Race-conscious proponents insist on the need for stronger enforcement of anti-discrimination laws and special concern to promote minority housing, on an integrated basis if possible. Color-blind advocates instead treat enforcement of federal housing laws as secondary in importance to market-oriented economic policies and warn against the dangers of "social conscience" lending.

Consistent with the modern Democratic strategy of stressing vigorous enforcement but not policies with overt racial targets, the Obama administration went on in 2009 to structure its economic stimulus and housing relief measures in "color-blind" terms, prompting criticism from some in the race-conscious alliance. John Powell of the Kirwan Institute for the Study of Race and Ethnicity complained that the administration's efforts might "end up worsening the racial disparity." The Obama administration responded that it had more than doubled aid to disadvantaged business enterprises and minority owners and that doing so was "a top priority of the President's."[115] Even during the presidential campaign, candidate Obama felt compelled to try to persuade members of the Congressional Black Caucus and the Congressional Hispanic Caucus to support the Emergency Economic Stabilization Act, as he did, because they saw it as rewarding instead of punishing bankers who had engaged in racially discriminatory lending.[116]

But rather than setting explicit racial targets or building racial preferences into its economic aid programs, the Obama administration's "signature policy" in housing is its focus on litigation designed to combat discrimination and to promote policies fostering residential racial integration. The Westchester

Chapter 5

case fits this pattern. As of 2010, the Obama administration has pursued these goals more energetically than any administration since the 1970s. In January 2010, at a conference sponsored by the Reverend Jesse Jackson's Rainbow/PUSH Coalition, Assistant Attorney General Thomas Perez of the Obama Justice Department's Civil Rights Division announced the creation of a new unit focused on "reverse redlining," the alleged practice of singling out minority neighborhoods for loans with inferior terms.[117] By March, the Obama DOJ had negotiated a settlement with the American International Group (AIG), the financially troubled insurance company whose subsidiaries included many firms engaged in home lending, to pay $6.1 million to about twenty-five hundred African Americans for having charged them higher fees than those offered to whites. In announcing the settlement, Perez indicated that other lenders using broker networks could be vulnerable to similar lawsuits. The National Association of Mortgage Brokers complained that only individual local brokers "who actually do the discriminating," not "lenders who acquired the loans with no knowledge of the discriminatory fees," should be punished.[118] But amidst evidence of predatory real estate and lending practices in most American cities, including New Orleans as African American evacuees sought to find housing in the wake of Hurricane Katrina, the administration headed by a former civil rights lawyer appeared determined to deploy aggressive anti-discrimination litigation strategies.[119]

If the Obama administration similarly seeks to make the Westchester settlement a model for jurisdictions receiving federal housing funds throughout the nation, moreover, it will place greater emphasis on achieving residential racial integration than most Democrats have been willing to do since the dawn of the Reagan era, even if still less than some race-conscious advocates would wish. Doing so will heighten both political and legal opposition to the administration's housing policies. The refusal of Westchester so far to live up to the terms of its settlement demonstrates a persistent lack of political will by many officials to expend resources in pursuit of integrated housing. And although the modern Supreme Court has yet to challenge the identification of racial residential integration as a public policy goal in the Fair Housing Act and other statutes and federal regulations, its decisions in other areas of civil rights law, particularly employment and education, show that its insistence on constitutional commitments to color blindness have the potential to call into question this race-conscious policy as well. Hence, clashes between the racial alliances will probably still loom large in housing debates in the years ahead.

In sum, though housing poses both philosophical and political challenges to members of each modern racial alliance, their conflicts have still done much to shape policy for decades. Color-blind proponents do not regard it as either morally or politically feasible to attack aspirations for an America with racially integrated residential sections. But they insist it must come, if it comes, through voluntary individual choices. They adamantly oppose all race-conscious efforts to mandate such integration. As a result, for the most part they oppose expansive and expensive federal enforcement efforts on behalf of the anti-discrimination principles they espouse.

Race-conscious proponents wish for nonwhites to be able to obtain quality housing wherever they prefer. But recognizing the daunting political obstacles to governmental efforts to promote such housing and the divisions in their own ranks about how much priority to give to residential integration, they have focused on supporting federal aid programs and vigorous anti-discrimination enforcement, while seeking to structure these to facilitate residential racial integration whenever and wherever it seems politically feasible to do so, in terms of both white and nonwhite sentiments.

As a result, disputes between the racial policy alliances have been less central in this area than in many others; but both housing segregation and racial gaps in housing persist. The Obama administration, again, has made clear that its typically mixed strategy is to advocate for generous and explicitly race-neutral federal aid programs while using anti-discrimination litigation both to ensure nonwhite access to homes, apartments, and loans, and to promote residential race and class integration in the process. As the polemics over the subprime mortgage crisis and the continuing resistance in Westchester indicate, it remains far from clear whether that strategy can succeed either as politics or as policy. The subprime crisis showed that although many color-blind advocates might welcome greater racial desegregation in America's housing, they are only willing to promote such a goal through market policies, which historically have done little to reduce segregation. The Obama mixed strategy sits upon a political world of housing policy in which the administration's aspirations to promote quality, integrated housing find far too little support to inspire confidence that they will succeed.

Chapter 6

"To elect one of their own"
Racial Alliances and Majority-Minority Districts

Persistent as racial housing segregation has been, 2000 census data showed that it was receding slightly in Chicago, and that the Latino presence was growing. Black city aldermen found it difficult to draw a new ward map that would preserve the existing twenty black-majority alderman districts. The chairman of the Chicago City Council's black caucus, Alderman Ed Smith, nonetheless expressed determination to maintain twenty wards that were at least 65 percent African American. His efforts won support from Illinois state senator Barack Obama. The Chicago-based state legislator observed that as long as "we have hardened racial attitudes reflected in our voting patterns for minorities—to elect one of their own—they still need to have a substantial voting-age majority in neighborhoods and communities."[1] As he did in his constitutional law courses at the University of Chicago, the future president defended the propriety, indeed the necessity, of creating substantial black "majority-minority" districts so that African American voters could gain meaningful political power. He worried "incremental integration" made achieving such power "harder to do."[2]

In his 2008 campaign, Obama criticized the Bush Justice Department for failing to file anti-discrimination cases on behalf of African American voters. Obama's campaign documents noted that as a civil rights lawyer, he had "defended minority voters who challenged redistricting plans that diluted their vote." But he did not explicitly advocate majority-minority districts.[3] Such districts had long been under attack both by proponents of color-blind decision making and by many proponents of race-conscious approaches who regarded majority-minority districts as often operating to weaken, not to enhance, the political influence of nonwhites.[4] These "strange bedfellow" critics are often considered counterparts to the "strange bedfellow" political proponents of majority-minority districts. Looking back at the politics of district drawing after the last two censuses, analysts from across the political spectrum reach conclusions that may appear to debunk any effort to analyze American racial issues in terms of the rival racial alliances we identify. They see these districts as born of "unholy alliances" between Republicans and black Democrats, in the very years in which we claim that the parties have been polarized on racial issues.[5]

In response, we argue that there is indeed evidence of efforts to foster such "strange bedfellow" coalitions. But they have generally failed, in part because political disputes over majority-minority districting have been extensively, indeed predominantly, shaped by the opposed modern racial alliances. Officially the districts represent efforts to conform to the 1965 Voting Rights Act (VRA), as amended in 1982. As we saw in chapters 1 and 2, the major issues involving race and suffrage from the slavery through the Jim Crow eras were not districting per se. They were the many means white supremacists used to disfranchise blacks, with districting a minor part of the story. Through the 1960s, racial egalitarians' primary aim for the franchise was to eliminate the veiled racial barriers to voting registration and to voting. Consequently, like the other major civil rights laws of the era, the 1965 VRA was discussed and structured in ways that expressed color-blind goals more plainly than race-conscious ones. Partly for that reason, its provisions have long had broad support from both modern racial alliances.

But the original VRA, concerned with voting rights enforcement, had limited success in getting nonwhite officials elected. Partly as a result, the act has been repeatedly amended and extended, most importantly in 1982. So in voting rights, the contestation between the rival racial alliances over how vigorously to enforce civil rights laws now focuses on clashes over the race-conscious districting practices that proliferated in the wake of the 1982 amendments. Despite exaggerated claims that Republicans created these districts in tactical alliance with African American Democrats, for the most part color-blind proponents in the GOP and allied groups have attacked race-conscious districting in general, while opposing the specific majority-minority districts proposed by black and Latino leaders. And on this important constitutional issue, too, color-blind proponents have increasingly prevailed, mainly through court decisions invalidating majority-minority districts.

The striking upshot is that today, American politicians can design districts in ways that serve multiple purposes. But courts will strike down their plans if their overriding aim is to achieve greater racial inclusiveness in the nation's elected representatives. Only when new majority-minority districts result from the pursuit of other purposes—such as conformity to traditional geographic divisions in areas that have become predominantly nonwhite, or efforts to achieve partisan advantages—will they be deemed constitutional.

The 1965 Voting Rights Act

The Voting Rights Act fought Jim Crow disfranchisement aggressively. It stipulated the suspension of voting tests and systems in jurisdictions that had below 50 percent registration or turnout of the resident voting-age population in the 1964 elections. Its Section 5 required Justice Department "pre-clearance" of new voting rules adopted by such jurisdictions, a dramatic and forceful expression of federal power. The act generated sizable increases in black voter registration and voting, but not in office holding.[6] In 1969, there were still only 9 African Americans in the U.S. House and only one in the Senate. Only 32 blacks served in southern state legislatures, and only 168 did so nationwide. But after amendments to the Voting Rights Act in 1970 and 1975, and particularly after the 1982 amendments promoted majority-minority districts, greater changes unfolded. When the 109th Congress opened in 2005, forty years after the original VRA, there were 42 African Americans in the House, though still only one in the Senate, all Democrats. In that year the House had 27 Hispanic members, 21 Democrats, and 6 Republicans, while the Senate had 3 Hispanics, two Democrats and one Republican. Including a Delegate, the House had 6 members of Asian or Native Hawaiian/other Pacific Islander ancestry, five Democrats and one Republican, and the Senate had 2, both Democrats. There was one Native American in Congress, a Republican in the House.[7] From 1980 to 2004, the number of Hispanic state legislators more than doubled, from under 90 concentrated in nine states to 221 serving in three times as many states. The number of black state legislators grew to over 600.[8]

Who brought about these changes during the last three decades? Who opposed them? Do the coalitions resemble the color-blind and race-conscious alliances as we have seen them in other areas? To answer, it is important to begin by recognizing that the 1965 Voting Rights Act was both the climactic triumph of the anti–Jim Crow coalition and the ultimate defeat for those southern and conservative Democrats who had long battled within their party to keep it the strongest supporter of segregation in the American political system. Furthermore, the VRA's enactment was not foreordained even after the 1964 Civil Rights Act. Though both parties had called for vigorous enforcement of the recent civil rights laws and some new legislation to secure voting rights in their 1960 platforms, with the Democrats doing so more emphatically, and majorities in both parties supported the 1964 Civil Rights Act, neither party urged further legislation in their platforms that year. The Democrats merely boasted of how the recently passed Civil Rights Act provided "effective procedures for assuring the right to vote in Federal elections."[9]

But in fact, Lyndon Johnson knew both that passage of the 1964 act had permanently discredited the Democrats in the eyes of white segregationists, and that it did *not* provide mechanisms sufficient to overcome the barriers still preventing the Democrats from replacing their lost white voters with new black ones, especially in the South.[10] The Kennedy administration had launched a Voter Education Project in collaboration with a number of civil rights groups already active in voter registration, including the Southern Christian Leadership Conference (SCLC), the Student Nonviolent Coordinating Committee (SNCC), the Congress on Racial Equality (CORE), and the NAACP. These efforts drove up African American voter registration from roughly 29 percent voting-age black southerners to approximately 43 percent between 1962 and 1964. But mounting southern white resistance, often violent, increasingly stymied civil rights workers, and many felt they were not receiving adequate federal support.[11] Voting reform efforts seemed destined to stall unless the federal government took further steps. But with the 1964 Civil Rights Act celebrated as the cure for all American racial problems, something further was needed to mobilize support for additional legislation.

That something proved to be the voting rights campaign in Selma, Alabama, in 1965. In January of that year, civil rights leader Martin Luther King Jr. described Selma as an effort "to arouse the federal government." The turning point came with the "Bloody Sunday" march in honor of a recently slain civil rights protestor that started out from Selma and headed for the state capital in Montgomery, Alabama, on March 7, 1965. Fifty Alabama state troopers on horseback and the local sheriff and his "posse" tear-gassed, clubbed, and whipped the protestors while yelling racist slurs in front of television cameras and microphones from the major networks, who replayed the ugly scenes and sounds for all America that evening. The same scenes of racist mayhem aired on national television networks around the world, much to Americans' chagrin.

A week later, President Johnson addressed a solemn joint session of Congress. He issued a moving call for a new federal voting rights bill, invoking the great anthem of the civil rights movement, "We Shall Overcome."[12]

Though most southern Democrats and some conservative Republicans still opposed the VRA, after the 1964 election they had diminished minorities in both the House and the Senate. The House voted for the initial bill 333 to 85, with Republicans voting 112–24 in favor, Democrats 221–61. In the Senate the vote was 77–19, with Republicans supporting the bill 30–2, Democrats 47–17. In the final votes on the conference report reconciling the two slightly different versions the chambers had passed, Senate Democrats voted in favor of the bill 49 to 17, with four southern Democrats supporting it, and Strom Thurmond (who had recently, and momentously, switched parties) the only negative Republican vote. House Democrats voted 217–54 in favor, House Republicans 111–20, with forty southerners now supporting the bill. The vestiges of the Jim Crow alliance now held real power only at the state level and in some congressional committees, particularly in the Senate.[13] They could still sometimes force delays and compromises. But at this point they could not stop the enactment of new laws and judicial decisions establishing formally equal rights in all arenas, including elections.

With only Justice Hugo Black of Alabama in partial dissent, the Warren Court swiftly upheld the constitutionality of the Voting Rights Act in *South Carolina v. Katzenbach* (1966). The Court rejected the claims of South Carolina and state attorneys general from Virginia, Louisiana, Alabama, Mississippi, and Georgia (opposed by their counterparts from fifteen northern, midwestern, and western states) that the law lacked a rational basis and intruded on state prerogatives protected by the Tenth Amendment.[14] In a companion case, *Katzenbach v. Morgan*, the Court also upheld Section 4(e) of the VRA. This ruling prevented New York and all other American jurisdictions from disfranchising citizens who had finished the sixth grade in Puerto Rico because of their inability to read or write English.[15] Few had any doubts after these rulings that the Court would support muscular enforcement of the Voting Rights Act and insist that lower courts throughout the country do the same.

Aided by this favorable judicial and political climate, the VRA had immediate and dramatic impact on voter registration: in Arkansas, Florida, Tennessee, and Texas, black voter registration rose from 60 percent in 1964 to 71.4 percent in 1968, and in the states composing the heart of the old Confederacy, Alabama, Georgia, Louisiana, Mississippi, North Carolina, South Carolina, and Virginia, the increase was from 33.8 percent of all eligible blacks in 1964 to 56.6 percent in 1968.[16] Once again, however, the decisive resolution of some racial issues quickly gave way to new and in many ways more difficult ones. Because the VRA did not address barriers to office holding, even as southern states and municipalities acquiesced in African American voter registration, many began restructuring their electoral systems to make the election of candidates preferred by blacks more difficult. Some created at-large local elections, since blacks were usually residentially concentrated minorities. Some redrew their boundaries to add white voters. Some required runoffs between the top two candidates for various positions, and some made key offices appointive, among many other devices.[17]

So in this area of constitutional and political rights, too, many civil rights reformers soon decided that banning Jim Crow subordinating and exclusionary practices was not enough. In 1968, a year in which the Republican platform said nothing about voting rights, the Democrats promised not to permit the Civil Rights Acts of 1964 and 1968 and the Voting Rights Act of 1965 to be "chipped away by opponents or eroded by administrative neglect," and affirmed that "if their compliance provisions fail to serve their purposes, we will propose new laws."[18] Prior to doing so, however, civil rights reformers began insisting in litigation that, in addition to preventing racial disfranchisement, the VRA as it stood should be understood to protect against vote "dilution" by banning all mechanisms structured to make the votes of nonwhites less effective in electing candidates than those of whites. In parallel to enforcement developments elsewhere, it was impossible to determine whether nonwhite votes were being "diluted," much less to devise remedies for such dilution, without engaging in race-conscious data collection, analysis, and decision making.

The fact that in this era, the late 1960s and early 1970s, racial liberals still predominated on the Supreme Court and in the lower federal courts meant that these "vote dilution" arguments initially received emphatic judicial approval. The first major decision, *Allen v. State Board of Elections*, considered four cases. These included instances in which southern governments had adopted at-large election systems and shifted to appointive offices to limit black influence. The southern states argued that the VRA's "pre-clearance" requirements for federal approval applied only to changes in systems of voter registration, not other alterations in the electoral laws of jurisdictions whose low registration or turnout percentages placed them under the act's provenance.[19] Chief Justice Earl Warren rejected the southerners' contentions. Only Justices Black and John Marshall Harlan dissented. Warren wrote that the act "was aimed at the subtle, as well as the obvious, state regulations which have the effect of denying citizens their right to vote because of their race," and that it gave "a broad interpretation to the right to vote, recognizing that voting includes 'all action necessary to make a vote effective.'"[20] It thereby proscribed anything that amounted to vote "dilution."

That decision provided ammunition for the Justice Department's Civil Rights Division. The department expanded to fulfill its "pre-clearance" duties under the VRA. This augmentation made the division a significant bureaucratic player in voting rights politics, with a professional staff that over time usually aligned with race-conscious advocates. As both federal voting rights officials and civil rights groups reported real progress but continuing resistance to reform efforts in the late 1960s, and with liberal Democrats still in control of Congress, in 1970 the VRA's proponents overcame the initial reluctance of the Nixon administration and extended the act for five years. The main concession to conservatives' claims that the act unfairly targeted the South was to *widen* its coverage, including a national ban on literacy tests.[21] In their 1972 platform, the Republicans noted Nixon's support for these "strong new amendments to the Voting Rights Act of 1965" and pledged "continued vigilance" to uphold those rights.[22] But the Democrats charged the Nixon Justice Department with failing to enforce the VRA. They also urged "further steps" to end "all barriers to participation in the political process," including bilingual registration, voting, and voter education programs; "no discriminatory districting"; and, in an issue that would not really surface until decades later, "restoration of civil rights to vote and hold public office" after criminals had completed their sentences and paroles.[23]

In a similar spirit, the Supreme Court in the early 1970s continued to read the VRA broadly. The Court held in *White v. Regester* (1973) that the adoption of multimember state legislative districts for two urban counties in Texas represented invidious "vote dilution" affecting Mexican Americans and African Americans.[24] By examining the "totality of circumstances," the justices concluded that extensive historic political and economic discrimination against Mexican Americans as well as blacks was present in those areas.[25] This "totality of circumstances" test appeared promising for litigating on behalf of voting rights for all groups that could show histories of discrimination against them. By the same token, to many it raised concerns that the Court might insist on the adoption of arrangements empowering particular racial and ethnic groups based only on very general findings of past discrimination.[26] Partly as a result of this judicial receptivity to their claims and the earlier *Katzenbach v. Morgan* ruling on the rights of Puerto Ricans, as well as the Democrats' new emphasis on bilingual voting procedures, Mexican Americans and other Latinos acquired key roles when the act came up for renewal in 1975.

There were then only eight Hispanics in the House and one Senator. President Gerald Ford sought to limit renewal of the act to five years instead of the ten proposed by civil rights proponents. Renewal for seven years was the compromise. The Mexican American Legal Defense and Educational Fund (MALDEF) urged new protections for Chicanos via language-based triggers for federal monitoring and pre-clearance requirements. Congress responded by requiring that voting materials be printed in the language of four groups—American Indians, Asian Americans, Alaskan Natives, and Hispanics—whenever they constituted 5 percent of the voting population of any political subdivision. Failures to provide such materials were deemed illegal literacy tests which, combined with low turnout, would trigger Justice Department election supervision and pre-clearance of any changes.[27]

Some black leaders were slow to support these proposals, initially fearing they might endanger the act's renewal.[28] But Barbara Jordan, elected the first African American representative from Texas in 1972, championed the cause of Hispanic and Native American voters. Jordan thereby facilitated a major expansion of civil rights forces in the face of declining white support. The addition of many Latinos helped generate the modern race-conscious alliance, making it more "multiracial" on an enduring basis than its anti–Jim Crow predecessor, even though tensions between black and Latino priorities soon became a recurrent feature of the alliance's internal politics.[29] In 1975, these coalescing race-conscious proponents and their Democratic allies in Congress had sufficient clout to defeat conservatives and color-blind advocates allied with the weakened post-Watergate Republicans.[30] In 1976, the GOP platform said nothing about these changes. But the Democrats' platform promised "vigorous enforcement of voting rights legislation to assure the constitutional rights of minority and language-minority citizens." This was a direct appeal to the emerging and broadening race-conscious alliance on voting issues.[31]

EXTENDING THE VRA

But the color-blind alliance regrouped. Its members mobilized against race-conscious voting rights enforcement, primarily through litigation. Soon, the successful nominations to the Supreme Court of Republican presidents Nixon and Ford started to bear fruit. The new Court initiated its shift away from approval of many race-conscious measures, including ones aimed at securing voting rights. Rejecting briefs from the Carter Justice Department and the Lawyers' Committee for Civil Rights Under Law, in *Mobile v. Bolden* (1980) the Court sustained an at-large election system in the white-majority city of Mobile, Alabama, against complaints that this structure made it hard for black candidates to win.[32] The Court insisted here, too, on a more color-blind reading of civil rights laws: the justices ruled that to violate the VRA, which derived its authority from the Fifteenth Amendment and the Fourteenth Amendment's equal protection clause, electoral systems not only had to have "disproportionate impact" on racial minorities; they must have been enacted demonstrably with an invidious "discriminatory purpose." To hold otherwise would imply that the Constitution requires "proportional representation" of all racial groups, which the Court rejected.[33] In the Court's eyes, such discriminatory purposes had been shown in *White v. Regester* but had not been shown for Mobile's system, adopted in 1911 with blacks already largely disfranchised.

The Democratic platform that year continued to court Latino voters by promising to "end discrimination against language minorities" with vigorous enforcement of "the Voting Rights Act of 1975 to assist Hispanic citizens," while the Republicans again said nothing on voting rights.[34] Amidst the economic and foreign policy travails of the Carter administration, the Democrats' race-conscious appeals were not nearly enough to prevent Ronald Reagan from winning his substantial presidential victory as the GOP gained a thin majority in the Senate. But with Democrats still dominant in the House, civil rights groups reacted quickly and aggressively to *Mobile v. Bolden*. They sought not just to renew the VRA when it expired in 1982 but to amend it to overturn the Court's limitation of the act to actions based on discriminatory intent.[35] The resulting conflicts further consolidated the modern rival alliances, while demonstrating the surviving power of the race-conscious coalition even during the dawn of the era of color-blind predominance.

The extension of the VRA that race-conscious proponents proposed included a modified Section 2 containing a "results-oriented" standard. The modification used language taken directly from the Supreme Court's ruling in *White v. Regester* that supporters and opponents of the amendment alike saw as likely to foster the creation of majority-minority districts. One factor in deciding whether an electoral system was equally open to participation by all citizens would be "the extent to which members of a protected class" were elected to office.[36] This criterion would again enable advocacy groups and DOJ officials to challenge state districting plans that made the election of blacks or Latinos improbable. The deliberate creation of majority-minority districts would then be the most obvious way to forestall such lawsuits.

Why did race-conscious advocates think they could enact this potent provision in 1982? They believed that an administration then plummeting in the polls would not oppose the VRA's prestige, its attraction to Latino voters, and the civil rights forces in Congress.[37] They turned out to be right. The coalitions on the issue were constituted much as they were on employment and housing (table 6.1). But since most in the color-blind alliance supported the original VRA, they found it hard to oppose renewal, even with the new, more overtly race-conscious Section 2.

The race-conscious alliance did not have the active support of large businesses as it did in the employment area. But many minority-owned businesses supported strengthening the VRA as did the newly active Latino advocacy groups (table 6.2).

Especially in the early 1980s, Ronald Reagan hoped to bolster his support from the expanding pool of Latino voters, whom he knew from his California political experiences to be conservative in many respects.[38] Consequently, he did not wish to appear opposed to renewal of either the original Voting Rights Act or its 1975 amendments. Race-conscious forces in 1982 benefited greatly from the Reagan administration's support for the act's renewal. But the executive branch emphatically did *not* favor the amended Section 2. Reagan's as-

TABLE 6.1
Color-Blind Alliance, 1978–2008: Anti Majority-Minority Districts

Most Republican Party officeholders and members

GOP presidents pro-VRA but against majority-minority districts

Conservative Democrats

Majority of Supreme Court

Most lower federal court judges, many state judges

Conservative and neoconservative think tanks / advocacy groups such as American Enterprise Institute, Institute of Justice

Some businesses (most not active on this issue)

Some Christian Right activists

Fringe white supremacist groups

Conservative foundations (e.g., Bradley Foundation)

Source: Abigail M. Thernstrom, *Whose Votes Count? Affirmatice Action and Minority Voting Rights*, (Cambridge, MA: Harvard University Press, 1987), 85, 97, 103, 107–110, 114–17 (most Republicans, GOP presidents, conservative Democrats); David Michael Hudson, *Along Racial Lines* (New York: Peter Lang, 1998), 143 (most Republicans, conservative Democrats); Institute for Justice, "State of the Supreme Court 2000: The Justices' Record on Individual Liberties," Washington, DC, http://www.ij.org/images/pdf_folder/other_pubs/supreme_court_report_2000. pdf; Edward Blum and Roger Clegg, "*Amici Curiae* Brief in *League of United Latin American Citizens v. Perry*," U.S. Supreme Court Nos. 04-204, 05-254, 05-276, 05-439 (2005) (conservative advocacy groups like the American Enterprise Institute; majority of the Supreme Court, lower court judges); Max Blumenthal, "Avenging Angel of the Religious Right," January 6, 2004, Salon. com, http://salon.com/story/news/feature/2004/01/06/ahmanson, (Christian Right activists); Swain, *New White Nationalism*, 77–81 (white supremacist groups); Lynde and Harry Bradley Foundation, 2007 Bradley Prize Recipients, http://www.bradleyfdn.org/bradley_prizes.asp (conservative foundations) (Bradley Prize awarded to Abigail Thernstrom).

sistant attorney general for civil rights, William Bradford Reynolds, repeatedly criticized the amendment's "results" standard until it became clear the amendments would pass anyway. Conservative Republicans including Strom Thurmond, North Carolina's Jesse Helms and John East, and Utah's Orrin Hatch opposed renewal by focusing on that provision. They claimed the bill set up a "quota" system, despite its express denial of any "right to have members of a protected class elected in numbers equal to their proportion in the population." But when efforts to decouple the new Section 2 from the original act

Chapter 6

Race-Conscious Alliance, 1978–2008: Pro Majority-Minority Districts

---

Most Democratic state and national officeholders, in control of House in 1982

Some Republicans, often pursuing partisan strategies

Some federal, state judges

Many civil service members of executive agencies

Some white and most nonwhite business groups (e.g., National Funeral Directors and Morticians Association)

Most labor unions (e.g., AFL-CIO)

Liberal and left groups such as Common Cause, ACLU, Democratic Socialists

Most nonwhite advocacy groups (e.g., NAACP, MALDEF)

Liberal media (e.g., *New York Times*)

Liberal religious groups (e.g., National Council of Churches, National Council of Catholic Women)

Liberal foundations: Rockefeller, Ford

Source: Thernstrom, *Whose Votes Count?* 80–81, 86–89, 94, 110–11, 118–19 (most Democrats, some Republicans, liberal groups including the ACLU; nonwhite groups including the NAACP and MALDEF; nonwhite business groups such as the National Funeral Directors and Morticians Association; religious groups including National Council of Catholic Women and others; labor unions including AFL-CIO; Ford, Rockefeller foundations); "New Jersey's Redistricting," *New York Times*, May 9, 2001, http://www.nytimes.com/2001/05/09/opinion/new-jersey-s-redistricting. html; "Equal Opportunity," The Leadership Conference, http://www.civilrights.org/equal-opportunity; and "Coalition Members of the Leadership Conference on Cival and Human Rights," The Leadership Conference, http://www.civilrights.org/about/the-leadership-conference/coalition_members (Common Cause, ACLU, unions, nonwhite advocacy groups, liberal religious groups); Democratic Socialists of America, "Where We Stand, Sec. 1: Solidarity," 2006, http://dsausa.org/about/ where.html; Hudson, *Along Racial Lines*, 141 (most Democrats, some Republicans); Valelly, *Two Reconstructions*, 240–43 (some judges).

failed, both chambers voted to extend the amended VRA by huge margins (389–24 in the House, 85–8 in the Senate).[39]

That final voting pattern does indeed cut across racial alliance lines. Nor does it fit the standard picture of modern polarized partisan politics. Does this mean that our racial alliance analysis fails to capture the politics of this major action? Did the Republicans' support indicate that they saw an opportunity in the amendments' stress on success in electing minority candidates? Perhaps they foresaw that legislators could devise apportionment plans that "packed" black and Latino voters into super-majority districts that would elect minorities but take Democratic voters out of competitive races.

There is no direct evidence for such claims. The vote for renewal does not decide the question, because most color-blind proponents as well as race-conscious advocates favored (and still favor) the original VRA. Again, the battles were now over race-conscious measures like majority-minority districting—and here the 1982 coalitions were as anticipated. The legislative history provides scant evidence of conservative plans to use majority-minority districts to hurt Democrats. Neither the White House nor DOJ officials hinted at any benefits from strategic district construction. Instead, Reagan's late and reluctant embrace of Section 2 came only when it clearly would pass in any case.

When Senate Republicans focused their opposition on the "results" provision, moreover, they had broad conservative support. But the GOP's slim Senate majority of fifty-three included liberal Republicans like Rhode Island's John Chafee, Pennsylvania's Arlen Specter, and Maryland's Charles Mathias, the Senate sponsor of the 1982 VRA renewal and amendments. With their aid, race-conscious advocates remained in command of the Senate as well as the House, ultimately compelling many to join their bandwagon. Still, success on Section 2 came in *opposition* to most conservative congressional Republicans and "Old South" Democrats, not in alliance with them.[40] In 1984, the Democratic platform therefore could proclaim that "the statute protecting voting rights has been extended through a massive bipartisan effort, opposed by the Reagan administration," while the Republicans took no credit for the VRA's renewal, much less its amendments.[41] In 1988 the Democrats restated their support for strong voting rights enforcement and in 1992 they urged "stronger protection of voting rights for racial and ethnic minorities, including language access to voting." The Republicans again said nothing about the topic in 1988. In 1992 the GOP condemned "Democrat efforts to perpetuate vote fraud through schemes that override the States' safeguards of orderly voter registration," via efforts to enhance minority voting.[42]

JUDICIALIZING THE 1982 AMENDMENTS: THE GINGLES GUIDELINES

Many of those efforts did help expand the number of nonwhite Democratic voters, and in this achievement, the 1982 amendments had ballast. Presented with a factual situation similar to that in *Mobile v. Bolden*, but now faced with Section 2's modified mandate, the Supreme Court voted 6–3 in *Rogers v.*

Chapter 6

Lodge (1982) to sustain invalidation of a rural Georgia at-large system that had never elected a black candidate. The NAACP LDF, the Lawyers' Committee for Civil Rights Under Law, the Georgia Association of Black Elected Officials, and the Center for Constitutional Rights filed amicus briefs in support of that result.[43] Then, writing for a 5–4 majority in *Thornburg v. Gingles* (1986), Justice William Brennan set out guidelines for finding impermissible vote dilution through multimember districting and other electoral devices, even without a showing of racially discriminatory intent.

Drawing on a 1982 law review article by liberal voting rights lawyers, Brennan stressed three factors. First, a minority group had to "demonstrate that it is sufficiently large and geographically compact to constitute a majority in a single-member district." Second, it must "show that it is politically cohesive," sharing common political interests that were being thwarted. And third, it had to show "that the white majority votes sufficiently as a bloc to enable it . . . usually to defeat the minority's preferred candidate."[44] In formulating these *Gingles* guidelines, the majority justices aimed to prevent racially exclusionary districting. But to avoid violating these new guidelines, designers of legislative districts would clearly have to be conscious of racial voting patterns and the probable racial consequences of different districting systems, and they were likely to design majority-minority districts to promote minority representation.

The *Gingles* case is significant for another reason: it is indeed an example of "strange bedfellow" coalitions on voting rights, more than "racial policy alliances." A North Carolina General Assembly controlled by largely white Democrats had drawn the multimember districts that black citizens challenged, and the state's Democratic attorney general, Lacy Thornburg, appealed the district court's initial ruling that the districts were discriminatory in the "totality of the circumstances." The Supreme Court affirmed the lower court. It rejected briefs representing "color-blind constitutionalism" from the Reagan Justice Department and the Washington Legal Foundation that supported the North Carolina Democrats. The Court's stance was urged by briefs from typical members of the race-conscious alliance, the ACLU, the Lawyers' Committee for Civil Rights Under Law, and Common Cause; but here they were joined by North Carolina's Republican governor James G. Martin and the Republican National Committee, both siding with the black voters' challenge to the white Democrats' districting, against the Reagan administration.[45] There can be little doubt that, unlike the Reagan Justice Department, these Republicans *did* see a strategic opportunity to divide and conquer Democrats and to overturn Democratic apportionment plans through supporting these strongly race-conscious "disparate impact" voting challenges.

180

The decisive issue, however, is not whether some Republicans supported more race-conscious positions because they *hoped* they would be able to forge alliances with blacks and Latinos on districting. It is whether Republicans in practice *were* able to do so—whether their ideas of desirable majority-minority districts matched those of African Americans and Latinos—and whether as a result, the GOP as a whole refused to champion color blindness in this area. The evidence does not suggest that either of these things occurred.

With the *Gingles* guidelines in place, state legislators used the 1990 census to redraw fourteen U.S. House districts to make it more possible for African Americans to get elected and to improve the chances of Latinos, while concurrently creating many new majority-minority state and local electoral districts.[46] Sixteen new black congressional representatives then won election in 1992, twelve from southern or border states (one new majority black district in Philadelphia elected a white Democrat, and new black representatives in Illinois and California replaced African American predecessors).[47] Eight new Latino representatives were elected, while two Latinos succeeded co-ethnic predecessors.[48] In state legislatures, the number of black lawmakers increased by almost 50 to 530 and Latinos to 156.[49] Undeniably, after the 1982 amendments and their initial interpretation by the Supreme Court, majority-minority legislative districts promoted much greater (though still not proportionate) racial representation in legislatures.

Even so, scholars Carol Swain, David Lublin, and others contend that Republicans seized the opportunity provided by the 1982 amendments to create "max-Black" and "max-Latino" districts from the early 1990s, with approval from the Republican-controlled Justice Department up to 1993, and in alliance with nonwhite Democrats.[50] These scholars argue that the new districts increased the numbers of nonwhite legislators but also enhanced the power of Republicans versus Democrats, contributing to the historic GOP takeover of Congress in the 1994 elections. Although neither Swain nor Lublin systematically documents such Republican schemes, their claim has force. Though most GOP leaders continued in principle to oppose race-conscious districting, the Republican National Committee and GOP partisans in many states did seek to maximize their power under the new VRA rules of the game, as the briefs in the *Gingles* case reveal.[51]

Rarely, however, did these efforts produce sustained "unholy alliances" of Republicans and blacks and Latinos working across racial alliance lines that actually agreed on particular ways to create majority-minority districts and successfully enacted them. We base that conclusion on case studies of the fourteen states that created majority-minority congressional districts between 1990 and 1992, and on surveys of all states that had majority-minority districts (table 6.3). In congressional districting, the Department of Justice's Civil Rights Division posed only three challenges to post-1990 state plans, in Alabama, Georgia, and North Carolina.[52] The DOJ's deliberate impact on the makeup of Congress therefore was slight. The Civil Rights Division did object to districting plans at some level in thirteen states overall. Many have argued that under the first President Bush until 1993, the division challenged only plans that helped Democrats, as in *Gingles*, while upholding "strange bedfellow" plans that benefited Republicans.[53]

But that claim requires the presumption that the Reagan Justice Department, which supported the Democratic multimember districts in *Gingles*, was much less partisan and more principled than the Bush DOJ a few years later. Bernard Grofman, Lisa Handley, and Mark Posner, among others, dispute this proposition. In a more plausible explanation they argue that while the top Justice Department leadership is politically appointed and sometimes partisan, the Civil Rights Division has long been staffed chiefly by civil service professionals, many liberals, who do the work on districting. These officials employed the 1982 amendments in the early 1990s chiefly to address long-standing problems of severe minority underrepresentation.[54] After 1993, moreover, the Clinton Justice Department was hardly likely to champion any Republican/black-Latino challenges to districts benefiting the Democratic Party, at least not on partisan grounds. Nor did the federal courts hear many cases brought by minority voters and race-conscious advocacy groups who were backed by Republican Party briefs. *Gingles* is atypical.

The tougher question is whether Republican legislators worked with nonwhite Democrats at the state level to create majority-minority districts that harmed white Democrats. In half of the fourteen states that created new congressional districts, we do find attempts at "unholy alliances." But usually these efforts failed, because GOP and black and Latino leaders had very different ideas of desirable majority-minority districts. Alliances created districts that Republicans and minorities jointly favored in, at most, three states.

These patterns are unsurprising. Nine of these were border or southern states that together accounted for thirteen of the fourteen new black districts and two of the nine new Latino districts. White Democrats controlled these legislatures sufficiently to override Republican/black alliances.[55] In 1992 Democrats still controlled every legislative chamber in the South except for the Florida Senate. By 2002 Republicans had gained control of thirteen out of thirty-two, showing clear GOP progress.[56] But this progress did not come because Republicans and nonwhite Democrats outvoted white Democrats on districting plans. Instead, these trends arose from the general gains of Republicans

TABLE 6.3

"Unholy Alliances" in States Creating New Majority-Minority Districts, 1990–92

State	Alliance Formed	DOJ Objection	GOP Helped
1. Alabama	no	yes	yes
2. California	no	no	no
3. Florida	**yes**	no	**unclear**
4. Georgia	**limited**	*yes*	**yes**
5. Illinois	no	no	yes
6. Louisiana	yes	no	no
7. Maryland	no	no	no
8. New Jersey	limited	no	no
9. New York	no	no	no
10. North Carolina	yes	yes	no
11. Pennsylvania	no	no	no
12. South Carolina	**yes**	no	**minimal**
13. Texas	no	no	no
14. Virginia	limited	no	no

Source: Richard L. Engstrom and Jason E. Kirksey, "Race and Representational Districting in Louisiana," in *Race and Redistricting in the 1990s*, ed. Bernard Grofman (New York: Agathon Press, 1998), 240–42 , David Lublin, *The Paradox of Representation* (Princeton, NJ: Princeton University Press, 1997), 104–6, 111–12 (Alabama); Morgan Kousser, "Reapportionment Wars: Party, Race, and Redistricting in California, 1971–1992," in Grofman, ed., *Race and Redistricting*, 187 (California); Bill Moss, "Redrawn Districts Help GOP, Minorities," *St. Petersburg Times*, November 15, 1992, 1B; Lublin, *Paradox*, 112 (Florida); Carol M. Swain, *Black Faces Black Interests* (Cambridge, MA: Harvard University Press, 1995), 232, Lublin, *Paradox*, 111; Robert A. Holmes, "Reappointment Strategies in the 1990s: The Case of Georgia," in Grofman, ed., *Race and Redistricting*, 216–17, 226–28 (Georgia); Charles N. Wheeler III, "Redistricting '91: "The World Series of Illinois Politics," http:// www.lib.niu.edu/1992/ii921110.html (Illinois); Engstrom and Kirksey, "Race and Representational Districting," 234–64, Lublin, *Paradox*, 112 (Louisiana); Donald Stokes, "Is There a Better Way to Redistrict?" in Grofman, ed., *Race and Redistricting*, 361–64 (New Jersey); Alan Gartner, "New York City Redistricting," in Grofman, ed., *Race and Redistricting*, 371; Mark A. Posner, "Post-1990 Redistrictings and the Preclearance Requirement of Section 5 of the Voting Rights Act" in Grofman, ed., *Race and Redistricting*, 103–4 (New York); Patrick J. Sellers, David T. Canon, and Matthew M. Schousen, "Congressional Redistricting in North Carolina," in Grofman, ed., *Race and Redistricting*, 269–89 (North Carolina); Lublin, *Paradox*, 31 (Pennsylvania); Burton, "Legislative and Congressional Districting," 294–311; Lublin, *Paradox*, 112 (South Carolina); Swain, *Black Faces Black Interests*, 198; Lublin, *Paradox*, 32 (Texas); Winnett W. Hagens, "The Politics of Race: The Virginia Redistricting Experience, 1991–1997," in Grofman, ed., *Race and Redistricting*, 322–36 (Virginia).

among white voters in the United States and especially the South, as even David Lublin concedes.[57]

Again, we agree that many "unholy alliances" were *tried*. A few succeeded. Florida Republicans and black Democrats joined to fight a plan written by the Democratic legislature. The courts threw out that plan and upheld a new one largely written by the GOP. It paired two black districts with two Cuban American ones that would vote Republican. The next election saw increases in black and Hispanic representatives at both the congressional and state levels, and it increased GOP representation.[58] Still, Lublin concedes that "it is not clear" how much the redistricting hurt Florida Democrats.[59]

Republicans and African Americans also voted together to support majority-minority districts in South Carolina, but black Democrats came to see that strategy as misguided.[60] In North Carolina, suspicious of the white Democratic majority, a few blacks joined Republicans on some redistricting issues; but most opposed all plans that might increase Republican power. The state added two black U.S. representatives while losing no Democratic seats in 1992, though Republicans did gain five seats in their sweeping 1994 capture of the House.[61] In Virginia, the creation of a black majority congressional district did not produce partisan change in the state's delegation. A GOP/black alliance briefly surfaced in Virginia State Senate districting, but the final plan did not obviously aid Republicans.[62] In 1991–92, Georgia Democrats sought to harm Newt Gingrich's chances via congressional redistricting, while black legislators pushed for more majority-minority districts. The Bush DOJ's objections did enable the black legislators to prevail. In the next election, both blacks and the GOP increased their representation. But by then the Supreme Court, dominated by Republican appointees and ever more committed to color-blind principles, had begun invalidating majority-minority districts. It ruled in *Miller v. Johnson* (1995) that the DOJ had pushed too hard to establish them.[63] That ruling required another redistricting round, when a black-GOP alliance again surfaced briefly, but the alliance disintegrated as it became clear that Republicans would benefit more than blacks.[64]

In Alabama, a federal court ordered adoption of a GOP plan that created one majority black district—*rejecting* an alternate plan put forth by African Americans. The plan helped Republicans in 1992, but there was no unholy alliance.[65] In Louisiana, conservative white Democrats and all House Republicans supported a plan for the state House that did not create the sort of majority-minority districts that black legislators sought. The Louisiana Legislative Black Caucus unanimously opposed this proposal and lost. The DOJ then objected to the Louisiana plan, siding with the black legislators *against* local Republicans. The legislature finally adopted a plan that distributed African

American voters more efficiently, with strong black legislative backing and divided support in both parties. An African American / Republican coalition versus white Democrats did materialize in support of a Louisiana congressional plan, but ensuing litigation resulted in a plan favored by most Republicans and white Democrats and opposed by most black legislators.[66] In Texas, though redistricting produced a new black and a new Latino majority district in 1992, black leaders did not support extensive creation of majority-minority districts, and Republicans gained no seats.[67]

In Maryland, which created a new black majority district, redistricting did cause an incumbent Democrat to lose to an incumbent Republican; but the redistricting was driven by the governor's desire to protect a different Democrat.[68] In California, some black Republicans spoke in favor of GOP apportionment plans in 1991. But those plans scattered African American and Latino voters far more than Democratic proposals, so most blacks and Latinos opposed them.[69] In Illinois, a GOP-majority Redistricting Commission redistricted the state legislature, and when the state's Democratic House and Republican Senate could not agree on a congressional plan, a three-judge panel adopted one favored by Republicans. The GOP plans for both the state legislative and congressional districts did create majority-minority black and Latino districts, but blacks and Hispanic plaintiffs attacked the state legislative plan, to no avail. All parties supported the Latino district in the GOP congressional plan. Republicans benefited from the new districts, but not via an unholy alliance.[70] In Pennsylvania, a district drawn by Democrats to have a nonwhite majority still reelected its white Democratic incumbent. In New Jersey, the GOP wooed NAACP support for their state legislative plan, and congressional redistricting made a Democratic seat vulnerable, so that a Republican held it briefly from 1995 to 1997. But the plans adopted by the state's Apportionment Commission did not give either Republicans or Democrats all they wanted.[71] In New York, Democrats *increased* their congressional representation in 1992, and districting struggles at other levels were minority versus minority—generally blacks versus Latinos—not unholy alliances.[72]

THE SUPREME COURT AND MAJORITY-MINORITY DISTRICTS

The deliberate creation of majority-minority districts, whether for purposes of increased nonwhite representation or partisan advantage, became increasingly difficult as the 1990s proceeded, in ways that have endured ever since. With the appointment of five justices by Republican presidents Reagan and Bush (Sandra Day O'Connor, Antonin Scalia, Anthony Kennedy, David

Souter, and Clarence Thomas), the Supreme Court quickly opposed the spate of majority-minority districts, both black and Latino, purposefully created after the 1990 census.

Justice Sandra Day O'Connor wrote the opinion for the Court and GOP appointees provided all five votes for the narrow majority in *Shaw v. Reno* (1993), restricting the use of race as a factor in constructing districts.[73] North Carolina had received an extra congressional seat after the 1990 census, and the state legislature had created one majority black district. Given that North Carolina had failed to elect any African Americans since the end of the nineteenth century, the DOJ Civil Rights Division urged the creation of an additional majority-minority district. The state legislature approved one, albeit one that was weirdly shaped in order to include geographically dispersed black voters. This time the briefs corresponded with the composition of the modern racial alliances: the Republican National Committee and the Washington Legal Foundation, joined as they increasingly have been by the American Jewish Congress, filed on behalf of white litigants challenging the additional majority-minority district, while the Democratic National Committee, the NAACP LDF, and the Lawyers' Committee for Civil Rights Under Law filed in opposition.[74] Though Justice O'Connor refused to hold that "race-conscious state decisionmaking is impermissible in all circumstances," as many of the briefs for the white litigants urged, she found the oddly shaped North Carolina district "irrational." She concluded that "it can be understood only as an effort to segregate voters into separate voting districts because of their race," violating the equal protection clause.[75]

Kindred judgments, mostly by 5–4 votes, have followed since that time, including *Holder v. Hall* (1994), *Miller v. Johnson* (1995), *Bush v. Vera* (1996), *Reno v. Bossier Parish School Board* (2000), *Georgia v. Ashcroft* (2003), and *Bartlett v. Strickland* (2009).[76] In *Holder v. Hall*, where a 5–4 majority found that a Georgia county had not violated the VRA when it refused to replace an at-large, single commissioner system of county governance with a multidistrict commission, Justices Clarence Thomas and Antonin Scalia supported the result, but pushed for an even more strongly color-blind position. They insisted that the whole idea that any form of vote "dilution" violated the VRA was misguided, and that efforts to design mechanisms to remedy vote dilution prompted federal courts "to segregate voters into racially designated districts to ensure minority electoral success. In doing so, we have collaborated in what may aptly be termed the racial 'balkaniz[ation]' of the Nation."[77] Though Thomas and Scalia have since regularly endorsed this position, the majority has never gone so far as to rule that race-conscious measures to defeat vote dilution, including majority-minority districts, are *always* unconstitutional. Few such measures, however, have survived judicial scrutiny, and the Court has resisted efforts to apply the VRA to other perceived forms of vote dilution. Although color-blind proponents have not fully prevailed, they have largely halted the race-conscious alliance's pursuit of more extensive majority-minority districting and kindred changes in electoral systems.

In *Miller v. Johnson*, for example, the Civil Rights Division under both Bush and then Clinton had used its pre-clearance authority to insist on the creation of further majority-minority congressional districts to enhance the effective voting power of black voters in Georgia. White voters objected, and in upholding their complaints, Justice Kennedy clarified for the Court's majority that majority-minority districts did not have to have a "bizarre" shape, as in *Shaw*, to be unjustified. If race was the "predominant, overriding factor" in districting, only the strongest possible showing of necessity to remedy proven discrimination could justify such districting, and the majority did not find it in the case at hand.[78] In *Bush v. Vera*, the Court affirmed that in most circumstances, legislative pursuit of a variety of apportionment goals including deliberate political gerrymandering, protection of incumbents, and the predominance of the two major parties would not invoke strict scrutiny and presumptive equal protection violations. The majority conceded that race could be one factor among these motives in legislative districting; but if race were the "predominant" motive, the demanding standards of *Shaw* and *Miller* would apply.[79]

In decisions since the 2000 census and subsequent redistricting, novel but related issues have arisen. The Court's response has been much the same. In *Georgia v. Ashcroft* (2003), the Court showed that if a Democratic legislature, with near-unanimous support of its black members and the opposition of all its Republican ones, chooses to limit the number of super-majority black districts and to create more districts in which black voters have substantial "influence," the Court will subject that race-conscious districting to strict scrutiny, even though it operates to increase, not limit, minority political influence.[80] But a 5–4 majority ruled in *Bartlett v. Strickland* (2009) that the Voting Rights Act did not require close scrutiny of a state legislative plan that failed to create many such "crossover" or "influence" districts, in which minority voters were likely to be able to elect their preferred candidates because they would be able to form coalitions with like-minded white voters.[81]

Throughout these cases, opponents and supporters of particular rulings have been consistently arrayed in accordance with the modern racial alliance, with few if any "strange bedfellows." It has been liberal black and white Democrats, liberal advocacy groups like Common Cause and the ACLU, and black, Mexican

American, and Puerto Rican civil rights groups who have supported majority-minority districts and other race-conscious means to empower minority voters.[82] Conservatives allied with the GOP and conservative foundations like the Washington Legal Foundation, the Institute for Justice, the American Enterprise Institute, and the Center for Equal Opportunity have opposed them.[83] And to many in the race-conscious coalition, these decisions present a pattern in which race-conscious efforts to design districts and electoral systems to increase the influence of minority voters have been subjected to a far higher and usually fatal standard of scrutiny than plans that officially ignore concerns for their racial consequences and simply seek to aid the party, parties, or officials in power.

That is why we conclude that, by and large the limited strange bedfellow politics on voting rights in the early 1990s did not last. After the 2000 census, Republicans did seek again to increase black majorities in certain districts in order to weaken their influence in others, and they once more sought African American allies. They might well have succeeded with even the limited black support they had in the 1990s. But many race-conscious advocates concluded that, even though they wished for the deliberate creation of majority-minority districts to be a legal option, often their interests were better served through different strategies. As in the *Georgia v. Ashcroft* case, the prevalent pattern was for blacks to join white Democrats in seeking to *reduce* some black "supermajority" population concentrations in order to strengthen the prospects of Democrats generally. In consequence, the theme of post-2000 redistricting was much more incumbency protection and creation of minority "influence" districts rather than the advancement of new majority-minority districts.[84]

Perhaps because the battle lines over voting rights became less sharply drawn in the latter part of the 1990s than they had been at the beginning of the decade, neither party said anything on the subject in their 1996 or 2000 platforms.[85] After the extraordinary 2000 election and its charges of suppression of minority voting in Florida and elsewhere, both parties in Congress supported and President Bush signed the Help America Vote Act (HAVA). HAVA established the bipartisan U.S. Election Assistance Commission to give guidance to states and localities on conducting fair and accurate elections.[86] In 2004 the Republican platform acknowledged that many "African Americans, Hispanics, and others fear they may lose the right to vote because of inaccurate or insecure technology or because of a rolling back in the gains made by the passage of civil rights legislation."[87] The Republicans presented HAVA as their answer. The Democrats, in contrast, called for further "legislative action" and for funding "to ensure that voting systems are accessible, independently auditable, accurate, and secure" and that "every vote is counted fully and fairly." They also promised to reauthorize the Voting Rights Act and "vigorously enforce all our voting rights laws."[88]

THE 2006 VRA RENEWAL

When the VRA then came up for renewal in 2006, as the extension passed in 1982 was due to lapse, the judicial rulings that had read its scope more narrowly probably only enhanced support for it. Race-conscious proponents believed the VRA was still needed in light of these decisions. Color-blind adherents had less fear that it would be used aggressively. The Bush administration supported the act's extension without evident reservations. Nonetheless, GOP members of Congress—no longer joined by many conservative southern Democrats, since many of those districts were held by Republicans—still sought to weaken the VRA, joined by conservative commentators and activist groups. It was still civil rights leaders in the race-conscious alliance including representatives John Lewis, Jesse Jackson, and Andrew Young, joined by Democratic liberals such as Edward Kennedy and moderate Republicans like Arlen Specter, who vigorously championed the act. So did civil rights groups and minority leadership groups like the National Hispanic Caucus of State Legislators and the National Black Caucus of State Legislators.[89]

Because the leadership in both parties agreed on renewal, Congress devoted little attention to the topic. It thereby neglected pertinent questions about whether the "triggering" criteria needed to be updated to address today's problems.[90] But in June 2006, House GOP leaders felt compelled to cancel a vote on the act because it was not clear that most rank-and-file Republicans would support renewal.[91] Republicans then introduced four amendments that would have shortened the period of extension to ten instead of twenty-five years; eliminated multilingual ballot provisions; and helped states to escape from the act's jurisdiction. Nearly 60 percent of House Republicans voted for the shorter extension. More than 80 percent voted for the ban on multilingual ballots, and a majority favored easier "bailout" provisions. Overwhelming Democratic opposition resulted in the defeat of all four amendments. Then the act passed 390–33, with all the negative votes coming from Republicans.[92]

These results show that the VRA remains an enduring achievement of the civil rights era that few color-blind proponents in either party oppose. Even so, the color-blind alliance succeeded in blunting the race-conscious mandate of the 1982 amendments. Many would curtail the act in other ways if they could.

Because they failed to do so, and Justices Thomas and Scalia have not persuaded a majority of the justices to read the VRA as inapplicable to vote dilution, the Supreme Court ruled in *League of United Latin American Citizens (LULAC) v. Perry* (2006) that Section 2 of the VRA voided an effort by Texas Republicans to add Anglo Republican voters to a strongly Latino district in order to aid its Latino GOP incumbent, Henry Bonilla, who had been losing Latino support in recent elections.[93] The Court rejected claims that there was anything inappropriate in the Texas Republicans undertaking a second reapportionment in between censuses after they had acquired more state legislative seats and wished to increase their partisan advantage. But it did apply the *Gingles* criteria and determined that Bonilla's district had been redrawn to limit the influence of a cohesive Latino voting bloc, so the decision was a rare, partial, but still real judicial victory for race-conscious forces.

That case, along with growing controversies over immigration and criminal justice, issues to which we will turn, contributed to the renewed attention both parties gave to voting rights in their 2008 platforms. The Democrats promised they would "fully fund the Help America Vote Act," including "ensuring that all registration materials, voting materials, polling places, and voting machines are truly accessible to . . . citizens with limited English proficiency." They also pledged they would "vigorously enforce our voting rights laws instead of making them tools of partisan political agendas," and they opposed "laws that require identification in order to vote or register to vote, which create discriminatory barriers to the right to vote." They championed a proposed "Count Every Vote Act."[94]

The Republicans' platform was far different in tone and content. It voiced opposition to "attempts to distort the electoral process by wholesale restoration of the franchise to convicted felons, by makeshift or hurried naturalization procedures, or by discretionary ballot-reading by election boards." And it supported "the right of states to require an official government-issued photo identification for voting" and "efforts by state and local election officials to ensure integrity in the voting process and to prevent voter fraud and abuse."[95] Their platform no longer expressed concern for or promised aid to minority voters. Partly due to the sustained opposition of a majority of the Supreme Court, partly due to recalibrations of their political utility, race-conscious proponents no longer pressed the desirability of majority-minority districts.

But these platforms show that disputes over voting rights that focused on the exercise of the suffrage by blacks and Latinos today remain very important to the two major parties and to the broader race-conscious and color-blind alliances with which they have become so closely associated.

The Elusive Postracial Grail

The politics of voting rights, then, reconfigured significantly after 1965, as issues of voting exclusion gave way to questions of vote dilution that many saw
as requiring race-conscious analysis and remedies, including the deliberate
creation of majority-minority legislative districts in some instances. In this
process, voting rights political disputes, like so many others, were structured
deeply though not exclusively by the clash of the modern color-blind and
race-conscious alliances: issues of the electoral structures that confer power
are all too foundational for many politicians to eschew personal or partisan
political advantages in the name of racial principles. The politics of voting
rights has been particularly important in persuading Latino advocacy groups
to become key members of the race-conscious coalition, albeit not without
tensions over whether electoral systems should be designed to benefit blacks
or Latinos most. And the same politics have sometimes meant that Republican politicians have sought to ally with nonwhites on race-conscious districting plans, though the evidence suggests they have had limited success. The
defections of some Republican legislators from commitments to color blindness on this issue have in any case been more than counterbalanced by the
increased insistence of the Supreme Court that race can play only a limited
role in the construction of electoral systems. But the justices have yet to go as
far as the keenest color-blind proponents would have them do: to hold that
race can never be a factor at all.

Here, as elsewhere, it is arguable that both jurisprudential and policy debates over race, districting, and voting rights have been distorted by the clash
of the modern racial alliances—with some color-blind proponents seeking to
invalidate concerns for racial equity even as they accept gross partisanship and
incumbency protection as legitimate districting goals, and some race-conscious
advocates seizing too enthusiastically at times on majority-minority districts as
the road to secure political empowerment for racial and ethnic minorities, as
well as partisan and incumbent advantages. What seems most clear, however,
is that even as issues of American electoral systems and voting rights shift in
their particular content, the broader questions of whether they are being designed in ways that are fair to both whites and nonwhites remain pressing and
contentious. On this most political of all issues, as in regard to so many others,
an America that is not sharply divided by race and on race is nowhere in sight.

Chapter 7

"Our goal is to have one classification—American"
Vouchers for Schools and the Multiracial Census

Redistricting, like a broad range of other legislative and administrative actions, depends on census data. But census measurement is itself an exercise deeply embroiled in the politics of racial equality. In this chapter, census category change is one of two very different issues that share a common feature. They are two of the many less familiar policies on which the modern racial alliances have played unexpected but consequential roles. And they are issues involving dimensions of two of the most important foundational systems in American life: public education, and governmental classification of the population in terms of race and ethnicity.

Education is recognized as fundamental to developing capacities for responsible citizenship, marketable skills, and resources for personal fulfillment in modern America. Governmental racial and ethnic classifications not only determine such key issues as congressional district size, federal grants to states, and affirmative action. They help both to express and to constitute the senses of identity of many Americans. Neither the structure of modern American schooling nor its systems of racial classifications can be grasped without appreciating the roles the modern racial alliances play in the politics that have shaped current policies and practices on those issues.

SCHOOL VOUCHERS

In *The Audacity of Hope*, Barack Obama defended an understanding of the American constitutional system as structured to foster "a conversation, a 'deliberative democracy,' in which all citizens engage in a process of testing their ideas against an external reality, persuading others of their point of view, and building shifting alliances of consent."[1] Obama acknowledged, however, that this vision of constitutional "deliberative democracy" potentially championed "compromise, modesty, and muddling through . . . logrolling, deal-making, self-interest, pork barrels, paralysis, and inefficiency." He did not add "flip-flopping" or "hypocrisy." Instead he argued that such a politics can be true to "our highest ideals." [2] But his efforts to find middle-ground accommodations of conflicting values and interests have often brought such charges. Nowhere has this been more true than in regard to perhaps the most controversial issue in modern educational policies, apart from racial desegregation and affirmative action admissions policies: school vouchers.

In 2007, presidential candidate Obama told both national teacher unions, the American Federation of Teachers and the National Education Association, that he did not support school vouchers—taxpayer-funded scholarships that parents might use to send their children to accredited private schools if they so chose. As Democrats had long contended, Obama expressed fear that such vouchers might endanger public schools. But during his 2008 campaign, Obama told newspaper editors in Milwaukee that if the evidence proved vouchers effective in helping children to learn, he might well change his mind.[3] Both in his campaign and in his first major education speech as president, Obama also supported allowing students to choose to attend publicly funded charter schools, if the schools were rigorously assessed and found to be high performing.[4]

There are many types of charter school and voucher programs. They are often quite distinct, varying in which types of schools are eligible for vouchers, how much public control is exercised over charter schools, and importantly, how much discretion schools have in accepting applicants. Still, politically they are often linked in the minds of both proponents and critics. Many proponents see charter schools and school vouchers as related efforts to improve public schools through the heightened competition and innovation that introducing "choice" is thought to spur—and both charter schools and voucher-funded private schools are generally nonunion institutions that teachers' unions oppose.[5]

But as president, Obama has sharply distinguished the two, favoring charters and opposing vouchers. In 2009 his ally, Illinois senator Dick Durbin, opposed reauthorizing a voucher program in the D.C. public schools created under George W. Bush, and Obama supported Durbin, while characteristically offering a compromise. The president and his secretary of education, Arne Duncan, decided that students currently enrolled in private schools with the aid of vouchers could continue to receive them, but unless Congress voted to reauthorize the program, no new students would receive vouchers.[6] Conservative critics said Obama's "compromise" was really a "political capitulation," an effort to "avoid more bad press" while he neglected "needy, talented minority children" to "please the union bosses."[7] Despite the controversy, with the administration's approval, Democrats in the Senate repeatedly voted not to reauthorize the program, insisting that any value in school choice could best be achieved by encouraging the further growth of public charter schools (a position that displeased teachers' unions).[8]

Here, in contrast to the other issues we have examined, Obama was *not* accused of being unduly "race-conscious." Rather, he was portrayed as a union tool and as an ideologue committed to government solutions to all problems. It might seem, therefore, that a racial alliances analysis can reveal little about the contemporary politics of school vouchers; and it is true that the voucher debate is in many ways *not* about race. Vouchers have always involved disputes over market solutions to public problems and over Catholic schools. The major "race" story in relation to modern public elementary and secondary schools is clearly the long and grim narrative of school racial segregation. That story shows that, more than fifty-five years after *Brown v. Board of Education*, American public schools remain racially segregated in practice, though no longer in law, and indeed in many districts schools are becoming more segregated.[9] In *Parents Involved in Community Schools v. Seattle* (2007), the modern Supreme Court, again elaborating a robust color-blind reading of American constitutional principles, constricted the authority of public school districts to consciously seek to create racially integrated schools.[10] As widely noted, the Court has also limited the use of race-conscious "affirmative action" admission policies in all institutions of higher education receiving public funding, though despite the urging of Justices Scalia and Thomas, it has not wholly invalidated race-conscious admissions.[11]

But precisely because those developments have been so extensively analyzed and because the clash of color-blind versus race-conscious proponents in them is so salient, we focus here on the apparently less obviously racial educational issue of school vouchers—because in reality, most of the groups and institutions active in this area see it as possessing racial dimensions, and they are aligned as on other race-conscious issues. The business sector, always divided, does side more strongly with color-blind forces here than on issues like employment. That defection might appear to ensure success for vouchers, given the general modern predominance of the color-blind alliance. Yet ironically, color-blind advocates have been much less successful in this area because their proposals do not appeal so strongly to white voters as is ordinarily the case.

Though the activists who form the modern racial alliances behave as if this was an issue of support or opposition to race-conscious measures, voters do not. The alliances are thus crucial to the politics of this area, but so far they are not decisive for policy outcomes.

Proposing Vouchers

The idea of school vouchers is not recent. In 1955, economist Milton Friedman urged that all families receive vouchers for each school-age child, to be used for partial financing of education at any public or private school meeting minimal state requirements.[12] Friedman's advocacy was part of his general philosophy to promote market systems. But four years later, Virginia's Prince Edward County closed its public schools to avoid court-ordered desegregation and provided parents with vouchers to attend private academies. Whites used them at segregated schools. Blacks refused them, and many received no education for five years.[13]

This ugly example undercut interest in Friedman's idea. But with the rise of Barry Goldwater's economic libertarian wing of the Republican Party, GOP platforms began to endorse various means of aiding private schools and assisting parents in choosing to send their children to them. In 1964 the Republicans criticized the Democrats for resisting "personal income tax credits for education." Their emphasis then was on higher education, but they later extended this idea to elementary and secondary tuition tax credits, tentatively in 1976, firmly after 1980, when the Republicans denounced Jimmy Carter for opposing them.[14] That year the GOP also criticized "Mr. Carter's IRS" for its "unconstitutional regulatory vendetta" against "independent schools," an apparent reference to the IRS's refusal to grant tax exemptions to private schools and universities thought to be engaged in racial discrimination. Private academies had proliferated in the South in the late 1960s and early 1970s, and they tended to be white, leading the IRS to challenge their tax-free statuses.[15] From 1968 on, the GOP also regularly urged federal aid "to non-public school children," though in 1976 they added the qualifier, "on a constitutionally acceptable basis," as the Supreme Court in the early 1970s proved unsupportive of many forms of aid to private schools.[16]

Ronald Reagan's election in 1980 signaled broader appeal for market alternatives. Republican endorsements of market-oriented education policies became more full-throated. In 1984, the GOP platform applauded "the President's proposal for tuition tax credits." It promised to convert federal "Chapter One grants to vouchers," while contending that civil rights "enforcement must not be twisted into excessive interference in the education process."[17] That year the Democrats addressed the topic of "school choice" for the first time. They acknowledged the importance of private schools, "particularly parochial schools," and supported "constitutional acceptable methods" of aiding "all pupils in schools which do not racially discriminate and excluding all so-called segregation academies."[18] Obviously, the issue of various forms of public aid to private schools remained racially charged. But without addressing those concerns, the Republicans in their 1988 platform repeatedly called for "Choice in education" including "tuition tax credits" and proposed, "States should consider enacting voucher systems or other means of encouraging competition among public schools."[19]

In 1989, Milwaukee, Wisconsin, responded. It pioneered a "Parent Choice" voucher program sponsored in part by an African American Democrat, State Representative Annette "Polly" Williams.[20] At the same time, political scientists John Chubb and Terry Moe published an elaborately argued policy brief for voucher systems, *Politics, Markets, and America's Schools*. Other than contending that race was not associated with student achievement, that book gave little attention to the topic.[21] But Chubb and Moe's work and a surge of related scholarship gave impetus to "school choice" initiatives in the 1990s.

As voucher debates grew, political elites and advocacy groups aligned into polarized camps consistent with the two modern racial alliances. But voters did not. Unlike our other cases, opinion polls have never shown any sharp racial divide on this issue. Though different questions generate different responses, blacks and Latinos seem to support vouchers as much as or more than whites. And from Polly Williams to erstwhile D.C. mayor Anthony Williams, some African American urban leaders have been instigators of voucher systems.[22] As a result, analysts see the fundamental divide in this area as falling between supporters of parochial schools, inner-city parents, and those philosophically committed to personal choice, on the one hand; and secularist civil liberties activists, teachers' unions, school administrators, and those committed to statist approaches to public problems on the other.[23]

Yet everyone—parents, teachers, politicians, judges—understands that, from the Prince Edward County experiment on, some of the main questions about vouchers are whether they facilitate efforts to escape public schools affected by desegregation efforts and whether they will thereby heighten racial inequalities—or whether they will instead improve educational options for nonwhites and help reduce racial gaps in educational achievement. Most recognize that most of the leading alternative proposals for improving inner-city, largely nonwhite schools, short of abandonment, involve increasing their funding in ways that many perceive as race-targeted assistance. Though People for the American Way is motivated partly by religious establishment issues, it has joined with the NAACP to combat vouchers via "Partners for Public Education." The partnership now also includes most, though not all, leading Latino advocacy groups, despite their large Catholic constituencies and documented Latino aversion to predominantly black schools. These groups regularly argue against vouchers on race-conscious grounds, among other reasons, insisting that they will work to the disadvantage of minority students.[24] On the other side, voucher proponent Terry Moe has argued that responsible African Americans and Latino parents would be the chief beneficiaries of market-oriented voucher systems. Moe published an analysis of public opinion in 2001 stressing their strong support.[25]

Vouchers and Racial Alliances

These facts suggest that racial policy concerns have mattered and still matter greatly in the voucher debates, as in other school controversies.[26] But there are other consequential factors at work here. Do the politically active forces allied for and against vouchers nonetheless map closely onto the modern color-blind and race-conscious alliances? If so, are they succeeding in building mass support for their positions in ways comparable to what they are achieving on other issues with racial dimensions?

The answer to the first question is yes. But the answer to the second question is yes and no. In referendum campaigns, race-conscious opponents of vouchers, predominantly Democrats, have proven successful in persuading their constituencies to reject proposals they often initially favored. But color-blind champions of vouchers, chiefly Republicans, have repeatedly failed to win the support of their usual white mass electoral base. The partisan pattern is undeniable: although beginning with Bill Clinton's reelection campaign in 1996, Democratic platforms have moved toward the Republicans by supporting "public school choice," particularly via "charter schools," the Democrats have still often attacked private school vouchers as Republican "efforts to bankrupt the public school system" by taking "American tax dollars from public schools" and giving them to private ones.[27] Republicans have urged the promotion of "choice" in education by numerous means in every platform from 1980 on. These include charter schools but also tax credits and scholarships to attend private schools. The Republicans hold up the D.C. school choice initiative passed under George W. Bush as a model for the nation, while attacking Democrats for opposing it.[28]

As that record indicates, voucher initiatives have been primarily sponsored by Republican legislative officials, often in alliance with conservative Christian religious groups, especially Catholics, and with free market business interests and conservative advocacy groups (table 7.1). But many business groups are noncommittal on vouchers, stressing instead standards and testing.[29] And in sharp contrast to what opinion polls show, again the surprising reality is that

Chapter 7

Table 7.1
Color-Blind Alliance, 1978–2008: Pro-Vouchers

Most Republican Party officeholders and members

Presidents, 1981–93, 2001–9

Most Republicans in Congress after 1994

Some conservative and neoconservative Democrats

Majority of Supreme Court after 1980

Most lower federal court judges, many state judges

Mostly conservative think tanks / advocacy groups, (e.g., Heritage Foundation, Institute of Justice)

Some white and nonwhite businesses

Most Catholic groups

Christian Right groups (e.g., Focus on the Family)

Conservative foundations: Bradley, Walton, others

Source: Along with the sources cited in the text, table 7.1 derives from Lance Fusarelli, *The Political Dynamics of School Choice* (New York: Palgrave Macmillan, 2003), 46–48, 62, 78–79, 101–7 (Most GOP in Congress, some Democrats, Supreme Court, lower courts, Catholics); Thad D. Hall, "Congress and School Vouchers," in *Public School Choice v. Private School Vouchers*, ed. Richard D. Kahlenberg, (New York: Century Foundation Press, 2003), 115–22 (Congress); Angela Gabriel, "School Voucher Program Backed by State Chamber," *Business Journal of Phoenix*, March 19, 1991, http://www.bizjournals.com/phoenix/stories/1999/03/22/story6.html; Glen Warchol, "Business Leaders Tell Latinos to Back Vouchers," *Salt Lake Tribune*, November 2, 2007; (some white and nonwhite businesses); Kevin Schmiesing, "School Choice and the Common Good of All Children," December 3, 2009, Catholic Exchange, http://catholic exchange.com/2009/12/03/124728/ (Catholic groups); Randall Balmer, *Thy Kingdom Come: How the Religious Right Distorts the Faith and Threatens America* (New York: Basic Books, 2006), 90–92 (Heritage Foundation, Christian Right); Walton Family Foundation, "K-12 Education Reform," http://www.waltonfamilyfoundation.org/educationreform/index.asp#3; Lynde and Harry Bradley Foundation, 2007 Bradley Prize Recipients, http://www.bradleyfdn.org/bradley_prizes.asp (Bradley Prize awarded to Clint Bolick of the Institute for Justice for championing vouchers).

when their support has been tested in referenda, most voters in all racial and ethnic groups have opposed vouchers. White voters have been crucial to these results and so to overall policy outcomes on the issue. Even so, the advocacy groups and governing institutions favoring vouchers are the familiar members of the color-blind alliance.

The policy alliance opposed to voucher initiatives, frequently on explicit race-conscious grounds, includes most Democratic state and national officeholders; most African American and Latino civil rights groups; most unions, especially teacher unions; and most liberal policy groups like the ACLU. Asian American voices can be found on both sides of the issue, but it has not been a major concern of leading Asian American political spokespersons or advocacy groups. Liberal and minority businesses have also been less active here (table 7.2).

Some analysts believe that not only nonwhite voters but also advocacy groups for African Americans, Latinos, and Asian Americans are more divided on this issue than on most others, with many increasingly coming to see vouchers as desirable experiments. But this trend is far from clear. The growth of voucher systems has been limited chiefly because white suburban voters often oppose them, whether or not they are included in the systems. No definitive study of these voters' motives exists, and there are many possible explanations for their preferences. Because most live in areas with schools that are overwhelmingly white and well-funded, some may fear that these schools would appear less superior if vouchers were effective in strengthening other schools, thus perhaps lowering their property values or the prestige these schools provide their children. Others may fear that voucher programs would give their tax dollars to religious schools they dislike, or to urban nonwhite students with whom they do not identify, or that the programs might open up their schools to those students. Whatever the reasons, their opposition is pivotal, since the alliances on vouchers resemble those on more explicitly racial issues.

The sharpest evidence suggesting that race is not really important in this area comes in polling data, which consistently confirm that ordinary Americans in all groups express support for vouchers in surveys. The Joint Center for Political and Economic Studies and Phi Delta Kappa / Gallup polls have for some years found that a majority of African Americans support school vouchers and do so in higher percentages than the general population. Polls also show strong Latino support.[30] But the Joint Center results also indicate that most of these respondents acknowledge that they know "very little" to "nothing" about vouchers. Analysts on all sides agree that voucher survey results are in consequence exceptionally affected by how questions are worded and by the alternatives for school reform listed.[31]

And in the eight state referenda on vouchers held from 1972 to 2000, voters rejected voucher plans by large margins, usually 64 percent to 74 percent. The aggregate vote was 68 percent against, 32 percent for, almost the reverse of typical opinion poll results.[32] In the last two major referenda, held in 2000, exit polls indicated that in California 68 percent of African Americans, 77 percent of Latinos, 66 percent of Asian Americans, and 70 percent of Anglo

Chapter 7

TABLE 7.2
Race-Conscious Alliance, 1978–2008: Anti-vouchers

Most Democratic Party officeholders and members

Some federal, state judges

Some liberal Republicans

Many administrators in education agencies

Most labor unions, especially teachers' unions

Minority and liberal businesses (not active)

Most nonwhite advocacy groups (e.g., NAACP, MALDEF)

Liberal advocacy groups (e.g., ACLU, People for the American Way)

Liberal media, some on church / state grounds (e.g., *New York Times*)

Pro-secular and anti-religious groups (Americans for Religious Liberty, American Atheists)

Many liberal religious groups (e.g., United Church of Christ, Hadassah)

Some liberal foundations (e.g., Century Foundation, Ford)

Source: Along with the other sources cited in the text, table 7.2 derives from Fusarelli, *School Choice*, 46–48, 101–8 (some judges, some Republicans, administrators, unions, some businesses, anti-Catholics); "Parochial School Vouchers," *New York Times*, August 29, 1999, http://www.ny times.com/1999/08/29/opinion/parochial-school-vouchers.html?emc=eta1; Edd Doerr, "School Vouchers: Give Us Your Money!" Americans for Religious Liberty, http://www.arlinc.org/articles/ article_giveyourmoney.html (Americans for Religious Liberty); American Atheists, "Atheist Group Cautions U.S. Civil Rights Commission on Voucher Schemes," http://www.atheists.org/ press_releases/Atheist_Group_Cautions_U.S._Civil_Rights_Commission_on_Voucher_ Schemes%2C_Defends_Ban_on_Public_Fundin (anti-religious groups); American Civil Liberties Union, "Coalition Letter to Omnibus Conference Opposing D.C. Vouchers," November 18, 2002, http://www.aclu.org/religion/vouchers/16099leg20031118.html (administrators, ACLU, UAW, teachers' unions, People for the American Way, religious groups); School Success Info.org, "About Us" (NAACP, MALDEF); Richard D. Kahlenberg, ed., *Public School Choice v. Private School Vouchers* (New York: Century Foundation Press, 2003) (Century Foundation); Janice Patrovich, "Strategies for Improving Public Education: A Foundation Returns to School, "Ford Foundation, 2008, http://www.fordfoundation.org/pdfs/library/strategies_improving_public_education .pdf.

200

voters opposed vouchers, while in Michigan 77 percent of African Americans and 69 percent of whites voted against them.[33] In the wake of these crushing defeats, voucher advocates largely stopped trying to win via popular referenda — the reverse of the pattern in regard to race-conscious employment programs. Though Utah voucher advocates did offer a new referendum in 2007, only to lose by 62 percent to 38 percent, since 2000 most proponents have shifted to legislative strategies in which vouchers are added to omnibus education bills.[34] The coalitions in these legislative processes clearly map onto today's racial alliances.

In 1992 two leading Republicans, Texas's Dick Armey in the House and Utah's Orrin Hatch in the Senate, first sponsored federal voucher proposals. They had support from a few moderate Democrats including Senators Joseph Lieberman (now an independent) and Bill Bradley (now a former senator), along with one African American Republican and one Hispanic Republican in the House. But liberal Republicans such as Senators Mark Hatfield, Jim Jeffords, and Arlen Specter (now a former Democratic senator), along with most Democrats, voted to defeat the voucher bills. The negative votes included twenty black, ten Hispanic, and two Asian American representatives.[35] That pattern held through annual votes on voucher bills from 1994 through 1997. Despite gaining control of Congress, Republicans did not have majorities for national voucher plans. Congress did pass a bill creating a voucher plan for the District of Columbia in 1998 that President Clinton vetoed. Armey then tried to add vouchers to the Bush administration's general education package in 2001, initially without success.

Voucher advocates faced strong opposition from nonwhites in Congress. To counter this resistance, voucher proponents in these years sought to show that they had support from nonwhite publics and their advocacy groups like the Black Alliance for Educational Options (BAEO), founded in 2000, and the Hispanic Council for Reform and Educational Options (HCREO), founded in 2001. Like Moe, they increasingly contend that vouchers are the best system to aid long-disadvantaged racial and ethnic minorities. But critics noted that the conservative Bradley Foundation and Walton Family Foundation heavily funded the BAEO, in just the way the Bradley Foundation had backed the initial Milwaukee voucher plan in 1989.[36] HCREO, also supported by those same foundations, describes itself as a D.C.-based lobbying group founded by a small number of wealthy Hispanics unhappy because most Latino advocacy groups oppose vouchers.[37]

In contrast, in accord with the NAACP / People for the American Way's joint anti-voucher campaign, leading Latino organizations including MALDEF, the League of United Latin American Citizens (LULAC), and a range of other minority organizations have organized against national and state voucher laws, with the National Council of La Raza officially taking no position but expressing concerns.[38] There can be little doubt that on the whole, the leading nonwhite advocacy groups have worked together against vouchers and have been winning with their voters, while the small black and Hispanic groups who champion vouchers rely heavily on support not from their communities but from conservative, predominantly white foundations.

That pattern is also visible in the litigation leading to the major Supreme Court decision on vouchers, *Zelman v. Simmons-Harris* (2002). There the Republican-dominated bench upheld a Cleveland voucher plan against objections that it improperly aided parochial schools. School officials, the NAACP, and groups championing separation of church and state filed briefs against the program. The U.S. Conference of Catholic Bishops, the Cato Institute, the Friedman Foundation, and other conservative groups filed for it.[39] The Court's affirmation bolstered the political elites and activists on the voucher side.

Republicans then pushed through another D.C. voucher plan, eventually termed the "D.C. Opportunity Scholarship Program," in 2003 by a House vote of 205–203. The Senate approved it in early 2004 as part of a general D.C. budget bill. President George W. Bush signed it into law. And the Republicans celebrated it in their 2008 platform—though many vouchers then went unused, and an early report by the Cato Institute faulted the program's efficacy, a view challenged by some later evaluators.[40] Passage came only after D.C. mayor Anthony Williams, the school superintendent, and a leading council member endorsed the voucher proposal, thereby legitimating it as supported by local black leadership. But most members on the D.C. Council still opposed it, as did D.C.'s nonvoting delegate to Congress, Eleanor Holmes Norton. Norton denied the plan had widespread local African American support. The Bush administration lobbied strongly for the bill, presenting it as a key test of party loyalty.[41] In the House, voting ran almost wholly on party lines, with only 4 Democrats voting with the 201 Republicans who supported the plan, and only 14 Republicans voting against it. Among those opposing the bill were 35 of 36 African Americans, as well as Hispanics (including 3 Republicans), 17–4. Asian Americans voted no 3 to 0.[42] Victory did come, then, with the aid of a black urban leader and four Hispanic congressmen, two from each party. But this was a GOP measure, introduced by a Virginia Republican, Tom Davis, and vigorously opposed by virtually all Democrats, blacks, and Latinos in the Congress. Republican control of the House and Senate ensured that they carried the day—until Obama and the Democrats came to power after the 2008 election. At this writing, when all the students already in D.C. private schools with the aid of these federal vouchers complete high school, the program will expire. Even so, voucher proposals are unlikely to die. But given their poor track record in referenda, it is probable that debates over educational reform will focus on other topics, including charter schools, at least for a time.

Despite the complexities of vouchers as a policy and political issue, in elite political action on voucher proposals, alignments have corresponded to the modern era's racial alliances. And it is the institutional center of the modern color-blind order, GOP control of state and national legislatures, that accounts for the slow but continuing progress of this controversial policy during the 1990s and early 2000s. But because voters know little about the issue, and white voters do not see it as presenting a choice between color-blind and race-conscious alternatives (indeed, they may see vouchers as most assisting non-whites), here the color-blind racial alliance lacks the electoral support that sustains its rise in other arenas. Whether this pattern represents an appropriate policy outcome, as most activists in the race-conscious alliance believe, or one that has been distorted by modern racial politics, as many in the color-blind coalition conclude, very much remains in dispute.

Census Categorizations

In 2008, the Democratic Party platform promised to make the U.S. census "more culturally sensitive, including outreach, language assistance, and increased confidentiality protections to ensure accurate counting of the growing Latino and Asian American and Pacific Islander populations." The party assured voters that those efforts would include "enforcement on disaggregation of Census data" to describe better racial and ethnic identities.[43] This provision represented the first time either of the two modern major parties had addressed the topic of race and the census in their quadrennial platforms. It implied a goal of achieving fuller official recognition of the racial and ethnic diversity of modern America.

On March 29, 2010, President Barack Obama answered question 9 on the U.S. census form, which asked him to identify his "race." Obama's mixed-race parentage entitled him to check "White"; "Black, African Am., or Negro"; or both categories, and he also had the choice of checking "some other race" and then, if he wished, specifying that "other race," either singly or in combination with either "White," "Black, African Am., or Negro," or both. The president had, then, a wide range of options. Filling out his form quickly while cameras clicked, Obama marked only one box, "Black, African Am., or Negro" (the last term reportedly maintained due to the Census Bureau's perception of the preferences of older blacks).[44] The president may have done so out of a strong sense of self-identification; or because he knew that if he checked that box at all, he would be counted as "Black" for most federal administrative purposes; or because he believed that many in his political base would be offended if he identified otherwise. He may have done so with some inner misgivings or, as his press secretary Robert Gibbs implied, without hesitation.[45] But in any case, as a political figure who has faced suspicions about being both "not black enough" and "too black," Obama must have been aware of how the choice before him had been shaped by the politics of today's racial alliances.[46]

Yet even though census racial classifications are obviously about race, it is not at first glance obvious why the racial alliances have taken the positions on census categories that they have and why race-conscious proponents, in particular, largely favor Obama answering as he did. More than a decade before, many with backgrounds similar to Obama's sought to structure census options, and choices of racial identity in the United States more broadly, differently. Beginning in the late 1980s and especially in the mid-1990s, a growing number of Americans who did not see themselves as belonging to either side of the black/white binary generated a movement to add a "mixed race" category to the 2000 census. That movement failed to achieve its goal but won a lesser change sustained on the 2010 census form: agreement to permit persons to check more than one racial box. Since then, and especially since Obama's election, commentators have speculated that these developments, along with others, portend the transcendence of traditional American racial identities. If so, these changes might mean that in the foreseeable future, we will come to view the sorts of racial alliances we depict here as, at best, fast-fading relics of a divided American past.

But President Obama's example and other evidence in fact show that something close to the opposite is the case. When it comes to mobilized political activities, rather than social self-identifications, people are still largely aligning themselves in terms of the racial alliances that emerged in the mid-1970s. Even as he offers the promise of greater racial harmony and national unity, President Obama still depicts himself and is commonly depicted as the first black president far more frequently than as the first mixed-race president. And though efforts to include "two or more races" categories on governmental forms and public opinion surveys have had real impact, in the wake of these changes, it is not the color-blind/race-conscious alliances, but the organizations that campaigned intensely for a "mixed race" census category in the 1990s, that have faded.

"Mixed race" campaigners correctly perceive the census as crucial for racial matters. By collating information about Americans in categories of groups, censuses compile the data with which to map group sizes and boundaries in the nation. And though de jure segregation and traditional racial discrimination are now illegal, racial classifications still play a central role in many public policies. To enforce anti-discrimination laws, protect voting rights, monitor educational, economic, and medical progress, promote inclusive housing, and implement affirmative action measures, among other programs, government agencies such as the Equal Employment Opportunity Commission, the Office of Federal Contract Compliance Programs, and the Department of Justice must differentiate among American citizens by race and ethnicity, principally through the nation's shifting decennial census categories.[47] All recent censuses and their inter-census published supplements prompt newspaper headlines about the most salient trends in racial and ethnic group sizes and the policy questions they pose.

Few deny today that census categories long served as a lynchpin of the white supremacist order. The census specifications of the degree of African ancestry, such as the 1890 categories of "quadroons" and "octoroons," provided states with the information they used to define eligibility and ineligibility for various political, legal, and economic rights. Despite the influence of the "one drop of black blood" conception of racial identities, state laws long differed in their definitions of whether one needed to be one-sixteenth, one-eighth, or one-quarter or more "African" to be "black."[48] The anti-segregation forces that gained power in the civil rights era rejected the uses to which those census categories had been put in the Jim Crow era. They were able to persuade federal policymakers to allow persons to choose their own racial designations on the census forms from 1960 on, rather than having their race assigned to them by census takers on the basis of their phenotypes.[49] That shift marked a rejection of biological conceptions of race—but not of racial categories, to which most Americans still voluntarily assigned themselves. And civil rights advocates soon decided that they needed data organized by race to pursue their egalitarian goals effectively.

THE OMB's DIRECTIVE NO. 15

Officials convened a Federal Interagency Committee on Education in 1964 to revise census classifications for their use in decisions about the allocation of federal funding in a nondiscriminatory way.[50] As advocates for nonwhites turned increasingly to race-conscious programs, it became crucial to define the racial identities of Americans in order to determine eligibility for voting rights protection, educational, employment, housing assistance programs, and other benefits. Eventually in 1977, the Office of Management and Budget (OMB) issued the now-famous Statistical Directive No. 15, specifying four "race" categories: American Indian or Alaskan Native, Asian or Pacific Islander, Black, and White. There were also two "ethnic" identities: Hispanic

Origin and Not of Hispanic Origin.[51] This 1977 scheme provided the definitional basis—or "official racial cosmology"—under which groups could seek recognition to be entitled to group-based federal funds. Though census forms permitted more varied designations, they were organized under these categories, so that Directive No. 15 determined and defined what data were available about race both to policy makers and to scholars.

But by that point, most Latino and Asian American advocacy groups were members of the race-conscious order. In 1980 these groups helped persuade the OMB to extend its directive to include subcategories in the Hispanic and Asian-Pacific Islander categories. Before the 1990 census, the Bureau of the Census condensed the specifications under the Asian American category to save space on the form, permitting respondents to write in related ethnic or subcultural affiliations. This change upset many Asian Americans; many Latinos also felt their identities were not well captured by the four race categories; and the census provided further evidence that many other Americans were unhappy with the available categories, particularly recent immigrants from a wide variety of backgrounds. Roughly a half million respondents ignored instructions to mark only one race and selected more than one designation.[52]

By itself, this number was not so large as to suggest that traditional racial self-categorizations were ceasing. But the dissatisfactions with the census questions expressed by many Latino, Asian American, and immigrant advocates came to be joined in the early 1990s by some small yet active new groups that emerged from 1986 on: the Association of MultiEthnic Americans (AMEA); A Place for Us (APFU); and Project RACE (for "Reclassify All Children Equally"). Political scientist Kim Williams argues that the new pro–mixed race classification advocacy groups "consisted predominantly of white women married to black men," generally middle-class and suburban, who wished to win recognition of their children as having "multiracial," not "black," racial identities.[53] The groups were also small, led by "about twenty people," and operated on "shoestring budgets."[54] Even so, they had some early successes in winning legislative adoption of the multiracial category in six states. They did so generally with Democrat support, because at this early stage, many perceived multiracialism as an extension of the race-conscious civil rights agenda that sought to include still more identities. And because these changes did not affect federal funding or districting or, indeed, many state policies, they mobilized few opposed interests or groups.[55]

All these developments prompted the OMB to ask Congress to hold hearings and authorize the agency to explore changes in its racial classification schemes. This process ran from 1993 through 1997, a period when Democrats controlled the White House but surging Republicans captured Congress. The upshot of this reconsideration was that the OMB adopted a somewhat modi-fied set of categories, "American Indian or Alaskan Native" including Central and South American indigenous peoples; "Asian"; "Black or African Ameri-can"; "Native Hawaiian or Other Pacific Islander"; and "White"; and one cat-egory labeled "ethnic": "Hispanic or Latino." Faced with opposition from older civil rights groups, the OMB refused to place a "multiracial" or "mixed race" box on the census. But it did decide in October 1997 to permit Ameri-cans to check more than one racial category in the 2000 census. The OMB also indicated "other Federal programs" should adopt methods for reporting more than one race "as soon as possible, but not later than January 1, 2003, for use in household surveys, administrative forms and records, and other data collections."[56] Then, in the election year of 2000, the agency adopted a tabula-tion scheme that counted most of those who selected more than one race as racial minorities for purposes of civil rights laws. That rule is why President Obama would have counted as black even if he had checked multiple boxes, so long as one of them was "Black, African Am., or Negro." About 6.8 million people, 2.4 percent of the population, eventually chose to list more than one racial identity in that year's census.[57]

From 2001 through 2005, the OMB call for new systems of racial classifica-tion led many agencies, including the Departments of Justice, Commerce, Agriculture, Health and Human Services, Defense, and Labor, along with the Federal Reserve Board, the Centers for Disease Control, the Food and Drug Administration, and the EEOC, to mandate or recommend that departmental surveys and funded research and employer reporting forms offer "multiracial" or "two or more races" categories, or opportunities to check multiple boxes. Then, in a major policy shift in 2007, the OMB required that by 2010–11, educational institutions from preschool through universities would have to gather and report data using the "two or more races" category. Some states have followed suit. They permit respondents to identify with more than one race on voting registration forms. Officials in most states, however, appear to regard such changes as needlessly costly, if not otherwise undesirable. But a number of public opinion surveys and polls have also begun permitting mul-tiple racial identifications.[58]

How Racial Alliances Persist

For some commentators such as the historian David Hollinger, this multiplication of racial and ethnic categories signals the emergence of a "post-ethnic America." It "favors voluntary over involuntary affiliations, balances an appreciation for communities of descent with a determination to make room for new communities, and promotes solidarities of wide scope that incorporate people with different ethnic and racial backgrounds."[59] Immigration scholar Peter Schuck adds that new "demographics and identities mean that as time goes on, the government's use of the standard racial categories as a pivot of social policy will become ever harder to justify logically and sustain politically."[60] Schuck believes that efforts to sustain those categories will just "further erode the already weak public support for preferences."[61] These views suggest that the multiracial controversy signals the future if not current breakdown of the existing framework of racial alliances in American politics, because new multiracial or postracial identities may be replacing older ones. And because these changes in the census have resulted partly from the emergence of new groups, it may appear that the framework of racial alliances that preceded those groups cannot explain these developments.

Though we agree that the new multiracial advocacy groups, along with concerns to develop classifications satisfactory to immigrants, have been important for this single issue, we disagree with these broader claims for their significance or the contemporary significance of multiracialism more generally. The controversy over mixed race or multiple race demographic categories emerged roughly fifteen years after the coalescence of the modern racial coalitions. It has not engaged or mobilized all groups long associated with both of those alliances: businesses, unions, churches, liberal foundations, and courts have not been active. And it was indeed new groups that spurred discussion of revising racial categories.

But more than many observers have recognized, when the issue reached the federal level, it was taken up and redefined by leaders of the two rival racial alliances in terms of color-blind and race-conscious objectives, with supporters for and against change aligned accordingly. The strength of the color-blind forces in Congress was sufficient to produce some innovations. Still, the alliance of the executive branch, particularly its administrative agencies, with race-conscious proponents meant that the changes were compromises designed to preserve the capacity of the census to inform race-conscious measures, while permitting more registration of multiracial identities.

In contrast to the states in previous years, at the federal level it was conservative GOP leaders and allied groups who proved to be the main political champions of these census category revisions and who have been responsible for the shifts in policies that have resulted (table 7.3).

Their opponents have chiefly been Democrats and the civil rights groups representing Latinos and Asian Americans as well as African Americans that form the core of the modern race-conscious alliance (table 7.4).

TABLE 7.3.
Color-Blind Alliance, 1978–2008: Pro–Mixed Race Census Category (1990–2008)

Most Republican Party officeholders and members after 1995

Some conservative, neoconservative Democrats

A minority of state legislatures

Conservative think tanks / advocacy groups

American Enterprise Institute, Cato Institute, Manhattan Institute

Mixed race advocacy groups (Project RACE, AMEA)

Source: Along with the sources cited in the text, table 7.3 derives from Ben J. Wattenberg, "Did the Confederacy Win?" AEI Online, March 29, 2000, http://www.aei.org/issue/11451 (American Enterprise Institute); Edward L. Hudgins, "Testimony on the Census," Cato Institute, http://www .cato.org/pub_display.php?pub_id=12333 (Cato Institute officer opposing existing racial categories though also racial categories generally, consistent with Newt Gingrich's goal for the mixed race movement); Stephan Thernstrom, "One Drop-Still: A Racialist's Census," April 17, 2000, http://www.manhattan-institute.org/html/_national_review-one_drop-stil.htm (Manhattan Institute, *National Review*).

At the 1993 congressional hearings convened by the Subcommittee on Census and Statistics, participants included many who were not part of the color-blind alliance but who wished to see the census changed to acknowledge specific racial and ethnic identities properly—precisely due to the race-conscious concerns that led them most often to act with the race-conscious alliance on issues generally. For example, Democratic senator Daniel Akaka's testimony about Native Hawaiians expressed widely shared worries about counting Asian Americans accurately. Under Directive 15, the category of Asian/Pacific Islander included Native Hawaiians, misleadingly in Akaka's view. He explained: "While culturally Polynesian, we are descendants of the aboriginal people who occupied and exercised sovereignty in the area that now constitutes the State of Hawaii. Like the varying cultures among the hundreds of American Indian tribes or Alaska Natives, Native Hawaiians also have a unique political and historical relationship with the United States."[62] The classification of Native Hawaiians as Asian/Pacific Islanders perpetuated "the misperception that Native Hawaiians, who number well over 200,000, somehow 'immigrated' to the United States like other Asian or Pacific Island groups, as well the erroneous impression that Native Hawaiians, the original inhabitants of the Hawaiian Islands, no longer exist."[63]

TABLE 7.4
Race-Conscious Alliance, 1978–2008: Anti–Mixed Race
Census Category (1990–2008)

Most Democratic Party officeholders and members after 1995

Many civil service members of executive agencies

Most state budgetary and administrative officials

Most nonwhite advocacy groups: NAACP, Urban League, National Council of La
Raza, MALDEF, Asian American Legal Defense fund

Liberal media (e.g., *New York Times*)

Source: Along with the sources cited in the text, table 7.4 is derived from Jennifer Hochschild and Vesla Weaver, "There's No One as Irish as Barack Obama: The Policy and Politics of American Multiculturalism," *Perspectives on Politics* 8 (2010): 749–50; "Multiracial Americans," *New York Times*, November 8, 1997, http://www.nytimes.com/1997/11/08/opinion/multiracial-americans .html?scp=1&sq=%22Multiracial+Americans%22&st=nyt (arguing for greater recognition of "racial complexity in racial identity" while also arguing that a multiracial category "would not have provided sufficiently specific information" and that care must be taken to avoid diluting "minority numbers" in ways that would impair "fighting discrimination."

All group representatives similarly championed the uniqueness of their group's identity. But these calls for change met little if any resistance from African Americans and their traditional civil rights allies. Such modifications did not threaten and indeed seemed capable of strengthening civil rights enforcement and government aid programs. They only posed queries about administrative feasibility. Even defenders of the extant categories, such as U.S. Commission on Civil Rights official Arthur Fletcher, the erstwhile proponent of the Philadelphia Plan, recognized that those calling for more nuanced classifications had a strong case. Fletcher noted that "the current categories are not adequate for most applications in the civil rights arena, such as civil rights enforcement, education, and outreach efforts."[64] Moreover, he added that "the broad race and ethnicity categories established by Directive 15 conceal extraordinary diversity in the characteristics and civil rights status of the distinct groups composing these categories. Within each of the major race categories and within the Hispanic population, there appear to be major differences in the nature and extent of discrimination as revealed by key socioeconomic outcomes."[65] Traditional civil rights advocates agreed that those differences should be tracked, though they did resist expanding the list of "races" in ways that might place those they considered white in the category of beneficiaries of racial preferences. That is why Hispanics/Latinos succeeded

in getting the census modified to obtain for their group the more specific inclusion afforded to African Americans, even as efforts by some Latinos to be
designated a race, not an ethnic group, did not bear fruit. Hispanic lobbying
to be declared a "race" also faded after tests suggested that fewer would identify with the category if it was termed a "race" rather than an "ethnicity."[66]

In contrast to their support of subcategories, most race-conscious alliance
members saw the movement to create a multiracial box on the census forms
not as a means of race-conscious recognition and assistance but as a threat to
traditional civil rights programs. They almost unanimously opposed it, while
conservative Republicans championed it as a means, ultimately, to color
blindness, in perfect constancy with the racial alliances framework. Starting
in 1993, a Republican representative, Thomas Petri of Wisconsin, began introducing bills to require the OMB to adopt the multiracial category (which
he called the "Tiger Woods" bill).[67] In the 1993 hearings on census categorizations, an OMB official, Norma V. Cantu, expressed the anxieties of many civil
rights advocates about such proposals. While the innovation might assuage
the concerns of parents of mixed race children, it would not help with civil
rights enforcement. Cantu concluded that it would mean creating "a number
of technical problems for OCR's [Office for Civil Rights'] data collections,
and increasing both data collection costs and data burden on respondents."[68]
Billy Tidwell of the Urban League also expressed concern about "the potential impact of such a modification on the representation of 'Blacks' or African
Americans" and on "gains that have accrued to them under the existing reporting system. It would be an unfortunate circumstance, indeed, if changes
in census data collection methodology effectively turned the clock back on
the well-being of a group that has had such distinctive and profound experiences with exclusion and deprivation in this society."[69] Experts who monitored
discrimination and implemented affirmative action policies joined with the
Urban League. Some experts argued that multiracial categories might create
problems in determining discrimination, because victims might be assigned to
a group inappropriately. Arthur Fletcher concluded: "The existing racial and
ethnic groups are extremely diverse. A multiracial category would be even
more so."[70] In 1997, with the executive branch in Democratic hands, a federal
task force representing thirty agencies sided with civil rights groups to oppose
the multiracial category.[71]

But that same year, Republican House Speaker Newt Gingrich saw an opportunity to make political capital from the issue. He responded to the Clinton administration's efforts to sustain alliances with civil rights groups by advocating a ten-point program on racial issues that included ending affirmative
action, adopting school vouchers, and adding the multiracial category to the

census—explicitly linking all of these issues to the goal of color blindness. Gingrich stressed that his advocacy of multiracialism represented not a form of race consciousness but promotion of what he saw as a step toward achieving race-neutral policies: "Ultimately our goal is to have one classification—American."[72] Gingrich contacted Franklin Raines, head of the OMB, to pressure the agency to make this change and also promised legislation to bring it about. Gingrich was supported by the Libertarian Party, which similarly hoped that with increased use of this novel category, "the politicians' framework for American Apartheid would crash to the ground."[73]

Once the multiracial category became identified with the color-blind alliance's goals, with few exceptions, Latino, Native American, and Asian American advocacy groups joined with African American leaders to oppose adding it to the census. The Japanese American Citizens' League was the only mainstream civil rights group that supported the change. Such groups as the National Council of La Raza, Asian Americans for an Accurate Count, and the Asian American Legal Defense Fund refused to do so. Some of their spokespersons indicated they acted not so much from strong opposition to multiracial categories as from a desire "to preserve the needs of our coalition partners."[74] Yet they did act in concert with African American civil rights groups, thereby attesting to the power of the modern race-conscious alliance in shaping conduct on this as on many other issues. There was also little division within the ranks of African American advocates. Representative John Conyers was the only black member of Congress to support the change. And though some in the multiracial advocacy groups identified as black, they were not numerous and were predominantly in mixed-race couples, with, again, white women, not their black husbands, providing the most active leadership.[75]

It was only the increased power in Congress of conservative Republicans in the 1990s that provided strong leverage on behalf of the multiracial option. These Republicans understood fully that this change might weaken governmental regulatory measures that sought to improve the political, educational, and economic position of, especially, African Americans, in ways that GOP leaders condemned as misguided. But with a Democratic president and bureaucratic opposition, not even strong congressional support enabled the multiracial movement to win more than a watered-down version of its goal, the option to check multiple boxes, while still being counted as a racial minority. This partial victory was won by familiar members of the color-blind alliance, joined by a few non-white advocates, arrayed against the core of the race-conscious alliance.

Subsequently, as the use of "two or more races" option has become more common in federal surveys and report forms, opposition to the practice has quieted but not disappeared. Both MALDEF and the Reverend Jesse Jackson spoke against the EEOC's adoption of the category in 2005. For them, the category "would not be meaningful for affirmative action purposes under OFCCP's [Office of Federal Contract Compliance Programs'] authority."[76] But because prominent persons of mixed African ancestry like Barack Obama, Halle Berry, and Tiger Woods have come to be widely seen as black as well as multiracial and have generally chosen to embrace identification as black, and government agencies do generally count persons with African ancestry as black for policy purposes, anxieties within the race-conscious alliances about multiracial identities diminished after the 1990s.

Those developments also reveal that efforts to establish "multiracial" as a politically salient identity have not succeeded and instead appear to be diminishing. Jennifer Hochschild and Vesla Weaver report that, though they identified over one hundred groups that claimed to promote multiracialism in 2008, only twenty-one had active websites. Many of those had not been updated in over a year, and most appeared to be more social than political. None of the groups had renewed the effort to create a "multiracial" category in testimony at hearings on the 2010 census or in other agency proceedings.[77]

Multiracial or Postracial Era?

Analyzing a variety of surveys, Hochschild and Weaver argue that multiracial self-identifications are on the rise, especially among younger Americans. But they also note that such self-identification remains low, endorsed by under 4 percent of the general population in all the "key surveys" they examined.[78] These two scholars think these percentages are likely to increase. Their analysis gives little reason to think that such identities will become less purely social and more consciously political in the future, however. It is, after all, not apparent what political agenda, beyond a desire to be able to self-identify as they wish, might unite African Asians, African Latinos, African–Native American, black-white, white-Asian, white–Native American, and other still more complexly mixed race Americans, in opposition to the positions of both the modern racial policy alliances. It is therefore likely that the multiracial groups as such will not be politically active on most racial issues at all. Many of their members will probably support the race-conscious alliance if they are active in their other capacities, though in the wake of the Gingrich efforts of the 1990s, some may instead support the positions of the color-blind alliance. But even on their core racial policy issue, multiracial classifications, the evidence indicates that the bulk of the opposing forces have lined up in ways consistent with the memberships of today's racial alliances, even if many members of those alliances did not get involved in the controversy.

To be sure, ultimately members of the race-conscious coalition may decide, as some did initially, that an embrace of multiracialist policies is consistent with their political vision and goals. And many advocates of mixed race categories may then in turn give more active support to the race-conscious alliance on other issues.[79] Arguably, the 1990s framing of multiracialism in terms of its ultimate implications for color-blind policies popularized by Gingrich and other conservative Republicans, prompting attacks by race-conscious proponents, distorted the goals and impacts of multiracial advocacy.

Still, there is no reason as yet to think that the small rise in multiracial self-identifications and the brief flowering of multiracial advocacy groups is fundamentally changing the structure of American racial politics. Certainly when the most successful multiracial politician in the nation's history filled out his census form in 2010 in his White House office, he gave no sign of thinking that, in this regard at least, a change had come in which he could believe. Instead, he chose to identify himself in a way that did not capture his full racial heritage, but one that did comply with the policy preferences of the race-conscious alliance that forms an essential part of his political base. In so doing, Barack Obama officially and unequivocally marked himself as America's first "black" president.

Chapter 8

"We can take the people out of the slums, but we cannot take the slums out of the people"
How Today's Racial Alliances Shape Laws on Crime and Immigration

Few issues recur more forcefully or regularly in U.S. politics than immigration and crime. And the impact of the racial alliances with their ideologically opposed policy agendas has been decisive in shaping how the issues of criminal policy and immigration are framed and how support for them is mobilized. Plainly these issues would be debated even if racial alliances did not exist. Many voters and politicians have acted on them for reasons having nothing to do with racial policy commitments. But for many others, the racial implications of policies in these areas have been vital. Racial politics have infused these issues with a content and significance they would not otherwise have. Most important, on these issues as on many others, conflicts over their racial dimensions hamper the making of beneficial policies.

As we argue throughout the book, though today's racial alliances affect contestation over a wide range of issues in American politics, they are far from the only players in American political arenas. Just as racial alliances are not reducible to economic or partisan conflicts, even if they have all become much more closely aligned, so economic and partisan alliances play independent roles in political conflicts; governmental institutions themselves shape the values and strategies of political actors; and a huge number of lesser groups, movements, and interests are also at work. We cannot hope to canvass here all the actors involved in major political controversies in modern America, including crime and immigration.

And because many other factors are indeed at work, crime and immigration issues are widely seen as either not being only about race or as not politically structured through the racial coalitions that we emphasize. Hence, both issues are further candidates to demonstrate that our portrait of racial alliances is wrong or at least that it is well on its way to becoming obsolete. We argue here that although there is more going on in the politics of both these issues than simply clashes between the era's two major racial coalitions, those alliances are and appear likely to remain major players in criminal justice and immigration policies, as in so many others.

CRIMINAL JUSTICE

We have stressed that Barack Obama, the president who aspires to forge senses of unity while valuing diversity, speaks about racial issues rarely and then carefully. Yet he stirred perhaps the most publicized controversy of his first year in office when on July 23, 2009, he animatedly declared at a press conference that the Cambridge, Massachusetts, police had "acted stupidly" when they arrested Harvard professor Henry Louis Gates as he tried to jimmy open the damaged front door to his own home. Obama added, "We know . . . that there is a long history in this country of African-Americans and Latinos being stopped by law enforcement disproportionately."[1] Cambridge and Massachusetts police associations leaped to the defense of the arresting officer, Sergeant James Crowley. The next day Obama made an unannounced trip to the White House pressroom to say that he "could've calibrated those words differently" and that he had called Sgt. Crowley to indicate that he did not mean to malign him.[2] The two men began arranging a subsequent brief but much-publicized "beer summit" at the White House with the equally conciliatory Professor Gates (along with an apparently thirsty Vice President Joe Biden, who drank a nonalcoholic beer).

By itself the incident was minor. And Obama's willingness to address race in the context of apparent racial profiling in policing was nothing new. He had campaigned on the fact that as a state senator, he had sponsored a law that required the Illinois Department of Transportation to record the race, age, and gender of all drivers stopped for traffic violations so that bias could be detected. As a U.S. senator, he cosponsored legislation to require federal, state, and local law enforcement agencies to take steps to end racial profiling.[3] Yet the story dramatized how in modern America, race is entangled with criminal justice issues in ways that deeply concern and yet confound proponents of each of the racial justice perspectives of the two modern racial alliances. At first glance, racial profiling appears to be an issue on which the rival policy coalitions might agree. Seeking to end it seems, after all, like an imperative to achieve a color-blind criminal justice system. It is also a goal that the members of the race-conscious policy alliance and all those who seek to overcome surviving patterns of traditional racial discrimination can and do endorse.

But as Obama's law in Illinois indicates, combating invidious racial profiling requires collecting racial data on law enforcement practices and questioning racially disproportionate official conduct. Many advocates of color blindness see these actions as steps toward mandating racially proportionate criminal justice punishments, even if African Americans and Latinos prove to be committing crimes more often than whites. Due to reports of its high rate of arrests for "Driving While Black," for example, New Jersey required all its state troopers to receive instructions on how to classify a motorist's race by skin color and facial characteristics, so they could track who they were arresting.[4] To race-conscious proponents, this response was misguided. Their objection was to New Jersey state police disproportionately stopping people the troopers perceived as African American. It was not about whether police were making those racial identifications correctly. Still, because anti-profiling techniques do require collection of racial data, and because they may discourage police from arresting "too many" nonwhites, race-conscious advocates can appear to be "soft on crime," particularly crime by nonwhites, when they argue as Obama does that it is important to combat police bias. Nonwhites are also not just disproportionately arrested but also disproportionately innocent victims of crimes. Many race-conscious advocates therefore feel obliged to stress that they are indeed strongly opposed to all criminal conduct, even as they see many kinds of racially discriminatory behavior as making up such conduct.

Crack Cocaine and Cracking Down on Crime

Those factors may well have been at work more than twenty years earlier, when on March 21, 1986, Congressman Charles Rangel of Harlem introduced into the *Congressional Record* an article by Peter Kerr published the day before in the *New York Times*, entitled "Extra-Potent Cocaine: Use Rising Sharply Among Teen-Agers."[5] It reported that from "the wealthiest suburbs of Westchester County to the Bedford-Stuyvesant section of Brooklyn," growth in the use of "crack," described as "an especially potent and addicting form of cocaine," was "so great that it is fast outpacing the ability" of authorities to "cope with the problem."[6]

Rangel's action was one of a flurry of similar submissions of articles and statements by members of Congress that day, marking the first appearance of the words "crack" and "cocaine" in the *Congressional Record*. Representatives bemoaned the sudden eruption of a crack "epidemic" that was perhaps "the most serious problem facing" the country.[7] Rangel went on to join the overwhelming bipartisan support for the rapidly enacted 1986 Anti-Drug Abuse Act, passed in the House on September 11 by a vote of 392–16 and in the Senate on September 30 by 97–2.[8] Among other provisions, the act mandated a five-year minimum federal prison sentence for possession of five grams of crack cocaine or five hundred grams of powder cocaine.[9]

Thirteen years later, after the searing effects of this measure became plain, Rangel was the author of the "Crack-Cocaine Equitable Sentencing Act of 2009." The bill aimed to end the "disparity in cocaine sentencing" created in 1986 because it had "failed as a deterrent." Instead, the 1986 law "unfairly condemned many to unreasonably long prison sentences." Said Rangel in 2009, "This policy isn't working. It's not working for Blacks; it's not working for minorities — it's not working for this country."[10]

The story of the shift on crack cocaine sentencing by Congressman Rangel, one of the nation's leading African American legislators for nearly four decades even though he was censured for being found guilty of ethics violations in 2010, is significant here for two reasons. First, the fact that he and others in the Congressional Black Caucus supported this punitive mandatory sentencing provision, with its foreseeable racially disparate impact, may seem to provide key evidence *against* analyzing modern criminal justice policies in terms of our "racial alliances" framework. Support for such policies among leading political actors appears bipartisan and biracial, not polarized by clashing racial coalitions. But second, the fact that Rangel came before long to shift dramatically on this issue, adopting a stance more in line with his typical positions and with those of most in the race-conscious alliance, shows that the structure of modern racial politics is at work in criminal justice disputes, as in most other policy arenas. We do not deny that, especially in the 1980s, electoral pressures generated a huge bipartisan elite consensus in favor of punitive criminal justice measures, including more mandatory sentences, death penalty crimes, and prison expansion. This consensus diminished for a time the role of the contemporary racial alliances, because so many Democrats running for office supported these measures, but also because some civil rights leaders and a range of new activist groups did as well.

Yet even as each of the modern racial alliances has favored anti-crime policies, they have favored distinct anti-crime policies. Both proponents and opponents of tougher crime measures have conceived of crime policy as, in part, a crucial arena for the nation's broader debates about whether its governments should deliberately assist racial minorities, or whether they should treat individuals in color-blind fashion, in this case protecting the law-abiding and punishing lawbreakers, whether or not the results are racially disparate. Color-blind proponents argue that it is a moral and policy error to focus on social "root causes" of crime to be addressed, in part, by race-targeted programs. They condemn any criticism of the racially disparate consequences of punitive laws as fostering permissive attitudes that disastrously deny personal responsibility for misconduct, and as failing to recognize the benefits minority communities receive from the incarceration of the criminals in their midst. In contrast, race-conscious alliance proponents insist that programs targeted on crime prevention and rehabilitation, especially for urban, poor, largely nonwhite communities, be included along with punitive provisions in a series of omnibus crime bills, which members of both alliances have in the end supported. Many in civil rights groups belonging to the alliance go further, contending that the patterns of racially disproportionate incarceration and disfranchisement that modern criminal justice policies have produced amount to a "new Jim Crow" system that is only masked by the rhetoric of color blindness.[11] Thus, as political scientist Marie Gottschalk has argued, race has "interacted with a complex array of other specific political and institutional developments" during these years, so that an account focused on race alone would be badly incomplete. But as she also contends, it is still true that criminal justice policies and politics cannot be discussed apart from issues of "race and social control."[12]

That pattern is not surprising. The intertwining of race and criminal justice policies in American history is long-standing. Antebellum pro-slavery southerners resisted penitentiaries in part because abolitionists favored them as preferable to permanent servitude. Hard-line Jim Crow supporters favored the convict leasing system in the early twentieth century to control blacks and boost the southern economy. Moderate racial Progressives thought rehabilitative prisons might help to "uplift" African Americans. At the national level, as we have seen, segregationists and anti-segregationists warred over the creation of federal anti-lynching laws throughout the New Deal.[13]

Crime after Civil Rights

In the latter part of the Jim Crow era, stances on crime came to be still more explicitly linked to positions on the emerging civil rights movement. Naomi Murakawa notes that soon after the publication of *To Secure These Rights*, the landmark report of the Truman Committee on Civil Rights in 1947 that signaled the momentous shift of the presidency into the enlarging anti–Jim Crow alliance, champions of segregation began contending that expanded civil rights for blacks would mean the unleashing of black "criminal tendencies," generating more "inter-racial crime," especially rape of white women.[14] During the course of the 1950s and early 1960s, as civil rights protests mounted and more public institutions became integrated, prominent segregationists such as Georgia congressman Elijah Forrester and South Carolina senator Strom Thurmond attacked the protests as themselves criminal and claimed that in newly integrated parks and schools, whites faced "assaults upon their person or the robbery of their personal effects" so that "political demands for integration" were creating a "wave of terror, crime, and juvenile delinquency."[15]

Barry Goldwater then made a dramatic linkage of civil rights reforms with "the way of mobs in the streets" a centerpiece of his 1964 Republican presidential campaign.[16] While promising to oppose racial discrimination, the GOP platform that year accused the Johnson administration of exploiting "interracial tensions by extravagant campaign promises without fulfillment . . . encouraging disorderly and lawless elements."[17] In contrast, just before disavowing racial quotas, the 1964 Democratic platform insisted that Democrats "will not tolerate lawlessness," but that they would also "seek to eliminate its economic and social causes."[18] In the November 1964 election, amidst the emotions spurred by Kennedy's assassination and fears of Goldwater's alleged nuclear weapons recklessness, the Republicans' coupling of civil rights laws with increases in crime appealed only in the Deep South. It was unable to prevent the historic triumphs of the anti-segregation alliance in the mid-1960s.

The Racial Alliances Realign

The GOP stances on race and crime did, however, begin the processes of the realignment of modern racial coalitions around new, post-segregation issues and the closer identification of those coalitions with the also-transforming two major parties.[19] The realigning processes took place in the context of a sharp rise in official crime statistics in the late 1960s, a rise whose sources criminologists still debate.[20] Then and thereafter, most Republicans and racial conservatives interpret heightened crime as evidence that civil rights laws, protests, and judicial decisions have indeed unleashed illegality, which needed to be met by punishment—but punishment that they now justify as aimed at individuals guilty of criminal conduct, not at regulation or coercion of nonwhites as a group (though their critics perceive a racial "subtext").[21]

For example, Democratic congressman Watkins Abbitt of Virginia argued in 1967 that "civil rights officials" had "encouraged lawlessness." He charged that these officials permitted "certain elements" to believe that "they have the right to take what they want" while "the judiciary . . . coddled" the offenders. Republican congressman Clarence Miller of Ohio said that "give-away programs" had "lulled a downtrodden element into the belief that society owes them a living."[22] Southern senators including Richard Russell, Herman Talmadge, and Russell Long all contended that toleration of civil rights protests and civil disobedience fostered "mob violence."[23]

In so arguing, these politicians paved the way for modern conservatives' re-focusing of racial issues away from legal segregation and from assistance programs to the need for color-blind policies that develop, protect, and reward good character and conduct while restraining and punishing bad character and conduct. As West Virginia senator Robert Byrd put it, poverty did not provide "a license for laziness or for lawlessness. We can take the people out of the slums, but we cannot take the slums out of the people."[24]

Racial liberals and, initially, many Democrats continued to insist instead in the late 1960s that, though the federal government did need to do more about crime, those actions had to feature "financing and administering the great social programs" that were "America's best hope of preventing crime and delinquency," as the report of Lyndon Johnson's President's Commission on Law Enforcement and Administration of Justice argued in 1967.[25] Doing so meant not only strengthening families "often shattered by the grinding pressures of urban slums," providing "enough" resources to "slum schools" to make them "as good as schools elsewhere" and enlarging employment opportunities. It also meant expanded efforts to "combat school segregation and the housing segregation that underlies it."[26] In the 1968 campaign, Democratic presidential candidate Hubert Humphrey argued that it was "dangerous nonsense to believe that social progress" toward "racial justice" and "respect for law are . . . in opposition to each other."[27] Civil rights advocates thereby moved toward the endorsement of racial assistance policies that would become the hallmark of the modern race-conscious alliance.

Still, those coalitions would not crystallize for nearly a decade. In 1968, Congress again gave overwhelming support to the Omnibus Crime Control and Safe Streets Act of 1968, which passed by a vote of 72–4 in the Senate and 368–17 in the House.[28] Foreshadowing an enduring pattern, its popularity came in part because this "omnibus" bill was designed to appeal to both camps. Its provisions included the establishment of the Law Enforcement Assistance Administration (LEAA). LEAA offered federal assistance to state and local police forces and channeled hundreds of millions of dollars into research studies, many intended to design ways to combat the social conditions liberals saw as "root causes" of crime. The act regulated firearms sales and possession, in part due to fears that radical black groups were stockpiling guns. It established procedures for how wiretapping could be done consistently with recent Supreme Court decisions holding that warrantless wiretaps violated the Fourth Amendment. And it sought to limit the scope of the Court's *Miranda* ruling on the admissibility of confessions.[29] The statute was a classic and very popular compromise that gave much to both conservatives and liberals and satisfied the desires of both parties to be seen as responding to rising crime rates.

It did not, however, reduce crime. Already that summer both parties were promising to do more, though still in distinctive ways that linked to their differences on American racial issues. Both the 1968 Democratic and Republican Party platforms gave massive attention to crime. The Democrats promised a "a vigorous and sustained campaign against lawlessness in all its forms." In stark contrast to the party's old states' rights traditions, they stated that "the federal government has a clear responsibility for national action" that included but went beyond aiding "state and local law enforcement agencies." In the Democrats' views, these national efforts should center on an "attack on the root causes of crime and disorder." The Republicans contended that the Johnson administration had ignored "our rising crime rates until very recently." And though they too pledged "a relentless attack on economic and social injustice in every form," the GOP stressed that "while the youth's environment may help to explain the man's crime, it does not excuse that crime." They called for "an all-out, federal-state-local crusade against crime."[30]

In subsequent elections, both parties highlighted anti-crime initiatives in partly overlapping but also contrasting ways. The Republicans insisted that their policies aimed to "protect the law-abiding citizenry . . . rather than absolve the criminal." Democrats maintained that "law and order" should not be used "as justification for repression" and emphasized "rehabilitation" and the "constitutional and human rights of prisoners."[31] By 1980, the emergence of the modern racial alliances was visibly shaping the ways the parties framed their criminal justice policies. The Democrats in that year defended race-conscious assistance programs in numerous respects, including as a means to combat the causes of crime, which they continued to link to denials of civil rights (including the rights of immigrants). As their platform put it:

> Our commitment to civil rights embraces not only a commitment to legal equality, but a commitment to economic justice as well. It embraces a recognition of the right of every citizen—Black and Hispanic, American Indian and Alaska Native, Asian/Pacific Americans, and the majority who are women—to a fair share in our economy. When that opportunity is denied, and the promise of social justice is unfulfilled, the risks of tension and disorder in our cities are increased. The Democratic Party condemns violence and civil disorder wherever they occur. But, we also pledge to attack the underlying injustices that contribute to such violence so that no person need feel condemned to a life of poverty and despair.

The platform went on to contend that because racial minorities "have been discriminated against" through "excessive or illegal police force," Americans needed "at the federal, state and local level . . . a renewed commitment to affirmative action in the hiring of law enforcement personnel."[32] The Republicans, in contrast, again stressed "the firm and speedy application of criminal penalties," including the death penalty, and the "right of citizens to keep and bear arms," while contending that "equal opportunity should not be jeopardized by bureaucratic regulations and decisions which rely on quotas, ratios, and numerical requirements to exclude some individuals in favor of others, thereby rendering such regulations and decisions inherently discriminatory."[33]

Democrats, then, interpreted fighting crime as including preventive and rehabilitative social and economic aid and drug treatment programs, along with heightened efforts to combat discrimination against minorities, in part via race-conscious police employment practices. Republicans emphasized the importance of punishment far more than preventive or rehabilitative social programs. They criticized affirmative action in criminal justice system hiring and presented the right to bear arms as the civil right most in need of protection against governmental discrimination, so that citizens could protect themselves against individuals with criminal characters.

In this configuration, the political parties represented here as on so many other issues the positions of the modern racial alliances, and they have since continued to do so—though the involvement of new groups active chiefly in the crime arena; genuine uncertainties about what policies would most benefit nonwhites; and electoral pressures to be tough on crime have affected the positions of many Democrats and many policy outcomes. The structure of the modern color-blind alliance in relation to criminal justice is shown in table 8.1.

That formidable coalition has been countered, though with less consistency than in some other areas and with less success, by the race-conscious alliance (see table 8.2).

The Reagan Shift

The Republicans, of course, won a thundering victory in 1980. But the Reagan administration soon confronted intractable economic problems and a recalcitrant Democratic House of Representatives. In 1982, at a low point in his popularity, Ronald Reagan announced new federal initiatives against drug trafficking and organized crime, launching his "War on Drugs."[34] Reagan attributed "the crime problem" to a "misguided social philosophy" holding that

Chapter 8

TABLE 8.1
Color-Blind Alliance, 1978–2008: Punitive Criminal Justice Policies

Most Republican Party officeholders and members after 1976

Presidents, 1981–93, 2001–9

Conservative, neoconservative, and electorally vulnerable Democrats

Majority of Supreme Court after 1980

Many lower federal court judges, state judges after 1980

Most prosecutors

Many businesses, private prison companies

Law enforcement employee advocacy groups, unions

Conservative community crime prevention groups

Some conservative think tank / advocacy groups (e.g., American Enterprise Institute)

Victims' rights groups (e.g., Parents of Murdered Children)

Women's groups concerned with rape, battered women

Fringe white supremacist groups (e.g., New Century Foundation)

Source: In addition to the other sources cited in the text, table 8.1 is based on Bruce Western, *Punishment and Inequality in America* (New York: Russell Sage Foundation, 2006), 59–79 (GOP officeholders and presidents); Katherine Beckett, *Making Crime Pay Law and Order in Contemporary American Politics,* (New York: Oxford University Press, 1997), 60–61, 98–101 (conservative and electorally vulnerable Democrats, prison companies, law enforcement advocacy groups); Katherine Beckett and Theodore Sasson, *The Politics of Injustice: Crime and Punishment in America,* 2nd ed. (London: Sage, 2004), 133–37, 140–48 (conservative community groups, victims' rights groups); Michael Novak, *Character and Crime: An Inquiry into the Causes of the Virtue of Nations* (Lanham, MD: University Press of America, 1987) (American Enterprise Institute); Marie Gottschalk, *The Prison and the Gallows* (New York: Cambridge University Press, 2006), 77–164, 216–27, 230–35, 253 (victims' rights groups, women's groups; Supreme Court, lower federal and state courts); Lisa L. Miller, *The Perils of Federalism: Race, Poverty, and the Politics of Crime Control* (New York: Oxford University Press, 2009), 49–84 (courts and prosecutors); Swain, *New White Nationalism,* 111–29 (fringe white supremacist groups).

TABLE 8.2
Race-Conscious Alliance, 1978–2008: Preventive and Rehabilitative
Criminal Justice Policies

More liberal Democratic Party officeholders and members

Congressional Black Caucus

President (mixed support), 1993–2001

Some liberal Republicans

Some federal, state judges

Liberal and some libertarian advocacy groups (e.g., ACLU)

Some unions (e.g., AFL-CIO)

Liberal community crime prevention groups

Prisoners' rights groups

Most nonwhite advocacy groups (NAACP LDF, National Council of La Raza, Asian American Legal Defense Fund)

Liberal media (e.g., *New York Times*)

Liberal religious groups (e.g., National Council of Churches)

Liberal foundations (e.g., Soros, Ford)

Source: In addition to the other sources cited in the text and for table 8.1, table 8.2 is based on Beckett and Sasson, *Politics of Injustice*, 51–52, 63–68, 130–31, 138–39, 151, 158 (more liberal Democrats, CBC, president, some liberal Republicans, liberal advocacy groups including ACLU, community crime prevention groups); AFL-CIO, "AFL-CIO Legislative Guide," 2009, http://www.aflcio.org/issues/legislativealert/upload/legislative_guide09.pdf, sec. 7.3–7.4; "Racial Inequity and Drug Arrests," *New York Times*, May 10, 2008, http://www.nytimes.com/2008/05/10/opinion/10sat1.html?emc=eta1; Gottschalk, *Prison and the Gallows*, 165–83, 216–27 (NAACP LDF, prisoners' rights groups, some federal, state judges); National Council of La Raza, "Latinos and the Criminal Justice System," http://www.nclr.org/index.php/issues_and_programs/civil_rights_and_justice-1/criminal_justice/criminal_justice_system/; Asian American Legal Defense and Education Fund, "Amici Curiae Brief in Massachusetts v. A.I. and A.W., Juveniles," Filed in the Supreme Judicial Court, Commonwealth of Massachusetts, No. SJC-10299, 2009; National Council of Churches, "Challenges to the Injustice of the Criminal Justice System," 1979, http://www.ncccusa.org/NCCdocs/criminaljusticepolicy.pdf; Judith A. Greene, "Smart on Crime: Positive Trends in State-Level Sentencing and Corrections Policy," Washington, DC, Families Against Mandatory Minimums (2003), http://www.soros.org/initiatives/usprograms/focus/justice/articles_publications/publications/smart_on_crime_20031101 (Soros); Ford Foundation, "Reforming Civil and Criminal Justice Systems," http://www.fordfoundation.org/issues/human-rights/reform-civil-and-criminal-justice-systems.

"society, not the individual, is to blame" due to "poor socioeconomic conditions or an underprivileged background." He insisted instead that "evil is frequently a conscious choice, and that retribution must be swift and sure."[35] To focus instead on socioeconomic inequalities or the disparate racial consequences of anti-crime measures was to encourage lawlessness. Many Americans responded favorably, and soon thereafter, many Democrats began moving closer to Republican anti-crime rhetoric and policies, especially when campaigning.[36]

In 1984 the Democrats' platform argued that "neither a permissive liberalism nor a static conservatism is the answer to reducing crime. While we must eliminate those elements—like unemployment and poverty—that foster the criminal atmosphere, we must never let them be used as an excuse."[37] By 1992, Democrats stressed that "crime is not only a symptom but also a major cause of the worsening poverty and demoralization that afflicts inner city communities," a signal reversal of their earlier emphasis. And in 1996, they promised to continue "putting more police on the streets and tougher penalties on the books," including "three-strikes-you're-out" mandatory sentences and the extension of the death penalty to many more crimes.[38] In 2000, with the rising influence of victims' rights groups discussed later, it was the Democrats who contended that too often American officials "bend over backward to protect the rights of criminals" without sufficient concern for "victims." They also adapted color-blind critiques of treating "Americans as members of groups instead of as individuals" by attacking "racial profiling," even as they argued for additional punishment of "hate crimes," defined in race-conscious terms.[39] Although in 2008 the Democratic platform again spoke of "getting tough on the root causes of crime" and continuing "to fight inequalities in our criminal justice system," it also continued to champion "the rights of victims" and a nonarbitrary death penalty, while promising that Democrats would be "tough on violent crime" and hold "offenders accountable."[40]

Despite the fact that Democrats were voting for anti-crime bills in massive numbers during these years, Republicans repeatedly claimed that their partisan opponents had not really changed, that Democrats "had more concern for abstract criminal rights than for the victims of crime" and would "coddle hardened criminals," preferring to "blame society." GOP platforms heralded the importance of tougher sentences including the death penalty; prisons with strong work requirements and conditions designed to deter crime; and a broad right to bear arms.[41] In 2008, the Republicans added that crime problems had "escalated with the rise of gangs composed largely of illegal aliens," who should be "removed as soon as possible."[42]

The Democrats, for whom the Latino members of the race-conscious alliance were an important and growing constituency, eschewed such anti-alien language. But in other respects, from the late 1960s to the late 1980s and subsequently, in the area of criminal justice, many Democrats shifted toward Republican stances. This movement is evident on victims' rights, on tougher sentencing policies including the death penalty, and on the dangers of overemphasizing rights of the accused. At times, Democrats also adopted the anti–group rights rhetoric of the color-blind alliance to critique racial profiling.

But although partisan differences did not always show up in final roll call votes on popular anti-crime bills, the Republicans were correct that important differences in the preferred approaches of the parties to crime persisted throughout these years. While the Democrats did not always highlight their support for race-conscious hiring practices to limit racially discriminatory police behavior, they did not renounce it. The Republicans never supported such practices. Though the Democrats placed less rhetorical emphasis on preventive and rehabilitative programs than they had in the past, most continued to favor such measures and to include them along with more punitive provisions in the omnibus crime bills they regularly voted for after 1984. And though the Democrats could and did employ the rhetoric of color blindness to oppose racial profiling, to call for stricter enforcement of civil rights laws, and to endorse tougher criminal penalties for hate crimes, these represented efforts to turn the broad public approval of anti-crime measures and for color-blind policies to support for policies that especially aided nonwhites, in ways that all recognized to be race-conscious.

Conversely, the Republicans routinely invoked the rhetoric of individual responsibility and the importance of rewarding good character and punishing bad that were staples of modern conservative ideology to support punitive policies without regard for racially disparate impacts. At the same time, many in the GOP favored the versions of color blindness that counseled against substantial funding for civil rights enforcement; that minimized the need to track the racial identities of suspects in order to combat racial profiling; and that opposed singling out for special punishments crimes motivated by racism. Quantitative evidence finds that prison expansion grew more rapidly under Republican presidents than Democrat ones prior to Bill Clinton, and particularly under Republican governors and state legislatures throughout the modern era.[43]

Rather than suggesting that the positions of the racial alliances have been irrelevant to understanding the parties' positions on crime in the modern era, then, the cumulative evidence demonstrates that the parties have indeed sought to claim the mantle of being most anti-crime. But they have done so in ways that have been framed to a great extent by the concerns of the racial alliances with which they have been affiliated.

The Tsunami of Congressional Criminal Laws

Despite observable partisan convergence on anti-crime policies, the deeper contrasts between the parties can be further seen by examining the positions advocated and the voting patterns on two types of legislation that have been central to the development of modern American criminal justice policies. These are mandatory minimum sentences for drug-related crimes and capital punishment for an increasingly wide range of crimes.

Laws mandating mandatory minimum sentences, especially for drug crimes, accelerated the explosive growth of America's prison population in the last three decades of the twentieth century, with a vastly disproportionate impact on blacks and Latinos and poorer Americans. By 2001, 21 percent of state prisoners and a massive 57 percent of those incarcerated in federal prisons had been convicted of drug crimes.[44] By the first decade of the twenty-first century, the U.S. incarceration rate had been increasing each year for over a quarter century, and at 737 per 100,000 residents, it was five to twelve times that of western European and most other advanced industrial societies. The black incarceration rate is currently over eight times that of non-Hispanic whites, with black males facing a one in three lifetime chance of being incarcerated, as compared to one in six for Hispanic men and one in ten for non-Hispanic white men.[45] Whites and blacks appear to use illegal drugs at comparable rates. These racial disparities have resulted largely from the ways that mandatory minimum drug crimes have been defined and enforced.[46] The death penalty, of course, represents the ultimate form of punishment, abandoning any possibility of future rehabilitation, and it, too, is applied in racially and ethnically disproportionate ways.[47] Though it is not likely that most supporters of mandatory sentences and death penalty actively sought such racially disparate consequences, their spread has nonetheless meant that the politics of crime has remained intertwined with the politics of racial alliances.

Since both parties began endorsing a greater federal role in crime control after 1968, and especially since the Reagan Revolution persuaded many Democrats that they, too, had to appear not just concerned about crime but tough on crime, federal crime laws have been enacted so prolifically that we cannot review all crime bills here. Naomi Murakawa has provided the most systematic historical analysis of congressional crime legislation.[48] She notes that although congressional impositions of mandatory minimum sentences date all the way back to the first Congress in 1790, the number of such provisions roughly tripled from Reagan's election to the end of the century. The figure rose from 61 in 1983, shortly after the launch of Reagan's "War on Drugs," to 168 in 2000.[49] Most of those convicted under such statutes during that period were prosecuted for drug-related offenses—91 percent between 1984 and 1990.[50] Congress also increased the number of federal crimes punishable by death from a mere two in 1986 to fifty-four by 1994.[51] Democrats contributed to these dramatic increases almost as much as Republicans. Yet the influence of the race-conscious alliance can still be discerned in efforts to include preventive, rehabilitative, and race-conscious provisions in bills that were more and more punitive overall—bills for which most Democrats felt compelled to vote, whether or not their preferred measures were included.

The accelerated enactment of punitive mandatory minimum laws and additional death penalties really began in 1984. As late as January 1980, with Democrats still in control of both chambers of Congress and a lame-duck Democratic president in the White House, Congress enacted a "Drug Abuse, Prevention, Treatment and Rehabilitation Act." The act mandated percentages of federal community programs funds to be spent on preventive and intervention programs aimed at groups with high risks of drug abuse.[52] But four years later, after Reagan and the Republicans sought to sustain their 1980 success by stressing their "tough on crime" posture, an overwhelming majority of the Senate (91–1) and a strong majority of the House (243–166) voted to include the Sentencing Reform Act, which created the U.S. Sentencing Commission, in the Comprehensive Crime Control Act of 1984.[53] Members of both parties had long objected to apparently arbitrary disparities in sentences for similar offenses, but the bill leaned toward conservative desires to resolve disparities punitively.[54] Opposition came chiefly from Democrats concerned about its preventive detention provisions.[55] The creation of the commission proved momentous. It was empowered to enact guidelines that many came to criticize as harsh and inflexible.[56]

But as noted, it was Congress itself that authorized the 100–1 crack / powder cocaine disparity in the 1986 Anti-Drug Abuse Act. Though ten of the House's twenty-one African American members refused to join Charles Rangel in voting for the act, many black leaders were genuinely uncertain about whether the proclaimed new crack "epidemic" was a real threat that required strong measures if their communities were to be protected.[57] A number of other Democrats, including then representative Charles Schumer, admitted they believed that "the policies are aimed at looking good rather than solving the problem." But even those expressing such sentiments voted for the bill, saying their opponents would "distort a no vote."[58] Two years later, Congress voted even more overwhelmingly for the Omnibus Anti-Drug Abuse Act of 1988. This act authorized funds for prevention and treatment programs but also applied the five-year minimum sentence to first conviction for simple possession of five grams of crack cocaine, without proven intent to sell. The bill also imposed the death penalty on those responsible when a person died in connection with a drug-related felony.[59] It passed the House 375–30 and the Senate 87–3, and then the House approved the final version that emerged from the congressional conference committee by a vote of 346–11, the Senate by voice vote.[60]

Such near-unanimity confirms that divisions between the racial alliances were subsumed under pressures to cast visible anti-crime votes. Even so, the concerns of the race-conscious alliance were visible, and not only in the continued preventive, treatment, and rehabilitative provisions in the act. The year before, the Supreme Court had ruled in *McCleskey v. Kemp* (1987) that properly structured death penalties were constitutional. This judgment came even as statistics showed that the application of death penalties had racially disparate impacts.[61] Representative John Conyers and others in the Congressional Black Caucus sought to persuade Congress not to enact new death penalties without adopting a "Racial Justice Act." This measure would have limited use of the death penalty when there was statistical evidence of its racially disproportionate application. But though Democrats would continue to advocate the Racial Justice Act for years to come, and versions of it would eventually be adopted by Kentucky in 1998 and by North Carolina in 2009, strong majorities in Congress rejected it in 1988 and repeatedly thereafter.[62]

And after many Democrats perceived George H. W. Bush as having won the 1988 election in part by portraying their presidential candidate Michael Dukakis as soft on crime, responsible for the violent crimes of furloughed prisoner Willie Horton, congressional Democrats sought even harder to establish their anti-crime credentials. None did so more ardently than Senator Joe Biden, the cosponsor, along with Strom Thurmond, of the Crime Control Act of 1990. This act passed the House 313–1 and the Senate by voice vote.[63] Along with provisions adding more serious penalties for various crimes, requiring gun-free school zones, and much more, it included measures attesting to the influence of some distinctive actors on crime legislation: victims' rights groups. As Marie Gottschalk documents, these groups formed from the late 1970s on as "formidable" supporters of "highly retributive and punitive" measures, often allied with women's groups seeking harsher penalties and longer incarceration for rapists and batterers of women.[64] Many in the women's groups supported race-conscious along with gender-conscious policies in other areas of public policy. But they were convinced of the need to be tough on violent assailants, regardless of whether this meant racially disparate patterns of convictions and incarcerations. Along with the victims' groups, the women's groups played significant roles in broadening the popular basis and winning Democratic legislative support for punitive crime policies. The 1990 bill gave victims rights to participate in the legal proceedings against those charged with harming them, along with other forms of assistance. Most expected such participation to work in favor of more severe sentences.

The election of Bill Clinton in 1992 only reinforced the bipartisan consensus in favor of stronger, more mandatory anti-drug laws and more death penalties, packaged to be sure with measures designed to promote prevention, treatment, and rehabilitation. A self-proclaimed "New Democrat" who believed it was political suicide not to be strongly anti-crime, Clinton had flown back to Arkansas in the midst of his presidential campaign to oversee the execution of Ricky Ray Rector, an African American convicted of murdering a white police officer who had since been mentally damaged by surgery.[65] Clinton praised the 1994 Violent Crime Control and Law Enforcement Act as "the toughest, largest, and smartest federal attack on crime" in the nation's history. It included a "three strikes and you're out" provision that mandated life imprisonment for repeated violent offenders, thereby sharpening the upward spike in American incarceration rates.[66] The act also increased again the number of federal crimes subject to the death penalty.

But though it was the most punitive federal crime law yet, the omnibus bill was still another result of logrolling that included elements for all camps. It authorized funds for programs to combat violence against women, for community policing, and for crime prevention programs, as well as prison expansion; and it imposed controls on semiautomatic assault weapons.[67] The House version of the bill also included the "Racial Justice Act," supported by the Congressional Black Caucus and most Democrats. But Republicans opposed the provision, claiming as they had in the past that it was really an effort to abolish the death penalty. Clinton persuaded congressional Democrats to abandon the measure.[68] Given the popularity of color-blind positions, the GOP won that battle. They were unable to eliminate the provisions limiting assault weapons, however. Consequently, the conference version of this bill passed only 235–195 in the House, with only 46 Republicans voting in favor and 131 opposed, joined by 64 Democrats. The Senate vote was 61–38–1 in favor, with all the nays except two coming from Republicans.[69]

The 1996 Anti-Terrorism and Effective Death Penalty Act provided further forms of aid to victims of terrorism. The act heightened and mandated various penalties, including the death penalty. It also limited habeas corpus appeals for those involved in terrorism.[70] Again the bill passed with broad bipartisan support, the conference report approved in the House by Republicans 188–46 and by Democrats 105–86, and in the Senate 91–8–1.[71] Though anti-crime laws continued to proliferate thereafter, first the impeachment controversy during President Clinton's second term, then the focus on terrorism after George W. Bush's election and the September 11, 2001, attacks, gave those concerned to oppose lawlessness some different targets.[72] Pursuing all those developments here would take us too far afield, but even on these topics the issues were framed very differently by leading figures in the rival racial camps.

The contrasts in the priorities of the modern racial alliances are if anything more glaring when we look beyond party platforms and legislative votes to alliance members' participation in crime-related litigation. In cases involving felon disfranchisement, the death penalty, jury composition, and sentencing practices, activist groups with consistent membership in the race-conscious alliance have regularly filed briefs on behalf of the rights of those accused and convicted of crimes, while more conservative groups have often weighed in on the side of prosecutors. In *Alexander v. Sandoval* (2001), for example, Justice Antonin Scalia wrote for a 5–4 majority ruling that Title VI of the 1964 Civil Rights Act did not authorize private suits against government actions with racially disparate impacts.[73] The decision has since made it far more difficult for victims of racial profiling to file the kinds of suits against local and state police forces that have been so powerful in enforcing other civil rights laws.[74] The NAACP Legal Defense Fund, the National Women's Law Center, the Puerto Rican LDF, the Lawyers' Committee for Civil Rights Under the Law, the Asian American LDF, the Center for Constitutional Rights, and other members of the race-conscious alliance filed on behalf of the private right to sue. Conservative litigation groups including the Washington Legal Foundation, the Center for Equal Opportunity, and the Eagle Forum Education and Legal Defense Fund, along with the National Association of Manufacturers and an anti-multicultural advocacy group, U.S. English, filed against permitting such suits. In *Hayden v. Pataki* (2006), a divided Second Circuit U.S. Court of Appeals ruled that the Voting Rights Act did not apply to New York's felon disfranchisement laws, even though (as Judge Sonia Sotomayor stressed in dissent) it applies on its face to all "voting qualifications."[75] New York was supported by the Bush Justice Department and by conservative litigation groups, including the Center for Equal Opportunity and the Criminal Justice Legal Foundation. It was opposed by the NAACP, the ACLU, the National Black Police Association, the National Latino Officers Association, the Center for Constitutional Rights, the People for the American Way Foundation, and a number of similar groups.

In modern death penalty cases, including *McCleskey v. Kemp*, groups such as the National Urban League, the NAACP, the Mexican American Legal Defense and Educational Fund (MALDEF), the ACLU, the National Organization for Women Legal Defense and Education Fund, and the Center for Constitutional Rights, among others, have frequently filed anti-capital punishment briefs. Pro–death penalty briefs have come from conservative litigation groups such as the Washington Legal Foundation and the Allied Educational Foundation, as well as government prosecutors.[76] In jury composition cases, the ACLU, the NAACP LDF, and MALDEF have all filed on behalf of defendants, opposed chiefly by justice departments in Republican administrations.[77] Because these groups are associated both with the distinctive positions of the racial alliances in which they commonly participate and with one or the other party, their roles in litigation have sustained perceptions that Democrats are pro-defendant, Republicans pro-prosecution of crime, despite the fact that most members of both parties have voted similarly on final roll calls for major crime bills since 1984.

Nonetheless, by the first decade of the twenty-first century, predominant American views on criminal justice policies had begun to shift.[78] In recent years, greater attention has been given to the consequences of the increase in, especially, mandatory minimum drug laws in the last two decades of the twentieth century. Their legacy is the increase in the number of Americans incarcerated at very high cost in greatly expanded numbers of prisons, with high percentages convicted of nonviolent drug-related crimes. More Americans have expressed concern, too, about the racially disproportionate character of those incarcerations, despite similar levels of illegal drug use among whites and nonwhites.[79] By 2009, even the conservative Heritage Foundation argued that Americans "must reverse the dangerous trend to criminalize almost everything. To do this" the nation had to limit the federal role in crime control and "restore the traditional protections afforded the accused by the criminal justice system."[80] With a divided court that included justices voting across the usual ideological lines, the Supreme Court ruled in *U.S. v. Booker* (2005) that sentencing guidelines could not be applied as inflexibly as many courts were doing. Just what that ruling implied for future sentencing is unspecified.[81]

The case provided evidence, however, of growing doubts about the policies that had produced massive, and massively racially disparate, incarcerations. The framing of criminal justice in ways that stigmatized all but color-blind punitive and retributive policies as counterproductive and permissive has now come to seem to many more Americans to be questionable if not mistaken. Even so, at this writing it is too early to say that the tides have definitively shifted on criminal justice policies.[82]

Chapter 8

The Framing Effects of Racial Alliances

We do not believe that most or even a great many of those who have supported a more punitive criminal justice system consciously intended the racial consequences visible today. We do not think these consequences would have occurred, however, without the intertwining of crime with the politics of race in America. The framing of criminal justice issues is shaped by the battles between the two modern racial alliances. First the links between crime and the clash of the pro- and anti-segregation racial alliances over the legitimacy of civil rights protests made in the 1960s by longtime segregationists like Strom Thurmond and Robert Byrd, and then the disputes between the modern color-blind and race-conscious alliances over whether policies should punish and reward individual conduct or aim at alleviating material inequalities, including racial inequalities, frame criminal justice issues in ways that made concern about disparate racial consequences appear to be in opposition to effective law enforcement. Absent this framing, fewer Americans might have been convinced that it made sense to minimize prevention, treatment, and rehabilitation in favor of retributive punishment against those deemed to have bad character. Fewer still might have thought it appropriate to ignore the disparate racial impacts of their nation's new crime policies.

IMMIGRATION

President Obama's signature concern in the area of criminal justice, racial profiling, also reared its contentious head during his second year in office in our final policy area, immigration. On April 23, 2010, Arizona governor Jan Brewer signed into law Senate Bill 1070, the "Support Our Law Enforcement and Safe Neighborhoods Act."[83] Its proponents presented the bill as a means to ensure that all Arizona governments and agencies would contribute to enforcement of federal immigration laws, rather than abstaining from or even obstructing enforcement. Among other provisions, the bill required all cities to aid immigration enforcement, first by collecting and reporting information on immigrant statuses to pertinent federal agencies, and second by requesting status information from federal immigration authorities. The law added state penalties for violations of some federal immigration laws and for the commission of various immigration-related crimes. Most controversially, it authorized Arizona law officers to require proof of immigrant status on the basis of "reasonable suspicion" and to arrest immigration law violators without warrants, so long as police had "probable cause" to believe them guilty of such violations. The bill carried further earlier Arizona measures against undocumented immigrants, including Proposition 200, the Arizona Taxpayer and Citizenship Protection Act, which required proof of citizenship to vote and obtain public benefits, and the 2007 Legal Arizona Workers Act, which prohibits businesses from hiring undocumented workers (but has been only sporadically enforced).[84] But SB 1070 stirred far more national furor.

If Obama's reaction to the Gates incident was poorly "calibrated" and partly recanted, the president steadfastly criticized the new Arizona law as "misguided" and a threat to American "core values." He immediately instructed the Justice Department to consider lawsuits against enforcement of the law, including its potential to foster civil rights violations by encouraging unfair targeting, indeed racial profiling, of Latinos.[85] Civil rights groups belonging to the race-conscious alliance, including the Mexican American Legal Defense and Educational Fund (MALDEF) and the National Coalition of Latino Clergy and Christian Leaders LDF, quickly vowed to file suit as well.[86]

Obama agreed that the nation faced major immigration issues and that Arizona was experiencing severe challenges. But he insisted that immigration called for "comprehensive" federal, not state, action. Governor Brewer responded by seeking to prove her own opposition to racial profiling. On April 30, the Arizona legislature enacted and the governor signed an additional bill to ensure that Arizona's new immigration law would not investigate complaints based on "race, color, or national origin," and Brewer requested her own summit meeting at the White House with the president on the issue.[87]

The summit occurred. But far more than in the case of the Gates-Crowley "beer summit," it was clear that in its wake, major policy differences over immigration persisted. The Obama Justice Department still sued Arizona, claiming that its law represented state interference with national policies concerning the enforcement of immigration laws and that it might encourage stops, searches, and arrests on the basis of suspicions that amounted to illegal racial profiling. And despite Arizona's new law designed to protect it against the latter charges, on July 28, 2010, a day before SB 1070 was to be activated, U.S. District Judge Susan Bolton issued a preliminary injunction against its authorizations to demand proof of status and to arrest without warrants, though she allowed most of the law to go into effect.[88] At this writing, Arizona is appealing her ruling before a Ninth Circuit panel.

Yet despite these tight links to controversies over racial profiling, there may be no issue that seems less conducive to analysis in terms of our racial alliances than immigration policy. It has long been characterized as the leading locus of "strange bedfellow" political coalitions. Economic conservatives and social liberals—usually arch rivals—have supported greater immigration. Social conservatives and some of those with whom they have often been at odds—left-leaning unions and many working-class African Americans—favor restrictions.[89] These coalitional descriptions oversimplify a bit, because immigration policies fall under two distinct if connected headings: overall levels of immigration and the severity of measures to enforce them against undocumented aliens, on the one hand, and the social and civil rights of immigrants who are already resident, on the other. Though "strange bedfellow" coalitions persist on each side today, on issues of immigration levels and enforcement, they are somewhat less "strange" than in the past, because many unions and African American civil rights groups have moved into the pro-immigration camp.[90] And on issues involving the social and civil rights of immigrants, where most economic conservatives shift to anti-immigrant stances, the pro- and anti-camps do not seem to us strange at all, because they map onto the modern racial alliances closely, and so also onto modern partisan and liberal/conservative divisions.[91] But for that very reason, these opposed coalitions do not appear likely to agree on any coherent federal "comprehensive immigration reform" in the foreseeable future, any more than they have been able to do during the last quarter century.

Racial Alliances and the Framing of Immigration

As on many other issues, a key effect of the modern racial alliances is the way they contribute to the framing of pro-immigration and anti-immigration positions generally. The relative predominance of color-blind positions means that here, as in the area of criminal justice, those who favor restricting immigration levels or limiting the rights of immigrants, or both, cannot advance their positions by explicitly denigrating the race or ethnicity of immigrants. Such denunciations often provided the best rhetorical strategy for restrictionists during the two previous racial eras in American history. Modern immigration opponents have instead focused on how some of the foreign-born enter the United States in violation of the nation's immigration laws and how others prove incapable of being economically self-supporting and become claimants for public assistance, and how they lack respect for the United States and its institutions. They therefore seek to criticize not the race or ethnicity but the character of many immigrants.

At times, however, the two types of criticisms are difficult to present as distinct. For example, on May 12, 2010, less than three weeks after enacting SB 1070, the very active Arizona legislature passed and Governor Brewer signed HB 2281, which banned Arizona school districts and charter schools from offering classes or courses that were "designed primarily for students of a particular ethnic group" or that "advocate ethnic solidarity instead of the treatment of pupils as individuals."[92] The state superintendent of public instruction said the bill was primarily aimed at ending the Chicano studies program in the Tucson schools.[93] The law carried further the educational goals of Arizona voters who gave overwhelming approval in 2000 to Proposition 203, which abolished bilingual education and replaced it with English-immersion classes. Both measures were cast as concerns to reject a race-conscious focus on group identities in favor of a focus on individual character, and to reject attachments to foreign cultures and languages as inappropriate for patriotic and economically productive Americans. Yet to many Hispanics, as well as to many others in the modern race-conscious alliance, these bans looked like proof that calls for color blindness and a focus on individual character often were veiled efforts to disparage minority ethnic, racial, and cultural identities and to privilege the traditional cultural identities and social advantages of white Americans.

But since it is indisputable that most immigrants come to do needed work, both skilled and unskilled, and that the majority seek to be as law-abiding as possible to avoid deportation, these "character" arguments have proven more effective in arguing for reduced rights for immigrants who can be said to have proven themselves unworthy than they have been in arguing for lower levels of overall immigration. That is all the more true because on this issue, proponents of race-conscious policies and of immigration find themselves in a rare fortunate position. Since modern immigration policies operate in practice especially to the benefit of nonwhite immigrants from Latin America, Asia, and Africa, instead of to the benefit of northern and western Europeans as in the past, pro-immigration advocates concerned to break down the legacies of white supremacy do not need to urge new race-targeted measures. They can defend the status quo and invoke widely accepted principles of nondiscrimination to criticize new immigration and social policy proposals and enforcement practices hostile to the aspirations of current nonwhite immigrants. Hence, in contrast to many other issues, on immigration, advocates of the goals of the race-conscious alliance need to depart much less from the language that their predecessors deployed to seek more inclusive immigration policies in America's previous racial eras.

In the antebellum period, to be sure, national policies left immigration largely unimpeded despite ideological, religious, and class pressures for more nativist measures. Still, the most restrictive national and state laws that were enacted on an enduring basis involved race—the abolition of the international (but not domestic) slave trade in 1808, supported both by anti-slavery forces and some domestic slave "producers," and the state policies denying entry to free blacks that proliferated as the antebellum era proceeded. State legislators openly enacted these laws in the name of maintaining white supremacy, and so some more egalitarian Americans opposed them as unjustly discriminatory.[94] After the Civil War, from the 1882 Chinese Exclusion Act, through the Johnson-Reed 1924 Immigration Act establishing the race-based national origins quota system, to the Immigration and Naturalization Act of 1952 affirming this form of racial discrimination, policies favoring restriction depended on coalitions knit together by concerns to maintain white dominance against the Chinese (in the West) and against African Americans (in the South), as well as "Anglo-Saxon" predominance against southern and eastern Europeans in the Northeast. Even though many African Americans feared competition from immigrant labor, as far back as the 1920s the NAACP denounced all such race-based immigration restrictions as wrongful discrimination.[95]

But by 1960, as the anti-segregation alliance entered its period of greatest success, both of the major parties favored more welcoming immigration policies and revisions in national origins quotas, just as they both embraced strong domestic civil rights planks. Here, however, the Democrats clearly went further. Republicans argued for doubling the annual number of immigrants to provide a "stimulus to growth" and also "a haven for the oppressed," particularly "victims of Communist tyranny." They favored only a limited alteration of the quota system. It still apportioned access to immigration based on the percentage of the American population that had come from a particular nation. The GOP sought to replace the "outdated 1920 census" with the 1960 census as the basis for assigning national quotas. This change would have softened the quota system's bias toward northern Europeans without repudiating its original racial aims. Democrats, in contrast, insisted the main concern of immigration reform should be "to eliminate discrimination" and "again implant a humanitarian and liberal spirit in our nation's immigration and citizenship policies," making them more consonant with "the rights of man," as well as "an important factor in the growth of the American economy."[96] Though by this time neither party sought to openly defend the racial basis of American immigration policy, the Republican emphasis was on economics and cold war priorities, the Democrats on the anti-discrimination goals of the anti–Jim Crow alliance whose undivided allegiance they now hoped to win.

The Legacies of Ending National Origins

Democratic presidents Kennedy and Johnson then proposed legislation ending the national origins system, bills the 1964 Democratic platform praised as means to "eliminate discrimination based upon race and place of birth." The

Goldwater Republicans in 1964 promised only to work for family reunification and asylum for refugees.[97] Congress went on to enact the 1965 Immigration Act, replacing the quota system with one that gave priority to family reunification, followed by immigrants with valuable economic skills, and then refugees from political oppression. For the first time, the act also placed a numerical ceiling of 120,000 on annual immigration from the Western Hemisphere.

The priority for family reunion reflected in part the price of winning labor support for the bill, as union leaders continued to worry about competition from immigrant workers.[98] But along with the ceiling on Western Hemisphere immigration, it responded to the main opponents of the bill, southern Democrats like Mississippi senator James Eastland and conservative Republicans like Goldwater's running mate, William Miller, who feared the coming of more "browns and blacks."[99] Conservatives who were on the fence, including powerful senators Sam Ervin of North Carolina and Everett Dirksen of Illinois, agreed to abolish national origins quotas only when the family reunification and Western Hemisphere ceiling provisions persuaded them that the new policies would not work against entry of our "traditional friends and allies in Western Europe." With their support, the final bill passed overwhelmingly, 76–18 in the Senate, 326–69 in the House. The opposition came mainly from the South.[100] In 1968, the platforms of both parties acclaimed the law's "non-discrimination" principles, just as both parties now officially endorsed the Great Society's major civil rights bills.[101]

But the family reunification and skills provisions proved more transformative than anticipated. Few Western European–descended Americans had immediate relatives seeking entry, while many Latino Americans did, and other Latinos came in as workers in occupations in short supply. Many Asian immigrants, especially from India, Korea, and the Philippines, took initial advantage of the priority for skilled occupations. They then brought in their relatives. Within a few years, roughly three-quarters of all immigrants were coming from Latin America, the West Indies, Asia, and Africa. And because unskilled immigrants needed to show that they had job offers to prove they were workers in short supply who would not become public charges—but few had any contacts with employers, much less employers willing to offer a job to persons far back in the immigration queue—the new policy perversely encouraged illegal immigration, especially from Mexico.[102]

Already in 1972, both parties' platforms expressed concern about this "illegal immigration." Republicans called for increased enforcement efforts. The Democrats sought programs to "remove the economic reasons" for illegal entry. These positions paralleled their stances on criminal justice issues.[103]

Still, immigration, both legal and not, mounted in ensuing years. As the nation entered the 1980s, with the modern racial alliances now formed, pressure for new immigration legislation became pronounced.

It was then that proponents of reducing the disadvantages facing nonwhites found that on most immigration issues, they did not need to argue for explicitly race-targeted policies. The nation's post-1965 "color-blind" immigration priorities by themselves worked to expand opportunities for nonwhites. Consequently, most in the race-conscious alliance argued, "immigration policies should be nondiscriminatory in term of race, ethnicity, and religion." They attacked restrictive policy proposals and stringent enforcement practices as expressing hostility to nonwhites.[104] The 1980 Democratic platform urged an end to "discriminatory" procedures "in enforcing the immigration laws." The 1984 platform contended that recent immigrants were being subjected to "new forms of discrimination," and the next two party platforms also stressed the "non-discrimination" theme.[105] Though many of the urban constituents of African American civil rights groups, especially, doubted the desirability of high immigration levels, few of their advocates openly urged immigration restrictions.[106] The Congressional Black Caucus joined the Congressional Hispanic Caucus in fighting against discriminatory treatment of immigrants.[107]

In contrast, in 1980 the Republican platform celebrated America's tradition of welcoming immigrants. There was a caveat. This welcome extended only to those "who will make a positive contribution to America and who are willing to accept the fundamental American values and way of life," and whose entry was consistent with "our national security and economic well-being."[108] Already many conservatives, including much of the color-blind alliance, criticized broad civil and social, much less political, rights for immigrants often deemed unworthy of public aid and unwilling to assimilate.[109] But social and economic conservatives divided sharply on the question of whether immigration itself should be reduced. And many of the libertarians and business advocates who favored high immigration levels resisted tougher enforcement policies, especially employer sanctions.[110] The 1984 and 1988 Republican platforms lamented the growing numbers of "illegal aliens" and called for immigration reforms "to regain control of our borders," but the party struggled to agree on immigration policy internally, much less with Democrats.[111]

To chart the resulting relationships of the modern racial alliances to modern immigration issues, we must distinguish issues of overall immigration levels and their enforcement from issues of the social and civil rights of immigrants.[112] On the first set of issues, as shown in tables 8.3 and 8.4, "strange bedfellow" patterns are more evident than on the second, shown in tables 8.5 and 8.6. As the tables make clear, those "strange bedfellows" operate in favor

TABLE 8.3
Color-Blind / Social Conservative / Native Black "Strange Bedfellows":
For Reducing Immigration

Many socially conservative Republicans (e.g., Pat Buchanan, Edward Gallegly)

Some socially conservative Democrats (e.g., Rep. John Bryant)

Neorestrictionist groups (e.g., FAIR, NumbersUSA)

Some conservative think tanks (e.g., Center for Immigration Studies)

Some African American advocates outside Congress (e.g., T. Willard Fair)

Fringe white supremacist groups (e.g., New Century Foundation, Pioneer Fund)

Source: Along with the sources cited in the text, especially James G. Gimpel and James R. Edwards, *The Congressional Politics of Immigration Reform* (Boston: Allyn and Bacon, 1995), 42–53, 113–308; Daniel J. Tichenor, *Dividing Lines: The Politics of Immigration Control in America* (Princeton, NJ: Princeton University Press, 2002), 242–88; and Aristide R. Zolberg, *A Nation by Design: Immigrant Policy in the Fashioning of America* (Cambridge, MA: Harvard University Press, 2006), 337–431, table 7.3 derives from "About FAIR," (FAIR), http://www.fairus.org/site/PageNavigator/about/; Dan F. Marsh, "Our National Tradition, Until the 1965 Congress Drastically Changed the Rules" (NumbersUSA), February 2, 2008, http://www.numbersusa.com/content/learn/overpopulation/our-national-tradition-until-1965-congre.html (accessed December 4, 2009); T. Willard Fair, "Mass Immigration v. Black America," http://www.cis.org/articles/2007/fairtestimony050907.html, and Carol M. Swain, "The Congressional Black Caucus and the Impact of Immigration on African American Unemployment," in *Debating Immigration* ed. Carol M. Swain (New York: Cambridge University Press, 2007), 175–88, (some African American advocates); "Immigration and the Demographic Transformation" (New Century Foundation), http://www.amren.com/siteinfo/rg-immigration.html.

of sustaining high levels of immigration. The fact that positions on immigrant rights conform to the positions of today's racial alliances to a greater degree than do positions on immigration levels and enforcement has meant that rights restrictionists have had greater success in shaping modern policies than immigration restrictionists or champions of stringent enforcement policies — outside of Arizona.

The 1986 Reform

With the lines thus drawn, reaching consensus on comprehensive immigration policies has proven difficult throughout the modern era. But in 1986, after several years of intense lobbying and negotiating, Congress passed the Immigration Reform and Control Act (IRCA). IRCA imposed mild sanctions

TABLE 8.4
Race-Conscious / Libertarian / Economic Conservative: "Strange Bedfellows":
Against Reducing Immigration

Most economically conservative, some liberal Republicans

Most Democratic Party officeholders and members

Ethnic advocacy groups (e.g., MALDEF, National Council of La Raza, LULAC, Asian American Legal Defense Fund, NAACP)

Congressional Hispanic Caucus

Congressional Black Caucus

Immigrant advocacy groups (e.g., National Immigration Forum, American Immigration Council)

Most employers (e.g., U.S. Chamber of Commerce, National Association of Manufacturers)

Most unions (e.g., AFL-CIO, Change to Win) (but against more guest workers, divided on employer sanctions)

Liberal advocacy groups (e.g., ACLU, People for the American Way)

Liberal media (e.g., *New York Times*)

Libertarian and economically conservative think tanks / advocacy groups (Cato Institute, American Enterprise Institute) (for more guest workers)

Many religious groups (e.g., National Council of Churches, Catholic Legal Immigration Network)

Liberal foundations (e.g., Soros, Ford)

Source: Along with the sources cited in the text, table 8.4 derives from National Immigration Forum, "Community Resources: National Organizations" (MALDEF, La Raza, LULAC, Asian American Legal Defense and Education Fund, NAACP, National Immigration Forum, American Immigration Council [formerly American Immigration Law Foundation], ACLU, People for the American Way, U.S. Chamber of Commerce, Catholic Legal Immigration Network) (links to the websites for these organizations confirm their positions), http://www.immigrationforum.org/directory; "Immigration and the Candidates," *New York Times*, December 30, 2007, http://www.nytimes.com/2007/12/30/opinion/30sun1.html?emc=eta1; Carolyn Wong, *Lobbying for Inclusion: Rights Politics and the Making of Immigration Policy* (Stanford, CA: Stanford University Press, 2006), 33–38 (ethnic groups) and 76–90 (unions, employers); "CBC's Commitment to America: Immigration" (Congressional Black Caucus), http://www.house.gov/cleaver/cloc/construction.html; "The Labor Movement's Framework for Comprehensive Immigration Reform"

TABLE 8.5
Against Full Social and Civil Rights for Immigrants: Includes Most
of Color-Blind Alliance, 1978–2008

Most Republican Party officeholders and members after 1976

Socially conservative Democrats

Neorestrictionist groups (e.g., FAIR, NumbersUSA)

Most employers (against immigrant welfare rights; e.g., U.S. Chamber of Commerce, National Association of Manufacturers)

Some African American advocates (e.g., T. Willard Fair)

Most conservative think tank / advocacy groups (e.g., Heritage Foundation, AEI, Washington Legal Foundation)

Conservative religious groups (e.g., Focus on the Family, American Values)

Fringe white supremacist groups (e.g., New Century Foundation)

Source: Along with the sources cited in the text and in support of table 8.3, table 8.5 derives from U.S. Chamber of Commerce, "Immigration Myths and the Facts Behind the Fallacies," (Chamber of Commerce), 6, http://www.uschamber.com/sites/default/files/issues/immigration/files/1448immigrationmythsfacts.pdf; Edwin Meese and Matthew Spalding, "Where We Stand: Essential Requirements for Immigration Reform," *Executive Summary Backgrounder* 2034, May 10, 2007, Washington, DC, Heritage Foundation; Jenna Baker McNeill and James Jay Carafano, "Fixing Border Security and Immigration: A Memo to President-elect Obama," *Heritage Foundation Memos* 8, December 16, 2008, Washington, DC, Heritage Foundation; "FRC Action's Values Voter Summit to Rally Activists Ahead of 08 Election," http://www.fraction.org/index.cfm?i=fR08H02.

on employers of undocumented aliens combined with an amnesty program for all such aliens living in the United States prior to 1982. It also included anti-discrimination provisions and funds for states to aid with their costs in implementing the bill.[113] The bill passed with sizable majorities. The House approved the conference report by 238–173, the Senate by 63–24. Most Democrats voted in favor of the law, as did many pro-employer Republicans. Latinos and African Americans were divided. Both groups approved of the anti-dis-

(continued from page 242)

(AFL-CIO, Change to Win), http://www.aflcio.org/issues/civilrights/immigration/upload/immigrationreform041409.pdf; Daniel Griswold, "Will Democrats Err in Immigration Reform?" 2009 (Cato Institute), http://www.cato.org/pub_display.php?pub_id-10972; Irwin M. Seltzer, "Immigration: Hard Facts," 1997 (American Enterprise Institute) http://www.aei.org/issue/7936; "A Social Creed for the 21st Century" (National Council of Churches), http://www.ncccusa.org/news/ga2007.socialcreed.html; Open Society Institute, "Grants, Scholarships, and Fellowships" (Soros), http://www.soros.org/grant; "Ford Foundation Annual Report 1998" (Ford Foundation), http://www.fordfound.org/archives/item/1998/text/82.

TABLE 8.6
For Full Social and Civil Rights for Immigrants: Includes Most of
Race-Conscious Alliance, 1978–2008

Most Democratic Party officeholders and members

Ethnic advocacy groups (MALDEF, National Council of La Raza, LULAC, Asian American Justice Center, NAACP)

Congressional Hispanic Caucus

Congressional Black Caucus

Immigrant advocacy groups (e.g., National Immigration Forum, American Immigration Council)

Most unions (e.g., AFL-CIO, SEIU, UNITE)

Some liberal Republicans

Liberal advocacy groups (e.g., ACLU, People for the American Way)

Liberal media (e.g., *New York Times*)

Liberal religious groups (e.g., National Council of Churches, Catholic Legal Immigration Network)

Liberal foundations (e.g., Soros, Ford)

Source: Along with the sources cited in the text and in support of table 8.4, table 8.6 derives from James Parks, "New Coalition Set to Push Immigration Reform Now" (AFL-CIO, SEIU, La Raza, NAACP, Asian American Justice Center, National Immigration Forum), http://blog.aflcio.org/2009/06/03/new-coalition-set-to-push-immigration-reform-now/ (December 5, 2009).

crimination provisions; some feared they might be undercut by the sanctions policies; Latinos especially supported amnesty. Opposition came chiefly from Republicans alarmed that immigrants would seek public aid and from conservative southerners, though some liberals also feared that the new sanctions would foster discrimination.[114]

Within a few years, virtually everyone agreed that the only successful part of IRCA was the amnesty program.[115] Undocumented immigration continued — fueled, in the eyes of critics, by both lax enforcement and the promise of eventual legalization the amnesty program symbolized. Surprisingly, a coalition of older ethnic associations, civil rights groups, churches, new immigrant groups, employer associations, and free market conservatives still succeeded in passing an immigration act in 1990 that did not lower immigration levels. Instead, it modified individual country caps, the overall ceiling on immigration, and the preference system in various ways, including "diversity visas" for underrepresented countries, which increased legal immigration. The Senate strongly supported the bill, and the House approved the final conference report 264–118, with Democrats heavily in favor and Republicans narrowly so. Opposition came chiefly from south and west border state representatives.[116]

But after 1990, the implementation of NAFTA, promoting further trafficking between the United States and Mexico and more Mexican immigration; the explosion of a bomb by Islamic immigrants at the World Trade Center in 1993; and controversies over Haitian and Cuban refugees all reinforced concerns about rising numbers of immigrants and, especially, undocumented Latino immigrants. Those concerns sparked intensified effort to reduce immigration levels, deport the undocumented, deny immigrants public benefits, and limit immigrant social and civil rights generally.[117] In 1992, the Republican platforms urged increased efforts to "stop illegal immigration," while the Democrats simply repeated their calls for "fairness, non-discrimination, and family reunification."[118] In 1994 Governor Pete Wilson of California, a champion of guest worker programs when he was a U.S. representative during the 1980s, successfully backed Proposition 187, a state referendum denying public benefits to undocumented aliens. A federal court struck down most of the law as violating federal authority over immigration and the Supreme Court's 1982 decision on immigrant access to public education, *Plyler v. Doe*.[119]

Undeterred, after gaining control of both houses of Congress in 1994, Republicans introduced a flurry of bills providing federal authorization for restrictions in immigrant rights.[120] Some aimed to expedite deportation of undocumented immigrants and aliens suspected of terrorism through limiting procedural rights. Some sought to deny immigrants access to public benefits, including economic aid, health care, and education. Some tried to lessen immigration overall. The 1996 Republican Party platform devoted extensive attention to immigration, criticizing the Democrats for opposing Proposition 187, urging more general denials to "non-citizens" of "welfare" and "public benefits other than emergency aid," and also advocating restrictions on birthright citizenship for children of alien parents who were not long-term residents.[121] As in regard to crime, Democrats now echoed much of the Republicans' character-oriented immigration rhetoric, advocating an "immigration policy that is pro-family, pro-work, pro-responsibility, and pro-citizenship," denouncing "illegal immigration" and "criminal aliens" and endorsing denials of "welfare benefits" to "illegal alien." The Democrats did still attack those who used immigration issues "as a pretext for discrimination."[122] The acceptance of color-blind and race-conscious advocates alike of the illegitimacy of racial discrimination explains why "respectable" restrictionists never argue in racist and nativist terms, making their efforts appear to be motivated chiefly by economic and national security concerns. But given the strength of the economy, some analysts contend, "racial prejudice played a much greater role than economic outlook in shaping attitudes toward immigration policy."[123]

Even so, a coalition of business, labor, civil rights, immigrant advocacy, and religious groups once again succeeded in fending off all efforts to lower the legal immigration ceiling.[124] Congress did, however, pass three laws in 1996 that put "the government seal of approval" on the "wave of widespread anti-immigrant feeling."[125] Not coincidentally, they also included tougher crime laws and the triumph of a decades-long effort to end a landmark New Deal social welfare program now seen as breeding dependency and as rewarding undeserving, largely nonwhite Americans.

Congress first passed the Antiterrorism and Effective Death Penalty Act of 1996 (AEDPA). AEDPA expedited the exclusion and arrest, punishment, and removal of those suspected of being alien terrorists or criminals by authorizing a special removal court, limiting judicial review of deportations, speeding up the timetable for deportation processes, limiting the discretion of the attorney general to admit or grant asylum to suspect aliens, and making many immigration law offenses subject to the expansive punitive measures authorized by RICO (the Racketeer Influenced and Corrupt Organizations Act).[126] Next, President Clinton signed the Personal Responsibility and Work Opportunity Reconciliation Act (PRWORA). It ended the AFDC program established in the original New Deal Social Security Act, replacing it with Temporary Assistance for Needy Families (TANF) block grants to the states. It made immigrants arriving after its enactment ineligible for all federally funded means-tested benefit programs like TANF and Medicaid for five years, with a state option to restore them thereafter; and it denied them Supplemental Security Income (SSI) and food stamps altogether. Immigrants could regain eligibility by naturalizing.[127]

Then in September 1996, the Illegal Immigration Reform and Immigrant Responsibility Act (IIRIRA) increased resources for immigration law enforcement, including detentions. It streamlined procedures to expedite exclusions and deportations. It limited the attorney general's discretionary authority to grant entry to the needy via "parole." It banned Social Security benefits for undocumented aliens. It gave the states the authorization to limit public assistance to aliens that anti-immigrant forces had long sought. It mandated new data collection on aliens, including requirements that educational institutions report on their foreign students. And it authorized heightened worksite investigations, among other measures.[128] After long negotiations, the bills that went to a conference committee received overwhelming bipartisan support in the Senate, passing 97–3, and Republican support in the House, 229–5, with House Democrats voting 76–117 against it. Black, Hispanic, and Asian Caucus House members overwhelmingly opposed the bill, but conservative Democrats, especially but not exclusively from the South and West, helped Republicans gain a comfortable victory.[129]

Collectively, these laws meant that even though the United States did not restrict legal admissions, it cut back sharply on the public benefits that immigrants as well as citizens could receive. For immigrants, the main consequence was to make it more likely that they would take any sort of employment on any terms offered. If they failed to find employment, the laws also made it easier to deport them. These measures heightened pressures to naturalize, and naturalization rates rose. But most scholars agree that the laws succeeded in sharply reducing the number of immigrants who received various forms of public aid, and many argue that problems of ill health, inadequate nutrition, and poverty rose in immigrant populations as a result.[130] They also prompted the states to undertake additional financial burdens of immigrant support that many have found difficult to sustain.[131] Even so, the laws placated some critics of high immigration levels while reducing many welfare and criminal procedural protections for all residents (citizens and aliens alike)—all without jeopardizing the availability of cheap immigrant labor favored by many employer interests and free market conservatives.

Though immigration continued to receive substantial attention in the subsequent presidential platforms of both parties, in bills introduced in Congress, and in the popular media, and though in 2003 the functions of the Immigration and Naturalization Service were redistributed to two agencies, Immigration and Customs Enforcement (ICE) and Citizenship and Immigration Services within the new Department of Homeland Security, the nation's basic immigration policies have since remained unchanged. In 2000, 2004, and 2008, Democrats promised to support punishment for employers of undocumented workers and to develop paths for otherwise unoffending undocumented aliens to obtain citizenship, while opposing guest worker programs.[132] Republicans in those years continued to stress the economic value of immigration and free trade while calling for immigrants' "cultural integration" and more effective enforcement of immigration restrictions, including a border fence and "sweeping new powers to deport." They also continued to oppose social benefits and amnesty for "illegal aliens."[133]

The nation's anti-terrorist political climate after the 9/11 attacks favored the tougher enforcement views within the governing Republicans. But the former Texas governor who was now president did not wish to alienate either employers of immigrant workers or Latino voters. As a result, the party's internal divisions on immigration continued, and the priority of other concerns meant that the Bush administration made little progress toward its oft-repeated goal of "comprehensive" immigration reform.[134] Restrictionists also made little headway in expanding their coalition. Black leaders like Wade Henderson of the Leadership Conference on Civil Rights made clear that they remained allied with "Latino and Asian communities and other progressive groups" because on issues like the "Voting Rights Act . . . education, Head Start, racial profiling, affirmative action, hate crimes," and other policies important to blacks, pro-immigration groups had supported African Americans, while most restrictionists had "stood squarely against us."[135] In return for their support, Democrats responded to pro-immigrant groups by championing the "Development, Relief and Education for Alien Minors" or DREAM Act. This act would provide many undocumented immigrants who had five years of residence in the United States and "good moral character" an opportunity for permanent residency status, if they completed high school and did military service or at least two years in an institution of higher education. Though a majority of the Senate expressed support, at this writing the bill still has fallen short of the sixty votes needed to avoid a filibuster.[136] The likelihood of the Obama administration fulfilling its broader promises for comprehensive immigration reform is doubtful.

It would be claiming too much to assert that on issues such as crime and immigration, all policymaking has been driven by the two modern racial alliances. It is impossible, however, to describe the politics or the policy outcomes in those areas accurately without recognizing that not only the overtly racial dimensions of these issues, but also the debates over them generally, have been profoundly shaped by the central ideological themes that bind the two modern alliances in opposition to each other. On the one hand, predominantly conservative and Republican forces repeatedly have sought to move the nation to color-blind policies that promise to encourage good character, punish misconduct, and diminish the significance of race in American life. Predominantly liberal and Democratic forces, including most advocacy groups for communities of color, have repeatedly instead supported policies that promise to redistribute resources and opportunities to America's long-disadvantaged nonwhite populations in the hopes of creating a more egalitarian society. These policies are often structured in race-targeted fashion, and they are always defended in race-conscious terms.

Neither side has succeeded in enacting policies to vindicate its positions or to fulfill its hopes. Instead, the inability of Americans to agree on responses to racial inequities has often meant that they have failed to define crime and immigration policies that are coherent and effective from any point of view. Instead, criminal justice policies have deepened gaps between whites and blacks, especially, and both immigration and criminal justice policies have deepened gaps between whites and Latinos. Nothing has done more to keep the America of the twenty-first century a house divided.

PART FOUR

America's Inheritance

Chapter 9

Prospects of the House Divided

THE STRUCTURE OF AMERICAN RACIAL POLITICS, THEN AND NOW

How can Americans achieve further progress in their long national struggle to reduce enduring material race inequalities? To aid reflection on this question, we have advanced in the preceding chapters a distinctive narrative of the past and present of American racial politics. That narrative has significant implications for understanding how politics has contributed to the construction of racial statuses and identities in America, and for thinking about how Americans might conduct their politics differently, in ways that offer better prospects for addressing inherited racial inequalities.

We have defended two chief empirical claims about how we should understand racial politics in the United States. First, we have sought to show that American racial politics has historically been structured as evolving systems of opposed racial policy alliances. Second, we have documented how modern American racial politics is characterized by a clash between generally cohesive color-blind and race-conscious alliances that are more aligned with the two major political parties and with opposed economic ideologies than ever before. Recall the pro- and anti-slavery alliances we saw in chapter 2 (tables 2.1 and 2.2):

Pro-slavery Alliance, 1787–1865	Anti-slavery Alliance, 1787–1865
Most Jeffersonian Republicans and Jacksonian Democrats	Some Free Soil Democrats, especially in the North (e.g., David Wilmot)
Most southern Federalists, Whigs (e.g., Alexander Stephens)	Some northern Federalists, Whigs; all Liberty Party, Free Soil Party, GOP
Most Supreme Court justices, many state courts	
Slave owners and most northern textile industrialists	Many northern state officials, judges, enforcing anti-slavery laws

Pro-slavery Alliance, 1787–1865	Anti-slavery Alliance, 1787–1865
Many artisans and working-class European immigrants	Many small farmers, merchants, craft manufacturers, esp. in the North, border states
Most white religious leaders, especially in the South	Some white religious groups (e.g., Quakers)
American School of Ethnology scholars	African American religious, educational, professional, and business groups
Some "civilized" Native American tribes	White abolitionists (e.g., American Anti-Slavery Society)
	Some intellectuals, popular writers (e.g., Harriet Beecher Stowe)

Recall also the pro– and anti–Jim Crow alliances we saw in chapter 3 (tables 3.1 and 3.2):

Pro–Jim Crow Racial Alliance, 1896–1954	Anti–Jim Crow Racial Alliance, 1896–1954
Southern and conservative Democrats	Racially egalitarian Democrats, overwhelmingly northern, mostly after 1932
Conservative Republican Party officeholders and members	Liberal Republicans
Presidents of both parties, either supportive or passive	Minority of Congress, federal bench, until 1950s
Most members of Congress, especially the Senate	Some federal agency officials, mostly after 1932
Majority of the Supreme Court to late 1940s	Minority of Supreme Court (i.e., Justice Harlan)
Most federal civil service officials	Some lower federal court, state judges
Most federal court judges, many state judges	A few white and most black businesses
Most white businesses	Black unions
Most white labor unions	Some liberal and socialist advocacy groups and parties
Most white churches	

Pro–Jim Crow Racial Alliance, 1896–1954	Anti–Jim Crow Racial Alliance, 1896–1954
Most academic institutions, disciplines until 1940	Liberal black and white religious groups
White supremacist groups (e.g., the KKK, the Pioneer Fund, White Citizen Councils)	Most nonwhite advocacy groups (e.g., NAACP, Urban League)
	Black fraternal organizations (e,g., Negro Fellowship League)
	Liberal white-black southern reform groups (e.g., Southern Conference for Human Welfare, Committee on Interracial Cooperation, Southern Electoral Reform League)
	Liberal foundations (e.g., Phelps-Stokes Foundation, Julius Rosenwald Fund)
	Liberal academics, especially after 1932

Throughout most of the anti-slavery era, until the Whigs gave way to the Lincoln Republicans, not only were the two major parties internally divided on the battleground issues of the maintenance and extension of slavery. There were also pro-slavery and anti-slavery proponents of economic ideologies favoring the use of central governmental power for national development, and pro- and anti-slavery advocates of more decentralized or laissez-faire economic policies. During the Jim Crow era, the two major parties were internally divided over segregation until large majorities in both finally converged on support for civil rights policies in the 1960s. And again, there were pro– and anti–Jim Crow Progressives and New Dealers who supported new economic regulatory and social aid policies, even if pro–Jim Crow Democrats were often anxious about the racial consequences of those policies. Similarly, there were pro– and anti–Jim Crow opponents of these economic initiatives.

It is only in the modern era that proponents of color blindness, pro-market economic policies, and the Republican Party largely align, while proponents of race-conscious policies, national regulatory and redistributive programs, and the Democratic Party also overlap extensively. As a result, although American racial politics has always been characterized by the opposition of rival racial policy alliances over battleground issues, interspersed with periods of transition after the issues of a particular era were decisively resolved, the modern opposition between today's color-blind and race-conscious alliances is playing a new role in contemporary American politics. The only real precedent is the period from 1856 to 1876, when partisan clashes over slavery and Reconstruction generated the most polarized politics in the nation's history. Fortunately, today's alignments do not map onto regional differences, as they did then. But if the United States does not face the prospect of sectional secession and another civil war today, it is nonetheless a political house that is more sharply divided than it has been for most of its history.[1]

Our contention that modern American politics displays distinctive and recurrent clashes between color-blind and race-conscious positions concurs with findings in many fields of scholarship, including constitutional jurisprudence, sociology, history, and to some degree political science.[2] But understandably, legal scholars, including most proponents of critical race theory, have tended to analyze "color-blind" and "race-conscious" positions as rival schools of constitutional jurisprudence. Sociologists have most discussed popular attitudes and social behavior. Modern historians, too, tend to focus on "ordinary citizens and civil rights activists" engaged in "social movements," while being wary of the generalizations found "in the pages of social science." And to our knowledge, no scholars working on electoral politics or public policymaking document the persistence of color-blind and race-conscious political coalitions across policy arenas in the way we do.[3]

Instead, some leading scholars in our own discipline, political science, stress that overt white racism receded in the latter third of the twentieth century—a point with which we agree. They therefore conclude that, at least in certain respects, class has come to play a more significant role in modern American politics than race—a point we regard as less clear. Representative of this perspective are studies by Byron Shafer and Richard Johnston, who argue that the momentous rise of the Republican Party in the South was due "first and foremost" to "economic development and an associated politics of social class."[4] In regard to the nation as a whole, Nolan McCarty, Keith Poole, and Howard Rosenthal similarly contend that "race as an issue has been absorbed into the main redistributive dimension of liberal-conservative politics" today.[5]

Other political scientists do stress the importance of race.[6] But many share often-justified suspicions of the kind of "grand narrative" we offer here. They emphasize the distinctive particularities of racial conflicts over different issues and in different national, state, and local political arenas, especially in the post-1965 era when immigration has made American racial and ethnic identities even more multiple.[7] Julie Novkov, for example, contends that a focus on national racial coalitions "provides some insights into large-scale change but does not generate much purchase on the intricacies of law and politics on the ground," including struggles over "particular visions of a racialized state order."[8] Because of these beliefs, or because they are simply more interested in social psychology, public opinion, voting behavior, or other topics, few political scientists have highlighted the persistence of racial alliances across America's foundational economic, residential, electoral, educational, criminal justice, immigration, and racial classification systems, among others, as we have done. Nor have they analyzed their significance.

Even so, we are far from wholly at odds with these positions. We acknowledge that the range of perspectives and attitudes on racial issues among the diverse American populace is far larger and more complicated than is captured by our focus on the positions of racial policy alliances. We agree as well that, while members of racial alliances are in fundamental agreement on how to resolve the central racial policy issues of their eras, alliance members nonetheless often have different motives to embrace those policies that reflect different visions of what race in America should become. Some color-blind proponents probably seek to covertly resist reductions in prevailing patterns of racial inequality in America. Others, probably most, sincerely believe both that race-neutral policies are inherently right and that they will prove broadly beneficial in the long run. On the other side, some proponents of race-conscious measures view them as temporary, to be used until meaningful material racial equality is achieved. Others believe that "multicultural" accommodations of racial and ethnic identities should be enduring features of American policy-making. Race-conscious advocates also differ in the weight they place on achieving many forms of racial integration. Though we have noted those different visions elsewhere, we have not explored them here.[9]

The preceding chapters do demonstrate that the modern racial policy alliances do not hold together in lockstep fashion on all issues. For example, mainstream Democrats are wary of appearing as "soft on crime" as the positions of some race-conscious proponents might have them do, and they support many crime laws shaped by color-blind ideology. Those business interests that support affirmative action in employment and education rarely champion integrated housing, and they may actively support school vouchers. Unions often support immigrant rights more enthusiastically than immigrant admissions, and many oppose guest worker programs. Latinos support majority-minority districts, but not always the same ones as blacks, and sometimes the same ones as Republicans. And blacks and Latinos have differed, though less fiercely, on census categories. When scholars look more closely at the politics of particular issues in particular locales, even greater variations appear, with Asian Americans in some cities and states more likely to oppose affirmative action,

and black and white Democrats or Latinos of different classes in greater conflict over districting, housing, and employment in some places than others.
Scholars who document and analyze race in America in ways that illuminate
these nuances and complexities contribute much of value.

At the extreme, however, there is a real danger of missing the forest for the
trees. A review of the tables and evidence in the preceding chapters shows that
on issue after issue involving a wide range of the most foundational structures
in American life, almost all of the same actors have lined up on one side or the
other of positions framed by support for or opposition to race-conscious policies designed to alleviate material racial inequalities. Tables 9.1 and 9.2 sum-
marize what the previous chapters have shown to be the core members of
each of the modern racial alliances—groups active on more than one racial
policy issue, and consistently on the same side when active—along with groups
that augment the ranks of each alliance on particular issues.

As with past racial policy alliances, the modern contending alliances have had
uneven success in gaining or retaining control of various American governing
institutions, each always in control of some but never all. Those variations,
along with some occasional defections or more frequently the disengagement
of some groups from particular controversies, mean that modern racial policy
contests have worked out differently on different issues. Modern courts endorsing color blindness have curtailed race-conscious measures in employment, education, and districting, for example. But race-conscious advocates in
Congress have reinstated some of those measures, and on balance they have
prevailed so far in contests over census categories and vouchers. The clash of
the modern racial coalitions continues precisely because neither has won
across the board. For that very reason, the alliance's conflicts have done much
to determine what American policies have been and what progress has or has
not been made in many areas.

We therefore think that much is missed if the continuing clashes of today's
racial policy alliances are not emphasized. We also think it misleading when
scholars suggest that either economic interests or economic ideologies or
some combination have displaced or "absorbed" race as an issue in American
politics today, especially in disputes between the two major parties. There is
no denying that partisan allegiances, economic ideologies, and racial policy
positions have become much more aligned in the modern era than in the past.
We have observed throughout how modern color-blind ideology, with its opposition to governmental favoritism and its emphasis on policies and institutions that reward good character and punish bad, has many affinities with
pro-market economic outlooks, as well as various forms of religious, military,
and cultural conservatism. Most modern race-conscious ideologies, in turn,

TABLE 9.1
Color-Blind Alliance, 1978–2008

Core members:

Most Republican Party officeholders and members after 1976

Presidents, 1981–93, 2001–9

Some conservative, neoconservative Democrats

Majority of Supreme Court after 1980

Most lower federal court judges, many state judges after 1980

Some senior bureaucrats after 1980

Some predominantly white-owned businesses and business lobbyists

Some traditional, predominantly white union locals

Conservative think tanks / advocacy groups (e.g., Center for Individual Rights, Cato Institute, AEI)

Conservative media (e.g., Rush Limbaugh, Anne Coulter, Charles Krauthammer)

Fringe white supremacist groups (e.g., New Century Foundation)

Christian Right groups (e.g., Family Research Council, Focus on the Family)

Conservative foundations (e.g., Bradley Foundation, Heritage Foundation)

Augmented for affirmative action in employment by:

Some single-issue employer advocacy groups (e.g., Equal Employment Advisory Council)

Augmented for color-blind housing policies by:

Some single-issue housing industry groups (e.g., National Association of Realtors, American Society of Appraisers, Independent Insurance Agents of America, National Association of Insurance Commissioners

Augmented for pro-vouchers by:

Catholic groups

(continued)

TABLE 9.1 *(continued)*

Augmented for pro–mixed race census category:

A minority of state legislatures

Mixed race advocacy groups (e.g., Project RACE, AMEA)

Augmented for punitive criminal justice policies:

Most prosecutors

Many businesses, private prison companies

Law enforcement employee unions, advocacy groups

Conservative community crime prevention groups

Victims' groups (e.g., Parents of Murdered Children)

Women's groups concerned with rape, battered women

Augmented for reducing immigration:

Neorestrictionist groups (e.g., FAIR, NumbersUSA)

Some unions (e.g., AFL-CIO) against guest workers, divided on employer sanctions

Some African American advocates outside of Congress (e.g., T. Willard Fair)

Augmented against full social and civil rights for immigrants:

Most employers (e.g., U.S. Chamber of Commerce, National Association of Manufacturers)

Neorestrictionist groups (e.g., FAIR, NumbersUSA)

Some African American advocates outside of Congress (e.g., T. Willard Fair)

---

have affinities with positions favoring government action to address persisting economic as well as social inequalities. As a result, we believe it only makes sense that various data show that party identifications, economic ideologies, and racial ideologies increasingly appear to be arrayed along a single spectrum. Most influentially in this vein, McCarty, Poole, and Rosenthal have used congressional roll call voting to show that most members of both parties have increasingly been distributed along, and clustered toward one or the other end of, a conservative-to-liberal ideological continuum. This ideological polarization, they contend, has followed an "unbroken upward trajectory"

TABLE 9.2
Race-Conscious Alliance, 1978–2008

Core members:

Most Democratic Party officeholders and members

President (mixed support), 1993–2001

Some liberal Republicans (e.g., Hamilton Fish)

Some federal, state judges

Many civil service members of executive agencies, some top executives

Many large businesses, minority-owned businesses

Most large labor unions, especially in public, service sector industries (e.g., SEIU, AFL-CIO, NEA)

Liberal media (e.g., *New York Times*)

Liberal advocacy groups (e.g., ACLU, Common Cause, People for the American Way)

Liberal think tanks (e.g., Urban Institute)

Most nonwhite and cross-racial advocacy groups (e.g., NAACP, National Council of La Raza, Asian American Legal Defense Fund, Leadership Conference on Civil Rights)

Liberal religious groups (e.g., National Council of Churches, National Catholic Council for Interracial Justice)

Liberal foundations (e.g., Soros Foundation, Ford Foundation)

Augmented for affirmative action in employment by:

Military leadership

Augmented for racial integration in housing by:

Housing advocacy groups (e.g., National Fair Housing Alliance, Housing Advocates, Inc.)

Augmented for pro-majority-minority districts by:

Some strategically minded Republican officeholders

(continued)

TABLE 9.2 *(continued)*

Augmented in opposition to vouchers by:

    Pro-secular and anti-religious groups (e.g., Americans for Religious Liberty, American Atheists)

Augmented to oppose mixed race census category by:

    Most state budgetary and administrative officials

Augmented for preventive and rehabilitative criminal justice policies:

    Liberal community crime prevention groups

    Prisoners' rights groups

Augmented against reducing immigration:

    Immigrant advocacy groups (e.g., National Immigration Forum, American Immigration Council)

    Most employers (e.g., U.S. Chamber of Commerce, National Association of Manufacturers)

    Libertarian and economically conservative think tanks (e.g., Cato Institute, AEI)

Augmented in favor of full social and civil rights for immigrants:

    Immigrant advocacy groups (e.g., National Immigration Forum, American Immigration Council)

---

since 1977—the same period in which we find that the modern racial alliances coalesced.[10] The 2010 midterm elections did not mark a break in the upward trajectory.

Yet these correspondences of party, economic, and racial positions are not total; and the disjunctions *matter*, because they are often consequential for policy outcomes. If many large businesses and major unions had not come to support affirmative action measures in employment and education, they might not survive in the restricted forms that they now do. Conversely, if more Democrats had supported the Congressional Black Caucus's Racial Justice Act, it might have passed. If Republicans had consistently held to their opposition to majority-minority districts in the name of color-blind principles, there might have been fewer such districts, and they might have been drawn differently.

Still more fundamental is the issue of how we should characterize the extensive alignments of racial ideologies, economic ideologies, and party allegiances we do observe. We question whether, even when partisan views, economic views, and racial views do correspond, this correspondence proves that racial positions have been "absorbed" by or subsumed under economic ideologies or interests, seen as the engines driving the party system, or that racial stances are now determined by party loyalties. On the relationship of racial and economic positions, consider for instance the argument of Byron Shafer and Richard Johnston about the American South in *The End of Southern Exceptionalism*. They offer a fresh interpretation of a phenomenon that all political scientists see as important. Among the greatest transformations in modern American electoral politics has been the end of the segregation-era Democratic Solid South and the rise of Republican support in the region, beginning most dramatically in presidential elections with Goldwater's success in the South (and nowhere else) in 1964; continuing with an increase in southern Republican members of Congress (including conversions of former Democrats like Strom Thurmond of South Carolina, Phil Gramm of Texas, and Trent Lott of Mississippi), leading to Republican majorities in the congressional delegations from the South after 1994; and culminating with the growth of Republican southern state governorships and legislatures since the early 1990s.[11]

For Shafer and Johnston, the key to this change is that, as the South moved from an agrarian to a service and industrial economy beginning in the 1950s, traditional white southern voting patterns began to reverse, first in presidential elections, then in House and Senate races. Whereas in the Jim Crow era wealthier southern whites were more likely to vote Democratic and poorer ones were somewhat more likely to vote Republican, in the modern era the South has become more like the rest of the nation, with wealthier whites endorsing conservative views on social welfare issues and voting more Republican, poorer whites more Democratic. After the 1960s, moreover, white racial conservatives, who formerly voted overwhelmingly Democratic, have voted Republican, and white racial liberals, once primarily Republican, have voted Democratic. Newly enfranchised blacks have voted far more often than they once could, and they have voted overwhelmingly for more liberal, "northern"-style Democrats, instead of traditionalist southern Democrats.[12]

We have no quarrel with these characterizations. To Shafer and Johnston, these depictions confirm their claim that the politics of social class and not race has been the primary engine of partisan change in the South, for two reasons. First, they stress the primacy of class in a chronological sense: they emphasize that economic development began to precipitate the growth of

263

wealthier southern Republican voters in the 1950s, while the impacts of race came later. Second, they contend that the "racial threat" hypothesis tracing back to the classic work of the political scientist V. O. Key, holding that white support for conservative racial positions should be strongest in those regions of the South where whites were a small ruling minority rather than a majority, is not sustained in their evidence of southern presidential and congressional voting.[13]

On the first point, we agree that support for Republicans began to grow in the South in the 1950s, largely due to the region's economic development. But Shafer and Johnston's data also show that *most* of the conversion of the South to support for Republicans came after the late 1960s, with the tipping point of Republican majorities in elections for both national and statewide offices in the South not coming until after 1990—years by which they acknowledge racial factors had become important.[14] On their second point, we have no position. Our argument is about the importance of modern coalitions on racial policies, not racial "threats."

What do Shafer and Johnston find in regard to the importance of racial policies? They divide their evidence into three unequally sized time blocs, 1952–60, 1962–90, and 1992–2000. With minor variations, they find that in elections for the presidency, the House, and the Senate, welfare policies did much to shape southern votes in the 1950s; from the 1960s through the 1980s, positions on racial policies became more important; and since the 1990s, "racial ideology" has been "a major voting influence."[15] They also find that by the 1990s, across House, Senate, and presidential elections, party allegiances and conservative versus liberal views on welfare policy and racial policy aligned.[16] These are really the patterns visible among white voters, they concede, since for modern southern black voters, "a politics of racial identity" has always been so powerful "that it left no effective room for an additional politics of class." Black voters have overwhelmingly been Democratic voters regardless of their income or wealth.[17]

Consider these results in light of the historical development of the rival racial policy alliances employed here. In the 1950s, with the Jim Crow segregation alliance in overwhelming control of the South, most blacks disfranchised, and the few credible southern Republican candidates unwilling to press racial issues, it is not surprising that the southern vote primarily reflected positions on whether voters supported New Deal–style welfare policies or not. The 1948 Dixiecrat revolt had already shown, however, that southerners would vote based on racial issues should segregation be challenged. Shafer and Johnston's second period, 1962 to 1990, is a long one encompassing major changes. At its start the national parties were close together on racial issues. Then there was an era of transition when neither racial issues nor the positions of the parties on them were clear. And finally, as the preceding case studies show, the modern racial policy alliances emerged in the late 1970s, identified with the major parties. It is not surprising that this heterogeneous period shows mixed patterns on the significance of racial policies for voting in the South, with evidence of its "rising relevance," particularly in presidential voting, where there was not the mix of what Shafer and Johnston term more "local," often more conservative, and more "cosmopolitan," often more liberal Democrats that could be found in House and Senate elections.[18] When we reach Shafer and Johnston's third era, the 1990s, with the rivalry between the two modern racial alliances now full-blown, their evidence shows preferences on racial policy were making "a single, consistent, and massively growing contribution" to southern voting behavior, so that economic attitudes no longer "clearly led racial attitudes as an influence."[19]

We conclude, then, that the data and analysis of Shafer and Johnston on the making of modern southern politics are wholly consistent with the account of evolving racial alliances explicated here. But it is, of course, not their purpose to document or characterize the coalitions on racial policies as we have done, so their work at best hints at the existence of these racial policy alliances. Their rhetorical emphasis on how "class continued to trump race as an engine for partisan change" as they analyze southern politics can moreover convey the impression that their analysis indicates declining significance for race in southern politics—far more than they argue or show to be the case.

What about broader national politics, as represented by McCarty, Poole, and Rosenthal's influential analysis of congressional voting, *Polarized America*? Though their interpretations sound more opposed, their evidence is if anything still more consistent with the racial alliances framework. They have created a widely used data set, termed NOMINATE scores, that positions members of Congress in relation to each other based on how often they vote together.[20] They argue that since 1876, which they date as the end of Reconstruction, members of Congress have generally voted with sufficient consistency to array along a single dimension ranging from most conservative to most liberal on virtually all issues. *Polarized America* does not directly analyze the content of this dimension. But the authors interpret it as primarily driven by "income and economics," because they note that in the late nineteenth and early twentieth century, both parties kept "voting on civil rights for African Americans . . . off the congressional agenda except for a scattering of votes on lynching."[21] Then in the late 1930s, when northern Democrats gained majorities in both houses of Congress for the first time, votes on civil rights became more frequent and a second dimension appeared, "separating northern and southern Representatives, regardless of party."[22]

They interpret this second dimension as the array of congressional positions on racial issues. It represents a distinct dimension because congressional members did not vote in the clusters and patterns that they did on economic ones. In particular, they observe that most southern Democrats who supported their party's New Deal economic liberalism on many issues did not support liberal racial positions, and a number of Republicans who were pro-business and conservative on most economic issues nonetheless backed racial reforms. McCarty, Poole, and Rosenthal find that the significance of this second, racial dimension to congressional voting expanded in "the post–WW II era" of the 1950s civil rights movement as "voting coalitions on racial issues" became ever more "distinct from those on other issues."[23] But as more and more members of Congress in both parties came to support civil rights in the late 1950s, "the second dimension began to disappear," a pattern that, these authors contend, "sped up dramatically" after the 1964 Civil Rights Act.[24] McCarty, Poole, and Rosenthal argue that "since the early 1970s," the importance of this "second dimension based on race" has receded steadily, and congressional voting has becoming increasingly one-dimensional. Racial issues formerly divided both parties internally but now have ceased to do so, rendering racial politics "more like the rest of American politics."[25] They also contend, in common with Shafer and Johnston, that these developments reflect in great part how southern voting in particular has come to resemble the patterns in the rest of the nation, with black southerners of all incomes voting Democratic, but for whites, the "richer the southerner, the more likely he is to vote Republican."[26]

These patterns again conform to those we have described in terms of evolving racial alliances: after the end of Reconstruction, the parties did not clash much over racial issues, only economic ones, until the increase of northern Democrats after 1932 began to divide the Democratic Party over segregation. That split was sharpest in the 1950s and early 1960s. But the triumphs of the civil rights movement then led to new racial issues and alliances—this time with the parties opposed to each other on *both* economic and racial issues. The fact that *Polarized America* breaks up the long middle period in Shafer and Johnston's analysis and identifies the late 1970s as the takeoff point for heightened partisan polarization means that its chronology matches ours even more precisely.

However, we dispute McCarty, Poole, and Rosenthal's contention that the modern convergence of partisan, economic, and racial positions means that economic positions have "absorbed" racial ones. They believe that "cleavages over race are converging to the preexisting economic cleavages, rather than the other way around."[27] Their main arguments for this claim are first, that

266

since "it is hard to see racism as hardening in the last quarter of the twentieth century," they doubt that modern political polarization can be traced to "racism."[28] Second, they contend that even voters often said to choose on the basis of social or moral issues, like conservative Christians, "do not completely ignore their economic interests," though low-income conservative Christians "do support the Republicans more than other low-income voters do."[29]

In our view, their first claim recklessly misses the boat (and a rather large boat) by presuming that racial issues can matter only if "racism" is "hardening." They do not consider that potent differences on racial policies might exist even if virulent overt racism is rare. And as we have seen, there is abundant evidence that clashes over racial policy issues did heighten in the last quarter of the twentieth century. The fact that congressional voting patterns on these racial policies conform to those on most economic issues and to party lines does not prove that economic positions (or, as others would have it, partisan allegiances) are what matter most. It simply proves that a polarizing convergence of partisan, economic, and racial positions has occurred, as we agree.

How are we to understand the sources of that convergence? *Polarized America* addresses that question obliquely. The authors observe that conservative Christians "do not completely ignore their economic interests"—though to some extent these voters "do." In so saying, McCarty, Poole, and Rosenthal imply an account of one of the central developments of late twentieth-century American politics: the forging of the Reagan coalition, linking economic, religious and cultural, racial, and pro-military foreign policy conservatives together more tightly than ever before (or since). As many conservative thinkers, among others, have noted, that coalition is far from automatic. Economic conservatives are often libertarians who oppose the social regulation, and sometimes even the large military spending, supported by many religious, cultural, racial, and foreign policy conservatives; and many in those ranks disagree over what regulations are best.[30]

We argue in the preceding chapters that modern conservatives united the Reagan coalition by linking discourses of character. These discourses presented conservative economic, religious, cultural, racial, and military policies as all serving to foster, recognize, protect, and reward good character and punish bad character—and that nothing did more to legitimate this blended "character conservatism" than its ability to invoke the moral, religious, and political prestige of the civil rights movement on its behalf.[31] McCarty, Poole, and Rosenthal appear to assume, without direct argument, that conservative leaders have used economic interests and ideology as the primary glue for this modern coalition—that as white Americans ceased to be racist, they all began voting with their pocketbooks or were quickly persuaded to do so. In particular, like Shafer and Johnston, they stress that wealthier southern whites that formerly voted against their economic interests on racial grounds now vote consistently for representatives who serve their economic goals.

But consider, first, that the elected representatives of wealthy white southerners, now Republicans, also favor more conservative color-blind positions on racial issues. Second, McCarty, Poole, and Rosenthal, like Shafer and Johnston, find that black voting *cannot* be explained chiefly in terms of economic interests. Third, they acknowledge that some conservative Christian voting, the backbone of the modern Religious Right in American politics, also cannot be explained in those terms. And finally, they provide no direct evidence on the content of the conservative/liberal ideological spectrum they find in modern congressional voting. In light of these points, it is at a minimum not clear why we should assume that economic policies have been much more fundamental than racial policies in forging the conservative and liberal coalitions in modern America's polarized politics. We believe the evidence we recount constitutes strong reason to believe that, as important as economic ideology and interests are, racial issues have mattered irrefragably as well. We see the modern conservative-to-liberal ideological spectrum that McCarty, Poole, and Rosenthal discern as comprising pro-market, pro-color-blind, pro-religiously and culturally traditionalist, and hawkish foreign policy positions, versus pro-government regulation, pro-race-conscious and multicultural, and more diplomacy-reliant positions, with color blindness in particular serving as a crucial conservative ideological glue. To be fair, *Polarized America* does note that race appears to be "related" to various public policy issues.[32] But like many, perhaps most, scholars of American politics, the three authors do not suggest that cohesive alliances on racial policies have been important contributors to modern political polarization, nor that these alliances have consistently been significant players in shaping outcomes on a wide range of issues. In common with Shafer and Johnston, their claims minimizing race as an explanatory variable exceed their evidence that racial concerns have ceased to be important.

THE CONSEQUENCES OF THE MODERN RACIAL ALLIANCES

That inattention to today's racial policy coalitions by many, though by no means all, scholars of American politics, particularly in political science, strikes us as severely damaging, because it fails to highlight a critical reality. The evidence reviewed here suggests that the effects of the clash of the modern racial alliances have been debilitating on many fronts. Color-blind proponents have long believed that promises of race-conscious assistance tempt blacks and Latinos away from doing what they need to do for themselves if they are to succeed in America. Race-conscious advocates have long believed that their color-blind opponents not only sharply restrict necessary race-targeted aid programs. They are accused further of cutting the funding, staffing, and commitment needed to enforce anti-discrimination laws effectively. What seems undeniable is that as legislators, executive branch officials, and courts at national, state, and local levels have battled over racial policies, they have produced a nation still marked by harsh, intractable racial inequalities in numerous arenas of American life. Before turning to the further implications of this analysis, it will be helpful to take stock of the data that show just how severe and pervasive those inequalities still are.

The story is far from wholly negative. Since the victories of the civil rights era, African Americans and Latinos have made progress on a number of fronts. In political representation, President Obama's election is only the tip of a dramatic iceberg of increased presence of nonwhites in elected offices at all levels. Systematically locked out of political power through most of U.S. history, African Americans and Latino Americans now have seats at the nation's governing tables, even if still disproportionately fewer seats than their shares of the population (see table 9.3).

As table 9.4 indicates, from 1940 to 2008, African Americans substantially increased their presence in various professions in both absolute and percentage terms, with the greatest increases coming after 1970 (the percentages of black doctors and college teachers actually declined from 1940 to 1970).

Similar patterns are visible in other professional fields, contributing to significant growth in the African American middle class. By way of comparison, though full historical data for Latinos are lacking, in 2008 Hispanics of all races made up more than 15 percent of the U.S. population—but they provided only 3.8 percent of American lawyers, 5.8 percent of American physicians, and 4 percent of American college teachers, relatively worse rates than African Americans.[33] Progress also occurred in the high school and college graduation rates for African Americans and to a lesser degree for Latinos by the age of twenty-five, accompanied by reductions in official dropout rates (tables 9.5–9.7):

Although these numbers confirm striking advances for African Americans and Latinos after 1970, with the major modern civil rights laws in place (and the beginning of affirmative action), they show that African Americans, who made up a little over 12.8 percent of the U.S. population in 2008, are still

TABLE 9.3

Black and Latino Legislators, National and State, 1940–2009

	Federal Legislators		State Legislators	
Year	Black	Latino	Black	Latino
1940	1	3	n/a	n/a
1950	2	3	n/a	n/a
1960	4	3	n/a	n/a
1970	11	6	169	n/a
1980	17	7	323	n/a
1990	24	14	423	144
2000	39	17	598	217
2009	42	26	628	242

Source: This table derives from Jennifer E. Manning and Colleen J. Shogan, "African American Members of the United States Congress: 1870–2009," February 2, 2010, Congressional Research Service 7-5700, http://www.fas.org/sgp/crs/misc/RL30378.pdf; "Hispanic Americans in Congress 1822–1995," http://www.loc.gov/rr/hispanic/congress/contents.html; Joint Center for Political and Economic Studies, "Black Elected Officials in the U.S. by Category of Office" (2000); National Conference of State Legislators, http://www.jointcenter.org/ publicationspublication-PDFs/BEO-pdfs/2001-BEO.pdf.

significantly underrepresented in relation to their population share in the higher paid educated professions, as in political offices. Latinos fare even worse.[34] Black Americans have closed much of the gap on whites in graduating from high school, though on this measure too, Latinos, particularly Mexican Americans, lag well behind. But blacks are still substantially behind whites in graduating from colleges, with Latinos and again Mexican Americans once more further back.

And even if more nonwhites are truly graduating from American high schools (many analysts find these numbers suspect), everyone recognizes that the schools most urban African Americans and Latinos attend remain far from equal to most suburban schools predominantly attended by whites.[35] Many analysts of American education are disturbed that the nation's schools are resegregating, in fact though not in law, in ways that make schooling continue to be separate and unequal, by both race and class. Table 9.8 depicts both

TABLE 9.4
Blacks in Selected Professions, 1940–2008

Year	Black Lawyers	Percent	Black Physicians	Percent	Black College Teachers	Percent	Black K–12 Teachers	Percent	Black Nurses	Percent
1940	1,000	0.5	4,160	2.5	2,680	3.5	67,580	6.4	7,880	2.2
1970	3,703	1.3	6,044	2.2	16,582	3.4	227,788	8.2	66,400	7.8
1990	27,320	3.5	20,874	4.5	37,867	4.8	435,558	9.6	165,520	8.9
2008	46,644	4.6	54,364	6.2	63,336	5.2	703,663	10.0	402,886	12.0

Source: Stephan Thernstrom and Abigail Thernstrom, *America in Black and White* (New York: Simon and Schuster, 1997), 187; Theodore Cross and Robert Bruce Slater, "Only the Onset of Affirmative Action Explains the Explosive Growth in Black Enrollments in Higher Education," *Journal of Blacks in Higher Education* 23 (1999): 114; U.S. Census Bureau, 2010 *Statistical Abstract of the United States*, "Table 603: Employed Civilians by Occupation, Sex, Race, and Hispanic Origin: 2008," http://www.census.gov/compendia/statab/2010/tables/10s0603.pdf.

TABLE 9.5

Percent High School Diploma or Higher, 1940–2009

Year	Total	White			Black			Hispanic		
		Total	Male	Female	Total	Male	Female	Total	Male	Female
1940	24.5	26.1	24.2	28.1	7.7	6.9	8.4	n/a	—	—
1950	34.3	36.4	34.6	38.2	13.7	12.6	14.7	n/a	—	—
1960	41.1	43.2	41.6	44.7	21.7	20.0	23.1	n/a	—	—
1970	55.3	57.4	57.2	57.7	36.1	35.4	36.6	n/a	—	—
1980	68.6	71.9	72.4	71.5	51.4	51.2	51.5	44.5	44.9	44.2
1990	77.6	81.4	81.6	81.3	66.2	65.8	66.5	50.8	50.3	51.3
2000	84.1	88.4	88.5	88.4	78.9	79.1	78.7	57.0	56.6	57.5
2009	86.7	91.6	91.4	91.9	84.2	84.2	84.2	61.9	60.6	63.3

Source: National Center for Education Statistics, "Table 8. Percentage of Persons Age 25 and Over and 25 to 29, by Race/Ethnicity, Years of School Completed, and Sex: Selected Years, 1910 through 2009," http://nces. ed.gov/programs/digest/d09/tables/dt09_008.asp.

the progress in desegregation in the late 1960s and the early 1970s and the subsequent return of segregated education:

As table 9.8 indicates, the percentage of black students in more than 90 percent minority schools dropped dramatically from 1968 to 1973 and fell as low as a third in 1991, but it has since increased. The percentage of Latinos in more than 90 percent minority schools has heightened as the Latino population has grown during those decades. In 2006–7, with federal courts no longer demanding desegregation in most jurisdictions, the numbers had risen to 38.5 percent of African Americans, 40 percent of Latinos. These patterns of some real progress accompanied by substantial persistent inequalities run throughout the data on contemporary America, with the main departures in areas where there has been little progress toward greater racial material equality at all, or even declines.

Despite the progress of African Americans in the professions, for example, both they and Latinos continue to lag behind whites in individual and especially in household income and net worth, while suffering persistently higher unemployment rates (tables 9.9–9.12).

TABLE 9.6
Percent Bachelor's Degree or Higher, 1940–2009

Year	Total	White			Black			Hispanic		
		Total	Male	Female	Total	Male	Female	Total	Male	Female
1940	4.6	4.9	5.9	4.0	1.3	1.4	1.2	n/a	—	—
1950	6.2	6.6	7.9	5.4	2.2	2.1	2.4	n/a	—	—
1960	7.7	8.1	10.3	6.0	3.5	3.5	3.6	n/a	—	—
1970	11.0	11.6	15.0	8.6	6.1	6.8	5.6	n/a	—	—
1980	17.0	18.4	22.8	14.4	7.9	7.7	8.1	7.6	9.2	6.2
1990	21.3	23.1	26.7	19.8	11.3	11.9	10.8	9.2	9.8	8.7
2000	25.6	28.1	30.8	25.5	16.6	16.4	16.8	10.6	10.7	10.6
2009	29.5	32.9	33.9	31.9	19.4	17.9	20.6	13.2	12.5	14.0

Source: National Center for Education Statistics, "Table 8. Percentage of Persons Age 25 and Over and 25 to 29, by Race/Ethnicity, Years of School Completed, and Sex: Selected Years, 1910 through 2009," http://nces .ed.gov/programs/digest/d09/tables/dt09_008.asp.

TABLE 9.7
Percent High School Dropouts, 1970–2008

Year	Total	White	Black	Hispanic
1970	15.0	13.2	27.9	n/a
1980	14.1	11.4	19.1	35.2
1990	12.1	9.0	13.2	32.4
2000	10.9	6.9	13.1	27.8
2008	8.0	4.8	9.9	18.3

Source: National Center for Education Statistics, "Table 108. Percentage of High School Dropouts among Persons 16 through 24 Years Old (Status Dropout Rate), by Sex and Race/Ethnicity: Selected Years, 1960 through 2008," http://nces.ed.gov/programs/digest/d09/tables/dt09_108.asp.

TABLE 9.8

Percent Students in Predominantly Minority Schools

Year	1968–69		1980–81		1991–92		2006–7	
Percent Nonwhite Students	50–100% Nonwhite	90–100% Nonwhite	50–100% Nonwhite	90–100% Nonwhite	50–100% Nonwhite	90–100% Nonwhite	50–100% Nonwhite	90–100% Nonwhite
Black	76.6	64.3	63.6	38.7	62.9	33.9	73.0	38.5
Latino	54.8	23.1	62.9	23.3	68.1	34.0	78.0	40.0

Source: Gary Orfield, "Reviving the Goal of an Integrated Society: A 21st Century Challenge," UCLA, The Civil Rights Project, January 2009, 12–13, http://www.civilrightsproject.ucla.edu/research/deseg/reviving_the_goal_mlk_2009.pdf; Gary Orfield and John T. Yun, "Resegregation in American Schools," UCLA, The Civil Rights Project "Table 9. Percentage of U.S. Black and Latino Students in Predominantly Minority and 90–100% Minority Schools, 1968–96".

TABLE 9.9
Median Income of Individuals, 1950–2009 (Constant 2009 Dollars)

Year	All Males, Median Income	All Females	White Males	White Females	Black Males	Black Females	Hispanic Males (all races)	Hispanic Females (all races)
1950	19,989	7,412	n/a	n/a	11,441	3,687	n/a	n/a
1960	25,859	7,992	n/a	n/a	14,324	5,305	n/a	n/a
1970	32,880	11,027	n/a	n/a	20,492	10,170	n/a	n/a
1980	31,054	12,194	33,906	12,342	19,849	11,351	23,939	10,917
1990	32,284	16,020	34,933	16,833	20,472	13,249	21,430	11,983
2000	35,303	20,007	39,245	20,757	26,584	19,781	24,286	15,256
2009	32,184	20,957	36,785	21,939	23,738	19,470	22,256	16,210

Source: U.S. Census Bureau, "Table P-2. Race and Hispanic Origin of People by Median Income and Sex: 1947 to 2009," http://www.census.gov/hhes/www/income/data/historical/people/index.html.

All groups declined in median household income between 2000 and 2009; but African Americans and Latinos declined more than whites. Table 9.11 shows the stark disparities in the median net worth of white, black, and Hispanic families at the end of that period, with non-Hispanic white families worth nearly sixteen times as much as black and Hispanic families. Those numbers reflect in part differences in homeownership. In 2007, 75.2 percent of whites were homeowners, compared with 47.2 percent of African Americans and 49.7 percent of Latinos.[36] Admittedly, a home became an asset of dubious reliability by the end of the decade. But if we exclude home equity from wealth calculations, the differences remain huge. From 1984 to 2007, the wealth gap between whites and blacks more than quadrupled, with wealth holdings for white families rising in those years from a median value of $22,000 to $100,000 in constant dollars, while the median wealth holdings of African American families went from $2,000 to roughly $5,000—increasing the gap from $20,000 to $95,000.[37] At the bottom end of the spectrum, in 2007, 9 percent of all non-Hispanic whites and 6 percent of non-Hispanic white families were below the poverty level, while 24.7 percent of all African Americans and 21.3 percent of African American families were poor, as were 20.7 percent of all Hispanics and 18.5 percent of Hispanic families.[38] Access to bank

TABLE 9.10
Median Income of Households, 1970–2009 (Constant 2009 Dollars)

Year	Median Income, All Households	White (not Hispanic)	Black	Latino (all Races)
1970	43,055	n/a	27,295	n/a
1980	43,892	47,126	26,677	33,832
1990	47,637	50,822	29,712	35,525
2000	52,301	56,826	36,952	41,312
2009	49,777	54,461	32,584	38,039

Source: U.S. Census Bureau, "Table H-5. Race and Hispanic Origin of Householder—Households by Median and Mean Income: 1967–2009," http://www.census.gov/hhes/www/income/data/historical/household/index.html.

accounts varies dramatically too according to an FDIC survey. The average percentage of Americans lacking bank accounts is 7.7 percent, and 3.3 percent, 19.3 percent, and 21.7 percent for whites, Latinos, and African Americans, respectively.[39]

There is ample evidence that the subprime mortgage crisis continues to deepen these racial economic inequalities. Because over half of the mortgages held by African American homeowners are subprime, at this writing many are faced with the loss of homes and home equity likely to amount to well over $100 billion nationally.[40] As a result of the housing crisis and the Great Recession more generally, by 2009 blacks and Latinos were 2.9 and 2.7 times as likely, respectively, to live in poverty as whites. Since the unemployment rate among African Americans at that time rose as high as 16.2 percent, among Latinos 12.9 percent, and among whites 9 percent, there were faint prospects for economic progress for nonwhites, much less a closing of the racial gaps.[41]

Health disparities today are also severe. These inequalities, too, will be compounded by the economic and psychological stress experienced by all Americans, and disproportionately nonwhite Americans, damaged by home foreclosures.[42] Already in 2005, African American men were from 1.3 to 2.4 times more likely than non-Hispanic white men to have various forms of cancer; 30 percent more likely to die of heart disease; 60 percent more likely to die of stroke; and African American babies had a 2.3 times higher infant mortality rate than non-Hispanic whites.[43] In many regards Latinos were actually less

TABLE 9.11
Median Net Worth of Families, 1983–2007 (Thousands of 2007 Dollars)

Year	Total	White	Black	Hispanic
1983	69.5	91.0	6.1	3.5
1989	74.3	108.1	2.8	2.3
1992	63.4	90.7	15.3	5.4
1995	62.1	83.0	10.0	6.8
1998	77.2	103.9	12.7	3.8
2001	86.1	124.6	12.5	3.5
2004	85.5	129.8	13.0	6.1
2007	102.5	143.6	9.3	9.1

Source: Edward N. Wolff, "Recent Trends in Household Wealth in the United States: Rising Debt and the Middle-Class Squeeze" (Working Paper 589, Levin Economics Institute, Bard College, March 2010), http://www.levyinstitute.org/pubs/wp_589.pdf.

likely to have various forms of cancer and heart disease than non-Hispanic whites, but they were twice as likely to have diabetes, and their infant mortality rates ranged significantly higher.[44]

Nowhere, however, is the worsening of conditions in nonwhite America more visible than in incarceration rates (table 9.13).

Though the racial disparities in incarceration rates have become a bit less lopsided since the end of the Reagan administration—when there were actually more African Americans in jail than whites even though over 80 percent of Americans were white and a little over 12 percent were black—today incarceration is vastly racially disproportionate. This inequality has wide-ranging consequences for African American and Latino communities.[45] These imprisonment rates both reflect and reinforce perceptions of nonwhites as prone to violent criminality; and according to audit studies, those perceptions in turn mean that even blacks without criminal records are half as likely to receive callbacks for jobs as equally qualified whites.[46]

When we consider historical and current statistics on political representation, employment, income, wealth, education, health, and control by the criminal justice system, then, it is impossible to avoid the conclusion that, though the United States has ended many formal racial inequalities and alleviated

TABLE 9.12
Unemployment Rates, 1980–2007

Year	Black Unemployed	Unemployed (%)	Latino Unemployed	Unemployed (%)	White Unemployed	Unemployed (%)
1980	1,553,000	14.3	620,000	10.1	5,884,000	6.3
1990	1,565,000	11.4	876,000	8.2	5,186,000	4.8
2000	1,241,000	7.6	954,000	5.7	4,121,000	3.5
2007	1,445,000	8.3	1,220,000	5.6	5,143,000	4.1

Source: Rates are for persons sixteen years and older. Many other unemployment estimates use higher ages. Table calculated from U.S. Census Bureau, *Statistical Abstract of the United States,* 2009, "Table 569. Civilian Population—Employment Status by Sex, Race, and Ethnicity: 1970–2007," http://www.census.gov/prod/2008pubs/09statab/labor.pdf.

TABLE 9.13

Number of Persons under Correctional Supervision, 1990–2008

Year	Total	White			Black			Hispanic		
		In Jail	Total (%)	White Population (%)	In Jail	Total (%)	Black Population (%)	In Jail	Total (%)	Hispanic Population (%)
1990	405,320	169,600	41.8	0.09	172,300	42.5	0.57	58,100	14.3	0.23
2000	621,149	260,500	41.9	0.11	256,300	41.3	0.72	94,100	15.1	0.27
2008	785,556	333,300	42.4	0.14	308,000	39.2	0.79	128,500	16.4	0.27

Source: U.S. Census Bureau, *Statistical Abstract of the United States,* "Table 337. Jail Inmates by Sex, Race, and Hispanic Origin: 1990 to 2008," http://www.census.gov/compendia/statab/2010/tables/10s0337.pdf.

some material ones, it is in many respects a "separate and unequal" society, far distant from a postracial nation.

These conditions represent failure to achieve the declines that many, probably most, Americans would like to see in racial inequalities. We acknowledge that, since accomplishing substantial egalitarian changes is rarely rapid or easy, the facts of inequality alone do not show that the United States is falling short of a reasonable overall rate of racial progress. We also recognize that full material equality is not the goal in a commercial market economy, adopted to spur productivity, innovation, and economic growth, not to achieve uniform economic statuses. Nonetheless, few could find much comfort in these statistics. We think on balance this evidence supports the conclusion that the clashes of today's racial alliances over many issues have posed obstacles to desirable changes, allowing harsh racial material inequities to persist or to accentuate.

The Modern Disorder

Yet the consequences of today's opposed racial coalitions for policy debates are in some ways even worse than these data suggest. It is not just the case that political calculations and pressures often lead advocates of both color blindness and race consciousness to impugn the motives and integrity of their opponents while ignoring the other sides' evidence and arguments, in ways that mount barriers to constructive policymaking. It is also true that proponents of each position often present their own side in misleading, sometimes self-contradictory fashion.

On the one hand, champions of color blindness who view most race-conscious policies as unjust and corrupting nonetheless often profess their respect for America's cultural diversity and promise that their policies will benefit racial and ethnic minorities. Even in the heart of the Reagan years, for example, the 1984 Republican platform proclaimed that the "healthy mix of America's ethnic, cultural, and social heritage has always been the backbone of our nation and its progress throughout our history. . . . For millions of black Americans, Hispanic Americans, Asian Americans, and members of other minority groups, the past four years have seen a dramatic improvement in their ability to secure for themselves and for their children a better tomorrow. . . . We Republicans are proud of our efforts on behalf of all minority groups, and we pledge to do even more during the next four years. . . . We honor and respect the contributions of minority Americans and will do all we can to see that our diversity is enhanced during the next four years."[47] Recently, Republicans have stressed instead the importance of "cultural integration" into common values, especially as immigration controversies have heightened. But the party still promises to respect many forms of cultural diversity.[48]

The 1984 platform went on to insist that Republican policies of low taxes, taxes designed to promote inner-city investments, and limited regulation provided the best routes to these ends, all officially race-neutral measures. Yet to recommend policies because they will specifically benefit racial and ethnic minorities, to pledge to do more, to celebrate ethnic and cultural diversity, and to promise to enhance it, is to defend positions in race-conscious terms, echoing the language of those who openly endorse race-conscious measures. Such rhetoric also suggests that policies can rightly be judged by whether they fulfill these promises of gains for racial and ethnic minorities. A genuine philosophic commitment to color blindness as an absolute moral requirement means that the racial consequences of a policy should not be grounds for assessing it. To be sure, there is nothing wrong with arguing that color-blind policies are intrinsically right and just, while adding the belief that they will prove more likely than any others to have broadly beneficial consequences, including for racial minorities. Yet the rhetoric of many color-blind proponents often veers from arguing that their approach is right in principle *and* will probably help minorities to arguments that their approach is desirable *because* it will help minorities. The more a policy is defended because of its racial consequences, the more evaluations of it necessarily move onto the pragmatic terrain of whether it is really improving the material conditions of nonwhites in measurable ways, as much as or more than race-targeted alternatives. That is a move that many color-blind advocates denounce when their opponents advance it. But the rhetoric of "efforts on behalf of all minority groups" means that at least sometimes, color-blind proponents can justly be accused of trying to have it both ways.

Modern defenses of race-conscious policy often appear even more disingenuous, as numerous commentators have noted with varying degrees of sympathy. Both philosophically and politically, advocates face the fundamental difficulty that they champion equality for all, generally on grounds expressing respect for the dignity and worth of all human beings as unique individuals. At the same time, they defend measures that give great weight to the racial identities Americans have ascribed to persons, and little or no weight to what individuals may see as the real bases of their identities, their merits, their dignity and worth. To many Americans, such treatment remains indistinguishable from the arbitrary mistreatment of nonwhites on the basis of their ascribed racial identities that racial egalitarians are supposed to oppose.

Recognizing this reality, many if not most contemporary proponents of race-conscious measures offer arguments that appeal to the value of "diversity," particularly when they defend affirmative action programs in employment and educational admissions. And some forms of diversity are plainly valuable in most such contexts, though others, such as the inclusion of persons incapable of doing the required work, plainly are not. But it is widely acknowledged that most "diversity" policies in employment and education do not really focus on all types of diversity that might have some pertinent value. They focus on expanding inclusion of nonwhites. As a result, the language of "diversity" often appears to be a kind of "dissimulation" or "subterfuge" designed to make policies of racial preference less transparent.[49]

Most scholars recognize that a major source of these tendencies to mask the reality of racial preferences has been the U.S. Supreme Court. This is especially apparent from the Court's rulings in cases involving affirmative action admissions programs in higher education from *University of California Board of Regents v. Bakke* (1978) to *Gratz v. Bollinger* and *Grutter v. Bollinger* (2003).[50] In his seminal *Bakke* opinion, Justice Lewis Powell famously argued that an admissions system in which racial and ethnic diversity counted as one among many "pluses" an applicant might offer was preferable to a system that set aside places in a medical school class for qualified minority applicants, even if its results were likely to be the same. In Powell's eyes, the first approach visibly displayed consideration for each applicant as an individual. He contended that justice "must satisfy the appearance of justice."[51] In a similar spirit, Justice Sandra Day O'Connor ruled against the University of Michigan's undergraduate "point system" of admissions but upheld its law school's less precise "plus" system.

Dissenting in the undergraduate case, Justice David Souter complained that it was "especially unfair to treat the candor" of the undergraduate admissions plan "as an Achilles' heel." He noted that the Court seemed to be encouraging admissions systems like those used at public universities in Texas, California, and Florida, in which "student diversity" is achieved by "guaranteeing admission to a fixed percentage of the top students from each high school." To Souter, these approaches had "the disadvantage of deliberate obfuscation. The 'percentage plans' are just as race-conscious as the point scheme (and fairly so) but they get their racially diverse results without saying directly what they are doing or why they are doing it. . . . Equal protection cannot become an exercise in which the winners are the ones who hide the ball."[52] But to many on both sides of the debate, in an era in which color-blind positions are politically dominant, Justice Souter's characterization describes just what efforts to defend policies aimed at achieving more materially egalitarian racial results have become.

Knowledgeable students of human political affairs are still entitled to ask, so what? Finding that political debate over an issue or set of issues is morally charged in ways that involve disregard for other points of view and contrary evidence, along with misleading, even self-contradictory presentations of favored positions, is neither novel nor uncommon. Arguably, these are inescapable features of efforts to conduct politics democratically. And despite their limitations, democratic political processes remain preferable to all alternatives. We recognize the sober realism of these observations.

Yet when we consider them in light of, first, the pervasive clashes of the modern racial alliances we have seen across the issues examined in this book, which are only a portion of the wide range of policies those conflicts have affected, and second, the evidence of persisting and sometimes even deepening material racial inequalities just reviewed, we find it difficult to accept that realistically, the status quo of American racial politics today is about the best that can be achieved. There is ample evidence that, even as "diversity" employment programs abound, concerns that vigorous enforcement of anti-discrimination laws will generate inappropriate racial quotas have permitted widespread employment discrimination to continue. At the same time, to some unknown extent, minority candidates who are not competent have probably been hired to meet racial goals. Few are likely to defend the latter result, though many might dispute what constitutes adequate competence for particular jobs. And whether or not one views the evidence of continuing traditional discrimination as justified by legitimate economic concerns, or as appropriate in light of the poor character of many nonwhites, or as understandable responses to affirmative action excesses, this discrimination contributes to maintaining racial inequalities in income and wealth that few applaud—though again, just how much it does so is unclear.

Similarly, there is undeniable evidence that nonwhites are suffering disproportionately and catastrophically from the housing and mortgage crisis, even if analysts dispute whether these results are due to misguided efforts to aid minorities or to underregulation and underpolicing of racially predatory lending. A focus on the uniquely suspect character of race-conscious districting has also probably stood in the way of achieving more racially inclusive legislative apportionments, a factor in causing nonwhites to still be underrepresented in political offices, at least in terms of descriptive representation (the election of members of their own groups). But it is also true that preoccupations with descriptive representation via majority-minority districting can at times militate against the election of legislative bodies willing to enact the kinds of policies desired by most nonwhite Americans.

There can also be little doubt that debates over public education, including school vouchers as well as school desegregation and affirmative action in admissions, and disputes over mixed race census categories, all would have taken different forms if the issues had not come to be framed and championed or opposed in significant measure by the polarized agendas of the two modern racial alliances. Perhaps the different forms might have led to more satisfactory outcomes. At any rate, it is hard to see how the outcomes could have been worse. We think it still more clear that concerns about whether criminal justice and immigration policies will either inappropriately benefit or unduly harm nonwhites have been major factors in the rise of imprisonment policies and practices that many conservatives now see as costly and unfair, and in the decline of the American political system's capacity to enact any sort of major immigration reform at all.

In sum, history demonstrates the United States can make progress on racial problems over time. But in all the policy disputes we have examined, there is little reason to believe that the nation will make much progress now by continuing along its current path.

Breaking Out of America's Racial Impasse

If it is true that the "stalemate" on race that Barack Obama perceived in 2008 results from the unresolved and wide-ranging contestation of today's racial alliances, and if it is correct that this contestation is marked by uncompromising moral attacks and sometimes disingenuous presentations of their positions by both sides, we draw clear implications for how Americans might better deal with their intractable racial difficulties. The fundamental implications are first, that American leaders all along the nation's ideological spectrum ought to focus attention on questions about the public *policies* that can offer hope of improving racially unequal material conditions, rather than belaboring undesirable social *attitudes* of American whites, Asians, blacks, and Latinos in ways that generate more anxiety than answers. The United States needs less talk of whether whites, blacks, and other Americans are "angry" or "racist" or "pathological," when those discussions are focused primarily on characterizing psyches and values, not on proposals for improvement. There should instead be more empirical analysis of policy alternatives aimed at achieving better conditions for all, accompanied by less stark material racial inequalities.[53]

Still more important, in their public rhetoric American opinion-shapers must cease to frame the basic racial public policy issues today as choices between purely color-blind and pervasively race-conscious measures. The truth is that Americans do not and never have faced that choice. Neither purely color-blind nor totally racial-targeted policies are real possibilities, either philosophically or politically. As their platforms and voting records make clear, in reality virtually all leaders have supported different mixes of more race-neutral and more race-conscious policy proposals, including defenses of race-neutral measures on race-conscious grounds. And necessarily so: as we have seen, the anti-discrimination laws that color-blind proponents endorse cannot be enforced without attending to racial practices and outcomes, even if doing so fosters dangers of race-targeted policies. Defenses of color-blind principles have won indispensable political support by contending that they will prove means to continue the racial progress partly achieved by the civil rights movement. The flip side is that it has never been plausible for race-conscious proponents to speak as if all policies should be judged primarily by their consequences for racial inequalities. In practice, most acknowledge that it is morally right as well as politically necessary for policymakers to consider many other goals, often best furthered through race-neutral measures.

The modern conservative Republican administrations of Nixon, Reagan, and both Presidents Bush condemned quotas and pushed for judicial rulings requiring color blindness. But they still offered programs that they said were designed to assist racial and ethnic minorities. Even Reagan ultimately supported the race-conscious 1982 Voting Rights Act amendments, and he and both his Bush successors disappointed those who thought they would abrogate all forms of affirmative action. Democrats from Carter through Clinton and now Obama, on the other hand, have always stressed the benefits of inclusive New Deal–style economic aid and stimulus measures for many goals, including efforts to close racial gaps. As Jennifer Hochschild confirms, "many public and private officials" appear in practice to "seek a middle ground" that would focus on the "actual workings" and results of different particular measures.[54] But as candidate Obama's speech in Philadelphia showed, even when seeking to build consensus, few if any of the nation's leaders have been willing to address the choice between color-blind and race-conscious approaches directly and to expose it as a false, harmful description of the options that Americans face.

As we have seen in each policy area, politicians in both parties have been reluctant to challenge the dominant framing of racial policy issues because, though overall American voters and opinion leaders display significant support for both principles of color blindness and goals of greater material racial equality, that support is sharply one-sided. It has long been far safer to champion principles of color blindness, to adopt obfuscated positions, or to say nothing about racial policy at all, than to be openly on the side of racial preferences of any sort. To advocate any kind of mixed or "middle-ground" approach, however, is to argue explicitly for measures that give more weight to the interests of some Americans because of their racial identities than to others, even if those measures are meant to be "soft" forms of "extra help" in various ways. Those weightings, that "extra help," are forms of racial preference.

As a result, candidates for office who favor "middle-ground" measures like Obama in 2008 generally seek to avoid discussing racial policies as much as they can. They know that to color-blind proponents, all race-conscious measures deserve castigation as "reverse racism"—and that these critics are not wrong to contend that all such measures violate pure color blindness. If America's racial alliances were to re-form into coalitions that presented different "mixed" policy packages, each with some sorts of race-conscious and race-neutral elements, as we think they should, it is true that to some degree, race-conscious proponents would have triumphed. That is not a popular prospect. A candidate must therefore have both great courage and skill to argue that this time, unlike in the days of slavery or Jim Crow, America need not and should not choose all one side or all the other of its racial policy alternatives if its house is to stand. The message that racial policies are not and cannot be as color-blind as one side would have it, but that it is misguided as well as impolitic to rely on race-targeted solutions for all existing racial inequalities, is a complicated, hard sell. But it is the message that the nation needs now.

Despite our stress on the need for this common message to be communicated by leaders across the political spectrum, we are not suggesting that the historical structuring of American racial politics into rival policy alliances is likely to end or that it should end. The possible mixes of race-neutral and race-conscious measures that can plausibly claim to provide desirable ways forward are many. Conservatives can continue to stress the desirability of private market-oriented solutions, liberals more public, regulatory, and redistributive ones. Nor does our call for all to acknowledge the reality that the nation needs mixed approaches imply that the most "middle-ground" solutions are the best solutions. It may be true that either more radically pro-market or more pro-government aid policies are needed to provide the economic context in which specific race-targeted measures can help to close racial gaps—and the race-conscious measures that prove effective may turn out to be large or small in scope. So racial alliances proposing dissimilar combinations of race-neutral and race-conscious policies seem inevitable, even if the need for some such combination comes to be widely accepted.

Moreover, these continuing disputes over different policy packages may well be desirable. It is probable that no one side will offer the best particular

when it comes to race, principles are more important than consequences is in our view the greatest damage wrought by the way racial issues have been framed through the modern racial alliances. To break the racial stalemate, partisans of all points of view need to ask themselves honestly whether, on the one hand, particular race-conscious policies really harm whites, and whether, on the other, race-conscious policies really help disadvantaged nonwhites more than race-neutral alternatives. It is particularly important to be clear who the immediate and longer-term beneficiaries of proposed measures are likely to be, and who will bear most of the costs. Programs that boast of being "race-neutral" but that are likely to benefit already well-off whites while leaving disadvantaged nonwhites further behind cannot be deemed acceptable. Neither should race-conscious programs that benefit only the best-off members of racial minority groups, even in the long run, while primarily burdening less affluent whites. If in certain arenas racially egalitarian progress can be achieved only at significant cost to poorer whites, all of the nation's more affluent citizens should be required to supply compensatory aid to those adversely affected. But there is good reason to believe that these are not the only options.

The limited evidence available suggests, for example, that affirmative action programs in employment and admissions often cause very little harm even to poorer whites.[58] There can be no denying, however, that firefighter Frank Ricci felt endangered when New Haven considered changing the rules and ignoring the high test score he had worked so hard to achieve. Even if the Supreme Court has now set the bar for justifications of change in employment policies unduly high, race-conscious advocates should recognize that it is often unfair to switch assessment horses in midstream. But color-blind advocates should also acknowledge that, if one sort of test for employment predicts meritorious job performance as well as or better than another and is likely to produce a more racially inclusive workforce, it is not wrong to adopt it for future hires and promotions simply because it is preferred on race-conscious grounds. It is instead imperative to do so. Had New Haven abandoned its questionable written exam before testing began, Frank Ricci might have practiced and done equally well on a performance-based assessment that better predicted success in emergency situations. If he did not, he would have had no claim against a more effective and more racially inclusive testing system.

Similarly, it is hard to see how advertising new, affordable Westchester housing units in zip codes known to have many poorer African American and Latino residents is likely to hurt whites, and particularly less affluent whites, in any substantial way. Unless evidence of such harms can be found, there is no strong case against conditioning receipt of federal funds on acceptance of recipients' duties to undertake such efforts. Race-conscious advocates should, however, acknowledge that there is little evidence that these measures alone will meet the needs of the nation's disproportionately nonwhite poor for well-constructed and maintained affordable housing. Reformers should also give weight to the reality that for many whom they seek to aid, decent, affordable housing is a higher priority than options for racially integrated housing, even if both are seen as desirable. Whether market-dominated or publicly provided or more likely some mix, housing policies must be concerned with more than just race-conscious goals.

In voting rights, it is understandable that aldermen representing Chicago's majority black districts sought to maintain as many such districts as possible after the 2000 census. But it is also likely that they will have more political success in the long run if henceforth they design districts that strengthen alliances with the rising number of Latino voters and leaders, rather than antagonizing them. Here, as on many other issues, the U.S. Supreme Court's still-rising insistence on ever-greater color blindness in public policymaking seems unnecessary and undesirable. Its restrictions stand in the way of the kinds of pragmatic political negotiations, compromises, and coalition building that work to cool rather than inflame racial antagonisms, even though there are likely to be many tensions involved in the process. To demand that racial concerns must always be sharply subordinated in districting is likely to produce only hypocrisy and more lawsuits. Yet here, too, race-conscious proponents need to recognize realistically that there is much that ought to go into democratically appropriate districting beyond racial goals. Even those goals may point to districting that strengthens the overall electoral power of nonwhite constituencies, rather than just their capacities to put nonwhites into office.

Americans would also benefit if debates over educational policies, including vouchers, school desegregation, and admissions, focused more seriously on what measures are backed by evidence that they improve schooling at all levels, rather than on which measures correspond with either market ideologies or goals of racial integration pursued in isolation from other standards in educational achievement. The Obama administration is making its call for reliance on such evidence of "what works" the chief theme of its educational policies. But genuine desires to focus on empirical evidence in this area represent a new and fragile phenomenon that has emerged in spite of, not because of, the influence on educational debates of today's racial alliances.[59] Turning to another policy front, those alliances now appear to have ceased to contend over race categories on the census. Yet it remains to be seen whether discussions of possible revisions can go forward without distortion by exaggerated hopes or fears that new categories will either foster a color-blind society or erode the constituencies for desirable race-conscious policies.

There may be no area where the color-blind insistence that it is inappropriate to pay attention to empirical evidence of racial consequences has done more harm than in criminal justice policies. Here, the difficulty of appearing to excuse criminals who have committed vicious offenses has meant that race-conscious proponents have played a limited role, while bipartisan support for tougher sentencing and more prisons has produced the nation's stratospheric incarceration rates and huge racial disparities. Even so, the Obama administration has thus far dared to do little more than to continue its leader's long-standing theme of eliminating racial profiling. Political leaders across the spectrum need to develop and offer policies with attention not only to what may reduce crime in general but also to the profound and enduring impact of those policies on America's black and Latino communities. In criminal justice policy debates, the views and the conditions of those communities should be heard and seen as fully as possible. At the same time, conscientious conservatives must strive to resist the political temptations of negative stereotyping, and conscientious liberals must not succumb to the counterpart dangers of defensive denials of criminality. Similarly, on the last issue area we have examined, immigration, it is imperative to combat the tendencies of public debates to be dominated either by officially color-blind but erroneous and stigmatizing depictions of "illegal" Latinos, or by disregard for the real burdens experienced by citizens in the areas of the United States in which new immigrants tend to be concentrated. Neither a color-blind denial that there is a racial component to current immigration anxieties nor a race-conscious dismissal of immigration concerns across the board is likely to move the nation toward effective policy-making in an area where it has for many years been politically unable to act.

One final point is worth underlining because today, the Supreme Court is the major governing institution most controlled by color-blind forces and most likely to challenge an executive branch advancing mixed, and therefore partly race-conscious, policies. If America's political leaders are to begin to devise and defend policies that combine color-blind and race-neutral measures in ways that they believe the evidence shows to be effective, it will be necessary for the Supreme Court's majority to cease its efforts to revise constitutional doctrines in order to require more extensive, if to date never full, color blindness. Thus, rather than making professions of color-blind objectivity prerequisites for appointment to the Supreme Court, as many in the Senate sought to do in the Sonia Sotomayor confirmation hearings, it would be preferable for judges, for those who appoint them, and for those who argue before them all to interpret the Constitution so that policies are assessed on whether they can reasonably be thought to contribute to achieving constitutional goals for all persons. Again, this means embrace of an overarching public philosophy in which there are still disputes between rival ideological camps, but in which all recognize that the real choices are not between color-blind or race-conscious principles, only between what combinations of color-blind and race-conscious policies will best serve Americans in the early twenty-first century.

To say all this is, admittedly, not to answer what that mix of policies should be in any area, let alone across the board. We take seriously our own admonitions that policy arguments should be based on evidence of what will work to alleviate the nation's entrenched racial inequalities and aid as many Americans as possible, and that all involved should embrace greater openness to a wider range of alternatives. The kinds of empirical studies needed to support specific policy proposals belong in another book, or many books.

But American scholars, policymakers, and political leaders are not likely to undertake or to heed such studies unless many more come to recognize that American politics is substantially shaped today, as it has been throughout the nation's history, by conflicts between rival racial policy alliances. They also will not make progress in dealing with racial issues so long as they fail to see and to communicate that unlike in the past, the clash of today's alliances does not mean that America's still-divided house must become all one thing or all another. The challenge today is for partisans of both the modern alliances to recognize that it is time to frame the nation's racial choices more accurately and honestly than they have done for the last three decades. Only then can Americans hope to discern how they can reduce the racial inequalities that so profoundly separate them. Only then can they hope to pursue their distinct yet interconnected dreams so that, in their commitments to racial progress, they may all be one.

Notes

CHAPTER 1. "THAT THEY MAY ALL BE ONE": AMERICA AS A HOUSE DIVIDED

1. United Church of Christ, "What is the United Church of Christ?" http://www .ucc.org/about-us/what-is-the-united-church-of.html.

2. Ibid.; Barbara Brown Zikmund, "Beyond Historical Orthodoxy," United Church of Christ, http://www.ucc.org/about-us/hidden-histories/beyond-historical-orthodoxy .html.

3. GreatSeal.com, "E Pluribus Unum—Origin and Meaning of the Motto Carried by the American Eagle," http://www.greatseal.com/mottoes/unum.html.

4. John Fischer, "Germantown Neighborhood of Philadelphia," About.com, http:// philadelphia.about.com/od/neighborhoods/p/germantown.html.

5. Ronald Kessler, "Obama's Mythology about Pastor Wright," *Cutting Edge*, April 21, 2008, http://www.thecuttingedgenews.com/index.php?article=446.

6. Barack Obama, *Dreams from My Father* (New York: Three Rivers Press, 1995, 2004), 282.

7. Biography.com, "Jeremiah A. Wright, Jr. Biography," http://www.biography.com/ articles/Jeremiah-A.-Wright-Jr.-29958.

8. Ibid.

9. James H. Cone, A *Black Theology of Liberation, Twentieth Anniversary Edition* (Maryknoll, NY: Orbis Books, 1990), 7, 21–22, 28.

10. "Transcript: Rev. Jeremiah Wright Speech to National Press Club," *Chicago Tribune*, April 28, 2008, http://www.chicagotribune.com/news/politics/chi-wrighttranscript- 04282008,0,3113697.story.

11. Barack Obama, *The Audacity of Hope* (New York: Three Rivers Press), 202–4, 207–8.

12. Brian Ross and Rehab El-Buri, "Obama's Pastor: God Damn America, U.S. to Blame for 9/11," March 13, 2008, ABC News, http://abcnews.go.com/Blotter/story?id= 4443788.

13. Barack Obama, "A More Perfect Union," National Constitution Center, March 18, 2008, http://constitutioncenter.org/amoreperfectunion/docs/Race_Speech_Transcript.pdf.

14. Ibid.; "Dr. Martin Luther King's 1963 WMU Speech Found," Archives and Regional History Collections, http://www.wmich.edu/library/archives/mlk/q-a.html.

15. Obama, "A More Perfect Union."

16. Ibid.

17. Ibid.

18. Wright went on to make speeches arguing that blacks and whites were "equal" but "different," relying on different sides of their brains to learn, and worse, comments widely seen as anti-Semitic. But he did so while acknowledging that he was no longer

in communication with the candidate. CNN Politics.com, "Transcript of Jeremiah Wright's Speech to NAACP," April 27, 2008, http://www.cnn.com/2008/POLITICS/04/28/wright.transcript/; "Transcript: Rev. Jeremiah Wright speech to National Press Club," *Chicago Tribune*; David Squires, "Reverend Wright Says 'Jews' Are Keeping Him from President Obama," *Daily Press.com*, June 10, 2009, http://www.dailypress.com/news/dp-local_wright_0610jun10,0,7603283.story.

19. *Brown v. Board of Education*, 347 U.S. 483 (1954); Civil Rights Act of 1964, Pub. L. 88-352, 78. Stat. 241, enacted July 2, 1964; Voting Rights Act of 1965, Pub. L. 89-110, 42 U.S.C. §1973-173-aa-6, enacted August 6, 1965.

20. See, e.g., Michelle Alexander, *The New Jim Crow: Mass Incarceration in the Age of Colorblindness* (New York: The New Press, 2010), 227–38; quoted passage is at 231.

21. Martin Luther King Jr., "I Have a Dream" Speech, U.S. Constitution Online, last modified March 3, 2010, http://www.usconstitution.net/dream.html.

22. *Regents of the University of California v. Bakke*, 438 U.S. 265 (1978); Thomas Byrne Edsall with Mary D. Edsall, *Racial Alliances Chain Reaction: The Impact of Race, Rights, and Taxes on American Politics* (New York: W.W. Norton, 1991), 3, 5, 18.

23. For an analysis of those circumstances, see Philip A. Klinkner with Rogers M. Smith, *The Unsteady March: The Rise and Decline of Racial Equality in America* (Chicago: University of Chicago Press, 1999).

24. As detailed in later chapters, the party platforms supporting these characterizations can be found at John Woolley and Gerhard Peters, *American Presidency Project*, http://www.presidency.ucsb.edu/platforms.php.

25. On Powell's support for affirmative action, see "Powell Defends Affirmative Action in College Admissions," CNN Politics.com, January 19, 2003, http://articles.cnn.com/2003-01-19/politics/powell.race_1_race-neutral-michigan-policy-affirmative-action?_s=PM:ALLPOLITICS; on Webb's opposition, see James Webb, "Diversity and the Myth of White Privilege," *Wall Street Journal*, July 22, 2010, http://online.wsj.com/article/SB10001424052748703724104575379630952309408.html. Webb argues that affirmative action for African Americans once was justifiable, and he still supports special efforts to assist African Americans in need.

26. E.g., Nolan McCarty, Keith T. Poole, and Howard Rosenthal, *Polarized America* (Cambridge, MA: MIT Press, 2006).

27. Compare, for example, Jim Sleeper, *Liberal Racism: How Fixating on Race Subverts the American Dream*, and Eduardo Bonilla-Silva, *Racism without Racists: Color-Blind Racism and Racial Inequality in Contemporary America*, 3rd ed. (Lanham, MD: Rowman and Littlefield, 2010).

28. Jennifer L. Hochschild, "The Strange Career of Affirmative Action," *Ohio State Law Journal* 59 (1998): 998.

29. Ibid, 1002.

30. Ibid., 1002–3. Since Hochschild wrote, law professor Richard Sander published a substantial empirical study of affirmative action admissions to law schools, which concluded that the nation might well have more black lawyers without affirmative action (Richard H. Sander, "A Systemic Analysis of Affirmative Action in American Law

Schools," *Stanford Law Review* 57 [2004]: 368–483). His argument was that if affirmative action did not "mismatch" black applicants with higher-ranked law schools for which they were not qualified, they would succeed more often. Critics charged that Sander overlooked evidence that blacks with similar scores often performed better in higher-ranked than in lesser law schools and that he made other optimistic assumptions while misstating some of his statistical findings. See, e.g., Ian Ayres and Richard Brooks, "Does Affirmative Action Reduce the Number of Black Lawyers?" *Stanford Law Review* 57 (2005): 1807–53; David L. Chambers, Timothy T. Clydesdale, William C. Kidder, and Richard O. Lempert, "The Real Impact of Eliminating Affirmative Action in American Law Schools: An Empirical Critique of Richard Sander's Study," *Stanford Law Review* 57 (2005): 1855–98. In our view, the critics had the better of the debate, but all participants deserve commendation for engaging the empirical issues seriously and for recognizing that affirmative action in law school admissions has both laudable goals and real limitations.

31. Jennifer L. Hochschild, "Affirmative Action as Culture War," in *The Cultural Territories of Race: Black and White Boundaries*, ed. Michèle Lamont (Chicago: University of Chicago Press, 1999), 346.

32. Peter H. Schuck, *Diversity in America* (Cambridge, MA: Harvard University Press, 2003), 163–69, 198; Daniel Sabbagh, *Equality and Transparency: A Strategic Perspective on Affirmative Action in American Law* (New York: Palgrave Macmillan, 2007), 139.

33. U.S. Census Bureau, "Table 36. Selected Characteristics of Racial Groups and Hispanic Population: 2007," http://www.census.gov/compendia/statab/2010/tables/10s0036.pdf; see also U.S. Department of Labor, Bureau of Labor Statistics, "Report 1005: Labor Force Characteristics by Race and Ethnicity," September 2008, 1–3.

34. U.S. Census Bureau, Table H-5, "Race and Hispanic Origin of Householder—Households by Median and Mean Income: 1967–2009," http://www.census.gov/hhes/www/income/data/historical/household/index.html.

35. NAACP, "NAACP Fact Sheet: Subprime and Predatory Mortgage Lending," http://naacp.3cdn.net/e8ad24da256549c740_sbm6bnq36.pdf. Early in 2011, U.S. Census Bureau data indicated that the gap in homeownership between black and white Americans was wider in the last quarter of 2010 than it had ever been in the sixteen years the bureau had been collecting these data. White homeownership was at 74.2 percent, while black homeownership was at 44.9 percent. Tom Braithwaite, "US Homeowners' Racial Gap Widens," FT.com, February 16, 2011, http://www.ft.com/cms/s/0/064c4870-3a01-11e0-a441-00144feabdc0.html#axzz1EnwuOVe5.

36. U.S. Department of Health and Human Services, Office of Minority Health, http://minorityhealth.hhs.gov/templates/browse.aspx?lvl+2&lvllD=51.

37. Gary Orfield, "Reviving the Goal of an Integrated Society: A 21st Century Challenge," UCLA, The Civil Rights Project, January 2009, http://civilrightsproject.ucla.edu/research/k-12-education/integration-and-diversity/reviving-the-goal-of-an-integrated-society-a-21st-century-challenge/orfield-reviving-the-goal-mlk-2009.pdf, 3.

38. U.S. Census Bureau, "Table 337. Jail Inmates by Sex, Race, and Hispanic Origin: 1990 to 2008," http://www.census.gov/compendia/statab/2010/tables/10s0337.pdf.

39. "Arthur Wergs Mitchell," Black Americans in Congress, http://baic.house.gov/member-profiles/profile.html?intlD=31; Nancy J. Weiss, *Farewell to the Party of Lincoln* (Princeton, NJ: Princeton University Press, 1983), 80–81, 242. Though Mitchell always professed allegiance to Booker T. Washington's philosophy, their relationship was troubled (Dennis S. Nordin, *The New Deal's Black Congressman* [Columbia: University of Missouri Press, 1997], 6–21).

40. Weiss, *Farewell to the Party of Lincoln*, 242–43; Nordin, *New Deal's Black Congressman*.

41. Quoted in Nordin, *New Deal's Black Congressman*, 250.

42. State-imposed racial segregation was first upheld by the Supreme Court in 1896 (and overturned in 1954). For an important account of the origins of segregated practices, see Barbara Y. Welke, "When All the Women Were White, and All the Blacks Were Men: Gender, Class, Race, and the Road to Plessy, 1855–1914," *Law and History Review* 13 (1995): 261–316; and Barbara Y. Welke, *Recasting American Liberty: Gender, Race, Law, and the Railroad Revolution, 1865–1920* (Cambridge: Cambridge University Press, 2001). Welke in particular underlines how Jim Crow segregation originated from the unexpected racial consequences of segregation by sex.

43. Nordin, *New Deal's Black Congressman*, 270; Kevin J. McMahon, *Reconsidering Roosevelt on Race* (Chicago: University of Chicago Press, 2004), 161.

44. *Mitchell v. United States et al.*, 313 U.S. 80, 94 (1941).

45. Ibid., 93.

46. Ibid., 94.

47. Harvard Sitkoff, *A New Deal for Blacks: The Emergence of Civil Rights as a National Issue: The Depression Decade*, 30th anniversary ed. (New York: Oxford University Press, 2009), 177–78.

48. Cf. Michael Omi and Howard Winant, *Racial Formation in the United States*, 2nd ed. (New York: Routledge, 1994), 77–79; Michael C. Dawson and Cathy J. Cohen, "Problems in the Study of the Politics of Race," in *Political Science: The State of the Discipline*, ed. Ira Katznelson and Helen V. Milner (New York: W. W. Norton, 2002), 495–96; Jennifer Hochschild and Vesla Weaver, "There's No One as Irish as Barack O'Bama: The Policy and Politics of American Multiculturalism," *Perspectives on Politics* 8 (2010): 738.

49. Omi and Winant, *Racial Formation*, 78.

50. We have been most influenced by Karen Orren and Stephen Skowronek, *The Search for Political Development* (New York: Cambridge University Press, 2004), although we stress broader political alliances and the ideas that unite them, rather than simply governing institutions, to an arguably greater degree.

51. See, e.g., *Hall v. DeCuir*, 95 U.S. 485 (1877) (holding that Louisiana's Reconstruction government had burdened interstate commerce when it banned racial segregation on steamboats traveling through the state) and *Louisville, New Orleans, and Texas Railway Co. v. Mississippi*, 133 U.S. 587 (1890) (holding that Mississippi could require intrastate railroad traffic to be segregated); *Chesapeake and Ohio Railway Co. v. Kentucky*, 218 U.S. 71 (1910) (upholding a similar Kentucky statute, even though it

applied to the intrastate operations of an interstate railroad); *Chiles v. Chesapeake and Ohio Railway Co.*, 218 U.S. 71 (1910) (holding that the railroad's decision also to segregate its interstate cars was its own decision, not due to the previously upheld Kentucky state, and so the state was not burdening interstate commerce).

52. That is why we originally referred to these alliances as "racial orders": see Desmond S. King and Rogers M. Smith, "Racial Orders in American Political Development," *American Political Science Review* 99 (2005): 75–92.

53. *Brown v. Board of Education II*, 394 U.S. 294 (1955), and see, e.g., Michael Klarman, *From Jim Crow to Civil Rights: The Supreme Court and the Struggle for Racial Equality* (New York: Oxford University Press, 2004).

54. Data limitations and changes in political practices (e.g., the invention of party platforms in the 1840s, the rise of *amicus* briefs in the latter half of the twentieth century) have led us to adopt mildly different counting practices for different eras. For the slavery era, for example, we document racial policy alliances in Congress by counting members who vote with one alliance or the other 80 percent to 100 percent of the time as core members of that alliance, and members who vote with one alliance or the other 60 percent to 80 percent of the time as more peripheral alliance members. For the Jim Crow era, where congressional votes on racial issues were rare until relatively late, we focus on the policies, institutions, and groups endorsed in official decisions, party platforms, and similar public documents.

In the modern "race-conscious" era, if we have found evidence that an institution, group, or political actor has adopted positions in their institutional decisions, public statements, congressional testimony, or *amicus* briefs on more than one of our seven racial policy issues, and consistently on the same side, we count it as an alliance member. For example, we will see that the *New York Times* has editorialized on behalf of the positions of the race-conscious alliance on every issue we examine, though in the case of school vouchers, it does so for separation of church and state, not for racial policy reasons. We have not tabulated explicitly the positions of all the many other institutions, groups, and actors we examine. The evidence for their adoption of alliance positions on multiple issues can be found in the sources we cite. If the institution, group, or actor has taken a position on only one of our issues, we count it as "augmenting" the alliance on that issue. We do not count an institution, group, or political actor's inactivity on an issue as evidence either for or against placing it in a particular racial alliance, since expecting all to be active on all issues is not realistic. Most have more focused concerns and responsibilities. We recognize that at times an institution or group's failure to be active on an issue may amount to a defection from its usual racial policy alliance, but decisive evidence as to the institution or group's reasons for inaction is rarely available. Similarly, we have not been able to document whether a group or actor has taken private positions contrary to its public ones; but public positions do display alliance affiliation.

55. Klarman, *Jim Crow to Civil Rights*, esp. 217–19. On FDR's appointments of more liberal justices, see Kevin J. McMahon, *Reconsidering Roosevelt on Race* (Chicago: University of Chicago Press, 2004), 110–44.

56. For evidence that racial considerations remain profoundly important in American public opinion in terms of policy positions, electoral behavior, and general attitudes, see, e.g., Donald R. Kinder and Lynn M. Sanders, *Divided by Color: Racial Politics and Democratic Ideals* (Chicago: University of Chicago Press, 1996); and Michael Tesler and David O. Sears, *Obama's Race: The 2008 Election and the Dream of a Post-Racial America* (Chicago: University of Chicago Press, 2010).

57. We are most indebted here to Omi and Winant, *Racial Formation*, again despite our preference not to speak of a unitary "racial state" and our focus on alliances in control of certain governing institutions, rather than on social movements treated as things external to "the state."

58. *Plessy v. Ferguson*, 163 U.S. 596 (1896).

59. For pertinent influential works see, e.g., Noel Ignatiev, *How the Irish Became White* (New York: Routledge, 1996); Matthew Frye Jacobson, *Whiteness of a Different Color: European Immigrants and the Alchemy of Race* (Cambridge, MA: Harvard University Press, 1999); Mae M. Ngai, *Impossible Subjects: Illegal Aliens and the Making of Modern America* (Princeton, NJ: Princeton University Press, 2004); David R. Roediger, *Working Toward Whiteness: How America's Immigrants Became White* (New York: Basic Books, 2006).

60. The idea that political conflicts and debates are framed by prevailing ideas and values is widely used in political science scholarship. With respect to how race frames and is framed by politics, the decisive work is Tali Mendelberg's *The Race Card* (Princeton, NJ: Princeton University Press, 2001); while more general usage is developed in Dennis Chong and James N. Druckman, "Framing Public Opinion in Competitive Democracies," *American Political Science Review* 101 (2007): 637–55.

61. Racial policy alliances may rightly be conceived as similar to the networks of groups of "intense policy demanders" described by Marty Cohen, David Karol, Hans Noel, and John Zaller in *The Party Decides: Presidential Nominations Before and After Reform* (Chicago: University of Chicago Press, 2008), 30. But they understand these networks as part of a redefinition of how we should understand modern political parties. We present them as currently overlapping with today's political parties, but historically and still today at bottom relatively autonomous from parties.

62. Nordin, *New Deal's Black Congressman*, 254, 264–77.

63. Ibid., 271; Sitkoff, *New Deal for Blacks*, 177.

64. W.E.B. Du Bois, *Black Reconstruction in America, 1860–1880* (New York: Atheneum, 1935, 1992), 178, 193, 195; William Gillette, *The Right to Vote: Politics and the Passage of the Fifteenth Amendment* (Baltimore, MD: Johns Hopkins University Press, 1965), 28–31; Michael Les Benedict, *A Compromise of Principle: Congressional Republicans and Reconstruction, 1863–1869* (New York: W. W. Norton, 1974), 210–43, 252–56; David McCullough, *Truman* (New York: Simon and Schuster, 1992); Mary Dudziak, *Cold War Civil Rights: Race and the Image of American Democracy* (Princeton, NJ: Princeton University Press, 2000); William C. Berman, *The Politics of Civil Rights in the Truman Administration* (Columbus: Ohio State University Press, 1970).

65. Cited in Nordin, *New Deal's Black Congressman*, 88.

66. Ibid., 247–48, 291–92.

67. This reality has been at best understated by accounts that treat race as an unfortunate overlay on a fundamental democratic, rights-protecting political society, e.g., S. M. Lipset, *The First New Nation* (New York: Anchor, 1967).

68. Dana Bash and Emily Sherman, "Sotomayor's 'Wise Latina' Comment a Staple of Her Speeches," CNN.com, June 8, 2009, http://www.cnn.com/2009/POLITICS/06/05/sotomayor.speeches/#cnnSTCTest, accessed September 30, 2009.

69. Jennifer Rubin, "'A Wise Latina Woman': The Context Shows that Judge Sotomayor Meant What She Said," *Weekly Standard*, June 15, 2009, http://www.weeklystandard.com/Content/Public/Articles/000/000/016/587tzqjm.asp.

70. Amy Goldstein, Robert Barnes, and Paul Kane, "Sotomayor Emphasizes Objectivity: Nominee Explains 'Wise Latina' Remark," *Washington Post*, July 15, 2009, http://www.washingtonpost.com/wp-dyn/content/article/2009/07/14/AR2009071400992_pf.html, accessed September 30, 2009.

71. See, e.g., Reva B. Siegel, "Equality Talk: Anti-Subordination and Anti-Classification Values in Constitutional Struggles over *Brown*," *Harvard Law Review* 17 (2003–4): 1470–547.

CHAPTER 2. "THAT IS THE LAST SPEECH HE WILL EVER MAKE":
THE ANTEBELLUM RACIAL ALLIANCES

1. There are few comparative examples, though many scholars have effective combined accounts of the United States with Brazil and South Africa. See, in particular, George M. Fredrickson, *White Supremacy: A Comparative Study in American and South African History* (New York: Oxford University Press, 1991); and Anthony W. Marx, *Making Race and Nation: A Comparison of the United States, South Africa and Brazil* (New York: Cambridge University Press, 1999).

2. Joseph J. Ellis, *Founding Brothers* (New York: Alfred A. Knopf, 2000), 88–89.

3. Philip A. Klinkner with Rogers M. Smith, *The Unsteady March: The Rise and Decline of Racial Equality in America* (Chicago: University of Chicago Press, 1999), 17–23.

4. Cited and discussed in Akhil Amar, *America's Constitution: A Biography* (New York: Random House, 2005), 150.

5. James Madison, *Notes of Debates in the Federal Convention of 1787* (New York: W. W. Norton, 1966), 548.

6. Amar, *America's Constitution*, 98.

7. Lois E. Horton, "From Class to Race in Early America: Northern Post-Emancipation Racial Reconstruction," *Journal of the Early Republic* 19 (1999): 637–39.

8. We owe this point to an unpublished paper by Stephan Stohler, "Slavery and the Origins of the Fifth Amendment's Taking Clause" (presented at the Penn Program on Democracy, Citizenship, and Constitutionalism Graduate Student Workshop, October 6, 2010), 14–15.

9. Jared Sparks, ed., *Letters and Recollections of George Washington* (New York: Doubleday, 1906), 38.

10. Fritz Hirschfeld, *George Washington and Slavery: A Documentary Portrayal* (Columbia: University of Missouri Press, 1997), 214–15.

11. David P. Currie, *The Constitution in Congress: The Federalist Period, 1789–1801* (Chicago: University of Chicago Press, 1997), 66–67, 230–32.

12. Mia Bay, *The White Image in the Black Mind* (New York: Oxford University Press, 2000), 14–15; Ronald Takaki, *A Different Mirror: A History of Multicultural America* (Boston: Little, Brown, 1993), 173–76.

13. Reginald Horsman, *Race and Manifest Destiny: The Origins of American Racial Anglo-Saxonism* (Cambridge, MA: Harvard University Press, 1981), 98–157.

14. Eugene H. Berwanger, *The Frontier Against Slavery: Western Anti-Negro Prejudice and the Slavery Extension Controversy* (Urbana: University of Illinois Press, 1967), 42–49, 140; Lawrence H. Fuchs, *The American Kaleidoscope: Race, Ethnicity and the Civic Culture* (Hanover, NH: University Press of New England, 1990), 91–93; Leon F. Litwack, *North of Slavery: The Negro in the Free States, 1790–1860* (Chicago: University of Chicago Press, 1961), 31, 70–93, 113–15.

15. Berwanger, *Frontier Against Slavery*, 93.

16. See also Louis Hartz, *The Liberal Tradition in America* (New York: Harcourt, Brace, 1955); for important works influenced by this perspective, see David F. Ericson, "Dew, Fitzhugh and Proslavery Liberalism," in *The Liberal Tradition in American Politics: Reassessing the Legacy of American Liberalism*, ed. David F. Ericson and Louisa Bertch Green (New York: Routledge, 1999); David F. Ericson, *The Debate Over Slavery* (New York: New York University Press, 2000); J. David Greenstone, *The Lincoln Persuasion: Remaking American Liberalism* (Princeton, NJ: Princeton University Press, 1993), 85–117; Karen Orren and Stephen Skowronek, *The Search for American Political Development* (New York: Cambridge University Press, 2004).

17. Michael Goldfield, *The Color of Politics* (New York: The New Press, 1997), 79–80, 92.

18. Fuchs, *American Kaleidoscope*, 24; Edward P. Hutchinson, *Legislative History of American Immigration Policy, 1798–1965* (Philadelphia: University of Pennsylvania Press, 1981), 24, 35–39.

19. Barbara Jeanne Fields, "Slavery, Race and Ideology in the United States of America," *New Left Review* 181 (1990): 95–118.

20. W.E.B. Du Bois, *Black Reconstruction in America* (New York: Atheneum, 1992 [1935]), 700–701.

21. Charles R. Kesler, "The Promise of American Citizenship," in. *Immigration and Citizenship in the 21st Century*, ed. Noah Pickus (Boston: Rowman and Littlefield, 1998), 13–23.

22. Eric Foner, *Reconstruction: America's Unfinished Revolution, 1863–1877* (New York: Harper and Row, 1988), 75–87, 124–26, 543–47; Takaki, *Different Mirror*, 129–30; and William M. Wiecek, *The Sources of Antislavery Constitutionalism in America, 1760–1860* (Ithaca, NY: Cornell University Press, 1977), 153–62, 216–48.

policy mix on every issue, so a competitive and coalition-building democratic politics may prove productive here, as on other topics. Our contention is only that neither side should pretend that Americans have any *credible* option that does not involve some mix of race-neutral and race-conscious measures. And our hope is that, between those who favor color-blind policies because they believe that they will work to achieve greater racial equality, and those who support race-conscious measures because they, too, are looking for what can succeed in improving racial conditions, it will be possible to build a coalition in favor of some sensible combination of their most tested and proven programs. We believe that a combined approach that resulted from clear-eyed policy evaluations and honest political negotiations, rather than from contests over measures crafted and presented via obfuscation and evasion, would prove, if less than perfect, far preferable to what Americans are doing now.

THE TASKS AHEAD

To deliver this unpopular message effectively, political leaders not only need the rare courage and will to attempt it. They also need to focus on two tasks. The first one is rhetorical, yet essential. As an example of the kind of rhetoric that is needed, consider one of the most moving passages in Barack Obama's memoir, *Dreams from My Father*: his account of how he came to embrace membership and faith in the Trinity United Church of Christ, in the black church more broadly, and in the larger Christian tradition of which it has been part:

> And in that single note—hope!—I heard something else; at the foot of that Cross, inside the thousands of churches across the city, I imagined the stories of ordinary black people merging with the stories of David and Goliath, Moses and Pharaoh, the Christians in the lion's den, Ezekiel's field of dry bones. Those stories—of survival, freedom, and hope—became our story, my story; the blood that was spilled was our blood, the tears our tears; until this black church, on this bright day, seemed once more a vessel carrying the story of a people into future generations and into a larger world. Our trials and triumphs became at once unique and universal, black and more than black; in chronicling our journey, the stories and songs gave us a means to reclaim memories that we didn't need to feel shamed about, memories more accessible than those of ancient Egypt, memories that all people might study and cherish—and with which we could start to rebuild.[55]

otes to Chapter 2

93–104; Thomas D. Morris, *Free Men All: The Per-
1780–1861 (Baltimore, MD: Johns Hopkins Univer-
; and Arthur Zilversmit, *The First Emancipation: The
Chicago: University of Chicago Press, 1967), 135–42.
, 70–75, 84–104, 153–70; and William S. McFeely,
W. W. Norton, 1991), 175–77.
1805–7), the U.S. House of Representatives held thir-
of slavery (five roll call votes contemplating issues sur-
e trade; five votes considering a ban on the importation
over the deliberation of the legality of domestic transpor-
all vote contemplating the punishment for the importa-
h Congress (1817–19), the U.S. House of Representatives
the issue of slavery (seven roll call votes contemplating
age twenty-five; three considering issues related to fugitive
s involving deliberations over the status of slavery in Mis-
ngress (1819–21), the U.S. House of Representatives held
the issue of slavery (eleven roll call votes contemplating
Missouri into the Union; two votes considering the remission
illegally; and one vote tabling a resolution that authorized the
h other countries on the means of abolishing the interna-
call vote data available at "Roll Call Data," Voteview.com,
nloads.asp#PARTYSPLITSDWNL, a site hosted by political

Dred Scott and the Problem of Constitutional Evil (New York:
Press, 2006), 127.
klin and Alfred A. Moss Jr., *From Slavery to Freedom: A History
h ed. (New York: McGraw-Hill, 1996), 161–62.
f the seventy-one slavery-related roll call votes held in the U.S.
atives during the Twenty-fourth Congress (1835–37), fifty-one
ery petitions. Several additional votes contemplated the status of
t of Columbia, debates triggered in part by the petitions. In the
ess (1837–39), the U.S. House of Representatives considered
related roll call votes. Of those, twenty-six roll call votes addressed
ectly; two roll call votes contemplated Congress's jurisdictional au-
generally; and one roll call vote addressed an issue involving per-
This trend continued in the Twenty-sixth and Twenty-seventh Con-
, when the U.S. House of Representatives voted on slavery petitions
and fifty-two times, respectively. The Thirty-first Senate (1849–51)
related to "personal liberty" laws and fugitive slaves on six occasions.
ple, sought to establish a criminal offense for any efforts to tempt or
slave in his escape, making the person liable to the owner for the full
e. S. 347 also contemplated similar measures. The Senate held twenty-
tes during the Thirty-first Congress (1849–51) on questions of state

admission and slavery that would have undermined the Missouri Compromise. The roll call vote data are available at "Roll Call Data," Voteview.com, http://voteview.com/downloads.asp#PARTYSPLITSDWNL.

29. For example, the Senate voted seven times on free speech issues triggered by abolitionist mailings during the Twenty-fifth Congress (1837–39). It addressed the issue of fugitive slaves on fourteen occasions during the Thirty-first Congress (1849–51). The House of Representatives contemplated the status of slavery in the territories on a number of occasions, especially during the Thirtieth and Thirty-first congressional sessions (1847–51), when its members debated the question of slavery in the territories acquired from Mexico through the Treaty of Guadalupe Hidalgo. The roll call vote data are available at "Roll Call Data," Voteview.com, http://voteview.com/downloads.asp#PARTYSPLITSDWNL.

30. To determine the consistency of any representative's voting behavior, the following method was used. First, all roll call votes held in the U.S. House of Representatives related to issues of slavery during the antebellum period (First through Thirty-sixth Congress) were identified. This was accomplished by using the keyword search function in Voteview for Windows, v. 3.0.3 (available at http://voteview.ucsd.edu/) using the search term "slav" (and checked against the "issue" search tool and manual counts of sample congressional sessions; no deviations in results were found). Second, two individuals coded each slavery-related roll call vote from a sample of the overall set of all slavery-related roll call votes during the antebellum period. That sample was composed of slavery-related roll call votes in the U.S. House of Representatives during the First, Second, Third, Ninth, Sixteenth, Twenty-fifth, and Thirty-first congressional sessions and the U.S. Senate for the Ninth, Sixteenth, and Thirty-first congressional sessions. Each slavery roll call vote was coded as either "pro-slavery," "anti-slavery," or "unclear." The coders agreed 91.18 percent of the time initially, and after clarification of two categories, coded identically. Third, one individual subsequently coded the remaining slavery-related roll call votes for the antebellum period. Fourth, an overall set of observations was compiled. The overall set of observations was composed of members' ($n = 3280$) behavior on slavery-related roll call votes. If a member did not cast a vote on either a pro- or an anti-slavery roll call vote, his membership status could not be determined ($n = 695$), and he was therefore dropped, leaving a remainder of 2,585 members. Fifth, a scoring system was designed according to the following rules: (1) a "yea" vote on a pro-slavery roll call vote was scored as a "+1"; (2) a "nay" vote on an anti-slavery roll call vote was scored as "+1"; (3) a "nay" pro-slavery roll call vote was scored as a "−1"; and (4) a "yea" vote on an anti-slavery roll call vote was scored as "−1." Fifth, the consistency of each member's voting pattern was determined by applying the scoring system, which was subsequently divided by the total number of pro- or anti-slavery roll call votes that a member issued. A positive score ($0 < x \leq 1$) indicated that the House member voted with the pro-slavery alliance; a negative score ($-1 \leq x < 0$) indicated that the House member voted with the anti-slavery alliance. The magnitude of the ratio produced a measure of consistency by which to compare the behavior of House members.

g senses of political community with shared purposes
d of telling of the story of a people in ways that enable
porters as possible to see their personal stories as part of
ative.[56] No one in modern American politics has been
at task or more skilled at accomplishing it than Barack
ma catapulted to national prominence through his link-
e personal story with that of all Americans, in his 2004
ntion speech as well as his best-selling memoir. Obama
ne in his 2008 National Constitution speech in response
ight controversy.
t the beginning of this book, there Obama fell short. He
his own saga while expressing understanding of the anger
th American blacks and whites feel. He then argued that all
ling African Americans, would benefit from common (and,
ot spell it out, race-neutral) policies designed to meet their
bama did not seek to persuade white Americans that they
wn stories, their hopes, fears, and values, best realized in an
ed some race-conscious policies as necessary means to carry
ng held back by both public and private discrimination—even
quietly but consistently shown that he believes this to be the
lso did not show how Americans might continue their story in
whites, too, could find greater pride as well as greater peace and
ough such mixed measures. Nor did he suggest how policies
ctured to apportion the costs of racial change more heavily on
l, as for example the Westchester housing litigation sought to do,
n less advantaged whites striving to get ahead, like Frank Ricci—
too would have been consistent with his general approach.
Obama failed altogether to raise the difficult topic of the clashing
today's rival racial alliances. Yet unless American political leaders
nd not just this master storyteller, address those racial policy dis-
nly argue that they are too starkly framed; and then provide ac-
which Americans can see their distinct stories advanced through the
an appropriate blend of racial policies, speeches like Obama's may
o help the American vessel navigate rough spots, but they will not
tes for substantial progress.
ecommendation in regard to where analyses should now be directed
ly if not more important. In designing, evaluating, and advocating
e mixes of racial policies, both candidates and governing officials
focus much less on moral principles of color blindness or racial repara-
d much more on material results, candidly assessed.[57] The notion that,

31. For instance, a bill in House No. 31 on January 6, 1851, "to suspend the rules and introduce a resolution calling for the repeal of the fugitive slave law passed at the last session of Congress" was defeated by 119 votes to 68 (with 42 not voting); the breakdown by region is important in revealing the power of the white supremacist political coalition and its significant support from beyond the South: Northeast had 47 for, 31 against; South no support and 62 against; Midwest 19 for and 26 against; and the West 2 for, none opposing.

32. American Presidency Project, http://www.presidency.ucsb.edu/ws/?pid=29572.

33. Ibid., www.presidency.ucsb.edu/ws/?pid=29576.

34. Ibid., www.presidency.ucsb.edu/ws/?pid=25852, 25855.

35. Ibid., www.presidency.ucsb.edu/ws/?pid=25856.

36. Ibid., www.presidency.ucsb.edu/ws/?pid=25857.

37. Ibid., www.presidency.ucsb.edu/ws/?pid=29619. Paragraph 5 of the platform was ferocious: "that the present Democratic Administration has far exceeded our worst apprehensions, in its measureless subserviency to the exactions of a sectional interest, as especially evinced in its desperate exertions to force the infamous Lecompton Constitution upon the protesting people of Kansas; in construing the personal relations between master and servant to involve an unqualified property in persons; in its attempted enforcement everywhere, on land and sea, through the intervention of Congress and of the Federal Courts of the extreme pretensions of a purely local interest; and in its general and unvarying abuse of power intrusted to it by a confiding people."

38. American Presidency Project, www.presidency.ucsb.edu/ws/?pid=29620.

39. Quoted in Berwanger, *Frontier Against Slavery*: 125–26.

40. Rogers M. Smith, *Civic Ideals* (New Haven, CT: Yale University Press, 1997), 174–81, 187–88, 226–28.

41. *Groves v. Slaughter* (15 Pet. 449, 1841).

42. *U.S. v. Schooner Amistad* (15 Pet. 518, 1841).

43. *Prigg v. Pennsylvania* (16 Pet. 539, 1842).

44. David J. Bederman, "The Cautionary Tale of Alexander McLeod: Superior Orders and the American Writ of Habeas Corpus," *Emory Law Journal* 41 (1992): 528.

45. *Strader v. Graham* (10 How. 82, 1851).

46. *Dred Scott v. Sandford* (19 How. 393, 1857).

47. Graber, *Dred Scott*, 30–31, 34.

48. Alexander H. Stephens, "Cornerstone Speech," Teaching American History.org, http://teachingamericanhistory.org/library/index.asp?documentprint=76.

49. Greenstone, *The Lincoln Persuasion*, 245–85.

50. Abraham Lincoln, *The Writings of Abraham Lincoln*, ed. Arthur B. Lapsley (New York: Lamb, 1905–6), 7:366.

51. James M. McPherson, *Battle Cry of Freedom: The Civil War Era* (New York: Oxford University Press, 1988), 852.

52. Richard M. Valelly, *The Two Reconstructions: The Struggle for Black Enfranchisement* (Chicago: University of Chicago Press, 2004), 27.

53. Eric Foner, *Reconstruction: America's Unfinished Revolution, 1863–1877* (New York: Harper and Row), 165–75, 215–16; Smith, *Civic Ideals,* 302–12; Valelly, *Two Reconstructions,* 28–32.

54. Valelly, *Two Reconstructions,* 27; Foner, *Reconstruction,* 216–27, 247–51.

55. Michael Les Benedict, *A Compromise of Principle* (New York: W. W. Norton, 1974), 23–30. As Richard Valelly notes (*Two Reconstructions,* 25), though Lincoln and the Radical Republicans differed on the Wade-Davis bill as a blueprint for the reconstruction of Louisiana, on March 3, 1865, Lincoln did sign a Radical-sponsored bill authorizing the Freedmen's Bureau to assign freedmen "not more than forty acres" of land as three-year rentals with an option to buy. On this issue he clearly differed from his successor.

56. Valelly, *Two Reconstructions,* 92.

57. Valelly, *Two Reconstructions,* 106–9.

58. Nicholas Lemann, *Redemption: The Last Battle of the Civil War* (New York: Farrar, Straus and Giroux, 2006); LeAnna Keith, *The Colfax Massacre* (New York: Oxford University Press, 2008).

59. Valelly, *Two Reconstructions,* 91–96.

60. American Presidency Project, http://www.presidency.ucsb.edu/ws/?pid=29579.

61. Ibid., http://www.presidency.ucsb.edu/ws/?pid=29622.

62. Ibid., http://www.presidency.ucsb.edu/ws/? pid=29580.

63. Ibid., http://www.presidency.ucsb.edu/ws/?pid=29623.

64. Valelly, *Two Reconstructions,* 47, 69; Smith, *Civic Ideals,* 325.

65. American Presidency Project, http://www.presidency.ucsb.edu/ws/?pid=29624.

66. Ibid.

67. Ibid., http://www.presidency.ucsb.edu/ws/?pid=29581.

68. Aristide R. Zolberg, *A Nation by Design: Immigrant Policy in the Fashioning of America* (Cambridge, MA: Harvard University Press, 2006), 183.

69. *Senator Aaron Sargent: Joint Special Committee on Chinese,* Senate Report No. 689, 44th Cong., 2nd sess. (Washington, DC: U.S. Government Printing Office, 1877); Daniel J. Tichenor, *Dividing Lines: The Politics of Immigration Control in America* (Princeton, NJ: Princeton University Press, 2002), 102.

70. John F. Morgan, "The Political Alliance of the South and the West," *North American Review* 126 (1878): 313–16, cited in Tichenor, *Dividing Lines,* 104.

71. Cited in Andrew Gyory, *Closing the Gate: Race, Politics and the Chinese Exclusion Act* (Chapel Hill: University of North Carolina Press, 1998), 3–4.

72. Quoted in Paul Gordon Lauren, *Power and Prejudice: The Politics and Diplomacy of Racial Discrimination* (Boulder, CO: Westview, 1996), 41.

73. American Presidency Project, http://www.presidency.ucsb.edu/ws/?pid=29582, 29625.

74. The numbers come from Gyory, *Closing the Gate,* 238–39.

75. Ibid., 253.

76. Ellen Carol Dubois, *Feminism and Suffrage* (Ithaca, NY: Cornell University Press, 1978), 53–104.

77. Charles Darwin, *The Origin of the Species and the Descent of Man* (New York: Modern Library, 1936), 530–31, 539–43, 552n57, 556.

78. Tomas Almaguer, *Racial Fault Lines: The Historical Origins of White Supremacy in California* (Berkeley: University of California Press, 1994); Fuchs, *American Kaleidoscope*, 96–98; and David M. Oshinsky, *Worse Than Slavery: Parchman Farm and the Ordeal of Jim Crow Justice* (New York: Free Press, 1996), 40–41. For this wider context and especially the embrace of eugenic arguments, see Desmond King, *Making Americans: Immigration, Race and the Origins of the Diverse Democracy* (Cambridge, MA: Harvard University Press, 2000), 127–95.

79. Robert W. Rydell, *All the World's a Fair* (Chicago: University of Chicago Press, 1984), 219, 220, and Rydell, *World of Fairs: The Century-of-Progress Expositions* (Chicago: University of Chicago Press, 1993); and James Gilbert, *Whose Fair? Experience, Memory and the History of the Great St. Louis Exposition* (Chicago: University of Chicago Press, 2009).

80. Tichenor, *Dividing Lines*, 83, 106–8, 118–19; Zolberg, *Nation by Design*, 194, 218–29.

81. Zolberg, *Nation by Design*, 184.

82. Tichenor, *Dividing Lines*, 105.

83. Smith, *Civic Ideals*, 391–92.

84. For accounts giving greater credence to the courts' good faith in interpreting the postwar statutes and amendments than we do here, see, e.g., Pamela Brandwein, *The Supreme Court, State Action, and Civil Rights* (New York: Cambridge University Press, 2011); Leslie F. Goldstein, "The Spectre of the Second Amendment: Re-reading *Slaughterhouse* and *Cruikshank*," *Studies in American Political Development* 21 (2007): 1–18.

85. Smith, *Civic Ideals*, 327–29; Valelly, *Two Reconstructions*, 110–11.

86. *U.S. v. Cruikshank*, 25 F. Case. 707, 712–13 (U.S.C.D. La., 1874).

87. *U.S. v. Cruikshank*, 92 U.S. 542 (1876); Valelly, *Two Reconstructions*, 111–20.

88. *Civil Rights Cases*, 109 U.S. 3, 13, 18–25 (1883).

89. American Presidency Project, http://www.presidency.ucsb.edu/ws/?pid=29626, 29627, 29628, 29629, 29630, 29631, 29632. (Note: Subsequent references to this site provide the document number only.)

90. Ibid., 29583, 29584, 29585, 29586, 29587, 29588, 29589.

91. Valelly, *Two Reconstructions*, 121.

92. Richard M. Valelly, "The Reed Rules and Republican Party Building: A New Look," *Studies in American Political Development* 23 (2009): 115–16.

93. Desmond S. King and Rogers M. Smith, "Racial Orders in American Political Development," *American Political Science Review* 99 (2005): 87.

94. Valelly, *Two Reconstructions*, 1, 131–33.

95. *Roberts v. City of Boston*, 5 Cushing 198, 296 (Mass., 1849).

96. *Plessy v. Ferguson*, 163 U.S. 537, 551, 552 (1896).

97. *Giles v. Harris*, 189 U.S. 475 (1903).

98. *Giles v. Teasley*, 193 U.S. 146 (1904).

99. Louis R. Harlan, *Booker T. Washington: The Wizard of Tuskegee* (New York: Oxford University Press, 1983), 246–47.

CHAPTER 3. "WE OF THE NORTH WERE THOROUGHLY WRONG":
HOW RACIAL ALLIANCES MOBILIZED IDEAS AND LAW

1. Christopher Waldrep, *African Americans Confront Lynching: Strategies of Resistance from the Civil War to the Civil Rights Era* (New York: Rowman and Littlefield, 2009), xix–xxvi.

2. Charles Francis Adams Jr., "'Tis Sixty Years Since," Project Gutenberg, http://www.gutenberg.org/dirs/etext06/8sxys10h.htm.

3. See, e.g., Glenda Elizabeth Gilmore, *Gender and Jim Crow: Women and the Politics of White Supremacy in North Carolina* (Chapel Hill: University of North Carolina Press, 1996); Jane Dailey, Glenda Elizabeth Gilmore, and Bryant Simon, eds., *Jumpin' Jim Crow: Southern Politics from Civil War to Civil Rights* (Princeton, NJ: Princeton University Press, 2000); Steven Hahn, *A Nation Under Our Feet: Black Political Struggles in the Rural South, from Slavery to the Great Migration* (Cambridge, MA: Harvard University Press, 2003); Kimberley Johnson, *Reforming Jim Crow: Southern Politics and State in the Age Before Brown* (New York: Oxford University Press, 2010); and Julie Novkov, *Racial Union: Law, Intimacy and the White State in Alabama, 1865–1954* (Ann Arbor: University of Michigan Press, 2008).

4. American Presidency Project, 29633, 29634, 29635, 29636, 29637, 29638, 29639.

5. Ibid., 29640.

6. Ibid., 29591, 29593, and cf. 29590, 29592, 29594, 29595, 29596.

7. Ibid., 29592, 29593, 29594.

8. Ibid., 29597.

9. Ibid., 29617, 29618.

10. Desmond S. King and Rogers M. Smith, "Racial Orders in American Political Development," *American Political Science Review* 99 (2005): 86; Philip A. Klinkner with Rogers M. Smith, *The Unsteady March: The Rise and Decline of Racial Equality in America* (Chicago: University of Chicago Press, 1999), 103, 110; see also Tichenor, *Dividing Lines*, 38–39, 119–33; Zolberg, *Nation by Design*, 234–38.

11. Lawrence H. Fuchs, *The American Kaleidoscope: Race, Ethnicity and the Civic Culture* (Hanover, NH: University Press of New England, 1990), 80–86; Mai M. Ngai, "The Architecture of American Immigration Law: A Re-examination of the Immigration Act of 1924," *Journal of American History* 86 (June 1999): 67–92.

12. Matthew Frye Jacobson, *Whiteness of a Different Color: European Immigrants and the Alchemy of Race* (Cambridge, MA: Harvard University Press, 1998), 203–45; David R. Roediger, *Working Toward Whiteness: How America's Immigrants Became White — The Strange Journey from Ellis Island to the Suburbs* (New York: Basic, 2005); Ronald Takaki, *A Different Mirror: A History of Multicultural America* (Boston: Little Brown, 1993), 148–54, 209–13; Walter L. Williams, "United States Indian Policy and the Debate over Philippine Annexation: Implications for the Origins of American Imperialism," *Journal of American History* 66 (1980): 810–31.

13. Kimberley Johnson, *Reforming Jim Crow*, 17.

14. See, e.g., *U.S. v. Wong Kim Ark,* 169 U.S. 649 [1898] (upholding Fourteenth Amendment birthright citizenship for Chinese children born in the United States); *Rogers v. Alabama,* 192 U.S. 226 [1904] (invalidating overt efforts to prevent blacks from serving on juries); *Buchanan v. Warley,* 245 U.S. 60 [1917] (invalidating a municipal ordinance preventing persons of one race from selling their real estate to persons of another).

15. Robert L. Zangrando, *The NAACP Crusade Against Lynching, 1909–1950* (Philadelphia: Temple University Press, 1980), 6.

16. Amii Larkin Barnard, "The Application of Critical Race Feminism to the Anti-Lynching Movement: Black Women's Fight Against Race and Gender Ideology, 1892–1920," *UCLA Women's Law Journal* 3 (1993): 15–20; Waldrep, *African Americans,* 46–50.

17. Donald G. Nieman, *Promises to Keep: African-Americans and the Constitutional Order, 1776 to the Present* (New York: Oxford University Press, 1991), 123.

18. Ibid., 124–25; Waldrep, *African Americans,* 51–52, 59–70.

19. George C. Rable, "The South and the Politics of Antilynching Legislation, 1920–1940," *Journal of Southern History* 51 (1985): 203–6; Waldrep, *African Americans,* 71–75.

20. Rable, "Politics of Antilynching," 206; Waldrep, *African Americans,* 76–77; Letter from James Johnson to Harding's secretary J. E. Spingarn, December 15, 1922, in NAACP Papers, Library of Congress, Manuscript Division NAACP I Box C-66, File: Special Correspondence J. W. Johnson September–December 1922.

21. Mae M. Ngai, *Impossible Subjects: Illegal Aliens and the Making of Modern America* (Princeton, NJ: Princeton University Press, 2004), 20.

22. Tichenor, *Dividing Lines,* 144–46, 150–51; Zolberg, *Nation by Design,* 258–64.

23. Johnson, *Reforming Jim Crow,* 43–65, 116–43; Rable, "Politics of Antilynching," 208.

24. Rable, "Politics of Antilynching," 209–20; Waldrep, *African Americans,* 81–85.

25. E. David Cronon, *Black Moses: The Story of Marcus Garvey and the Universal Negro Improvement Association* (Madison: University of Wisconsin Press, 1969 [1955]), 189–95.

26. Lawrie Balfour, "Unreconstructed Democracy: W.E.B. Du Bois and the Case for Reparations," *American Political Science Review* 97 (2003): 33–44; John Hope Franklin and Alfred A. Moss Jr., *From Slavery to Freedom: A History of Negro Americans,* 6th ed., (New York: Alfred A. Knopf, 1988), 244–50.

27. Franklin and Moss, *From Slavery to Freedom,* 6th ed., 306.

28. Ibid., 339–40; Klinkner with Smith, *Unsteady March,* 145.

29. Ira Katznelson, *When Affirmative Action Was White: An Untold History of Racial Inequality in Twentieth-Century America* (New York: W. W. Norton, 2005), 20–22.

30. Franklin and Moss, *From Slavery to Freedom,* 6th ed., 342–44.

31. Ibid., 345–46; Lawrence S. Wittner, "The National Negro Congress: A Reassessment," *American Quarterly* 22 (1970): 884; Klinkner with Smith, *Unsteady March,*

144–46; Robin D. G. Kelley, *Hammer and Hoe: Alabama Communists During the Great Depression* (Chapel Hill: University of North Carolina Press, 1990).

32. Franklin and Moss, *From Slavery to Freedom*, 6th ed., 339–48; August Meier and Elliot Rudwick, "The Origins of Nonviolent Direct Action in Afro-American Protest: A Note on Historical Discontinuities," in *Along the Color Line: Explorations in the Black Experience*, ed. August Meier and Elliot Rudwick (Urbana: University of Illinois Press, 1976), 314–32. The manner in which, in response to domestic and international pressures, key actors and institutions joined the anti-segregation racial alliance seems even more central to explaining change than the heightened "resource mobilization" or the adoption of new concepts of "black identity" by "minority movements" rights stressed by scholars using "social movements and the state" frameworks. See, e.g., Doug McAdam, *Political Process and the Development of Black Insurgency* (Chicago: University of Chicago Press, 1984); Michael Omni and Howard Winant, *Racial Formation in the United States*, 2nd ed. (New York: Routledge, 1994), 98–99.

33. Johnson, *Reforming Jim Crow*, 19–42.

34. Robert C. Lieberman, *Shifting the Color Line: Race and the American Welfare State* (Cambridge, MA: Harvard University Press, 2001); Jill Quadagno, *The Color of Welfare: How Racism Undermined the War on Poverty* (Oxford: Oxford University Press, 1996); Katznelson, *Affirmative Action*; Deborah E. Ward, *The White Welfare State: The Racialization of U.S. Welfare Policy* (Ann Arbor: University of Michigan Press, 2005); and Mary Poole, *The Segregated Origins of Social Security: African Americans and the Welfare State* (Chapel Hill: University of North Carolina Press, 2006).

35. Katznelson, *Affirmative Action*, 44, also citing Lieberman, *Shifting the Color Line*.

36. Margaret Weir, "States, Race and the Decline of New Deal Liberalism," *Studies in American Political Development* 19 (2005): 157–72.

37. The standard account is Lieberman, *Shifting the Color Line*, 26–64.

38. Ibid., 36–37.

39. Quoted in ibid., 39, from an editorial on March 9, 1935.

40. Ibid., 40.

41. Ibid., 44–45.

42. Katznelson, *Affirmative Action*.

43. Beth Tompkins Bates, *Pullman Porters and the Rise of Protest Politics in Black America, 1925–1945* (Chapel Hill: University of North Carolina Press, 2001).

44. Ira Katznelson, Kim Geiger, and Daniel Kryder, "Limiting Liberalism: The Southern Veto in Congress, 1933–1950," *Political Science Quarterly* 108 (1993): 283–306; Lieberman, *Shifting the Color Line*; Kevin J. McMahon, *Reconsidering Roosevelt on Race: How the Presidency Paved the Road to Brown* (Chicago: University of Chicago Press, 2004).

45. Carl N. Degler, *In Search of Human Nature: The Decline and Revival of Darwinism in American Social Thought* (New York: Oxford University Press, 1991), 176–211; Johnson, *Reforming Jim Crow*, 104–5.

46. Greg Robinson, *By Order of the President: FDR and the Internment of Japanese Americans* (Cambridge, MA: Harvard University Press, 2001), 119–20.

47. *U.S. v. Wong Kim Ark,* 169 U.S. 649 (1898).

48. See, e.g., *United States v. Ju Toy,* 198 U.S. 253 (1905), and for discussion, Smith, *Civic Ideals,* 444–46.

49. See, e.g., *Downes v. Bidwell,* 182 U.S. 244 (1901); *Balzac v. Porto Rico,* 258 U.S. 298 (1922); Smith, *Civic Ideals,* 433–39.

50. Cf., e.g., *Carter v. Texas,* 177 U.S. 442 (1900) (sustaining an accused black because the state court would not hear his witnesses to the exclusion of blacks from a grand jury) and *Rogers v. Alabama,* 192 U.S. 226 (1904) (sustaining an accused black because the lower court did not examine evidence that a ban on black voters affected juror selection) with *Tarrance v. Florida,* 188 U.S. 519 (1903), *Brownfield v. South Carolina,* 189 U.S. 426 (1903), *Martin v. Texas,* 200 U.S. 316 (1906), and *Franklin v. South Carolina,* 218 U.S. 161 (1910) (all finding insufficient evidence of exclusion of blacks from juries).

51. See, e.g., *Hodges v. United States,* 203 U.S. 1 (1906); *Clyatt v. U.S.,* 197 U.S. 207 (1905); *Bailey v. Alabama,* 219 U.S. 219 (1911); *U.S. v. Reynolds,* 235 U.S. 133 (1914); Smith, *Civic Ideals,* 452; Nieman, *Promises to Keep,* 126.

52. *Guinn v. United States,* 238 U.S. 347 (1915).

53. See, e.g., *Nixon v. Herndon,* 273 U.S. 536 (1927); *Nixon v. Condon,* 286 U.S. 73 (1932); *Grovey v. Townsend,* 295 U.S. 45 (1935); *Smith v. Allwright,* 321 U.S. 649 (1944).

54. *Buchanan v. Warley,* 245 U.S. 60 (1917).

55. *Corrigan v. Buckley,* 271 U.S. 323 (1926).

56. Douglas S. Massey and Nancy A. Denton, *American Apartheid: Segregation and the Making of the Underclass* (Cambridge, MA: Harvard University Press, 1993), 187–88.

57. See, e.g., *Moore v. Dempsey,* 261 U.S. 86 (1923); *Powell v. Alabama,* 287 U.S. 45 (1932); *Norris v. Alabama,* 294 U.S. 587 (1935); *Chambers v. Florida,* 309 U.S. 227 (1940); *Smith v. Texas,* 311 U.S. 128 (1940); and for discussion, Nieman, *Promises to Keep,* 129–36; Dan T. Carter, *Scottsboro: A Tragedy of the American South,* rev. ed. (Baton Rouge: Louisiana State University Press, 1979).

58. See, e.g., *University of Maryland v. Murray,* 169 Maryland 478 (1936); *Missouri ex rel. Gaines v. Canada,* 305 U.S. 337 (1938).

59. Degler, *In Search of Human Nature,* 203.

60. See, e.g., Klinkner with Smith, *Unsteady March*; Mary L. Dudziak, *Cold War Civil Rights: Race and the Image of American Democracy* (Princeton, NJ: Princeton University Press, 2002); Daniel Kryder, *Divided Arsenal: Race and the American State During World War II* (New York: Cambridge University Press, 2002); Cary F. Fraser, "Crossing the Color Line in Little Rock: The Eisenhower Administration and the Dilemma of Race for U.S. Foreign Policy," *Diplomatic History* 24 (2000): 233–64.

61. American Presidency Project, http://www.presidency.ucsb.edu/ws/?pid=29640.

62. Ibid., http://www.presidency.ucsb.edu/ws/?pid=29597.

63. Francis L. Broderick and August Meier, eds., *Negro Protest Thought in the Twentieth Century* (Indianapolis: Bobbs-Merrill, 1965); August Meier and Elliot Rudwick, "The Origins of Nonviolent Direct Action in Afro-American Protest: A Note on Historical

Discontinuities," in *Along the Color Line: Explorations in the Black Experience*, ed. August Meier and Elliot Rudwick (Urbana: University of Illinois Press, 1976); Klinkner with Smith, *Unsteady March*, 144–79.

64. American Presidency Project, 25835.

65. Ibid., 29598.

66. Klinkner with Smith, *Unsteady March*, 128–35; McMahon, *Reconsidering Roosevelt on Race*, 110–44.

67. *Smith v. Allwright*, 321 U.S. 649 (1944). The earlier case, not involving African Americans, was *U.S. v. Classic*, 313 U.S. 299 (1941).

68. *Korematsu v. United States*, 323 U.S. 214, 216 (1944).

69. *Morgan v. Virginia*, 328 U.S. 373 (1946); *Shelley v. Kraemer*, 334 U.S. 1 (1948).

70. American Presidency Project, 25836.

71. Ibid., 29599.

72. Klinkner with Smith, *Unsteady March*, 202–26.

73. Ibid.; W. Edward Orser, "Racial Attitudes in Wartime: The Protestant Churches During the Second World War," *Church History* 41 (1972): 337–53.

74. American Presidency Project, 25851.

75. Ibid., 25837.

76. Ibid., 29600.

77. *Sweatt v. Painter*, 339 U.S. 629 (1950). See also McMahon, *Roosevelt on Race*, 193; Nieman, *Promises to Keep*, 139–47.

78. *Brown v. Board of Education*, 347 U.S. 483 (1954).

79. Tony Badger, "'The Forerunner of Our Opposition': Arkansas and the Southern Manifesto of 1956," *Arkansas Historical Quarterly* 56 (1997): 353–60.

80. Ibid.; Dan T. Carter, *The Politics of Rage: George Wallace, the Origins of the New Conservatism, and the Transformation of American Politics* (Baton Rouge: Louisiana State University Press, 1995), 82–105; Taylor Branch, *Parting the Waters: America in the King Years, 1954–1963* (New York: Simon and Schuster, 1988), 222–25.

81. American Presidency Project, 25838.

82. Ibid., 29601.

83. Johnson, *Reforming Jim Crow*, 16–17, 25–26.

84. Azza Salam Layton, *International Politics and Civil Rights Policies in the United States, 1941–1960* (New York: Cambridge, 2000), 92; Herbert Brownell with John P. Burke, *Advising Ike: The Memoirs of Attorney General Herbert Brownell* (Lawrence: University Press of Kansas, 1993); Paula Wilson, ed., *The Civil Rights Rhetoric of Hubert H. Humphrey, 1948–1964* (Lanham, MD: University Press of America, 1996); Mary Dudziak, *Cold War Civil Rights* (Princeton, NJ: Princeton University Press, 2000); David Alan Horowitz, "White Southerners' Alienation and Civil Rights: The Response to Corporate Liberalism, 1956–1965," *Journal of Southern History* 54 (May 1988): 173–200.

85. Alexander Keyssar, *The Right to Vote: The Contested History of Democracy in the United States* (New York: Basic Books, 2000), 260.

86. Franklin and Moss, *From Slavery to Freedom*, 6th ed., 438–41.

87. American Presidency Project, 25839.

88. Ibid., 29602.

89. Branch, *Parting the Waters*, 846–87; Franklin and Moss, *From Slavery to Freedom*, 6th ed., 441–45; Klinkner with Smith, *Unsteady March*, 243, 256–70.

90. *Public Papers of the Presidents of the United States: Lyndon B. Johnson, 1963–64* (Washington, DC: U.S. Government Printing Office, 1965), 8–10.

91. For a useful overview of the passage of the act, see Sean Farhang, *The Litigation State: Public Regulation and Private Lawsuits in the U.S.* (Princeton, NJ: Princeton University Press, 2010), 94–128. Additional vote totals can be found at *Congressional Quarterly Weekly Report* 21, no. 27 (1964): 1414–15.

92. Ibid.

93. This 'Operation Dixie' Goldwater strategy is recounted in Philip A. Klinkner, *The Losing Parties: Out-Party National Committees, 1956–1993* (New Haven, CT: Yale University Press, 1994), 41–70; and on the parties' positions in 1960, see Theodore H. White, *The Making of the President, 1960* (New York: Atheneum Press, 1961), 247–48, 348–50.

94. After his victory in the Kentucky Republican Senate primary in May 2010, libertarian "Tea Party" proponent Rand Paul did express reservations about those parts of the 1964 Civil Rights Act that ban discrimination by private businesses (which include Title II and Title VII). When criticized, he issued a press release stating "unequivocally . . . that I will not support any efforts to repeal the Civil Rights Act of 1964." Adam Nagourney, "Paul's Views on Civil Rights Cause a Stir," *The Caucus* (blog), *New York Times*, May 20, 2010, http://thecaucus.blogs.nytimes.com/2010/05/20/pauls-views-on-civil-rights-cause-a-stir/?hpw.

95. American Presidency Project, 25840.

96. Ibid., 29603.

CHAPTER 4. "THIS BACKDROP OF ENTRENCHED INEQUALITY":
AFFIRMATIVE ACTION IN WORK

1. The quotation in the chapter title is from Justice Ruth Ginsburg, dissenting, in *Ricci v. DeStefano*, 557 U.S. 2 (2009).

2. 557 U.S. 2; 129 S. Ct. 2658 (2009).

3. "*Ricci v. DeStefano*, Brief for the United States as Amicus Curiae Supporting Vacatur and Remand," 22–32 (2009).

4. Justice Anthony Kennedy, *Ricci v. DeStefano*, 557 U.S. 2, 19 (2009).

5. The "strong basis in evidence" standard first appears in *Wygant v. Jackson Board of Education*, 476 U.S. 367 (1986) at 277, in the majority opinion by Justice Lewis Powell.

6. As Paul Frymer stresses, the judiciary helped attack discrimination in labor markets, notably with respect to desegregating unions: *Black and Blue: African Americans, the Labor Movement and the Decline of the Democratic Party* (Princeton, NJ: Princeton University Press, 2008), 3.

7. Daniel Kryder, *Divided Arsenal: Race and the American State During World War II* (Cambridge: Cambridge University Press, 2000).

8. Thomas J. Sugrue, *Sweet Land of Liberty: The Forgotten Struggle for Civil Rights in the North* (New York: Random House, 2008), 3.

9. Data from Roberta Spalter-Roth and Terri Ann Lowenthal, *Race, Ethnicity and the American Labor Market: What's at Work?* (Washington, DC: American Sociological Association, June 2005), 2. Available online at http://www.asanet.org/images/research/docs/pdf/RaceEthnicity_LaborMarket.pdf.

10. U.S. Department of Labor, Bureau of Labor Statistics, "Table A-2. Employment Status of the Civilian Population by Race, Sex, and Age," last modified January 7, 2011, http://www.bls.gov/news.release/empsit.t02.htm (figures not seasonally adjusted).

11. Jennifer M. Gardner, "Worker Displacement: A Decade of Change," *Monthly Labor Review* (April 1995): 49, at http://www.bls.gov/opub/mlr/1995/04/art6full.pdf.

12. Douglas S. Massey, *Categorically Unequal: The American Stratification System* (New York: Russell Sage Foundation, 2007), 85.

13. For both points of view, see, e.g., Cindy Rodriguez, "Attitudes Soften but Blacks, Whites, See Bias Differently," *Detroit News*, July 19, 2007, http://detnews.com/article/20070719/METRO/707190419/; and Pew Research Center for the People and the Press, "Social and Political Attitudes About Race," http://people-press.org/report/?pageid=1520.

14. Massey, *Categorically Unequal*, 89; Massey cites several empirical studies including Marianne Bertrand and Sendhiil Mullainathan, "Are Emily and Greg More Employable Than Lakisha and Jamal? A Field Experiment on Labor Market Discrimination," *American Economic Review* 94 (2004): 991–1013; and an unpublished paper by Devah Pager and Bruce Western to the New York City Commission on Human Rights, "Race at Work: Realities of Race and Criminal Record in the New York City Jobs Market," released December 9, 2005, available online at http://www.nyc.gov/html/cchr/html/raceatwork.html.

15. Devah Pager, "The Mark of a Criminal Record," *American Journal of Sociology* 108 (2003): 937–75, 959.

16. Ibid., 959–60.

17. Linda Chavez, *Out of the Barrio: Towards a New Politics of Hispanic Assimilation* (New York: Basic Books, 1991), 5, 56, 169.

18. Daniel Kryder, *Divided Arsenal*, 52–55, 65–66, 90–94.

19. Kevin J. McMahon, *Reconsidering Roosevelt on Race* (Chicago: University of Chicago Press, 2004), 155–16.

20. Anthony S. Chen, *The Fifth Freedom: Jobs, Politics and Civil Rights in the United States, 1941–1972* (Princeton, NJ: Princeton University Press, 2009), 44.

21. Ira Katznelson, *When Affirmative Action Was White* (New York: W. W. Norton, 2005), 8.

22. Chen, *Fifth Freedom*.

23. Anthony S. Chen, "The Party of Lincoln and the Politics of State Fair Employment Practices Legislation in the North, 1945–1964," *American Journal of Sociology* 112 (May 2007): 1713–74.

24. Anthony S. Chen, "'The Hitlerian Rule of Quotas': Racial Conservatism and the Politics of Fair Employment Legislation in New York State, 1941–1945," *Journal of American History* 92 (March 2006): 1238–64.

25. Quoted in Chen, *Fifth Freedom*, 119.

26. Chen, *Fifth Freedom*, 131.

27. Hugh Davis Graham, *Collision Course: The Strange Convergence of Affirmative Action and Immigration Policy in America* (New York: Oxford University Press, 2002), 28–29.

28. Robert C. Lieberman, *Shaping Race Policy: The United States in Comparative Perspective* (Princeton, NJ: Princeton University Press, 2005), 159–63.

29. Paul Burstein, *Discrimination, Jobs and Politics: The Struggle for Equal Employment Opportunity in the United States since the New Deal* (Chicago: University of Chicago Press, 1985), 106–7.

30. Lieberman, *Shaping Race Policy*, 158–63.

31. Frank Dobbin and John R. Sutton, "The Strength of a Weak State: The Rights Revolution and the Rise of Human Resources Management Divisions," *American Journal of Sociology* 104 (1998): 441–76, 447.

32. John David Skrentny, *The Ironies of Affirmative Action: Politics, Culture and Justice in America* (Chicago: University of Chicago Press, 1996), 69–76; Linda Faye Williams, *The Constraint of Race: Legacies of White Skin Privilege in America* (University Park: Pennsylvania State University Press, 2003), 120, 170–79.

33. Michael Crane, *The Political Junkie Handbook: The Definitive Reference Book on Politics* (New York: S.P.I. Books, 2004), 13.

34. American Presidency Project, "Political Party Platforms: Parties Receiving Electoral Votes (1840–2008), www.presidency.ucsb.edu/platforms.php.

35. Skrentny, *Ironies of Affirmative Action*, 3.

36. Graham, *Collision Course*, 30–33, 65–66.

37. Skrentny, *Ironies of Affirmative Action*, 133–35.

38. U.S. Department of Labor, Executive Order 11246 as amended, http://www.dol.gov/ofccp/regs/statutes/eo11246.htm.

39. Skrentny, *Ironies of Affirmative Action*, 7.

40. Sean Farhang, *The Litigation State: Public Regulation and Private Lawsuits in the U.S.* (Princeton, NJ: Princeton University Press, 2010), 106.

41. Skrentny, *Ironies of Affirmative Action*, 90–91.

42. Frymer, *Black and Blue*, 41–42; Paul Frymer, "Acting When Elected Officials Won't: Federal Courts and Civil Rights Enforcement in U.S. Labor Unions, 1935–1985," *American Political Science Review* 97 (2003): 483–99.

43. Skrentny, *Ironies of Affirmative Action*, 123.

44. Lieberman, *Shaping Race Policy*, 185–87; and Robert C. Lieberman, "Civil Rights and the Democratization Trap: The Public-Private Nexus and the Building of American Democracy," in *Democratization in America: A Comparative-Historical Analysis*, ed. Desmond King, Robert C. Lieberman, Gretchen Ritter, and Laurence Whitehead (Baltimore, MD: Johns Hopkins University Press, 2009).

45. Cited in Skrentny, *Ironies of Affirmative Action*, 124.

46. John David Skrentny, *The Minority Rights Revolution* (Cambridge, MA: Harvard University Press, 2002), 145–46; Executive Order 11375, 3 CFR 684 (1966–1970 Comp.); Executive Order 11518, 3 CFR 907 (1966–1970 Comp.); discussed in *Fullilove v. Klutznick*, 448 U.S. 448, 464 (1980).

47. Graham, *Collision Course*, 33.

48. Graham, *Collision Course*, 69–71; Williams, *Constraint of Race*, 174–77; Skrentny, *Ironies of Affirmative Action*, 136–39, 193–211.

49. See David Hamilton Golland, "Arthur Fletcher and the Philadelphia Plan, 1969–1971" (paper presented at the Monmouth Conference on Race, November 12, 2010, West Long Branch, NJ), 5. For further details, see Golland, *Constructing Affirmative Action: The Struggle for Equal Employment Opportunity* (Lexington: University of Kentucky Press, 2011).

50. Golland, "Arthur Fletcher," 6–7; Graham, *Collision Course*; Desmond S. King, *Actively Seeking Work? The Politics of Unemployment and Welfare Policy in the United States and Great Britain* (Chicago: University of Chicago Press, 1995); Jill Quadagno, "Social Movements and State Transformation: Labor Unions and Racial Conflict in the War on Poverty," *American Sociological Review* 57 (1992): 616–34.

51. Quoted in Skrentny, *Ironies of Affirmative Action*, 139, from Fletcher memoirs.

52. Quoted in Skrentny, *Ironies of Affirmative Action*, 200, from the *Hearings on the Philadelphia Plan before the Subcommittee on Separation of Powers of the Senate Judiciary Committee*, 91st Cong., 1st sess., 1969.

53. Graham, *Collision Course*, 72.

54. Ibid., 67, 73–74; Golland, "Arthur Fletcher," 7–8; *Contractors' Association of Eastern Pennsylvania v. Secretary of Labor*, 442 F. 2d 159 (3d. Cir. 1971), cert. denied, 404 U.S. 854 (1971).

55. Golland, "Arthur Fletcher," 9–10.

56. U.S. Civil Service Commission, *The Federal Civil Rights Enforcement Efforts*, 1974, 385, cited in Frymer, *Black and Blue*, 38.

57. Charles R. Epp, *The Rights Revolution: Lawyers, Activists, and Supreme Courts in Comparative Perspective* (Chicago: University of Chicago Press, 1998).

58. Frymer, *Black and Blue*, 87–88.

59. *Griggs v. Duke Power Co.*, 401 U.S. 424 (1971).

60. Ibid., 425.

61. Ibid., 432.

62. Frymer, *Black and Blue*, 88; *Alexander v. Gardner-Denver Co.*, 415 U.S. 36 (1974).

63. Farhang, *Litigation State*, 145–46.

64. Peter H. Schuck, *Diversity in America: Keeping Government at a Safe Distance* (Cambridge, MA: Harvard University Press, 2003), 172–73.

65. Dobbin and Sutton, "Strength of a Weak State," 447, 456.

66. Frymer, *Black and Blue*, 7; *Grutter v. Bollinger*, 539 U.S. 306 (2003); *Gratz v. Bollinger*, 539 U.S. 244 (2003); "Brief for Amici Curiae 65 Leading American Busi-

nesses," FindLaw, http://conlaw.usatoday.findlaw.com/supreme_court/briefs/02-241/02-241
.mer.ami.sixtyfive.pdf.

67. James W. Ceaser, *Presidential Selection: Theory and Development* (Princeton,
NJ: Princeton University Press, 1979), 276–91; Skrentny, *Ironies of Affirmative Action*, 216.

68. American Presidency Project, 29605.

69. Ibid., 3537; Skrentny, *Ironies of Affirmative Action*, 217.

70. American Presidency Project, 25842.

71. Michael K. Brown, Martin Carnoy, Elliot Currie, Troy Duster, David B. Op-
penheimer, Marjorie M. Shultz, and David Wellman, *Whitewashing Race: The Myth
of a Color-Blind Society* (Berkeley: University of California Press, 2003), 161–66.

72. Graham, *Collision Course*, 65–66.

73. Schuck, *Diversity in America*, 138.

74. Steven M. Teles, *The Rise of the Conservative Legal Movement* (Princeton, NJ:
Princeton University Press, 2008), 86.

75. American Presidency Project, 25843.

76. Ibid., 29606.

77. Ibid., 25844.

78. Ibid., 29607.

79. Ibid.

80. See the pertinent platforms at the American Presidency Project, and for the Democrats in 1996, see American Presidency Project, 29611. The Democrats did drop their
explicit support for mandatory pupil transportation to achieve school integration.

81. We are indebted to Michael Graetz for this point.

82. Daniel A. Smith, "Howard Jarvis, Populist Entrepreneur: Reevaluating the
Causes of Proposition 13," *Social Science History* 23 (1999): 174, 196–97.

83. Graham, *Collision Course*, 4.

84. Ibid., 88–90.

85. Ibid., 72.

86. Ibid., 88–90; THOMAS, Library of Congress, http://thomas.loc.gov/cgi-bin/
bdquery/z?d095:HR00011:@@@R|TOM:/bss/d095query.html.

87. Ibid.

88. Graham, *Collision Course*, 91; Skrentny, *Minority Rights Revolution*, 162–63.

89. Mitchell F. Rice, "Government Set-Asides, Minority Business Enterprises, and
the Supreme Court," *Public Administration Review* 51 (1991): 117.

90. *Steelworkers v. Weber*, 443 U.S. 193 (1979), 197–98.

91. Ibid., 196.

92. Ibid., 196–97.

93. For the conservative legal foundations in general and their anti-affirmative action litigation in particular, see Teles, *Rise of the Conservative Legal Movement*, esp.
62–89, 258–62. For the Pacific Legal Foundation's endorsement of color-blindness, see
Pacific Legal Foundation, "PLF Cases: Preferences Based on Race or Gender," http://
www.pacificlegal.org/page.aspx?pid=258#race.

94. Equal Employment Advisory Council, "About," http://www.eeac.org/about/about.asp.

95. *Steelworkers*, 200.

96. *Fullilove v. Klutznick*, 448 U.S. 448 (1980).

97. See, e.g., David Bacon, "California Labor Prepares to Defend Affirmative Action," http://dbacon.igc.org/PJust/01LabDef.html.

98. *Fullilove*, 452.

99. *Fullilove*, 452–53.

100. Peggy Noonan, *When Character Was King: A Story of Ronald Reagan* (New York: Viking Adult, 2001).

101. For a similar summary of Reagan's appeal, see Edwin Meese III, "Rebuilding the Reagan Coalition," Heritage Foundation, January 31, 2007, http://www.heritage.org/Research/Lecture/Rebuilding-the-Reagan-Coalition.

102. Quoted in Skrentny, *Minority Rights Revolution*, 340. See also Farhang, *Litigation State*, 173.

103. American Presidency Project, 25844.

104. Ibid., 40708.

105. Farhang, *Litigation State*, 174–75.

106. Graham, *Collision Course*, 91, 156, 173. For an overview of the transition to diversity goals in work programs, see Frank Dobbin, *Inventing Equal Opportunity* (Princeton, NJ: Princeton University Press, 2009).

107. Graham, *Collision Course*, 174; Schuck, *Diversity in America*, 173; Brown et al., *Whitewashing Race*, 184; Skrentny, *Minority Rights Revolution*, 340.

108. Farhang, *Litigation State*, 176–78.

109. Ibid., 176–78, 180–82.

110. *General Building Contractors Association, Inc. v. Pennsylvania*, 458 U.S. 375, 382–84, 388–91, 407–18 (1982).

111. Ibid., 377.

112. *Guardians Association v. Civil Service Commission of the City of New York*, 463 U.S. 582, 584 (1983).

113. Ibid., 582–83.

114. American Presidency Project, 25845.

115. Ibid., 29608.

116. *Wards Cove Packing Co. v. Atonio*, 490 U.S. 642, 643 (1989).

117. Ibid., 645; Skrentny, *Ironies of Affirmative Action*, 226–27.

118. *Richmond v. J.A. Croson Co.*, 488 U.S. 469, 477 (1989).

119. Ibid., 475–76.

120. Farhang, *Litigation State*, 178–80.

121. Charlotte Steeh and Maria Krysan, "Trends: Affirmative Action and the Public, 1970–1995," *Public Opinion Quarterly* 60 (1990): 128–58, 146–47; Barbara F. Reskin, *The Realities of Affirmative Action in Employment* (Washington, DC: American Sociological Association, 1998), 83–84; Martin Gilens, Paul M. Sniderman, and James H.

Kuklinski, "Affirmative Action and the Politics of Realignment," *British Journal of Political Science* 28 (1998): 167, 169, 173.

122. Skrentny, *Minority Rights Revolution*, 90–164.

123. Leadership Conference, Americans for a Fair Chance, http://www.civilrights .org/equal-opportunity/about/; Albert M. Camarillo and Frank Bonilla, "Hispanic in a Multicultural Society: A New American Dilemma?" in *America Becoming: Racial Trends and Their Consequences*, vol. 1, ed. Neil J. Smelser, William Julius Wilson, and Faith Mitchell (Washington DC: National Academy Press, 2001).

124. Russell Thornton, "Trends Among American Indians in the United States," in Smelser, Wilson, and Mitchell, eds., *America Becoming* (Washington, DC: National Academy Press, 2001), 152–55.

125. On the Issues, "Colin Powell on Civil Rights Issues," last modified December 25, 2010, http://www.issues2000.org/Cabinet/Colin_Powell_Civil_Rights.htm; see also, e.g., Charles Moskos, "Affirmative Action: The Army's Success . . . ," *Washington Post*, March 15, 1995, http://www.washingtonpost.com/wp-srv/politics/special/affirm/stories/ aaop031595.htm; *Grutter v. Bollinger*, 539 U.S. 306 (2003); "Consolidated Brief of Lt. General Julius W. Becton et al.," FindLaw, http://conlaw.usatoday.findlaw.com/ supreme_court/briefs/02-241/02-241.mer.ami.military.pdf.

126. Frank Dobbin, John R. Sutton, John W. Meyer and W. Richard Scott, "Equal Opportunity Law and the Construction of Internal Labor Markets," *American Journal of Sociology* 99 (1993): 396–427, 401–8.

127. Burstein, *Discrimination, Jobs and Politics*, 106.

128. Dobbin, *Inventing Equal Opportunity*, 2.

129. Ibid.

130. For advocacy of ending federal antidiscrimination laws, see Richard A. Epstein, *Forbidden Grounds: The Case Against Employment Discrimination Law* (Cambridge, MA: Harvard University Press, 1992).

131. Tali Mendelberg, *The Race Card: Campaign Strategy, Implicit Messages, and the Norm of Equality* (Princeton, NJ: Princeton University Press, 2001).

132. Farhang, *Litigation State*, 183–85.

133. Ibid., 198.

134. Ibid., 188.

135. Skrentny, *Ironies of Affirmative Action*, 227.

136. U.S. House of Representatives, Office of the Clerk, "Final Vote Results for Roll Call 386," November 7, 1991, http://clerk.house.gov/evs/1991/roll386.xml; U.S. Senate, "Roll Call Votes 102d Congress—1st Session, On Passage of the Bill (S. 1745)," October 30, 1991, http://www.senate.gov/legislative/LIS/roll_call_lists/roll_call_vote_ cfm.cfm?congress=102&session=1&vote=00238.

137. Farhang, *Litigation State*, 200–201.

138. U.S. House of Representatives, "Republican Contract with America," http://www. house.gov/house/Contract/CONTRACT.html; "A New Tack on Affirmative Action," *Los Angeles Times*, August 8, 1995, http://aad.english.ucsb.edu/docs/gingrich.integ.html.

139. Tamar Lewin, "Colleges Regroup After Voters Ban Race Preferences," *New York Times,* January 26, 2007.

140. Peter Schmidt, "Election 2006: A Referendum on Race Preferences Divides Michigan," *Chronicle of Higher Education,* October 27, 2006, 21, http://chronicle.com/article/A-Referendum-on-Race/24828.

141. American Civil Rights Institute, http://www.acri.org/.

142. *Adarand Constructors v. Pena,* 515 U.S. 200, 203, 204 (1995).

143. Ibid., 225; see also *Metro Broadcasting, Inc. v. FCC,* 497 U.S. 547 (1990).

144. Williams, *Constraint of Race,* 298–309; J. Edward Kellough, *Understanding Affirmative Action* (Washington, DC: Georgetown University Press, 2006), 111–15.

145. *Adarand Constructors Inc. v. Federico Pena, Secretary of Transportation,* 515 U.S. 200 (1995), 237.

146. For elaboration, see Rogers M. Smith and Desmond S. King, "Barack Obama and the Future of American Racial Politics," *Du Bois Review* 6 (2009): 25–35.

147. Lewis-Beck, Tien, and Nadeau report polls indicating that 56 percent of respondents nationally "said yes, Obama would favor blacks," and of these, "only 32% said they would support Obama," in contrast to 80 percent among those who said Obama would not favor blacks. Michael S. Lewis-Beck, Charles Tien, and Richard Nadeau, "Obama's Missed Landslide: A Racial Cost?" *PS: Political Science & Politics* 43 (2010): 69–76.

148. Howard Kurtz, "McCain Spot Asks: 'Who is Barack Obama?'" http://voices.washingtonpost.com/44/2008/10/06/mccain_spot_asks_who_is_barack.html; Chuck Raasch; "McCain's 'American' Claim Sparks Critics," *USA Today,* April 3, 2008, http://www.usatoday.com/news/opinion/columnist/raasch/2008-04-03-raasch_N.htm/.

149. See Mendelberg, *Race Card.*

150. See, e.g., Peter Wallsten, "In Virginia, Tackling Race Before It Tackles Obama," *Los Angeles Times,* October 5, 2008, A-1; Chris Simkins, "US Voters Offer Opinions about Barack Obama, His Race, and Its Impact on the Upcoming Election," *VOA News.com,* October 14, 2008, http://www.voanews.com/english/news/a-13-2008-10-14-voa36-66791107.html.

151. Barack Obama. *The Audacity of Hope: Thoughts on Reclaiming the American Dream* (New York: Three Rivers Press, 2006), 232.

152. Ibid., 244.

153. Ibid., 247.

154. Ibid., 248, and see Barack Obama, "2004 Democratic National Convention Keynote Address," http://www.americanrhetoric.com/speeches/convention2004/barackobama2004dnc.htm.

155. Obama, *Audacity of Hope,* 248.

156. Lewis-Beck, Tien, and Nadeau, "Obama's Missed Landslide."

157. Dana Bash and Emily Sherman, "Sotomayor's 'Wise Latina' Comment a Staple of Her Speeches," CNN.com, June 8, 2009, http://www.cnn.com/2009/POLITICS/06/05/sotomayor.speeches/#cnnSTCTest, accessed September 30, 2009.

CHAPTER 5. TO "AFFIRMATIVELY FURTHER FAIR HOUSING":
ENDURING RACIAL INEQUALITIES IN AMERICAN HOMES AND MORTGAGES

1. In order to conform with the Civil Rights Act of 1964 and the Fair Housing Act provisions added to it in 1968, recipients of certain federal funds, including Community Development Block Grants, are required to certify to the Department of Housing and Urban Development that they will "affirmatively further fair housing," sometimes referred to as the AFFH requirement (*U.S.A. ex rel Anti-Discrimination Center of Metro New York Inc. v. Westchester County*, NY, 06 Civ. 2860 [DLC], 2009, at http://www.anti biaslaw.com/sites/default/files/files/SJDecision.pdf).

2. Ibid., 32–45.

3. Sam Roberts, "Westchester Adds Housing to Desegregation Pact," *New York Times*, August 11, 2009, http://www.nytimes.com/2009/08/11/nyregion/11settle.html; Joshua Bernstein, "Westchester Board Approves a Housing-Integration Pact," *New York Times*, September 23, 2009, http://www.nytimes.com/2009/09/23/nyregion/23 housing.html.

4. Dana Goldstein, "Shaking Up Suburbia," *American Prospect*, August 25, 2009, http://www.prospect.org/cs/articles?article=shaking_up_suburbia.

5. John Caulfield, "New York's Westchester Count Yields to Pressure to Desegregate Its Affordable Housing," *Builder 2009*, August 10, 2009, http://www.builderonline.com/affordable-housing/new-yorks-westchester-county-yields-to-pressure-to-desegregate-its-affordable-housing.aspx.

6. Howard Husock, "The Affordable-Housing Pact: A Flawed Remedy for Suburbs," Manhattan Institute for Policy Research, *Journal News*, August 30, 2009, http://www .manhattan-institute.org/html/miarticle.htm?id=5239.

7. Gerald McKinstry, "With Landmark Housing Settlement, Many Questions Remain— Like Where Are the Units Going," *Journal News–White Plains*, NY, August 12, 2009, AWP.8. In 2010, Russell again ran unsuccessfully for Congress as a Republican and Conservative Party nominee, although the New York Republican Party sought to have its designation for him removed from the ballot after learning that he had published an article in 2001 that party leaders deemed racist. Justin Elliott, "GOP Denounces Racist GOP Congressional Hopeful," Salon.com, September 21, 2010, http://www.salon.com/news/politics/war_room/2010/09/21/ny_gop_distances_from_jim_russell.

8. Sam Roberts, "Federal Monitor Rejects Westchester's Plan to Address Segregation with Fair Housing," *New York Times*, February 11, 2010, http://www.nytimes.com/2010/02/12/nyregion/12westchester.html.

9. See, e.g., Ben S. Bernanke, "The Subprime Mortgage Market," Board of Governors of the Federal Reserve System, May 17, 2007, http://www.federalreserve.gov/news events/speech/bernanke20070517a.htm; Ben S. Bernanke, "Mortgage Delinquencies and Foreclosures," Board of Governors of the Federal Reserve System, May 5, 2008, http://www.federalreserve.gov/newsevents/speech/Bernanke20080505a.htm.

10. Amaad Rivera, Brenda Cott-Escalera, Anisha Desai, Jeannette Huezo, and Dedrick Muhammad, "State of the Dream 2008: Foreclosed," United for a Fair Economy,

January 15, 2008, http://www.faireconomy.org/files/StateOfDream_01_16_08_Web.pdf., 15–16. See also Ajamu Dillahunt, Brian Miller, Mike Prokosch, Jeannette Huezo, and Dedrick Muhammad, "State of the Dream 2010: Drained: Jobless and Foreclosed in Communities of Color," United for a Fair Economy, January 13, 2010, http://www .faireconomy.org/files/SoD_2010_Drained_Report.pdf.

11. Rivera et al., "State of the Dream 2008: Foreclosed," 15.

12. See "NAACP Files Landmark Lawsuit Against Major Home Mortgage Companies for Discriminatory Lending," NAACP, http://www.naacp.org/press/entry/naacp-files-landmark-lawsuit-against-major--home-mortgage-companies-for-discriminatory-lending/; E. Scott Reckard, "NAACP Suits Claim African Americans Were Targeted for Subprime Mortgages," Los Angeles Times, March 14, 2009.

13. Michael Powell, "Blacks in Memphis Lose Decades of Economic Gains," New York Times, May 30, 2010, http://www.nytimes.com/2010/05/31/business/economy/31 memphis.html.

14. Earlier NAACP lawsuits were filed against Ameriquest Mortgage Company of Orange, Fremont Investment & Loan of Brea, and Option One Mortgage of Irvine.

15. Elizabeth Laderman and Carolina Reid, "Lending in Low- and Moderate-Income Neighborhoods in California: The Performance of CRA Lending During the Subprime Meltdown," Working Paper 2008-05, November 2008, Federal Reserve Bank of San Francisco, 13–14, http://www.frbsf.org/publications/community/ wpapers/2008/wp08-05.pdf; "The Mortgage Meltdown, Financial Markets, and the Economy," Federal Reserve Bank of San Francisco Economic Letter 35-36, November 7, 2008.

16. Rivera et al., "State of the Dream 2008: Foreclosed," 45.

17. Andrew Haughwout, Christopher Mayer, and Joseph Tracy, "Subprime Mortgage Pricing: The Impact of Race, Ethnicity, and Gender on the Cost of Borrowing" (Staff Report 368, Federal Reserve Bank of New York, April 2009), 21, http://www .newyorkfed.org/research/staff_reports/sr368.pdf.

18. Rep. Michele Bachmann (R-Minn.), Testimony to House Financial Services Committee, "Hearing on Treasury Action on GSEs," September 25, 2008; Emily Heil and Elizabeth Brotherton, "Heard on the Hill: Finger-Pointing," Roll Call, September 26, 2008, http://www.rollcall.com/issues/54_40/hoh/28769-1.html.

19. Michele Bachmann, Interview with Larry King, September 16, 2008, CNN.com, http://transcripts.cnn.com/TRANSCRIPTS/0809/16/lkl.01.html.

20. Doug Grow, "Ellison Angered and Shocked That Some Are Blaming the Poor and Blacks for Wall Street's Troubles," MinnPost.com, September 24, 2008, http:// www.minnpost.com/douggrow/2008/09/24/3634/ellison_angered_and_shockd_that_ some_are_blaming_the_poor_and_blacks_for_wall_streets_troubles#13-3634.

21. See "Cavuto Suggests Congress Should Have Warned That '[l]oaning to Minorities and Risky Folks Is a Disaster,'" Media Matters for America, September 19, 2008, http://mediamatters.org/items/200809190021; see also Cynthia Tucker, "Viewpoint: Minorities a Convenient Scapegoat," Palm Beach Post, October 1, 2008, 12A.

22. Charles Krauthammer, "Catharsis, Then Common Sense," *Washington Post*, September 26, 2008, A23, http://www.washingtonpost.com/wp-dyn/content/article/2008/09/25/AR2008092503600.html.

23. Ann Coulter, "They Gave Your Mortgage to a Less Qualified Minority," anncoulter.com, September 24, 2008, http://www.anncoulter.com/cgi-local/printer_friendly.cgi?article=275.

24. Ibid.

25. "Report to Congress on the Root Causes of the Foreclosure Crisis," Office of Policy Development and Research, U.S. Department of Housing and Urban Development, January, 2010, http://www2.huduser.org/portal/publications/hsgfin/foreclosure_09.html, 29–36, 41–42.

26. E.g., Helen Thompson, "The Political Origins of the Financial Crisis: The Domestic and International Politics of Fannie Mae and Freddie Mac," *Political Quarterly* 80 (January–March 2009): 17–24.

27. *U.S.A. ex rel Anti-Discrimination Center of Metro New York Inc. v. Westchester County*, 25.

28. Douglas S. Massey, "Segregation and Stratification: A Biosocial Perspective," *Du Bois Review* 1 (2004): 9, 10–11.

29. Margery Austin Turner and Lynette Rawlings, "Promoting Neighborhood Diversity: Benefits, Barriers, and Strategies," Urban Institute, August 2009, 5, http://www.urban.org/UploadedPDF/411955promotingneighborhooddiversity.pdf.

30. "Homeownership Rates by Race and Ethnicity of Householder," Infoplease, http://www.infoplease.com/ipa/A0883976.html.

31. Powell, "Blacks in Memphis."

32. *Buchanan v. Warley*, 245 U.S. 60 (1917); *Corrigan v. Buckley*, 217 U.S. 323 (1926).

33. For a superb study that captures these elements, see Thomas J. Sugrue, *The Origins of the Urban Crisis: Race and Inequality in Postwar Detroit* (Princeton, NJ: Princeton University Press, 1996); for the evolution of federal urban policy from the 1930s, see John H. Mollenkopf, *The Contested City* (Princeton, NJ: Princeton University Press, 1983).

34. Desmond S. King, *Separate and Unequal: African Americans and the US Federal Government* (New York: Oxford University Press, 2007), 189; John T. Woolley and Gerhard Peters, American Presidency Project, http://www.presidency.ucsb.edu/ws/?pid=29638.

35. Sugrue, *Sweet Land of Liberty*, 204.

36. Massey and Denton, *American Apartheid*, 51–52.

37. For details, see ibid., 51–55; King, *Separate and Unequal*, 192–93.

38. Gregory D. Squires, "Community Reinvestment: An Emerging Social Movement," in Gregory D. Squires, ed., *From Redlining to Reinvestment: Community Responses to Urban Disinvestment* (Philadelphia: Temple University Press, 1992), 5; Massey and Denton, *American Apartheid*, 54.

39. Massey and Denton, ibid.; American Presidency Project, 29597; *Shelley v. Kraemer*, 334 U.S. 1 (1948). *Shelley* was decided under the equal protection clause, which

applies only to the states. But the Court went on to hold that the Civil Rights Act of 1866, which guaranteed all citizens the same rights as white citizens to engage in real estate transactions, also made racially restrictive covenants in the District of Columbia unenforceable in federal courts (*Hurd v. Hodges*, 334 U.S. 24 [1948]).

40. Sugrue, *Origins of the Urban Crisis*, 44–45.

41. American Presidency Project, 25839, 29602.

42. Reference in King, *Separate and Unequal*, 190, 318.

43. American Presidency Project, 25836, 25837, 25838; 29599, 29600, 29601. And see Mollenkopf, *Contested City*, chap. 3, and Jewel Bellush and Murray Hausknecht, eds., *Urban Renewal: People, Politics and Planning* (Garden City, NY: Anchor Books, 1967).

44. Brown et al., *Whitewashing Race*, 92–94.

45. Sugrue, *Origins of the Urban Crisis*, 62–63.

46. John R. Logan and Harvey L. Molotch, *Urban Fortunes: The Political Economy of Place*, 2nd ed. (Berkeley: University of California Press, 2007); and Harvey Molotch, "The City as a Growth Machine: Toward a Political Economy of Place," *American Journal of Sociology* 82 (September 1976): 309–32.

47. Charles M. Lamb, *Housing Segregation in Suburban America since 1960: Presidential and Judicial Politics* (New York: Cambridge University Press, 2005).

48. U.S. Department of Housing and Urban Development (HUD), "History of Fair Housing," http://www.hud.gov/offices/fheo/aboutfheo/history.cfm; Nieman, *Promises to Keep*, 181–82, 185–86.

49. HUD, "History of Fair Housing"; Massey and Denton, *American Apartheid*, 3–4, 59.

50. HUD's regulations to implement anti-discrimination in housing stated that "it shall be unlawful, because of race, color, religion, sex, handicap, familial status, or national origin, to restrict or attempt to restrict the choices of a person by word or conduct in connection with seeking, negotiating for, buying or renting a dwelling so as to perpetuate, or tend to perpetuate, segregated housing patterns, or to discourage or obstruct choices in a community, neighborhood or development" (24 CFR Part 14, Section 100.70(a)).

51. Massey and Denton, *American Apartheid*, 192–98; Nieman, *Promises to Keep*, 186.

52. American Presidency Project, 29604. The Republican platform that year did not address race and housing (American Presidency Project, 25841).

53. *Jones v. Alfred H. Mayer Co.*, 392 U.S. 409, 412 (1968).

54. Ibid., 411, 440.

55. Ibid., 415–17; J. Harlan, dissenting, 478.

56. See, e.g., *Trafficante v. Metropolitan Life Insurance Park Merced Apartments*, 409 U.S. 205 (1972) (holding that white tenants had standing to sue because their landlords' discrimination against nonwhites deprived them of a multiracial living environment); *U.S. v. City of Black Jack*, 508 F. 2d 1179 (1974) (holding that a zoning ordinance banning new multiple-family dwellings had a racially discriminatory effect that violated the Fair Housing Act); *Zuch v. Hussey*, 394 F. Supp. 1028 (1975) (granting injunction against realtors engaged in "blockbusting," seeking to accelerate neighbor-

hood transitions to racial homogeneity); *Hills v. Gautreaux,* 425 U.S. 284 (1976) (where, reinforced by briefs from the National Committee Against Discrimination in Housing, the Lawyers' Committee for Civil Rights Under Law, and the National Education Association, the Court rejected Republican solicitor general Robert Bork's argument that a remedy for discrimination in public housing by the Chicago Housing Authority could not extend to the entire metropolitan area); *Laufman v. Oakley Building and Loan,* 72 F.R.D. 116 (1976) (granting discovery request to gain evidence of "redlining" in home loans); *Dunn v. Midwestern Indemnity,* 88 F.R.D. 191 (1980) (granting discovery request for evidence of racial discrimination in homeowners' insurance).

57. Massey and Denton, *American Apartheid,* 46.

58. Kevin L. Yuill, *Richard Nixon and the Rise of Affirmative Action* (Lanham, MD: Rowman and Littlefield, 2006), 172.

59. Lamb, *Housing Segregation,* chap. 3; Chris Bonastia, "Hedging His Bets: Why Nixon Killed HUD's Desegregation Efforts," *Social Science History* 28 (2004): 26–33.

60. Yuill, *Richard Nixon.*

61. "199—Statement About Federal Policies Relative to Equal Housing Opportunity, June 11, 1971," American Presidency Project, http://www.presidency.ucsb.edu/ws/index.php?pid=3042&st=&st1=.

62. *Public Papers of the Presidents: Richard Nixon* (Washington, DC: U.S. Government Printing Office, 1972), 730, cited in Lamb, *Housing Segregation,* 9; see also Sugrue, *Sweet Land of Liberty,* 444–45.

63. "199—Statement About Federal Policies Relative to Equal Housing Opportunity, June 11, 1971," American Presidency Project, http://www.presidency.ucsb.edu/ws/index.php?pid=3042&st=&st1=. The Third Circuit Court of Appeals had ruled the previous year that such consideration was a statutory requirement (*Shannon v. HUD,* 436 F. 2d 809 [3d Cir. 1970]).

64. Bonastia, "Hedging His Bets," 32–33.

65. American Presidency Project, 25842.

66. Ibid., 29605.

67. Bonastia, "Hedging His Bets," 38–39. Bonastia adds the plausible claims that federal bureaucrats concerned with fulfilling their statutory mandates to spur more housing production sometimes resisted civil rights goals, and that even more important, HUD's Office of Equal Opportunity lacked the institutional stature and powers to push effectively for desegregation goals (39–41). On the failure of Section 8 and the more recent HOPE VI voucher program to serve desegregation purposes, see, e.g., Florence Wagman Roisman, "Keeping the Promise: Ending Racial Discrimination and Segregation in Federally Financed Housing," *Howard Law Journal* 48 (2005): 917–26. But for discussion of an instance when Section 8 housing vouchers accompanied by a mobility counseling program produced more integrated suburban housing, with mixed but many positive results, see Peter H. Shuck, *Diversity in America* (Cambridge, MA: Harvard University Press, 2003), 228–29, 258–59.

68. *Village of Arlington Heights v. Metropolitan Housing Development Corporation,* 429 U.S. 252 (1977).

69. Ibid., 257, 265.

70. "Arlington Heights v. Metropolitan Housing Corp.—Impact," Law Library—American Law and Legal Information, http://law.jrank.org/pages/24366/Arlington-Heights-v-Metropolitan-Housing-Corp-Impact.html.

71. The Court did strike down a town's effort to curb "white flight" from integrating neighborhoods by banning For Sale signs on lawns while expressing support for the goal of racial integration. See *Linmark Associates v. Township of Willingboro*, 431 U.S. 85, 94, 97 (1977). The case divided the ACLU, which urged invalidation of the ban, from the NAACP LDF, which supported it; Justice Thurgood Marshall wrote for a unanimous Court in favor of the ACLU position. See also *Gladstone, Realtors v. Village of Bellwood*, 441 U.S. 91, 111, 115 (1979) (upholding standing of "testers" to challenge realtor racial discrimination even if they did not intend actually to purchase housing); *Havens Realty Corp. v. Coleman*, 455 U.S. 363 (1982) (upholding the standing to sue of a black "tester" exploring racial steering in apartment rentals).

72. American Presidency Project, 25843, 25844, 25845, 25846.

73. Ibid., 29606, 29607.

74. Ibid., 29608, 29609.

75. National Fair Housing Alliance, *Housing Discrimination in Detroit, Michigan* (Washington, DC: NFHA, January 25, 2007).

76. National Fair Housing Alliance, *Unequal Opportunity—Perpetuating Housing Segregation in America* (Washington, DC, NFHA, April 5, 2006), 17, http://www.mvfairhousing.com/pdfs/2006%20Fair%20Housing%20Trends%20Report.PDF.

77. The National Fair Housing Alliance (*Unequal Opportunity*, 16) writes: "By steering Whites away from schools and entire school districts, the real estate industry limits demand for homes in those communities. This artificial manipulation of the real estate market depresses home values in those communities. School performance is inextricably tied to the funding it receives. The funding for schools is based on property taxes, which are in turn based on property values. Steering White families away from 'bad' schools becomes a tragically self-fulfilling prophecy for those schools. Deprived of valuable capital in the form of home values, those schools suffer in the funding matrix critical to school performance."

78. See, e.g., George Galster, "Racial Steering in Urban Housing Markets: A Review of the Audit Evidence," *Review of Black Political Economy* 18 (1990): 105–30; Margery Austin Turner, Stephen L. Ross, George C. Galster, and John Yinger, with Erin B. Godfrey, Beata A. Bednarz, Carla Herbig, Seon Joo Lee, Rezaul Hossain, and Bo Zhao, "Discrimination in Metropolitan Housing Markets: National Results from Phase I HDS 2000: Final Report," Washington, DC: Urban Institute, November 2, 2002, http://www.huduser.org/portal/publications/pdf/Phase1_Report.pdf.

79. Kim Kendrick, Assistant Secretary for the Office of Fair Housing and Equal Opportunity, written statement before the Subcommittee on the Constitution, Civil Rights, and Civil Liberties, Committee on the Judiciary, U.S. House of Representatives, June 12, 2008, 1; http://archives.hud.gov/testimony/2008/test080612.cfm.

80. Remarks by Kim Kendrick, Assistant Secretary HUD, The Housing Advocates Inc. Fair Housing and Lending Conference, October 20, 2006, 7–8.

81. Ibid., 4.

82. For a review of such criticisms with extensive citations to supporting studies, see Michael S. Barr, "Credit Where It Counts: The Community Reinvestment Act and Its Critics," *New York University Law Review* 80 (2005): 527–33.

83. Ibid., 516–17; G. William Domhoff, "The Ford Foundation in the Inner City: Forging an Alliance with Neighborhood Activists," September 2005, 10, Who Rules America.net, http://sociology.ucsc.edu/whorulesamerica/local/ford_foundation.html.

84. Hugh Davis Graham, "The Surprising Career of Federal Fair Housing Law," *Journal of Policy History* 12 (2000): 215–32; House Judiciary Committee's Subcommittee on Civil Rights, chaired by Californian representative Don Edwards. Edwards's committee continued its investigations throughout the 1970s into the efficacy of Title VIII.

85. Nadine Cohodas, "Battle Lines Drawn Over New Enforcement Powers by HUD," *Congressional Quarterly Weekly Report* 38, May 3, 1980, 1175–77.

86. Alabama: 4 Democrats voted against the enforcement powers amendment, Florida: 6, Georgia: 5, Kentucky: 3, Louisiana: 4, Mississippi: 3, North Carolina: 8, Texas: 11. Nadine Cohodas, "Fair Housing Bill Passed by House," *Congressional Quarterly Weekly Report* 38, June 14, 1980, 1613, and "CQ House Votes 274–281," *Congressional Quarterly Weekly Report* 38, June 14, 1980, 1680–81.

87. Now joined by Lloyd Bentsen, Texas; David Boren, Oklahoma; Howell Heflin, Alabama; Walter Huddleston, Kentucky; J. Bennett Johnson, Louisiana; Russell B. Long, Louisiana; Robert Morgan, South Carolina; and Sam Nunn, Georgia. Nadine Cohodas, "Failure to Vote Cloture Kills Fair Housing Bill," *Congressional Quarterly Weekly Report* 38, December 13, 1980, 3544.

88. Massey and Denton, *American Apartheid*, 207.

89. Ibid., 208.

90. Gordon H. Sellon Jr. and Deana VanNahmen, "The Securitization of Housing Finance," Federal Reserve Bank of Kansas City *Economic Review* 14 (1988): 17–20, http://kansascityfed.org/PUBLICAT/ECONREV/EconRevArchive/1988/2q88sell.pdf.

91. Domhoff, "Ford Foundation in the Inner City," 11.

92. Massey and Denton, *American Apartheid*, 209–11.

93. Graham, "Surprising Career of Federal Fair Housing Law."

94. Macon Morehouse, "Fair-Housing Bill Approved by House Judiciary Committee," *Congressional Quarterly Weekly Report* 46, April 30, 1988, 1159.

95. Nadine Cohodas, "Prognosis Good as Housing Bill Goes to Senate," *Congressional Quarterly Weekly Report* 46, July 2, 1988, 1838; Cohodas, "Backed by Reagan, Senate OKs Fair Housing Law," *Congressional Quarterly Weekly Report* 46, August 6, 1988, 2204.

96. George C. Galster, "The Evolving Challenges of Fair Housing Since 1968: Open Housing, Integration, and the Reduction of Ghettoization," *Cityscape: A Journal of Policy Development and Research* 4 (1999): 124–26; American Presidency Project, 25847.

97. American Presidency Project, 29610; Galster, "Evolving Challenges"; Roisman, "Keeping the Promise," 924.

98. Galster, "Evolving Challenges"; Roisman, "Keeping the Promise"; Anthony D. Taibi, "Racial Justice in the Age of the Global Economy: Community Empowerment and Global Strategy," *Duke Law Journal* 44 (1995): 948–53.

99. Taibi, "Racial Justice," 953; National Association of Home Builders, "A Century of Progress," 8.

100. Barr, "Credit Where It Counts," 524–26; U.S. Civil Rights Commission, "Redefining Rights in America: The Civil Rights Record of the George W. Bush Administration, 2001–2004," Draft Report for Commissioners' Review, September 2004, 62, University of Maryland School of Law, http://www.law.umaryland.edu/marshall/usccr/documents/cr12r24.pdf.

101. American Presidency Project, 25848.

102. Ibid., 25849.

103. Ibid., 29612.

104. U.S. Civil Rights Commission, "Redefining Rights in America," 64.

105. American Presidency Project, 25850.

106. Ibid., 29613.

107. National Fair Housing Alliance, "Dr. King's Dream Denied: Forty Years of Failed Federal Enforcement," 2008 Fair Housing Trends Report, April 8, 2008, 58, http://nfha.objectwareinc.com/Portals/33/reports/2008%20Fair%20Housing%20Trends%20Report.pdf.

108. Ibid., 57; U.S. Civil Rights Commission, "Redefining Rights in America," 64–72; Eunice Moscoso, "Civil Rights Enforcement Falls in Bush Term, Study Says," Cox News Service, November 22, 2004, http://www.seattlepi.com/national/200584_civil22.html.

109. United States Government Accountability Office, "Report to Congressional Requestors: U.S. Department of Justice, Information on Employment Litigation, Housing and Civil Enforcement, Voting and Special Litigation Sections' Enforcement Efforts from Fiscal years 2001 through 2007," GAO-10-75, October 2009, http://www.gao.gov/highlights/d1075high.pdf; Charlie Savage, "Report Examines Civil Rights During Bush Years," *New York Times*, December 2, 2009, http://www.nytimes.com/2009/12/03/us/politics/03rights.html.

110. Kendrick, congressional testimony, before the Subcommittee on the Constitution, Civil Rights and Civil Liberties of the Committee on the Judiciary, U.S. House of Representatives, June 12, 2008, 2.

111. American Presidency Project, 78283.

112. "Barack Obama and Joe Biden: Creating Equal Opportunity and Justice for All," Barackobama.com, http://www.barackobama.com/pdf/issues/Fact_Sheet_Civil_Rights_and_Criminal_Justice_FINAL.pdf.

113. American Presidency Project, 78545.

114. Jake Tapper, "McCain: Obama Called Subprime Loans a 'Good Idea,'" *Political Punch* (blog), ABC News, October 6, 2008, http://blogs.abcnews.com/politicalpunch/

2008/10/mccain-obama-ca.html; see Stanley Kurtz, "Planting Seeds of Disaster: ACORN, Barack Obama, and the Democratic Party," *National Review Online*, October 7, 2008, http://article.nationalreview.com/374045/planting-seeds-of-disaster/stanley-kurtz.

115. Tim Padgett, "Are Minorities Being Fleeced by the Stimulus?" *Time*, November 23, 2009, http://www.time.com/time/nation/article/0,8599,1940338,00.html.

116. Julie Hirschfield Davis and David Espo, "Congress OKs Historic Bailout Bill," *Associated Press*, October 4, 2008, http://www.breitbart.com/article.php?id=D93J5NJO0 &show_article=1.

117. Charlie Savage, "Justice Dept. Fights Bias in Lending," *New York Times*, January 14, 2010, http://www.nytimes.com/2010/01/14/us/14justice.html.

118. Kenneth R. Harney, "Obama Administration Adopts Get-Tough Stance on Mortgage Bias," *Los Angeles Times*, April 11, 2010, http://articles.latimes.com/2010/apr/11/business/la-fi-harney11-2010apr11/2.

119. Testimony by Shanna L. Smith, President and CEO of NFHA, before the House Financial Services Committee, Subcommittee on Housing and Community Opportunity, February 28, 2006, 1, http://democrats.financialservices.house.gov/media/pdf/022806ss.pdf. See Monique W. Morris, "Discrimination and Mortgage Lending in America: A Summary of the Disparate Impact of Subprime Mortgage Lending on African Americans," NAACP, March 2009, http://naacp.3cdn.net/4ca760b774f81317c4_klm6i6yxg.pdf, for the NAACP's evidence of racial and ethnic disparities in real estate and lending practices. The NAACP and the National Council of La Raza urged (unsuccessfully) a national six-month moratorium on foreclosures as a measure to recognize that the crisis is falling disproportionately upon African Americans and Latinos, and to provide services to the thousands of households on the brink of financial disaster in their housing debts.

Minority advocacy groups were not alone in these claims. A HUD report based on the American Housing Survey from 1998, 2002, and 2004 investigated why interest rates appear to differ according to race, with Latinos and blacks consistently paying higher interest rates than their white counterparts. For first-time borrowers, even when controlling for differences in household, loan, and property characteristics, "blacks and Hispanics (particularly nonwhite Hispanics) have significantly higher interest rates than comparable white households. For African-Americans this differential is 21 to 42 basis points, while for nonwhite Hispanics the range is 13 to 15 basis points" (Thomas P. Boehm, Alan M. Schlottmann, and ABT Associates, Inc., "Mortgage Pricing Differentials Across Hispanic, Black, and White Households: Evidence from the American Housing Survey," prepared for the U.S. Department of Housing and Urban Development, Office of Policy Development and Research, February 2006, http://www.huduser.org/Publications/PDF/hisp_homeown5.pdf). A case study of Washington Mutual's lending practices found that it used its subsidiary company the Long Beach Mortgage Company (LBMC) to sell subprime mortgages. In 2006 Mutual was the third largest lender of new mortgages, but a mere 1 percent of its loans were subprime; in contrast, 90 percent of Long Beach's mortgages were subprime. Thus, the parent company camouflaged its subprime exposure—the kind of practice that the Obama administration sought to combat in its AIG settlement. We note, however, that although the study does provide evidence to show that African Americans and Latinos do receive a disproportionate share of high-cost loans, it does not attempt to take into account financial factors that might explain a significant extent of the disparity, such as the occupational and income spread of borrowers. Jim Campen, Saara Nafici, Adam Rust, Geoff Smith, Kevin Stein, and Barbara van Kerkhove, "Paying More for the American Dream: A Multi-State Analysis of Higher Cost Home Purchase Lending," March 2007, 3, 5, Neighborhood Economic Development Advocacy Project, http://www.nedap.org/resources/documents/2007_Report-2005_HMDA.pdf.

Chapter 6. "To Elect One of Their Own": Racial Alliances and Majority-Minority Districts

1. David Mendell and Gary Washburn, "Race Shifts Seen in Remap Efforts: Leaders Struggle to Retain Wards," *Chicago Tribune*, October 14, 2001, http://articles.chicago tribune.com/2001-10-14/news/0110140403_1_ward-map-political-power-black.

2. Ibid.; Thomas J. Sugrue, *Not Even Past: Barack Obama and the Burden of Race* (Princeton, NJ: Princeton University Press, 2010), 40.

3. "Barack Obama and Joe Biden: Creating Equal Opportunity and Justice for All," Barackobama.com, http://www.barackobama.com/pdf/issues/Fact_Sheet_Civil_Rights_ and_Criminal_Justice_FINAL.pdf.

4. See, e.g., Abigail M. Thernstrom, *Whose Votes Count? Affirmative Action and Minority Voting Rights* (Cambridge, MA: Harvard University Press, 1987), 227–31; Michael Omi and Howard Winant, *Racial Formation in the United States: from the 1960s to the 1990s*, 2nd ed. (New York: Routledge, 1994), 74.

5. Richard L. Berke, "G.O.P. Tries a Gambit with Voting Rights," *New York Times*, April 14, 1991, D1; Carol M. Swain, *Black Faces, Black Interests: The Representation of African Americans in Congress* (Cambridge, MA: Harvard University Press, 1995), 205.

6. Richard M. Valelly, *The Two Reconstructions: The Struggle for Black Enfranchisement* (Chicago: University of Chicago Press, 2004), 4.

7. Mildred Amer, "Membership of the 109th Congress A Profile," Congressional Research Service, November 29, 2006, http://www.senate.gov/reference/resources/pdf/RS22007.pdf; Library of Congress, "Hispanic Americans in Congress, 1822 to 1995," 2005, http://www.loc.gov/rr/hispanic/congress/chron.html; YourCongress.com, "Asian Americans in Congress," http://www.yourcongress.com/viewarticle.asp?article_ID=1662.

8. David A. Bositis, *Black Elected Officials* (Washington, DC: Joint Center for Political and Economic Studies, 2002), 5–6; Library of Congress, "Hispanic Americans in Congress, 1822 to 1995"; Kim Geron, *Latino Political Power* (Boulder, CO: Lynne Rienner, 2004), 7; National Black Caucus of State Legislators, "Membership," http://www.nbcsl.org/membership.html (accessed June 9, 2010).

9. American Presidency Project, http://www.presidency.ucsb.edu/ws/?pid=25839, 25840, 29602, 29603.

10. Alexander Keyssar, *The Right to Vote: The Contested History of Democracy in the United States* (New York: Basic Books, 2000), 263.

11. Valelly, *Two Reconstructions*, 186–93.

12. Ibid., 193–96; Keyssar, *Right to Vote*.

13. Valelly, *Two Reconstructions*, 197; Keyssar, *Right to Vote*, 264; David Michael Hudson, *Along Racial Lines: Consequences of the 1965 Voting Rights Act* (New York: Peter Lang, 1998), 82; *Congress and the Nation: A Review of Government and Politics*, vol. 2, *1965–1968* (Washington, DC: Congressional Quarterly Service, 1969), 356–64.

14. *South Carolina v. Katzenbach*, 383 U.S. 301, 306–7 (1966).

15. *Katzenbach v. Morgan*, 384 U.S. 641 (1966).

16. Valelly, *Two Reconstructions*, 4.

17. Ibid., 200.

18. American Presidency Project, 25841, 29604.

19. *Allen v. State Board of Elections*, 393 U.S. 544, 550–54 (1969).

20. Ibid., 565–66; Valelly, *Two Reconstructions*, 214.

21. Valelly, *Two Reconstructions*, 203; Thernstrom, *Whose Votes Count?* 31–37, 47; Hudson, *Racial Lines*, 82.

22. American Presidency Project, 25842.

23. Ibid., 29605.

24. *White v. Regester*, 412 U.S. 755 (1973).

25. Ibid., 769.

26. Thernstrom, *Whose Votes Count?* 70–73.

27. Hudson, *Racial Lines*, 110; Keyssar, *Right to Vote*, 265.

28. Thernstrom, *Whose Votes Count?* 50–53.

29. Valelly, *Two Reconstructions*, 204.

30. Hudson, *Racial Lines*, 109–16.

31. American Presidency Project, 25843, 29606.

32. *Mobile v. Bolden*, 446 U.S. 55 (1980).

33. Ibid., 69–70, 75–76.

34. American Presidency Project, 25844, 29607.

35. Thernstrom, *Whose Votes Count?* 110–12.

36. Hudson, *Racial Lines*, 137.

37. Richard Reeves, *President Reagan: The Triumph of Imagination* (New York: Simon and Schuster, 2005), 119.

38. See, e.g., Ronald W. Reagan, "Remarks at a White House Ceremony Celebrating Hispanic Heritage Week," September 15, 1982, American Presidency Project, http://www.presidency.ucsb.edu/ws/print.php?pid=42983.

39. Hudson, *Racial Lines*, 137–45.

40. Thernstrom, *Whose Votes Count?* 117, 126, 133; Library of Congress, THOMAS, http://thomas.loc.gov/cgi-bin/bdquery/z?d097:HR03112:@@@R.

41. American Presidency Project, 25845, 29608.

42. Ibid., 24846, 25847, 29609, 29610.

43. *Rogers v. Lodge*, 458 U.S. 613, 615 (1982).

44. *Thornburg v. Gingles*, 478 U.S. 30, 50–51 (1986).

45. *Thornburg v. Gingles*, 34; Valelly, *Two Reconstructions*, 242.

46. David Lublin, *The Paradox of Representation: Racial Gerrymandering and Minority Interests in Congress* (Princeton, NJ: Princeton University Press, 1997), has slightly different numbers (at 7). By our count, Florida created three black majority-minority districts and one Latino one; North Carolina and Georgia each created two black majority-minority districts; Alabama, Louisiana, Maryland, Pennsylvania, South Carolina, Virginia, and Texas each created one black majority-minority district, and Texas created one Latino one (Kevin A. Hill, "Does the Creation of Majority Black Districts Aid Republicans?" *Journal of Politics* 57 [1995]: 386). California created four Latino districts, and New York, New Jersey, and Illinois each created one (Bob Benenson, "Arduous Ritual of Redistricting Ensures More Racial Diversity," *Congressional Quarterly Weekly*, October 24, 1992, 3355, 3361). We have not counted existing districts that had their percentages of nonwhites heightened, as occurred with Mississippi's majority black Second District, or districts producing nonvoting delegates (see Lublin, *Paradox*, 33; Swain, *Black Faces, Black Interests*, 283n1).

47. Lublin, *Paradox*, 21–36. The count is seventeen black Congress members, thirteen from the South, if one counts Eva Clayton, elected in a special election in 1992 from North Carolina's First District.

48. Ibid.; Library of Congress, "Hispanic Americans in Congress."

49. Morgan J. Kousser, *Colorblind Injustice* (Chapel Hill: University of North Carolina Press, 1999), 13; Bositis, *Black Elected Officials*, 17.

50. Swain, *Black Faces, Black Interests*; Lublin, *Paradox*.

51. David T. Canon, *Race, Redistricting and Representation: The Unintended Consequences of Black Majority Districts* (Chicago: University of Chicago Press, 1999), 76–77.

52. Mark A. Posner, "Post-1990 Redistrictings and the Preclearance Requirement of Section 5 of the Voting Rights Act," in *Race and Redistricting in the 1990s*, ed. Bernard Grofman (New York: Agathon Press, 1998), 90.

53. E.g., Canon, *Race, Redistricting and Representation*, 75–76, 110.

54. Bernard Grofman and Lisa Handley, "Voting Rights in the 1990s," in Grofman, ed., *Race and Redistricting*, 72n7; Posner, "Post-1990 Redistrictings," 88–98.

55. Canon, *Race, Redistricting and Representation*, 73–77.

56. Tim Storey and Gene Rose, "GOP #1: First Time in Fifty Years," National Conference of State Legislatures, http://web.archive.org/web/20040325042221/http://www.ncsl.org/programs/pubs/1202GOP.htm.

57. Lublin, *Paradox*, 113.

58. Moss, "Redrawn Districts Help GOP."

59. Lublin, *Paradox*, 112.

60. Burton, "Legislative and Congressional Districting," 290, 309–12.

61. Matthew M., Schousen, David T. Canon, and Patrick J. Sellers, "Congressional Redistricting in North Carolina," in Grofman, ed., *Race and Redistricting*, 273–89.

62. Winnett W. Hagens, "The Politics of Race: The Virginia Redistricting Experience," in Grofman, ed., *Race and Redistricting*, 322–36.

63. *Miller v. Johnson*, 515 U.S. 900 (1995), discussed further later on.

64. Swain, *Black Faces, Black Interests*, 232; Lublin, *Paradox*, 125–29; Robert A. Holmes, "Reapportionment Strategies in the 1990s," in Grofman, ed., *Race and Redistricting*, 201–9, 216–28.

65. Richard L. Engstrom and Jason E. Kirksey, "Race and Representational Districting in Louisiana," in Grofman, ed, *Race and Redistricting*, 240–42; Lublin, *Paradox*, 104–6, 111–12.

66. Engstrom and Kirksey, "Race and Representational Districting," 234–64.

67. Swain, *Black Faces, Black Interests*, 198; Lublin, *Paradox*, 32.

68. Lublin, *Paradox*, 112.

69. Morgan Kousser, "Reapportionment Wars: Party, Race, and Redistricting in the California, 1971–1992," in Grofman, *Race and Redistricting*, 166–74, 187.

70. *Legislative Redistricting Commission v. LaPaille*, 786 F. Supp. 704 (N.D. Ill. 1992); *Hastert v. Board of Elections*, 777 F. Supp. 634 (N.D. Ill. 1991).

71. Lublin, *Paradox*, 114; Donald Stokes, "Is There a Better Way to Redistrict?" in Grofman, *Race and Redistricting*, 359–66.

72. Alan Gartner, "New York City Redistricting: A View from Inside," in Grofman, *Race and Redistricting*, 371.

73. *Shaw v. Reno*, 509 U.S. 630 (1993).

74. Ibid., 631, 637.

75. Ibid., 656.

76. *Holder v. Hall*, 512 U.S. 874 (1994); *Miller v. Johnson*, 515 U.S. 900 (1995); *Bush v. Vera*, 517 U.S. 952 (1996); *Reno v. Bossier Parish School Board*, 528 U.S. 320 (2000); *Georgia v. Ashcroft*, 539 U.S. 461 (2003); *Bartlett v. Strickland*, 129 S. Ct. 1231 (2009).

77. *Holder v. Hall*, 892.

78. *Miller v. Johnson*, 907–9, 912, 920.

79. *Bush v. Vera*, 964–65.

80. *Georgia v. Ashcroft*.

81. *Barttlett v. Strickland*.

82. Frank Askin, "Statement of ACLU General Counsel," 1998, American Civil Liberties Union, http://www.aclu.org/scotus/1998/22660prs19981001.html; Common Cause, "FAQ: The Effect of Georgia v. Ashcroft on the Voting Rights Act and Why Congress Must Change It," 2003, http://www.commoncause.org/atf/cf/%7BFB3C17E2-CDD1-4DF6-92BE-BD4429893665%7D/FAQ-GEORGIAVSASHCROFT.PDF.

83. See, e.g., Institute for Justice, "State of the Supreme Court 2000: The Justices' Record on Individual Liberties," Washington, DC, http://www.ij.org/images/pdf_folder/other_pubs/supreme_court_report_2000.pdf; Edward Blum and Roger Clegg, "*Amici Curiae* Brief," *League of United Latin American Citizens v. Perry*, 548 U.S. 399 (2006), at http://www.jenner.com/files/tbl_s69NewsDocumentOrder/FileUpload500/625/Brief_Blum_Clegg.pdf.

84. National Committee for an Effective Congress, "What's the Latest on Redistricting?" 2004, http://www.ncec.org/redistricting/latest.html.

85. American Presidency Project, 25848, 25849, 29611, 29612.

86. United States Federal Election Commission, http://www.eac.gov/.

87. American Presidency Project, 25850.

88. Ibid., 29613.

89. Bob Kemper and Tom Baxter, "Voting Rights Act: Renewal of Good Faith," *Atlanta Journal-Constitution*, August 5, 2005, A1; Civilrights.org, "Our Coalition," 2006, http://www.civilrights.org/about/lccr/coalition_members.

90. Charles S. Bullock and Ronald Keith Gaddie, "Good Intentions and Bad Social Science Meet in the Renewal of the Voting Rights Act," *Georgetown Journal of Law and Public Policy* 5 (2007): 1–27.

91. Carl Hulse, "Rebellion Stalls Extension of Voting Act," *New York Times*, June 22, 2006, A-23.

92. Raymond Hernandez, "After Challenges, House Approves Renewal of Voting Act," *New York Times*, July 14, 2006, A13; "Final Vote Results for Roll Call 374," July 13, 2006, http://clerk.house.gov/evs/2006/roll374.xml.

93. *League of United Latin American Citizens v. Perry*, 548 U.S. 399 (2006).

94. American Presidency Project, 78283.

95. Ibid., 78545.

CHAPTER 7. "OUR GOAL IS TO HAVE ONE CLASSIFICATION—AMERICAN":
VOUCHERS FOR SCHOOLS AND THE MULTIRACIAL CENSUS

1. Barack Obama, *The Audacity of Hope: Thoughts on Reclaiming the American Dream* (New York: Three Rivers Press, 2006), 92.

2. Ibid., 94.

3. Elizabeth Green, "Obama Open to Private School Vouchers," *New York Sun*, February 15, 2008, http://www.nysun.com/national/obama-open-to-private-school-vouchers/71403/.

4. Obama's campaign website stated: "Barack Obama and Joe Biden will double funding for the Federal Charter School Program to support the creation of more successful charter schools. An Obama-Biden administration will provide this expanded charter school funding only to states that improve accountability for charter schools, allow for interventions in struggling charter schools and have a clear process for closing down chronically underperforming charter schools. An Obama-Biden administration will also prioritize supporting states that help the most successful charter schools to expand to serve more students." (Barackobama.com, http://www.barackobama.com/issues/education/index_campaign.php), and "Remarks to the United States Hispanic Chamber of Commerce," March 10, 2009, American Presidency Project, http://www.presidency.ucsb.edu/ws/index.php?pid=85836&st=education&st1=.

5. See, e.g., Jay P. Greene, "The Union War on Charter Schools," *Wall Street Journal*, April 16, 2009, http://online.wsj.com/article/SB123985052084823887.html.

6. "A Plea to Mr. Duncan," *Washington Post*, July 10, 2009, http://www.washingtonpost.com/wp-dyn/content/article/2009/07/09/AR2009070902542.html.

7. "Topic A: Obama's Compromise on D.C.'s School Voucher Program," Joseph E. Robert, Jr., Ed Rogers, Lisa Schifren, *Washington Post*, May 10, 2009, http://www.washingtonpost.com/wp-dyn/content/article/2009/05/08/AR2009050803546.html.

8. Susan Anne Hiller, "Democrats Officially Kill Successful DC Voucher Program," Big Government, December 31, 2009, http://biggovernment.com/sahiller/2009/12/31/democrats-officially-kill-successful-dc-voucher-program/; Michael Birnbaum, "Senate Votes Against Reopening D.C. Voucher Program," *Washington Post*, March 17, 2010, http://www.washingtonpost.com/wp-dyn/content/article/2010/03/16/AR2010031604034.html.

9. Though there has been progress toward integration in some school districts, Gary Orfield and Chungmei Lee report that "the percentage of black students attending majority nonwhite schools increased in all regions from 66 percent in 1991 to 73 percent in 2003–4." Gary Orfield and Chungmei Lee, *Racial Transformation and the Changing Nature of Segregation* (Cambridge, MA: The Civil Rights Project at Harvard University, 2006), 9.

10. *Parents Involved in Community Schools v. Seattle School District No. 1*, 551 U.S. 701 (2007).

11. See, e.g., *Gratz v. Bollinger*, 539 U.S. 244 (2003); *Grutter v. Bollinger*, 539 U.S. 306 (2003).

12. Milton Friedman, "The Role of Government in Education," in *Economics and the Public Interest*, ed. Robert A. Solow (New Brunswick, NJ: Rutgers University Press, 1955).

13. J. Harvie Wilkinson III, *From Brown to Bakke: The Supreme Court and School Integration, 1954–1978* (New York: Oxford University Press, 1979), 98–100.

14. American Presidency Project, 25840, 25843, 25844.

15. "Private Schools: The Last Refuge," *Time*, November 14, 1969, http://www.time.com/time/magazine/article/0,9171,840365,00.html. In *Green v. Connally* (330 F. Supp. 1150 [1971]), African American parents in Mississippi sued to enjoin U.S. Treasury officials from according tax-exempt status to private schools in the state that discriminated against their children. In response to the suit, the IRS announced it would no longer allow tax-exempt status or permit deductions for contributions in the case of any private schools that practiced racial discrimination. They could not be viewed as "charitable" institutions, for they operated "contrary to declared Federal public policy," as embodied in the Civil Rights Act of 1964. Ultimately even a more conservative Supreme Court sided with the IRS in the most publicized of these controversies, *Bob Jones University v. United States*, 461 U.S. 574 (1983). The case played a major role in the mobilization of the modern Religious Right: see, e.g., Rogers M. Smith, "An Almost Christian Nation? Constitutional Consequences of the Rise of Christian Conservatism," in *Evangelicals and Democracy in America*, vol. 1, *Religion and Society*, ed. Steven Brint and Jean Reith Schroedel (New York: Russell Sage Foundation, 2009), 329–55. For recent accounts of southern private white schools, see, e.g., Carla Crowder, "Private White Academies Struggle in Changing World," *Birmingham News*, October 27, 2002, http://www.al.com/specialreport/birminghamnews/index.ssf?blackbelt/black

belt16.html; Charles T. Clotfelter, "Private Schools, Segregation, and the Southern States," *Peabody Journal of Education* 79 (2004): 74–97.

16. American Presidency Project, 25842, 25843, 25844. Beginning with *Lemon v. Kurzman* (403 U.S. 602, 614 [1971]), the Supreme Court struck down many forms of financial aid for, especially, parochial schools; but many of the private white schools were "Christian academies" and felt threatened by these rulings. See, e.g., *Levitt v. Commission for Public Education and Religious Liberty* (413 U.S. 472 [1973]); *Committee for Public Education and Religious Liberty v. Nyquist* (413 U.S. 756 [1973]); *Sloan v. Lemon* (413 U.S. 825 [1973]); *Meek v. Pittenger*, 421 U.S. 349 [1975]); *Wolman v. Walter* (433 U.S. 229 [1977]).

17. American Presidency Project, 25845.

18. Ibid., 29608.

19. Ibid., 25846.

20. Bob Lowe, "The Hollow Promise of School Vouchers," *Rethinking Schools Online*, http://www.rethinkingschools.org/special_reports/voucher_report/v_sosholw.shtml.

21. John E. Chubb and Terry M. Moe, *Politics, Markets and America's Schools* (Washington, DC: Brookings Institution, 1990), 126–27.

22. David L. Leal, "Latinos and School Vouchers: Testing the 'Minority Support' Hypothesis," *Social Science Quarterly* 85 (2004): 1227–28; Matthew I. Pinzur, "Looking for a Better Choice," *Hispanic* 16 (2003): 28.

23. Sheila Seuss Kennedy, "Privatizing Education: The Politics of Vouchers," *Phi Delta Kappan* 82 (February 2001), http://www.pdkintl.org/kappan/kken0102.htm; R. Kenneth Godwin and Frank R. Kemerer, *School Choice Tradeoffs* (Austin: University of Texas Press, 2002), 228–33; Lance Fusarelli, *The Political Dynamics of School Choice* (New York: Palgrave Macmillan, 2003), 4.

24. Godwin and Kemerer, *School Choice*, 120–21, 231; "School Voucher Controversy Escalates as National African American Leaders Coalesce Around Issue," *People for the American Way*, September 10, 1998, https://www.pfaw.org/press-releases/1998/09/school-voucher-controversy-escalates-national-african-american-leaders-coales.

25. Terry Moe, *Schools, Vouchers, and the American Public* (Washington, DC: Brookings Institution Press, 2001).

26. Jeffrey R. Henig, Richard C. Hula, Marion Orr, and Desiree S. Pedescleaux, *The Color of School Reform* (Princeton, NJ: Princeton University Press, 1999), 6–7.

27. American Presidency Project, 29610, 29611, 29612, 29613, 78283.

28. Ibid., 25847, 25848, 25849, 25850, 78545.

29. National Association of Manufacturers, "HRP-01 Education and the Workforce," 2009,http://www.nam.org/Issues/Official-Policy-Positions/Human-Resources-Policy/HRP-01-Education-and-the-Workforce.aspx#101.

30. Paul Street, "The Case Against School Vouchers," July 1, 2002, http://www.zcommunications.org/the-case-against-school-vouchers-by-paul-street; Leal, "Latinos and School Vouchers," 1227–28; Fusarelli, *School Choice*, 4.

31. Street and Kaas, "School Vouchers," 4; Leal, "Latinos and School Vouchers," 1230.

32. People for the American Way, "History of Failed Vouchers and Tax Credits," https://www.pfaw.org/media-center/publications/history-of-failed-vouchers-and-tax-credits/voucher-referenda.

33. Leal, "Latinos and School Vouchers," 1228.

34. Utah Election Results, "State Referendum," 2007, http://www.electionresults.utah.gov/xmlData/30000.html; Fusarelli, *School Choice*, 147.

35. All congressional voting results in this section are obtained from the Library of Congress's THOMAS website, http://thomas.loc.gov (accessed October 6, 2006).

36. The Black Commentator, "Bush Funds Black Voucher Front Group Your Tax Dollars Pay for Propaganda Blitz," 2002, http://www.blackcommentator.com/16_thw_pr.html.

37. Hispanic Council for Reform and Educational Options, "At a Glance," http://www.hcreo.com/index.php.

38. See, e.g., "Resolution 4: School Vouchers," League of United Latin American Citizens, http://www.lulac.net/advocacy/resolutions/voucher.html; "MALDEF GA Legislative Update: Week of February 16, 2009," G.A.L.E.O, February 16, 2009, http://www.galeo.org/agenda.php?agenda_id=0000000562; DCPSWATCH, "Press releases by various organizations at House of Representatives Committee on Government Reform hearing on "School Choice in the District of Columbia: Opening Doors for Parents and Students," June 24, 2003, http://www.dcpswatch.com/vouchers/030624g.htm; ACSD, "INFObrief: Private School Vouchers: Helping Students or Harming Schools?" January 2001 #24, http://www.ascd.org/publications/newsletters/infobrief/jan01/num24/toc.aspx.

39. *Zelman v. Simmons-Harris*, 536 U.S. 639 (2002).

40. Sewell Chan, "Many D.C. School Vouchers Go Unused," *Washington Post*, September 1, 2004, B1; Tarron Lively, "Study Urges Restructuring of D.C. School Vouchers," *Washington Times*, February 1, 2006; "Democrats and Poor Kids: Sitting on Evidence of Voucher Success, and the Battle of New York," *Wall Street Journal*, April 6, 2009, http://online.wsj.com/article/SB123897492702491091.html.

41. Associated Press, "National Desk: House Approves a Voucher Plan for Poor Washington Students," *New York Times*, September 6, 2003, A-12; Spencer S. Hsu, "How Vouchers Came to D.C.," *Education Next*, 2004, http://educationnext.org/howvoucherscametodc.

42. Melanie Hunter, "House Approves DC School Voucher Program," CNSNews.com, July 7, 2008, http://www.cnsnews.com/node/29267; Library of Congress, THOMAS: Legislative Information from the Library of Congress, 2005, http://thomas.loc.gov/.

43. American Presidency Project, 78283.

44. Sam Roberts and Peter Baker, "Asked to Declare His Race, Obama Checks 'Black,'" *New York Times*, April 2, 2010, http://www.nytimes.com/2010/04/03/us/politics/03census.html; "US Census Day Today—Barack Obama Fills 2010 Census Form," *Merinews*, April 2, 2010, http://www.merinews.com/article/us-census-day-today-barack-obama-fills-2010-census-form/15802839.shtml.

45. "Obama Answers Census Question on Race: African-American," *The Oval* (blog), *USA Today*, April 2, 2010, http://content.usatoday.com/communities/theoval/post/2010/04/obamas-census-question-on-race/1.

46. Sugrue, *Not Even Past*, 7, 9.

47. Melissa Nobles, *Shades of Citizenship: Race and Census in Modern Politics* (Stanford, CA: Stanford University Press, 2000); Matthew C. Snipp, "Racial Measurement in the American Census: Past Practices and Implications," *Annual Review of Sociology* 29 (2003): 563–88; Kim M. Williams, *Mark One or More: Civil Rights in Multiracial America* (Ann Arbor: University of Michigan Press, 2006), 22–29; Jennifer L. Hochschild and Brenna Marea Powell, "Racial Reorganization and the United States Census, 1850–1930: Mulattoes, Half-Breeds, Mixed Parentage, Hindoos, and the Mexican Race," *Studies in American Political Development* 22 (2008): 62–63.

48. Stetson Kennedy, *Jim Crow Guide: The Way It Was* (Boca Raton: Florida Atlantic University Press, 1990), 48–50; Nobles, *Shades of Citizenship*; F. James Davis, *Who Is Black: One Nation's Definition* (University Park: Pennsylvania State University Press, 1991).

49. Nobles, *Shades of Citizenship*, 78.

50. Margo J. Anderson and Stephen E. Fienberg, *Who Counts? The Politics of Census-Taking in Contemporary America* (New York: Russell Sage Foundation, 1999).

51. Office of Management and Budget, *Directive No. 15, Race and Ethnic Standards for Federal Statistics and Administrative Reporting* (Washington, DC: U.S. Office of Management and Budget, 1977); Williams, *Mark One or More*, 27–28.

52. Sharon M. Lee, *Using the New Racial Categories in the 2000 Census* (Annie E. Casey Foundation and Population Reference Bureau, 2001), 5.

53. Kim M. Williams, "Multiracialism and the Civil Rights Future," *Daedalus* 134.1 (2005): 53–60; Williams, *Mark One or More*, 86.

54. Williams, *Mark One or More*, 15.

55. Ibid., 65–83; Williams, "Multiracialism," 55.

56. Office of Management and Budget, *Revisions to the Standards for the Classification of Federal Data on Race and Ethnicity* (Washington, DC: U.S. Office of Management and Budget, 1997).

57. Williams, "Multiracialism," 54–54.

58. Jennifer L. Hochschild and Vesla Mae Weaver, "'There's No One as Irish as Barack O'Bama': The Politics and Policy of American Multiculturalism," *Perspectives on Politics* 8 (2010): 743. Department of Education officials and various citizen groups continue to struggle, however, over the adequacy and administrative practicality of the new standards. Susan Saulny, "Counting by Race Can Throw Off Some Numbers," *New York Times*, February 9, 2011, http://www.nytimes.com/2011/02/10/us/10count.html.

59. David A. Hollinger, *Postethnic America: Beyond Multiculturalism*, rev. ed. (New York: Basic Books, 2000), 3.

60. Peter H. Schuck, *Diversity in America* (Cambridge, MA: Harvard University Press, 2003), 146.

61. Ibid., 145.

62. Testimony of Senator Daniel Akaka, U.S. House of Representatives, Committee on Post Office and Civil Service, Subcommittee on Census and Statistics, *Federal Measurements of Race and Ethnicity*, 103rd Cong., 1st sess., July 29, 1993.

63. Ibid.

64. Testimony of Arthur Fletcher, U.S. House of Representatives, Committee on Post Office and Civil Service, Subcommittee on Census and Statistics, *Federal Measurements of Race and Ethnicity*, 103rd Cong., 1st sess., November 3, 1993.

65. Ibid.

66. Clara E. Rodriquez, *Changing Race: Latinos, the Census and the History of Ethnicity in the United States* (New York: New York University Press, 2000).

67. Williams, "Multiracialism," 56–57.

68. Testimony of Norma Cantu, U.S. House of Representatives, Committee on Post Office and Civil Service, Subcommittee on Census and Statistics, *Federal Measurements of Race and Ethnicity*, 103rd Cong., 1st sess., November 3, 1993.

69. Testimony of Billy Tidwell, U.S. House of Representatives, Committee on Post Office and Civil Service, Subcommittee on Census and Statistics, *Federal Measurements of Race and Ethnicity*, 103rd Cong., 1st Sess., July 29, 1993.

70. Testimony of Arthur Fletcher, U.S. House of Representatives, note 6.

71. Steven A. Holmes, "Panel Balks at Multiracial Census Category," *New York Times*, July 9, 1997, http://www.nytimes.com/1997/07/09/us/panel-balks-at-multiracial-census-category.html.

72. Steven A. Holmes, "Gingrich Outlines Plan on Race Relations," *New York Times*, June 19, 1997, http://www.nytimes.com/1997/06/19/us/gingrich-outlines-plan-on-race-relations.html.

73. Jennifer L. Hochschild and Traci Burch, "(Purposes + Unintended Consequences) x 2 Policy Changes + Large Effects: Contingency and Intention in American Racial and Ethnic Categories" (paper presented at conference on "Contingency in the Study of Politics," Yale University, December 3–5, 2004), 25.

74. Williams, *Mark One or More*, 114.

75. Rebecca Chiyoko King, "Racialization, Recognition, and Rights: Lumping and Splitting Multiracial Asian Americans in the 2000 Census," *Journal of Asian American Studies* 3 (2000): 204–5; Williams, "Multiracialism," 59; Williams, *Mark One or More*, 74; Hochschild and Burch, "Purposes," 26–28.

76. Hochschild and Weaver, "There's No One as Irish," 750.

77. Ibid.

78. Ibid., 747–49, 751–52. The fact that the numbers of mixed race Americans is nonetheless on the rise has received increasing attention in the media, but most press coverage confirms that there is much "debate among mixed-race people about what the long-term goals of their advocacy should be," with some wanting greater acknowledgment of multi-racial identities, some a "color-blind society." See, e.g., Susan Saulny, "Black? White? Asian? More Young Americans Choose All of the Above," *New York Times*, January 29, 2011, http://www.nytimes.com/2011/01/30/us/30mixed.html.

79. Williams, *Mark One or More*, 121–31.

CHAPTER 8. "WE CAN TAKE THE PEOPLE OUT OF THE SLUMS,
BUT WE CANNOT TAKE THE SLUMS OUT OF THE PEOPLE":
HOW TODAY'S RACIAL ALLIANCES SHAPE LAWS ON CRIME AND IMMIGRATION

1. Katharine Q. Seelye, "Obama Wades into a Volatile Racial Issue," *New York Times*, July 23, 2009, http://www.nytimes.com/2009/07/23/us/23race.html.

2. Huma Khan, Michele McPhee, and Russell Goldman, "Obama Called Police Officer Who Arrested Gates, Still Sees 'Overreaction' in Arrest," ABC News, July 24, 2009, http://abcnews.go.com/Politics/story?id=8163051&page=1.

3. "Barack Obama and Joe Biden: Creating Equal Opportunity and Justice for All," Barackobama.com, http://www.barackobama.com/pdf/issues/Fact_Sheet_Civil_Rights_and_Criminal_Justice_FINAL.pdf.

4. Peter H. Schuck, *Diversity in America* (Cambridge, MA: Harvard University Press, 2003), 146.

5. 132 Cong. Rec. E944-01 (daily edition, March 21, 1986).

6. Peter Kerr, "Extra-Potent Cocaine: Use Rising Sharply Among Teen-Agers," *New York Times*, March 20, 1986, http://www.nytimes.com/1986/03/20/nyregion/extra-potent-cocaine-use-rising-sharply-among-teenagers.html.

7. Doris Marie Provine, *Unequal Under Law: Race in the War on Drugs* (Chicago: University of Chicago Press, 2007), 112.

8. Anti-drug Abuse Act of 1986, H.R. 5484, http://thomas.loc.gov/cgi-bin/bdquery/z?d099:HR05484:@@@L&summ2+m&.

9. Provine, *Unequal Under Law*, 109.

10. "Press Release: Rangel Testifies Against Cocaine Sentencing Disparity," website of Congressman Charles B. Rangel, http://rangel.house.gov/news/press-releases/2009/05/rangel-testifies-against-cocaine-sentencing-disparity.shtml. The bill was not reported out of committee.

11. See, e.g., Michelle Alexander, *The New Jim Crow: Mass Incarceration in the Age of Colorblindness* (New York: New Press, 2010).

12. Marie Gottschalk, *The Prison and the Gallows* (New York: Cambridge University Press, 2006), 13–16.

13. Ibid., 48–51, 63–67.

14. Naomi Murakawa, "The Origins of the Carceral Crisis: Racial Order as 'Law and Order' in Postwar American Politics," in *Race and American Political Development*, ed. Joseph Lowndes, Julie Novkov, and Dorian T. Warren (New York: Routledge, 2008), 238.

15. Ibid., 239, 241, 243; Vesla M. Weaver, "Frontlash: Race and the Development of Punitive Crime Policy," *Studies in American Political Development* 21 (2007): 240–42.

16. Richard Hofstadter and Beatrice K. Hofstadter, eds., *Great Issues in American History*, vol. 2, *From Reconstruction the Present Day, 1864–1981*, rev. ed. (New York: Vintage Books, 1982), 502.

17. American Presidency Project, 25840.

18. Ibid., 29603.

19. Katherine Beckett, *Making Crime Pay: Law and Order in Contemporary American Politics* (New York: Oxford University Press, 1997), 40–43, 85–88.

20. Bruce Western, *Punishment and Inequality in America* (New York: Russell Sage Foundation, 2006), 59; Weaver, "Frontlash," 244–46.

21. Beckett, *Making Crime Pay*, 32, 85.

22. Murakawa, "Carceral Crisis," 250–51.

23. Weaver, "Frontlash," 247–48.

24. Ibid., 248.

25. President's Commission on Law Enforcement and Administration of Justice, *The Challenge of Crime in a Free Society*, ed. Isidore Silver (New York: Avon Books, 1968); Beckett, *Making Crime Pay*, 36–37, 91; Weaver, "Frontlash," 240.

26. President's Commission, 40.

27. Weaver, "Frontlash," 249.

28. P.L. 90-351, 82 Stat. 197.

29. Thomas M. Hilbink, "Omnibus Crime Control and Safe Streets Act of 1968," Enotes.com, http://www.enotes.com/major-acts-congress/omnibus-crime-control-safe-streets-act.

30. American Presidency Project, 29604, 25841.

31. Ibid., 25842, 29605, 25843, 29606.

32. Ibid., 29607.

33. Ibid., 25844.

34. Provine, *Unequal Under Law*, 103–4; Ronald W. Reagan, "Radio Address to the Nation on Federal Drug Policy," October 2, 1982, American Presidency Project, 43805; Ronald W. Reagan, "Remarks Announcing Federal Initiatives Against Drug Trafficking and Organized Crime," October 14, 1982, American Presidency Project, 43127.

35. Reagan, "Remarks Announcing Federal Initiatives."

36. Katherine Beckett correctly notes that popular attitudes toward crime policy have been "complex, equivocal, and contradictory," with most Americans favoring educational and job training programs over more prisons, but she also acknowledges that "the punitive tone of the law and order discourse clearly resonates with salient sentiments in American political culture" (Beckett, *Making Crime Pay*, 4).

37. American Presidency Project, 29608.

38. Ibid., 29610, 29611.

39. Ibid., 29612.

40. Ibid., 78283.

41. Ibid., 25845, 25846, 25847, 25848, 25849, 25850.

42. Ibid., 78545.

43. Western, *Punishment and Inequality*, 61, 71; Kevin B. Smith, "The Politics of Punishment: Evaluating Political Explanations of Incarceration Rates," *Journal of Politics* 66 (2004): 925–38.

44. Katherine Beckett and Theodore Sasson, *The Politics of Injustice: Crime and Punishment in America*, 2nd ed. (London: Sage, 2004), 5.

45. Western, *Punishment and Inequality*, 12–18; Lawrence D. Bobo and Victor Thompson, "Unfair by Design: The War on Drugs, Race, and the Legitimacy of the Criminal Justice System," *Social Research* 73 (2006): 452–52; Marie Gottschalk, "Hiding in Plain Sight: American Politics and the Carceral State," *Annual Review of Political Science* 11 (2008): 236.

46. Western, *Punishment and Inequality*, 50.

47. Lawrence D. Bobo and Devon Johnson, "A Taste for Punishment: Black and White Americans' Views on the Death Penalty and the War on Drugs," *Du Bois Review* 1 (2004): 151–80.

48. Naomi Murakawa, "Electing to Punish: Congress, Race, and the Rise of the American Criminal Justice State" (Ph.D. diss., Department of Political Science, Yale University, 2005), UMI No. 3168958.

49. Ibid., 4–5.

50. Ibid., 9.

51. Ibid., 25–26.

52. P.L. 96-181, 93 Stat. 1309, enacted January 2, 1980.

53. P.L. 98-473, 98 Stat. 1987; Murakawa, "Electing to Punish," 19–20.

54. Beckett, *Making Crime Pay*, 95–96.

55. Murakawa, "Electing to Punish," 19.

56. Lord David James George Hennessy Windlesham, *Politics, Punishment, and Populism* (Oxford: Oxford University Press, 1998), 22–23.

57. Provine, *Unequal Under Law*, 113–17.

58. Murakawa, "Electing to Punish," 20–21.

59. P.L. 100-690.

60. Anti-Drug Abuse Act of 1988, H.R. 5210, http://thomas.loc.gov/cgi-bin/bdquery/z?d100:HR05210:@@@L&summ2=m&#major%20actions; Windlesham, *Politics, Punishment, and Populism*, 26.

61. *McCleskey v. Kemp*, 481 U.S. 279 (1987).

62. Provine, *Unequal Under Law*, 116–17; "Racial Justice Act Becomes Law: Not Soft on Crime, But Strong on Justice," *Advocate* 20, no. 4 (July 1998), http://www.e-archives.ky.gov/pubs/public_adv/july98/racial.html; "Perdue Signs Racial Justice Act," WRAL.com, http://www.wral.com/news/state/story/5769609.

63. P.L. 101–647.

64. Gottschalk, *Prison and the Gallows*, 77–164.

65. Brendan O'Connor, "Policies, Principles, and Polls: Bill Clinton's Third Way Welfare Politics, 1992–1996," *Australian Journal of Politics and History* 48 (2002): 401.

66. Franklin E. Zimring, "Imprisonment Rates and the New Politics of Criminal Punishment," *Punishment and Society* 3 (2001): 162, http://pun.sagepub.com/content/3/1/161.short.

67. P.L. 103–322; http://www.policyalmanac.org/crime/archive/crs_federal_crime_policy.shtml (accessed October 9, 2009); Gottschalk, *Prison and the Gallows*, 248.

68. Gottschalk, *Prison and the Gallows*, 247; Murakawa, "Electing to Punish," 28–29.

69. U.S. House of Representatives, Office of the Clerk, Final Results for Roll Call 416, H.R. 3355, August 21, 1994, http://clerk.house.gov/evs/1994/roll416.xml (accessed October 9, 2009); Violent Crime Control and Law Enforcement Act, Enotes.com,http://www.enotes.com/major-acts-congress/violent-crime-control-law-enforcement-act/ (accessed October 9, 2009).

70. P.L. 104-132, 110 Stat. 1214.

71. U.S. House of Representatives, Office of the Clerk, Final Results for Roll Call 126, S. 735, April 18, 1996, http://clerk.house.gov/evs/1996/roll126.xml (accessed October 9, 2009).

72. Beckett and Sasson, *Politics of Injustice*, 68–70.

73. *Alexander v. Sandoval*, 532 U.S. 275 (2001).

74. Alexander, *New Jim Crow*, 134–35.

75. *Hayden v. Pataki*, 449 F. 3d 305 (2006).

76. See, e.g., *Furman v. Georgia*, 408 U.S. 238 (1972); *Gregg v. Georgia*, 428 U.S. 153 (1976); *Coker v. Georgia*, 488 U.S. 584 (1977); *McCleskey v. Kemp*, 481 U.S. 279 (1987).

77. See, e.g., *Batson v. Kentucky*, 476 U.S. 79 (1986); *Hernandez v. New York*, 500 U.S. 352 (1991).

78. Beckett and Sasson, *Politics of Injustice*, 70–71.

79. Western, *Punishment and Inequality*, 50; Gottschalk, "Hiding," 249–51.

80. Heritage Foundation, "Rule of Law: Statement of Purpose," 2009, http://www.heritage.org/LeadershipForAmerica/Rule-of-Law.cfm.

81. *U.S. v. Booker*, 543 U.S. 220 (2005).

82. For an argument that recent state actions to reduce mandatory sentences reflect fiscal concerns but leave "the racial ideology that gave rise to these laws" undisturbed, see Alexander, *New Jim Crow*, 14, 217–22.

83. The text of the bill can be found at Arizona State Legislature, http://www.azleg.gov/legtext/49leg/2r/bills/sb1070s.pdf.

84. Eric V. Meeks, *Border Citizens: The Making of Indians, Mexicans, and Anglos in Arizona* (Austin: University of Texas Press, 2007), 244–45; Nicole Santa Cruz, "Arizona Has Rarely Invoked Its Last Tough Immigration Law," *Los Angeles Times*, April 19, 2010, http://articles.latimes.com/2010/apr/19/nation/la-na-employer-sanctions19-2010apr19.

85. Laura Meckler and Miriam Jordan, "Obama Blasts Arizona Law," *Wall Street Journal*, April 24, 2010, http://online.wsj.com/article/SB10001424052748703709804575202110136576160.html?KEYWORDS=obama+blasts+arizona+law; Peter Nicholas, "Obama Criticizes Arizona Immigration Law," *Los Angeles Times*, April 28, 2010, http://articles.latimes.com/2010/apr/28/nation/la-na-obama-midwest-20100429; Richard A. Serrano and Peter Nicholas, "Obama Administration Considers Challenges to Arizona Immigration Law," *Los Angeles Times*, April 29, 2010, http://articles.latimes.com/2010/apr/29/nation/la-na-obama-immigration-20100430; Kelly Chernenkoff, "President Fires Again at Arizona Immigration Law, Sets Sights on Federal Legislation," *Los Angeles Times*, May 5, 2010, http://articles.latimes.com/2010/apr/29/nation/la-na-obama-immigration-20100430.

86. "Civil Rights Groups Fight Ariz. Immigration Law," MSNBC News, April 24, 2010, http://www.msnbc.msn.com/id/36735281.

87. David Jackson, "Obama And Brewer Hold Arizona Immigration Summit," USA Today, June 3, 2010, http://content.usatoday.com/communities/theoval/post/2010/06/obama-and-brewer-hold-arizona-immigration-summit/1.

88. Randal C. Archibold, "Judge Blocks Arizona's Immigration Law," New York Times, July 28, 2010, http://www.nytimes.com/2010/07/29/us/29arizona.html.

89. Tichenor, 8; Zolberg, Nation by Design, 19.

90. James G. Gimpel and James R. Edwards, The Congressional Politics of Immigration Reform (Boston: Allyn and Bacon, 1995), 46.

91. Ibid., 144–45.

92. The full text of the bill is at Arizona State Legislature, http://www.azleg.gov/legtext/49leg/2r/bills/hb2281s.pdf.

93. Nicole Santa Cruz, "Arizona Bill Targeting Ethnic Studies Signed into Law," Los Angeles Times, May 12, 2010, http://articles.latimes.com/2010/may/12/nation/la-na-ethnic-studies-20100512.

94. Gerald L. Neuman, Strangers to the Constitution: Immigrants, Borders, and Fundamental Law (Princeton, NJ: Princeton University Press, 1996), 20–43.

95. Desmond S. King and Rogers M. Smith, "Racial Orders in American Political Development," American Political Science Review 99 (2005): 88–89; Mae M. Ngai, "The Architecture of American Immigration Law: A Reexamination of the Immigration Act of 1924," Journal of American History 86 (1999): 67–92.

96. American Presidency Project, 25839, 29602.

97. Ibid., 29603, 25840.

98. David M. Reimers, Still the Golden Door: The Third World Comes to America (New York: Columbia University Press, 1985), 72–73.

99. Zolberg, Nation by Design, 324, 329–32.

100. Reimers, Still the Golden Door, 78–81.

101. American Presidency Project, 25841, 29604.

102. Zolberg, Nation by Design, 335–39.

103. American Presidency Project, 25842, 29605.

104. Tichenor, Dividing Lines, 252–55.

105. American Presidency Project, 29607, 29608, 29609, and 29610.

106. Zolberg, Nation by Design, 359.

107. Tichenor, Dividing Lines, 254.

108. American Presidency Project, 25844.

109. Tichenor, Dividing Lines, 256–57.

110. Gimpel and Edwards, Congressional Politics, 178; Tichenor, Dividing Lines, 256.

111. American Presidency Project, 25845, 25846.

112. Tichenor, Dividing Lines, 276. Immigration litigation through these years has almost always concerned the social and civil rights of immigrants, because courts have not been involved in setting overall immigration levels. The alliances visible in amicus briefs are those visible in the legislative contests discussed in the text. Organizations

like the Asian American Legal Defense and Education Fund, the Catholic Legal Immigration Network, the Hispanic National Bar Association, MALDEF, La Raza, the American Immigration Law Foundation, the ACLU, the National Immigration Forum, the NAACP Legal Defense Fund (though less often), and others regularly file on behalf of immigrant rights. Opposition briefs are frequently filed by FAIR and the Washington Legal Foundation, joining in support of immigration enforcement agencies and, in some cases, state and local officials. See, e.g., *Matthew v. Diaz* , 426 U.S. 67 (1976); *Hampton v. Mow Sun Wong*, 426 U.S. 88 (1976); *Plyler v. Doe*, 457 U.S. 202 (1982); *Jean v. Nelson*, 472 U.S. 846 (1985); *INS v. Cardoza-Fonseca*, 480 U.S. 421 (1987); *INS v. Yueh-Shaio Yang*, 519 U.S. 26 (1996); *Reno v. American-Arab Anti-Discrimination Committee*, 525 U.S. 471 (1999); *INS v. St. Cyr*, 533 U.S. 289 (2002); *Zadvydas v. Davis*, 533 U.S. 678 (2002); *Demore v. Hyung Joon Kim*, 538 U.S. 510 (2003); *Clark v. Suarez Marti*, 543 U.S. 371 (2004); *Jama v. Immigration and Customs Enforcement*, 543 U.S. 335 (2005); *Muehler v. Mena*, 544 U.S. 93 (2005); *Fernandez-Varga v. Gonzalez*, 548 U.S. 30 (2006); *Lopez v. Gonzalez*, 549 U.S. 27 (2006). The overall pattern that emerges from these cases is that modern courts continue to uphold the primacy of federal policy over the states in immigration and to protect and sometimes expand minimal due process rights for immigrants; but they have not placed any major barriers in the way of modern legislation providing for expedited deportation, imposing restrictions on social benefits, and authorizing or mandating states to enact similar restrictions.

113. Tichenor, *Dividing Lines*, 261.

114. Gimpel and Edwards, *Congressional Politics*, 177–80; Zolberg, *Nation by Design*, 369–70.

115. Zolberg, *Nation by Design*, 371.

116. Ibid., 377–81; Tichenor, *Dividing Lines*, 267–74; Gimpel and Edwards, *Congressional Politics*, 194–97.

117. Tichenor, *Dividing Lines*, 275–77; Zolberg, *Nation by Design*, 382–86.

118. American Presidency Project, 25847, 29610.

119. Zolberg, *Nation by Design*, 404–8.

120. Gimpel and Edwards, *Congressional Politics*, 212–43.

121. American Presidency Project, 25848. The Republican call for restrictions on birthright citizenship was inspired in part by Peter H. Schuck and Rogers M. Smith, *Citizenship without Consent: The Illegal Alien in the American Polity* (New Haven, CT: Yale University Press, 1985). Though that work argued for Congress's power to adopt such restrictions, neither author subsequently endorsed them as desirable policies.

122. American Presidency Project, 29611.

123. Zolberg, *Nation by Design*, 386–87, 395.

124. Ibid., 410–11.

125. Audrey Singer, "Welfare Reform and Immigrants: A Policy Review," 2004, 26, Brookings, http://www.brookings.edu/reports/2004/05demographics_singer.aspx.

126. See bill at Federation of American Scientists, http://www.fas.org/irp/crs/96-499.htm.

127. In fact, PRWORA originally made even many immigrants present at the time of its enactment ineligible for SSI and food stamps, but Congress restored eligibility to most pre-enactment immigrants via the 1997 Balanced Budget Act, the 1998 Agricultural Research Extension and Education Act, and the Farm Security and Rural Investment Act of 2002. The states have chosen to provide TANF and Medicaid benefits to most pre-enactment immigrants, and the courts have also restricted some of the IIRIRA's harsh procedural provisions (Singer, "Welfare Reform," 23, 27–28; Zolberg, *Nation by Design*, 416–17, 420).

128. See, e.g., VisaLaw.com—The Immigration Law Portal, "IIRIRA 96—A Summary of the New Immigration Bill," http://www.visalaw.com/96nov/3nov96.html.

129. Gimpel and Edwards, *Congressional Politics*, 281–88; Tichenor, *Dividing Lines*, 283–85; Zolberg, *Nation by Design*, 417–19.

130. Michael Fix and Ron Haskins, "Welfare Benefits for Non-Citizens," 2002, Brookings, http://www.brookings.edu/papers/2002/02immigration_fix.aspx; Shawn Fremstad, "Recent Welfare Reform Research Findings: Implications for TANF Reauthorization and State TANF Policies," 2004, Center on Budget and Policy Priorities, http://www.cbpp.org/cms/index/cfm?fa=view&id=1536.

131. Singer "Welfare Reform," 29–30.

132. American Presidency Project, 29612, 29613, 29614.

133. Ibid., 25849, 25850, 78545.

134. See, e.g., "Senate Buries Immigration Bill," *Los Angeles Times*, June 29, 2007, http://articles.latimes.com/2007/jun/29/nation/na-immig29 (accessed December 13, 2009).

135. Wade Henderson, "Testimony on the U.S. Economy, U.S. Workers, and Immigration Reform," Hearing before the Subcommittee on Immigration, Citizenship, Refugees, Border Security, and International Law of the Committee on the Judiciary, House of Representatives, 110th Cong., 1st Sess., May 3, 2007, Serial No. 110-34, 70, at http://www.gpo.gov/fdsys/pkg/CHRG-110hhrg35117/pdf/CHRG-110hhrg35117.pdf.

136. DREAM Act Portal, http://dreamact.info.

Chapter 9. Prospects of the House Divided

1. A conclusion strengthened by Michael Tesler and David O. Sears's account of the 2008 presidential election, *Obama's Race: The 2008 Election and the Dream of a Post-Racial America* (Chicago: University of Chicago Press, 2010), in which they argue that the election was affected by more polarized racial attitudes than in any previous presidential election.

2. See, for example, Neil Gotanda, "A Critique of 'Our Constitution is Color-Blind,'" *Stanford Law Review* 44 (1991): 1–68; Michael Omi and Howard Winant, *Racial Formation in the United States*, 2nd ed. (New York: Routledge, 1994), 113–36; Eduardo Bonilla-Silva, *Racism without Racists: Color-Blind Racism and the Persistence of Racial Inequality in the United States*, 2nd ed. (Lanham, MD: Rowman and Littlefield, 2006); Thomas J. Sugrue, *Sweet Land of Liberty* (New York: Random House, 2008); Michael K. Brown, Martin Carnoy, Elliott Currie, Troy Duster, David B. Op-

penheimer, Marjorie M. Shultz, and David Wellman, *White-Washing Race: The Myth of a Color-Blind Society* (Berkeley: University of California Press, 2003).

3. Ibid. The quotations are from Sugrue, *Sweet Land of Liberty*, xxiii–xxv.

4. Byron E. Shafer and Richard Johnston, *The End of Southern Exceptionalism: Class, Race, and Partisan Change in the Postwar South* (Cambridge, MA: Harvard University Press, 2006), 2.

5. Nolan McCarty, Keith T. Poole, and Howard Rosenthal, *Polarized America: The Dance of Ideology and Unequal Riches* (Cambridge, MA: MIT Press, 2006), 11.

6. See, among others to whom we are indebted, Khalilah L. Brown-Dean, "Permanent Outsiders: Felon Disenfranchisement and the Breakdown of Black Politics," *National Political Science Review* 11 (2007): 103–20 (2007); Anthony S. Chen, *The Fifth Freedom: Jobs, Politics, and Civil Rights in the United States, 1941–1972* (Princeton, NJ: Princeton University Press, 2009); Cathy J. Cohen, *The Boundaries of Blackness: AIDS and the Breakdown of Black Politics* (Chicago: University of Chicago Press, 1999); Cathy J. Cohen, "From Kanye West to Barack Obama: Black Youth, the State and Political Alienation," in *The Unsustainable American State*, ed. Lawrence Jacobs and Desmond King (New York: Oxford University Press, 2009), 255–99; Michael Dawson, *Black Visions: The Roots of Contemporary African-American Political Ideologies* (Chicago: University of Chicago, 2001); Paul Frymer, *Black and Blue: African Americans, the Labor Movement, and the Decline of the Democratic Party* (Princeton, NJ: Princeton University Press, 2008); Michael Goldfield, *The Color of Politics: Race and the Mainsprings of American Politics* (New York: Free Press, 1997); Frederick C. Harris, Valeria Sinclair-Chapman, and Brian D. McKenzie, *Countervailing Forces in African-American Civic Activism, 1973–1994* (New York: Cambridge University Press, 2006); Jennifer Hochschild, *Facing Up to the American Dream: Race, Class, and the Soul of the Nation* (Princeton, NJ: Princeton University Press, 1996); Richard Iton, *In Search of the Black Fantastic: Politics and Popular Culture in the Post-Civil Rights Era* (New York: Oxford University Press); Ira Katznelson, *When Affirmative Action Was White: An Untold History of Racial Inequality in Twentieth-Century America* (New York: W. W. Norton, 2005); Donald R. Kinder and Lynn M. Sanders, *Divided by Color: Racial Politics and Democratic Ideals* (Chicago: University of Chicago Press, 1996); Robert C. Lieberman, *Shaping Race Policy: The United States in Comparative Perspective* (Princeton, NJ: Princeton University Press, 2005); Paula D. McClain and Joseph Stewart Jr.,*"Can We All Get Along?" Racial and Ethnic Minorities in American Politics*, 5th ed. (Boulder, CO: Westview Press, 2009); Sanford F. Schram, "Contextualizing Racial Disparities in American Welfare Reform: Toward a New Poverty Research," *Perspectives on Politics* 3 (2005): 253–68; Tesler and Sears, *Obama's Race*; Deborah E. Ward, *The White Welfare State: The Racialization of US Welfare Policy* (Ann Arbor: University of Michigan Press, 2005). As the preceding chapters make clear, we have also been aided by more scholars in other disciplines than we can list.

7. See, e.g., Claire Jean Kim, "Imagining Race and Nation in Multiculturalist America," *Ethnic and Racial Studies* 27 (2004): 987–1005; Julie Novkov, *Racial Union* (Ann Arbor: University of Michigan Press, 2008), 5–9; Kimberley S. Johnson, "Jim Crow

Reform and the Democratization of the South," in *Race and American Political Development*, ed. Joseph Lowndes, Julie Novkov, and Dorian T. Warren (New York: Routledge, 2008), 155–79.

8. Novkov, *Racial Union*, 7.

9. The most extensive discussion of different political visions among African Americans is Dawson, *Black Visions*. Also particularly illuminating in this regard are Cohen, *Boundaries of Blackness* and "From Kanye West"; Harris, Sinclair-Chapman, and McKenzie, *Countervailing Forces*; Iton, *Black Fantastic*; and Nikhil Pal Singh, *Black Is a Country* (Cambridge, MA: Harvard University Press, 2004). For our views, see Rogers M. Smith and Desmond S. King, "Barack Obama and the Future of American Racial Politics," *Du Bois Review* 6 (2009): 33–35.

10. McCarty, Poole, and Rosenthal, *Polarized America*, 7.

11. Ibid., 108; Shafer and Johnston, *End of Southern Exceptionalism*, 17; Tim Storey and Gene Rose, "GOP #1: First Time in Fifty Years," 2002, National Conference of State Legislatures, http://web.archive.org/web/20040325042221/http://www.ncsl.org/programs/pubs/1202GOP.htm.

12. Shafer and Johnston, *End of Southern Exceptionalism*, 12, 26–50, 52–53, 95–99, 174–77.

13. Ibid., 63–73, 176–77.

14. Ibid., 16–17, 176.

15. Ibid., 119–23.

16. Ibid., 125.

17. Ibid., 93.

18. Ibid., 119, 150–62.

19. Ibid., 91, 125.

20. McCarty, Poole, and Rosenthal, *Polarized America*, 5, 18–21.

21. Ibid., 10–11, 50.

22. Ibid., 51.

23. Ibid., 22.

24. Ibid., 51.

25. Ibid., 50, 52.

26. Ibid., 54, 76, 90.

27. Ibid., 11, 52.

28. Ibid., 10.

29. Ibid., 101.

30. See, e.g., Dr. Donald J. Devine, "Why We Are Conservative," American Conservative Union Foundation, http://www.conservative.org/acuf/why-we-are-conservative/, discussing the challenges of sustaining a coalition of conservative "traditionalists and libertarians."

31. For a related but distinct analysis of how racial tropes played a key role in uniting different forms of conservatism to create the modern "New Right" from which we have benefited, see Joseph L. Lowndes, *From the New Deal to the New Right: Race and the*

Southern Origins of Modern Conservatism (New Haven, CT: Yale University Press, 2008), esp. 157–62.

32. McCarty, Poole, and Rosenthal, *Polarized America*, 10.

33. Ibid.; Sugrue, *Sweet Land of Liberty*, 536–37.

34. U.S. Census Bureau, "Table 10. Resident Population by Race, Hispanic Origin, and Single Years of Age: 2008," http://www.census.gov/compendia/statab/2010/tables/10s0010.pdf.

35. James E. Ryan, *Five Miles Away, a World Apart: One City, Two Schools and the Story of Educational Opportunity in Modern America* (New York: Oxford University Press, 2010).

36. NAACP, "NAACP Fact Sheet: Subprime and Predatory Mortgage Lending," http://naacp.3cdn.net/e8ad24da256549c740_sbm6bnq36.pdf.

37. Thomas M. Shapiro, Tatjana Meschede, and Laura Sullivan, "The Racial Wealth Gap Increases Fourfold," Institute on Assets and Social Policy, Heller School for Social Policy and Management, Brandeis University, May 2010, http://iasp.brandeis.edu/pdfs/Racial-Wealth-Gap-Brief.pdf.

38. U.S. Census Bureau, "Table 36. Selected Characteristics of Racial Groups and Hispanic Population: 2007," http://www.census.gov/compendia/statab/2010/tables/10s0036.pdf.

39. Federal Deposit Insurance Corporation, *National Survey of Unbanked and Underbanked Households* (Washington, DC: FDIC, December 2009), 16–18, http://www.fdic.gov/householdsurvey/full_report.pdf.

40. Monique W. Morris, "Discrimination and Mortgage Lending in America," National Association for the Advancement of Colored People, March 2009, http://naacp.3cdn.net/4ca760b774f81317c4_klm6i6yxg.pdf.

41. Ajamu Dillahunt, Brian Miller, Mike Prokosch, Jeannette Huezo, and Dedrick Muhammad, "State of the Dream 2010: Drained: Jobless and Foreclosed in Communities of Color," United for a Fair Economy, January 13, 2010, v, http://www.faireconomy.org/files/SoD_2010_Drained_Report.pdf.

42. Craig E. Pollack and Julia Lynch, "Health Status of People Undergoing Foreclosure in the Philadelphia Region," *American Journal of Public Health* 99 (2009): 1833–39, http://ajph.aphapublications.org/cgi/content/short/99/10/1833.

43. Office of Minority Health, http://minorityhealth.hhs.gov/templates/browse.aspx?lvl=2&lvllD=51.

44. Office of Minority Health, http://minorityhealth.hhs.gov/templates/browse.aspx?lvl=2&lvllD=54.

45. U.S. Census Bureau, "Table 1. United States—Race and Hispanic Origin: 1790 to 1990," http://www.census.gov/population/www/documentation/twps0056/tab01.pdf. On the social effects, see Mary Patillo, David Weiman, and Bruce Western, eds., *Imprisoning America: The Social Effects of Mass Incarceration* (New York: Russell Sage Foundation, 2004); and Western, *Punishment and Inequality*.

46. Devah Pager, "The 'Stickiness' of Race in an Era of Mass Incarceration" (paper presented at the conference "Racial Inequality in a Post-Racial World?" Russell Sage Foundation, May 21–22, 2010), 1, 13–14.

47. American Presidency Project, 25845.

48. See, e.g., ibid., 78545.

49. Peter H. Schuck, *Diversity in America* (Cambridge, MA: Harvard University Press, 2003), 163–69, 198; Daniel Sabbagh, *Equality and Transparency: A Strategic Perspective on Affirmative Action in American Law* (New York: Palgrave Macmillan, 2007), 139.

50. *University of California Board of Regents v. Bakke*, 438 U.S. 265 (1978); *Gratz v. Bollinger*, 539 U.S. 244 (2003); *Grutter v. Bollinger*, 539 U.S. 306 (2003).

51. *University of California Board of Regents v. Bakke* at 319n53.

52. *Gratz v. Bollinger*, 297–98.

53. In this vein, see Cathy J. Cohen, *Democracy Remixed: Black Youth and the Future of American Politics* (New York: Oxford University Press, 2010).

54. Hochschild, "Affirmative Action as Culture War," 357–58.

55. Obama, *Dreams from My Father*, 294.

56. For an exploration of these themes, see Rogers M. Smith, *Stories of Peoplehood* (Cambridge: Cambridge University Press, 2003).

57. Schuck, *Diversity in America*, 332–33.

58. Ibid., 177–78; Hochschild, "Strange Career of Affirmative Action," 1002–3.

59. For the Obama administration's emphasis on developing "new, state-of-the-art assessment and accountability systems that provide timely and useful information" about student learning, see "Education," White House.gov, http://www.whitehouse .gov/issues/education. For a discussion of modern educational politics and policies by a scholar and policymaker who has aligned with different sides over time, see Diane Ravitch, *The Death and Life of the Great American School System: How Testing and Choice Are Undermining Education* (New York: Basic Books, 2010).

Index

An *f*, *n*, or *t* indicates a figure, footnote or table, respectively.

Abbitt, Watkins, 220
Abernathy, Ralph, 84
abolitionism, 37, 41t, 43–44, 46, 48, 219, 254t, 302n29
academic institutions, 65, 68t, 73, 78, 255t, 292. *See also* science; *specific institutions*
Acheson, Dean, 82
ACLU (American Civil Liberties Union): and alliance, race-conscious, 261t; and crime, 232, 233; and employment, 120, 122, 125, 126, 129; and housing, 150, 155t, 159, 324n71; and immigration, 242t, 343n112; and majority-minority districts, 187–88; and voting rights, 178t; and vouchers, 199, 200t
Adams, Henry, 62, 89
Adams, John, 3
Adams, John Quincy, 38
Adams Jr., Charles Frances, 62–63, 66, 89
Adarand Constructors v. Pena (1995), 131
Addams, Jane, 69
ADEPA (Anti-Terrorism and Effective Death Penalty Act of 1996), 231–32, 246
AEI (American Enterprise Institute), 188, 209t, 224t, 242t, 259t, 262t
AFDC (Aid for Dependent Children), 75, 246
affirmative action: basics, 9; and conservatism, 110, 111, 130; and Democrats, 10–12, 133, 162; and housing, 160, 166; and mortgage crisis, 162; and Republicans, 124, 211–12; results of, 269–70, 289. *See also* education; employment; equal opportunity; quotas
"affirmatively further fair housing" (AFFH) requirement, 319n1
AFL-CIO, 56, 120, 121, 155t, 159, 178t, 242t, 260t, 261t
African American groups and leaders: and alliances, modern, 257, 258, 269; and

alliances, segregation era, 72, 254t; and alliances, slavery era, 41t, 254t; and civil rights, 260t; and crime, 229; and employment, 118t, 120–21, 258; and housing/mortgages, 139, 258; and identity categories, 208, 212; and immigration, 236, 240, 241t, 244, 247, 248, 260t; and majority-minority districts, 187–88, 257, 258; office holders, 14, 105, 170–79, 172, 176, 181, 184–85, 269, 270t (*see also individual office holders*); and prison populations, 228; and Republicans, 181; and vouchers, 196, 199, 202. *See also individual leaders; specific groups*
African Americans: census views, 207; and education, 12–13, 269, 270–74t, 333n9; and employment, 269–71t, 278t; health, 13, 276–77; housing/mortgage statistics, 13, 143–44, 163, 275, 276, 295n35, 327n119; and identity categories, 211; immigration views, 236; incomes, 13, 272, 275–76; political visions of, 346n9; prison populations, 277, 279t. *See also* African American groups and leaders; inequalities; *individual African Americans; specific issues*
African American voters: and economic classes, 268; and education, 130; and equal protection, 60; and northern states, 72, 78; and political parties, 27, 101–2, 171, 263; and property taxes, 116; registration statistics, 172; and southern states, 73, 85, 266; and U.S. Supreme Court, 77, 81, 309n50; and vouchers, 198, 199–200, 201, 203. *See also* voting rights
Afro-American League (Council), 69
AFT (American Federation of Teachers), 150, 155t, 193
Agricultural Research Extension and Education Act of 1998, 344n127

Aid for Dependent Children (AFDC), 75, 246
AIG (American International Group), 166
Akaka, Daniel, 209
Alabama: and housing, 325nn86,87; juries, 307n14, 309n50; and majority-minority districts, 182, 183t, 184, 330n46; Scottsboro cases, 77–78; and voting rights, 60, 171–72, 175. *See also individual Alabamans*
Alabama, Rogers v. (1904), 307n14, 309n50
Alaska, 126
Alaskan Natives, 207, 209
Aleuts, 104, 119
Alexander v. Sandoval (2001), 232
Alfred Mayer Co., Jones v. (1968), 149–50
Allen v. State Board of Elections (1969), 173
alliance, color-blind: alliance, race-conscious *versus*, 110; basics, 7–14, 112–16, 255–60t, 269, 281, 285–86; and Democrats, 227 (*see also* Obama *this entry*); and economic alignments, 116, 258–59t; and foundations, 121, 315n93; and morality, 33, 112, 122–23; and Obama, 7–8, 132–35, 165, 285, 288; and polarization, 11, 112–16, 284–85; and public opinion, 19; and Republicans, 10, 23, 109–10, 115, 127–28, 260, 281, 285; and results, 281, 289; and southern states, 268; and U.S. Supreme Court, 124, 126–27, 131, 166, 194, 258, 282, 291–92. *See also* alliances, modern (race-conscious) era (1978–2008); *specific issues*
alliance, race-conscious: amicus briefs, 120–32; basics, 8–14, 116, 255, 257–62t, 269, 281–82, 286; and Civil Rights Act of 1991, 130; and Democrats, 10, 31, 132–36, 227, 285, 288, 318n147; and economic alignments, 128, 258, 260, 263–64; and Latinos, 175; and polarization, 11, 111–12, 284–85; and racial profiling, 216, 217; and Republicans, 10–11, 107, 124, 162–63; and results, 290; and U.S. Congress, 120, 258; and U.S. Labor Department, 106; and U.S. Supreme Court, 29, 94–95, 107–8, 131–32, 282; and whites, 127, 132. *See also* alliances, modern (race-conscious) era (1978–2008); *specific issues*

alliances, egalitarian, 67
alliances, modern (race-conscious) era (1978–2008): basics, 8–31, 29, 88–89, 110, 207–15, 255–68, 297n54; consequences of, 268–84; and conservatives/liberals, 256, 260; and Democrats, 115, 127, 132–35, 223, 257, 258–59t, 261t, 288, 298n61; and the future, 13–14, 29, 31, 136, 284–92; and identity categories, 20–21; and Obama, 7–8, 10, 31, 132–36, 284, 285, 286; persistence of, 207–13; and Republicans, 103–4, 152, 162, 223, 298n61; and results, 282–83, 289; and southern states, 264–65; unity of, 23–28, 30; and U.S. House, 59; and U.S. Supreme Court, 19–20, 93–96. *See also* alliance, color-blind; alliance, race-conscious; alliances, racial policy; polarization; *specific issues*
alliances, racial policy, 8–31, 136, 253, 256–57, 297n54. *See also specific alliances; specific eras*
alliances, segregation (Jim Crow) era and transitions (1865–1978): background, 19th century, 10, 50–63; basics, 9, 14–16, 63–78, 254–55t, 297n54; and foundational structures, 22, 59; organizations, 65, 68t (*see also specific organizations*); and political parties, 10, 11, 82–86; and science, 56; and southern states, 205; and U.S. House, 59; and U.S. Supreme Court, 14–15, 19, 20, 60, 76–78, 80–81, 83. *See also* alliances, racial policy; alliance, segregation (Jim Crow), anti-; alliance, segregation (Jim Crow), pro-; *specific issues*
alliance, segregation (Jim Crow), anti-: basics, 9, 71–73, 78–88, 308n32; and business, 101; and Civil Rights Act of 1964, 87; and political parties, 80, 86, 88, 102; and World War II, 78–80. *See also* alliances, segregation (Jim Crow) era and transitions (1865–1978); *specific issues*
alliance, segregation (Jim Crow), pro-: basics, 26, 61, 63–72, 65t, 68t; and conservatives, 254t; and LBJ, 87, 99; and Nazism, 78. *See also* alliances, segregation (Jim Crow) era and transitions (1865–1978); *specific issues*

alliances, slavery era (1787–1865): basics, 3–4, 8–9, 35–40, 253–55, 297n54; and Civil War, 39–40, 50; and Declaration of Independence, 35; and foundational structures, 22; and political parties, 10, 11, 39t; and U.S. Constitution, 36, 46–47, 48. *See also* alliances, racial policy; alliance, slavery, anti-; alliance, slavery, pro-; *specific issues*

alliance, slavery, anti-, 35–37, 40–51, 56, 237, 253–54t. *See also* alliances, slavery era (1787–1865)

alliance, slavery, pro-, 35–36, 37–40, 43–44, 45–46, 48, 253–54t. *See also* alliances, slavery era (1787–1865); slavery

Allied Educational Foundation, 233

Allwright, Smith v. (1944), 81

Amar, Akhil, 36

AMEA (Association of Multiethnic Americans), 206, 260t

American Advertising Council, 154t

American Anthropological Association, 75

American Anti-Slavery Society, 41t, 43, 56, 254t

American Apartheid (Massey and Denton), 150

American Atheists, 200t, 262t

American Civil Liberties Union. *See* ACLU

American Civil Rights Institute, 130

American Enterprise Institute (AEI), 188, 209t, 224t, 242t, 259t, 262t

American Equal Rights Association, 56

American Federation of Labor, 56. *See also* AFL-CIO

American Federation of Teachers (AFT), 150, 155t, 193

American Immigration Council, 242t, 262t

American Immigration Law Foundation, 343n112

American Indians. *See* Native Americans

American International Group (AIG), 166

American Jewish Congress, 186

American Negro Labor Congress, 72

American Savings and Loan League, 122

American School of Ethnology, 39t, 254t

Americans for Religious Liberty, 200t, 262t

American Society for Personnel Administration, 126

American Society of Ap...

Ameriquest Mortgage C... 320n14

amicus briefs, 109, 120... 297n54, 342n112

Amistad (ship), 48

anger, 6–8, 284, 288

Anglo-Saxons, 38

antebellum period, 2... 302n30. *See also* a... (1787–1865)

Anthony, Susan B., ...

Anti-Discriminatior... York, 137, 142

Anti-Drug Abuse A...

anti-peonage law (...

anti-slavery moven...

anti-tax uprisings, ...

Anti-Terrorism an... Act of 1996 (A...

apartheid, 65

apprenticeships, ...

"Are Emily and ... Lakisha and ... Labor Marke... and Mullain...

Arizona, 234–... *vidual Arizo...*

Arkansas, 14, ... *individual* ...

Arlington He... Developm...

armed servic... action, 10... of 1991, ... employn... housing... 146, 148

Armey, Di...

arms (gu...

Articles o...

artisans, ...

Ashcroft,

Asian Ar... firma... ern, ... 120–

sian American groups and leaders (*cont.*)
and immigration, 248, 343n112; and
vouchers, 201, 202, 206
sian American Justice Center, 127
sian American Legal Defense Fund, 118t,
120, 122, 125, 212, 225t, 242t, 261t; and
identity categories, 210t
ian Americans: and census, 207; and employment, 98, 104, 119; housing statistics,
143–44, 157; and identity categories, 209;
and minority businesses, 115; office holders,
70; and vouchers, 199. *See also* Asian
American groups and leaders
n Americans for an Accurate Count, 212
n Caucus House, 247
n immigrants, 239
ns, 66, 76, 85
ciated General Contractors of America,
1
iated Specialty Contractors, 126
iation of General Contractors, 124
iation of Multiethnic Americans
MEA), 206, 260t
iation of Southern Women for the Pre-
tion of Lynching, 71
a Exposition Address (B. Washington),
61
c Legal Foundation, 131
, *Wards Cobe Packing Co. v.* (1989),

dacity of Hope (Obama), 5, 133,
93

Black Alliance for Educational Op-
, 201
University of California Board of
ts v. (1978), 10, 282
d Budget Act of 1997, 344n127
ounts, 275–76
e specific banks
lla, 84
hael S., 325n82
rion, 85
Strickland (2009), 186, 187
atherine, 339n36
Ruth, 75
loyd, 325n87

Berry, Halle, 213
Bertrand, Marianne, 312n14
Biddle, Francis, 15
Biden, Joe, 230, 332n4
bilingual education, 237
biological differences, 20
Birth of a Nation (film), 66
Black, Hugo, 172, 173
Black Alliance for Educational Options
(BAEO), 201
Black and Blue: African Americans, the Labor
Movement and the Decline of the Demo-
cratic Party (Frymer), 311n6
black capitalism, 107
Black Caucus, Congressional, 119
Black Codes, 51, 67
black groups. *See* African American groups
and leaders
Black legislators
Black Panthers, 101
blacks. *See* African Americans
blacks, free, 38
Blaine, James G., 55
"blockbusting," 322n56
block grants, 137–38
Board of Education I and II, Brown v. (1954,
1955), 9, 18, 19, 83–84
Boas, Franz, 66, 75
Bob Jones University v. U.S. (1983), 333n15
Bolden, Mobile v. (1980), 175, 176
Bolick, Clint, 114
Bollinger, Gratz v. (2003), 109, 282
Bollinger, Grutter v. (2003), 109, 282
Bolton, Susan, 235
Bonastia, Chris, 151, 323n67
Bonilla, Henry, 190
Booker, U.S. v. (2005), 233
Booth, John Wilkes, 51
border states, 41t
Boren, David, 325n87
Bork, Robert, 323n56
Bossier Parish School Board, Reno v. (2000),
186
Bradley, Bill, 201, 259t
Bradley, Joseph, 11, 57–58
Brandwein, Pamela, 305n84
Brazil, 299n1

Brennan, William, 121, 124, 131, 180
Brewer, Jan, 234, 235, 236–37
Brock, William, 124
Brooke, Edward, 120
Brotherhood of Sleeping Car Porters, 72
Brown, Henry Billings, 60, 63
Brownfield v. South Carolina (1903), 309n50
Brown v. Board of Education I and II
    (1954,1955), 9, 18, 19, 83–84
Bryant, John, 241t
Buchanan, James, 49
Buchanan, Pat, 241t
Buchanan v. Warley (1917), 77, 144, 307n14
Buckley, Corrigan v. (1926), 77, 144
Bureau of Indian Affairs, 56
Burger, Warren, 108
Bush, George H.: and alliance, race-conscious,
    285; and crime, 230, 232; and employ-
    ment, 129; and housing, 160, 161–63; and
    majority-minority districts, 182, 187; racial
    policies, 128; and U.S. Supreme Court,
    185; and vouchers, 197
Bush, George W.: and alliance, race-conscious,
    285; and housing/mortgages, 141, 162–63,
    164t; and immigration, 248; and voting
    rights, 163, 188, 189; and vouchers, 193,
    202
Bush v. Vera (1996), 186, 187
business: and alliance, color-blind, 259t; and
    alliances, modern, 11, 257; and alliance,
    race-conscious, 102, 105, 106, 108–9, 124,
    128, 261t; and alliances, segregation era,
    65, 68t, 144, 254t; and alliances, slavery
    era, 253t, 254t; and Chinese immigration,
    56; and civil rights, 130, 260t; and crime,
    224t, 260t; and diversity, 124; and EEOC,
    101; and employment, 98, 100, 117t, 118t,
    121, 122, 128, 131, 262; and housing, 144,
    154t, 158, 161; and immigration, 240, 242t,
    243, 245, 246, 262t; and multiracialism,
    208; and Title VII enforcement, 104; and
    voting rights, 178t; and vouchers, 194, 197,
    198t, 199. See also commerce, interstate
    and foreign; industrialists/manufacturers;
    minority-owned small businesses; specific
    corporations; specific employer groups and
    leaders

busing, forced, 114, 115
Byrd, Harry, 73
Byrd, Robert, 160, 221, 234
Byrnes, James, 81

California: and education, 130, 282; and em-
    ployment, 100, 127; and housing, 139; and
    immigration, 54, 56, 66, 245; and majority-
    minority districts, 176, 181, 183t, 185,
    330n46; and taxes, 10, 116; and vouchers,
    199, 201. See also individual Californians
California Correctional Officers' Association,
    121
Cantu, Norma V., 211
capital punishment, 230
Carter, Jimmy, 120, 158, 159, 195, 285
Carter v. Texas (1900), 309n50
categories, racial. See identity categories;
    specific categories
Catholic groups: and alliance, color-blind,
    259t; and alliance, race-conscious, 261t;
    and housing, 150, 155t; and immigration,
    242, 244t, 343n112; and majority-minority
    districts, 178t; and vouchers, 196, 197, 198t,
    202. See also specific groups
Catholic Legal Immigration Network,
    343n112
Catholic schools, 194
Cato Institute, 117t, 154t, 202, 209t, 242t,
    259t, 262t
CCC (Civilian Conservation Corps), 26, 74
CDBGs (Community Development Block
    Grants), 137–38, 146t
census: and alliances, modern, 13, 203–13,
    258, 260t, 262t; and alliances, segregation
    era, 205; basics, 13, 30, 203–7, 284; and
    conservatism, 208–9t, 212, 214; and hous-
    ing, 168; and identity categories, 203–7,
    213–14; and majority-minority districts,
    180, 187, 188; and vouchers, 203–5
Center for Constitutional Rights, 180, 232,
    233
Center for Equal Opportunity, 188, 232
Center for Individual Rights, 117t, 126, 259t
Centers for Disease Control, 207
Century Foundation, 200t
Chafee, John, 179

change, 26–27

Change to Win, 242t

character conservatism, 248, 267, 269, 283, 284. *See also* morality

charter schools, 193, 203, 332n4

Chen, Anthony, 99

Chesapeake and Ohio Railway Co., Chiles v. (1910), 297n51

Chiles v. Chesapeake and Ohio Railway Co. (1910), 297n51

Chinese Exclusion Act of 1882, 238

Chinese immigration, 25, 51, 54–57, 76, 238, 307n14

Christian Right groups, 117t, 198t, 333n15

Christians: alliances, slavery era, 36, 37, 40; and alliances, modern, 268; and alliances, segregation era, 65; economic alignments, 267, 268; and education, 334n16; and immigration, 235; and vouchers, 197. *See also* religion; *individual Christians; specific groups*

Chubb, John, 196

CIO, 72. *See also* AFL-CIO

citizenship, 47, 49, 67–69, 73, 76, 343n121. *See also* immigration; *specific rights*

Citizenship and Immigration Services, 247

Citizenship without Consent: The Illegal Alien in the American Polity (Schuck and R.M. Smith), 343n121

Civilian Conservation Corps (CCC), 26, 74

civil rights: and alliances, modern, 27, 130, 221, 260t, 262t, 285; and alliances, segregation era, 25, 72, 81–83, 255; antebellum era, 23; and crime, 218–20, 229–34; and foundational structures, 22; and identity categories, 210, 211; and immigration, 236, 244–45, 246; and Obama, 8; and political parties, 27, 72, 83–84; and World War II, 79. *See also* civil rights movement; discrimination; *specific legislation; specific rights*

Civil Rights Act of 1866, 51, 57, 124, 150, 322n39

Civil Rights bill of 1871 (Ku Klux Klan Act), 52

Civil Rights Act of 1874, 53–54

Civil Rights Act of 1875, 58

Civil Rights Act of 1957, 3–4, 85

Civil Rights Act of 1964: and alliances, modern, 9; and alliances, segregation era, 87; basics, 311n91; and business, 87, 100; and crime, 232; and education, 333n15; and employment, 93, 95–97, 100–112, 121, 124; and federal funding (Title VI), 125, 126; and housing, 139, 148, 319n1; and political parties, 87–88, 115, 123, 125, 311n94; and voting rights, 170–71. *See also* Title VII

Civil Rights Act of 1968, 145t, 149

Civil Rights Act of 1991, 128–30

Civil Rights bill (Ku Klux Klan Act) (1871), 52

Civil Rights Cases (1883), 58

Civil Rights Division, U.S. Department of Justice, 163–64

civil rights movement, 9–10, 96, 110, 113–14, 123–24, 171, 219, 266, 267. *See also individual leaders*

Civil Rights Section, Justice Department, 80–81, 85

Civil Service Commission of the City of New York, Guardians Association v. (1983), 125

Civil War, 37, 39–40, 50

classes, economic, 63–64, 137, 142, 143–44, 256, 265, 266–68. *See also* economic structures; poverty

Clay, Henry, 11

Cleveland, Grover, 59

Clinton, William J.: and affirmative action, 115–16; and alliance, race-conscious, 130, 285; and crime, 231–32; and employment, 131; and housing/mortgages, 141, 161–62, 164t; and immigration, 246; and majority-minority districts, 187; and vouchers, 197, 201

coalition building, 22, 23, 290

Coalition for Economic Equity, 131

cocaine, 217–19, 218, 338n10. *See also* drugs

Cohen, Marty, 298n61

cold war, 78–79

Colorado, 130

commerce, interstate and foreign, 22, 36, 42, 47, 48, 87, 296n51. *See also Mitchell v. United States et al.* (1941); *Morgan v. Virginia* (1946)

Index

Committee on Economic Security, 74, 75

Committee on Equal Employment Opportunity (J. Kennedy), 100

Common Cause, 178t, 187–88, 261t

Commons, John R., 66

communism/Communist Party, 72, 77, 78, 79, 85, 86, 122

communitarians, 122

community, 287–88

Community Development and Financial Institutions Act of 1994, 162, 164t

Community Development Block Grants (CDBGs), 137–38, 146t

Community Reinvestment Acts, 141, 142, 146t, 159, 162

Comprehensive Crime Control Acts, 229

Cone, James Hal, 5

Confederate States of America, 49

Confederation Congress, 35

Congress. *See* U.S. Congress

Congressional Asian Pacific American Caucus, 131

Congressional Black Caucus, 119, 131, 165, 225t, 230, 231, 240, 262

Congressional Hispanic Caucus, 165, 240, 242t

Congress of Industrial Organization, 72

Congress on Racial Equality (CORE), 85, 171

Connally, Green v. (1971), 333n15

Connecticut, 36–37, 48, 93–96, 289

Connerly, Ward, 130

Connor, Eugene "Bull," 86

consequences of policies, 13–14, 111, 177, 269–70, 281–84, 288–91

conservatism: and the future, 291; and alliances, modern, 258–62t, 263, 285, 286; and alliances, segregation era, 25, 52, 65t, 80, 85, 86, 87, 254t; basics, 14, 25, 356nn30,31; and morality, 23, 221, 248, 267; and Republican Party, 319n7; southern, 264; and U.S. Congress, 264, 265; and U.S. Supreme Court, 19, 109, 333n15. *See also specific issues*

Constitution. *See* U.S. Constitution

construction industry, 105, 124

Continental Congress, 3

"contract labor," 51

"Contract with America," 130

Conyers, John, 212, 230

CORE (Congress on Racial Equality), 85, 171

"Cornerstone Speech" (Stephens), 49

Corrigan v. Buckley (1926), 77, 144

Cote, Denise, 137–42

cotton gin, 38

Coulter, Ann, 141, 154t, 259t

Count Every Vote Act, 190

courts and judges: and affirmative action in work, 118t; and alliance, color-blind, 122, 259t; and alliances, modern, 258; and alliance, race-conscious, 261t; and alliances, segregation era, 60, 65, 67, 68t, 76, 84, 254t, 305n84; and alliances, slavery era, 41t; antebellum, 47–48; and crime, 224t, 225t, 232, 235; and desegregation, 272; and egalitarianism, 57; and employment, 94, 108, 117t, 124; and housing, 150, 152, 154t; and immigration, 245; and majority-minority districts, 169, 173, 182, 185; and 1956 Republican platform, 84; and slavery era, 253t; and voting rights, 178t; and vouchers, 198t, 200t. *See also* U.S. Supreme Court; *individual judges*

Crack-Cocaine Equitable Sentencing Act of 2009, 218, 338n10

craft manufacturers, 41t

Cranston-Gonzalez National Affordable Housing Act of 1990, 164t

"Credit Where It Counts: The Community Reinvestment Act and Its Critics" (Barr), 325n82

crime: and alliance, color-blind, 218, 221, 224t, 226, 227, 231, 232, 233, 234, 260t, 291; and alliances, modern, 13, 215–34, 241–49; and alliance, race-conscious, 11, 225t, 230, 232, 234, 235, 262t, 291; and alliances, segregation era, 66, 77, 215–23, 234; and alliances, slavery era, 229; after civil rights, 218–20, 229–34; and cocaine, 217–19; and Communist Party, 77; and conservatives, 220, 221, 224t, 226, 227, 229, 232–33, 284, 291; and immigration, 247; and NAACP, 77; and Obama, 8,

crime (*cont.*)
216–17; popular opinion, 339n36; prison populations, 227, 228, 231, 233, 277, 279t, 284, 291, 339n36; Reagan shift, 223–29; and 20th century political platforms, 64; and U.S. Congress, 228–34, 246. *See also* lynching
Crime Control Act of 1990, 230
Criminal Justice Legal Foundation, 232
criminal records, 98
Crowley, James, 216
Cruikshank, U.S. v. (1876), 57
Cuban Americans, 184
Cuban immigrants, 245
Cuomo, Andrew, 141

Darwin, Charles, 56
Davis, Tom, 202
Dawson, William, 26, 27
Day, William, 60
death penalty, 228, 230, 231–32, 233, 246
Declaration of Independence, 35, 46, 76
DeCuir, Hall v. (1877), 296n51
Degler, Carl, 78
Democratic Party: and affirmative action, 10–12, 133, 162; and African American voters, 27, 171, 263; and alliance, color-blind, 10, 109–10, 127, 227; and alliances, modern, 115, 127, 132–35, 223, 255, 257, 258, 259t, 261t, 262–66, 288, 298n61; and alliance, race-conscious, 227; and alliances, segregation era, 26, 51, 53, 54, 68t, 72, 147, 254t, 255; and alliances, slavery era, 10, 11, 39t; and anti-lynching bills, 70, 71; background, 19th century, 50, 54, 55, 58; and census, 206; and civil rights, 81–82, 221; and Civil Rights Acts, 85, 115, 125, 128–29; and crime, 218, 220, 222–23, 224t, 225t, 226, 227, 229, 231, 233, 239, 257; and death penalty, 230; and education, 83, 84, 109–10, 115, 290, 315n80; and employment, 98, 99, 100, 103–7, 109–10, 117t, 118t, 125, 127–28, 131, 132–36, 223, 258; and housing, 137–43, 147–53 *passim*, 154–55t, 158–59, 160–62 *passim*, 163–67, 258, 325n86; and identity categories, 202, 208, 209t, 210t, 211; and immigration, 64, 70, 82, 238–48; and majority-minority districts, 169, 182, 184–89; and NAACP, 24, 82; and northern states, 72, 266; and policies, 10; and quotas, 10, 88, 102, 106, 109–10, 114–16, 120, 129, 131, 159, 220; and religion, 80, 82, 287–88; and schools, 315n80; and slavery era, 46, 48; and southern states, 72, 77, 81, 82, 263, 266; and U.S. Supreme Court, 19; and voting rights, 59, 84, 175, 178t, 190; and vouchers, 193–94, 195–96, 197, 198t, 199, 201, 202; and white supremacy, 63; and women's suffrage, 56; and World War II, 79. *See also* Democratic Party platforms; political parties; U.S. Congress; *individual Democrats especially Presidents*
Democratic Party platforms: 1900–1930 platforms, 64; 'thirties, 73, 78; 'forties, 79, 80, 82, 99, 147; 'fifties, 83, 84; 'sixties, 86, 87–88, 102, 149, 172–73, 220, 222, 239; 'seventies, 109–10, 114–15, 120, 151, 153, 239; 'eighties, 115, 153, 175, 179, 195, 222–23, 226, 240; 'nineties, 115–16, 162, 179, 197, 226, 315n80; 2000–2008 platforms, 190, 203, 226, 247
Democratic Socialists, 178t
Denton, Nancy, 150
Departments of U.S. Government. *See entries beginning* U.S. Department of . . .
the Depression, 26, 71
DePriest, Oscar, 26, 72
Descent of Man (Darwin), 56
desegregation, 83–84, 86, 284, 311n6. *See also* integration; segregation
DeStefano, Ricci v. (2009), 93–94, 130, 132, 135, 136
Development, Relief and Education for Alien Minors Act (DREAM), 248
Dillingham Commission, 66
Dirksen, Everett, 149, 239
disabilities, 163
discrimination: and alliances, modern, 282–83; and alliances, segregation era, 66–67; and Democrats, 80; and economic alliances, 156, 283; and employment, 97; and federal government, 158; and housing, 143, 153, 157; Obama on, 7; and political

parties, 64; and U.S. Supreme Court, 77, 125. *See also* civil rights; racism; segregation

disfranchisement, 50, 60, 66, 77

"disparate impact": and alliance, color-blind, 281; and G.W. Bush, 163; and Civil Rights Act of 1991, 129–30; and crime, 218, 227, 228, 229, 232, 234; and death penalty, 230; and employment, 93–94, 95, 123, 124–25; 126; and housing, 152, 160, 163; and voting rights, 175, 180

"disparate treatment," 101

districting. *See* majority-minority districts

District of Columbia: and alliances, slavery era, 43, 45, 46, 301n28; desegregation of, 84; and education, 193, 197, 201, 202; and enfranchisement, 51; and housing, 322n39

diversity: and alliances, modern, 13, 108, 281–82, 283; and business, 121, 124; and census, 203; and individualism, 113; and Republicans, 114, 280–81; and U.S. Supreme Court, 282. *See also* unity

Divided by Color: Racial Politics and Democratic Ideals (Kinder and Sanders), 298n56

Dixiecrats, 82, 264

Dixon, Frank, 24

Dixon, Thomas, 66

Dobbin, Frank, 128

Doe, Plyler v. (1982), 245

DOJ. *See* U.S. Department of Justice

Donovan, Raymond, 124

Douglas, Stephen, 11

Douglass, Frederick, 24–25

DREAM (Development, Relief and Education for Alien Minors Act), 248

Dreams from My Father (Obama), 287–88

Dred Scott decision, 47, 49

Druckman, James N., 298n60

Drug Abuse, Prevention, Treatment and Rehabilitation Act (1980), 229

drugs, 228, 233. *See also* cocaine

Du Bois, W.E.B., 69, 72

due process clause, 49

Duke, David, 129

Duke Power Co., Griggs v. (1971), 108

Duncan, Arne, 193

Dunmore, Lord (John Murray), 35

Dunn v. Midwestern Indemnity (1980), 323n56

Durbin, Dick, 193

Dyer, Leonidas, 70, 71, 82

Dyer bill, 70, 72

Eagle Forum Education and Legal Defense Fund, 232

East, John, 177

Eastland, James, 239

economic alignments: and alliance, color-blind, 116, 258–59t; and alliance, race conscious, 128, 258, 260, 263–64; and alliances, modern, 11, 27–28, 116, 255–56, 258, 285–86; and alliances, segregation era, 73; and alliances, slavery era, 255; and discrimination, 156, 283; institutions *versus*, 17, 18; Obama's, 165; and racial ideologies, 27–28, 38–39, 256, 258, 263–68; and results, 289; southern states, 256, 264, 268. *See also* economic classes; economic structures; morality; taxes; *specific policy issues*

economic classes, 63–64, 137, 142, 143–44, 256, 265, 266–68. *See also* economic structures; poverty

Economic Policy Institute, 144

economic structures, 22, 280. *See also* business; economic alignments; economic classes

education: affirmative action results, 290, 294n30; and African Americans, 12–13, 269, 270–71, 272t, 273t, 274t, 333n9; and alliance, color-blind, 12–13, 258; and alliances, modern, 31, 237, 258, 262, 284, 290; and alliance, race-conscious, 10–11, 13, 258, 282; and alliances, segregation era, 60, 66, 75; and armed forces, 128; and conservatism, 109; and Democrats, 83, 84, 109–10, 115, 290, 315n80; and desegregation, 270, 272, 274t; and housing, 324n77; and identity categories, 109, 192, 237; and immigration, 245, 247, 248; and majority-minority districts, 330n46; and northern states, 42; and Republicans, 53, 83, 84, 86, 114–15, 130; separate but equal, 60, 78, 83, 107, 270; and U.S. Supreme Court, 78, 83–84, 195, 282, 333n15, 334n16. *See also* affirmative action; quotas; vouchers, school

Edwards, Don, 325n84
efficacy of policies, 13–14, 269–70, 281, 284,
    288–91
egalitarianism: and alliances, segregation era,
    9, 51–59, 63, 67, 69; and alliances, slavery
    era, 36–37, 40–41, 47, 50; and immigra-
    tion, 25; and politcal parties, 50, 52, 53–54,
    55, 58. *See also* equality
Eisenhower, Dwight D., 83, 100
elections. *See* voting rights
Emergency Economic Stabilization Act, 165
empirical evidence, 12, 13–14, 30, 111,
    288–91, 295n30. *See also* results of policies
employment: and alliance, color-blind, 96,
    110–14, 117t, 121, 125–26, 130–32, 258,
    259t; and alliances, modern, 30, 93–107,
    112–36, 258, 262, 283; and alliance, race-
    conscious, 10, 96–98, 104–7, 110–21, 114,
    121–24, 128, 132–36, 258, 261t, 281–82;
    and alliances, segregation era, 66, 75, 79,
    84, 96, 98–100, 99, 104; amicus briefs, 109,
    120–22; and armed services leaders, 261t;
    background, 93–101; broader language,
    110–12; and conservatism, 99, 101, 102,
    103–4, 106, 108, 117t, 121–26; and courts,
    258; and Democrats, 98, 99, 100, 103–7,
    109–10, 117t, 118t, 125, 126–28, 127, 131,
    132–36, 223, 258; and economic align-
    ments, 116–19, 123; enforcement, 100,
    101–3; and Fair Employment Practices
    Committee (FEPC) (Roosevelt), 73, 79–80,
    82, 86, 98–99; and federal government, 84,
    96, 105, 107, 121; and housing, 153; and
    identity categories, 205; inequalities, 95,
    96–98, 101, 269, 278t; and NAACP, 75;
    narrowing, 124–27; and polarization,
    112–16; and political parties, 52, 81, 83,
    84, 86, 122–32, 163, 223; set-aside employ-
    ment, 119–20; and U.S. Supreme Court,
    107–10, 117t, 120–22, 124–25, 126,
    130–32, 289, 311n6. *See also* affirmative
    action; labor; quotas
Employment Opportunity Committee
    (Kennedy), 100
The End of Southern Exceptionalism (Shafer
    and Johnston), 263–64
Enforcement Act (1870), 124

enfranchisement, 50–51, 52, 53, 54, 55, 58,
    59, 64. *See also* majority-minority districts;
    voting rights; *specific legislation*
E Pluribus Unum, 3, 31, 134, 135. *See also*
    diversity; unity
Equal Employment Advisory Council, 117t,
    121–22, 124–25, 126, 259t
Equal Employment Opportunity Commission
    (EEOC): and alliance, race-conscious, 129;
    and alliances, segregation era, 96; and dis-
    parate impact, 108, 123; and employment,
    111; and identity categories, 205, 207, 213;
    and political parties, 123, 125, 127; and
    Title VII, 100–104
Equal Employment Opportunity programs,
    115
equality: and alliances, segregation era, 49,
    50, 67; and economic structures, 280; and
    empirical evidence, 14; and polarization,
    13; and political parties, 11–12, 80, 86; and
    women's rights, 56. *See also* egalitarianism
Equality in Enterprise Opportunities, 131
equal opportunity, 86, 114, 115. *See also*
    affirmative action; Equal Employment
    Opportunity Commission (EEOC)
equal protection, 60, 94, 152, 175, 186, 187,
    282, 321n39. *See also* U.S. Constitution:
    Fourteenth Amendment
Ervin, Sam, 106, 239
Eskimos, 104, 119
ethnicity. *See* identity categories; *specific
    ethnicities*
eugenics, 305n78
European immigrants, 254t
evolution, 66. *See also* Darwin, Charles

FAIR, 241t, 260t, 343n112
Fair, T. Willard, 260t
Fair Employment Board, 100
Fair Employment Practices Committee
    (FEPC) (Roosevelt), 73, 79–80, 82, 86,
    96, 98–99
fair housing. *See* housing
Fair Housing Act of 1968, 139, 145t, 149,
    150, 152, 159, 163, 319n1
Fair Housing Amendments Act of 1988, 160,
    164t

Fair Housing Assistance Program, 163
Fair Housing Council, 162, 164t
Fair Housing Laws, 115. *See also* Fair
    Housing Act of 1968
False Claims Act, 137
Family Research Council, 117t, 259t
Fannie Mae, 141, 154t, 162, 164t
Farhang, Sean, 103, 311n91
Farmer, James, 84–85
farmers, 41t, 52, 66
Farm Security and Rural Investment Act of
    2002, 344n127
Fascism, 78
Faubus, Orval, 84
FCC, Metro Broadcasting, Inc. v. (1990), 131
Federal Council of Churches, 82
federal funding: and civil rights, 125, 126; and
    education, 332n4; and housing/mortgages,
    74, 144–45t, 146–48, 153, 156, 158, 160,
    163, 289–90; and immigrants, 344n127; of
    minority-owned small businesses, 114–15,
    119. *See also specific agencies and programs*
federal government: and alliances, racial pol-
    icy, 23; and alliances, segregation era, 65,
    73, 144–45t, 146–47, 254t; and alliances,
    slavery era, 255; and discrimination, 64;
    and education, 336n58; and employment,
    84, 96, 105, 107, 121; and identity cate-
    gories, 205; and immigration, 242t; and
    labor unions, 66, 107; and racism, 66; and
    voting rights, 178t. *See also entries starting
    U.S. . . .;* federal funding; *specific agencies,
    branches, legislation, officials and programs*
Federal Home Loan Bank Board, 146
Federal Housing Administration (FHA), 26,
    145t, 146–47, 151, 155t, 160, 164t
Federal Interagency Committee on Edu-
    cation, 205
Federalists, 10, 37, 39t, 41t, 131, 253t
Federal Reserve, 139, 207
federal subsidies, 160
Ferguson, Plessy v. (1896), 20–21, 60
FHA (Federal Housing Administration), 26,
    145t, 146–47, 151, 155t, 160, 164t
50 percent minority ownership (MBEs),
    119–20
filibusters, 59, 85

Filipinos, 66
financial crisis of 2007, 138, 144. *See also*
    mortgages: subprime
Financial Institutions Reform, Recovery, and
    Enforcement Act of 1989, 164t
Fish, Hamilton, 155t, 161, 261t
Fitzsimons, Thomas, 37
Fletcher, Arthur, 105, 107, 210
Florida, 59, 172, 182, 183t, 184, 188, 309n50,
    325n86, 330n46
Florida, Tarrance v. (1903), 309n50
Focus on the Family, 198t, 259t
Food and Drug Administration, 207
forced labor, 50, 51
Ford Foundation, 155t, 160, 200t, 261t
Foreign Assistance Act of 1983, 120
foreign governments, 48
foreign policy, 86, 88. *See also* commerce,
    interstate and foreign
Forrester, Elijah, 219–20
Fortune, Thomas, 69
foundational structures, 22–23, 30, 59, 192,
    258
foundations, charitable: and alliances, mod-
    ern, 259t, 261t; and alliances, segregation
    era, 73, 255t; and crime, 225t; and employ-
    ment, 117t, 118t, 121, 315n93; and hous-
    ing, 154t, 155t, 160; and immigration, 242t;
    and majority-minority districts, 188; and
    multiracialism, 208; and voting rights, 178t;
    and vouchers, 198t, 200t, 202. *See also
    specific foundations*
"Framing Public Opinion in Competitive
    Democracies" (Druckman), 298n60
franchise. *See* enfranchisement
Franklin, Benjamin, 3, 37
Franklin v. South Carolina (1910), 309n50
Freddie Mac, 141, 146t, 154t, 164t
free blacks, 38, 42, 47
Freedmen's Bureau, 51, 53, 304n55
free labor, 40, 41, 47, 57
Free Soil Democrats, 41t, 47, 253t
free states, 42, 45, 48. *See also* northern states
Fremont Investment and Loan of Brea,
    320n14
Friedman, Milton, 195
Friedman Foundation, 202

From the New Deal to the New Right: Race and the Southern Origins of Modern Conservatism (Lowndes), 346n31
Frymer, Paul, 108, 311n6
Fullilove v. Kultznick (1980), 121–22

Gallegly, Edward, 241t
GAO (U.S. Government Accountability Office), 163
Garrison, William Lloyd, 24–25, 43
Garvey, Marcus, 72
Gates, Henry Louis, 216, 235
Gautreaux, Hills v. (1976), 323n56
General Building Contractors Association v. Pennsylvania (1982), 124
George, Henry, 54, 184
Georgia, 172, 180, 182, 183t, 186, 187, 325nn86,87, 330n46
Georgia v. Ashcroft (2003), 186, 187, 188
gerrymandering, 187
Gibbs, Robert, 29, 204
GI forum, 148
Giles, J, 60–61
Giles v. Harris (1903), 60, 61
Giles v. Teasley (1904), 60, 61
Gingles, Thornburg v. (1986), 180, 181, 182, 190
Gingrich, Newt, 130, 184, 211–12, 213
Ginsburg, Ruth Bader, 95
Gladstone, Realtors, v. Village of Bellwood (1979), 324n71
Goldwater, Barry, 87, 195, 220, 239, 263
"good faith," 103, 105–6
GOP. *See* Republican Party
Gottschalk, Marie, 219, 230
governmental structures, 22. *See also specific structures*
Government Contract Employees' Association, 121
Graetz, Michael, 315n81
Graham, Hugh Davis, 110, 117, 160
Graham, Strader v. (1851), 48–49
Grant, Madison, 66, 70
Grant, Ulysses, 52
grants, block, 137–38, 319n1
Gratz v. Bollinger (2003), 109, 282
Great Society, 107, 239

Green v. Connally (1971), 333n15
Griggs v. Duke Power Co. (1971), 108
Grofman, Bernhard, 182
Groves v. Slaughter (1841), 48
Grovey v. Townsend (1935), 77
Grutter v. Bollinger (2003), 109, 282
Guardians Association v. Civil Service Commission of the City of New York (1983), 125
guns (arms), 221, 223, 230, 231

habeas corpus, 23
Habeas Corpus Act of 1842, 48
Hadassah, 200t
Haden v. Pataki (2006), 232
Haiti, 245
Hall, Holder v. (1994), 186
Hall v. DeCuir (1877), 296n51
Handley, Lisa, 182
Harding, Warren G., 70
Harlan, John Marshall, 25, 68t, 173, 254t
Harris, Giles v. (1903), 60, 61
Harrison, Benjamin, 59
Hatch, Orrin, 159–60, 161, 177, 201
Hatfield, Mark, 201
HAVA (Help America Vote Act), 188, 190
Hawaiian Natives, 207, 209
Hawkins, Augustus, 106
Hayes, Rutherford, 55
health and health care, 13, 75, 120, 276–77. *See also* Medicaid
Heflin, Howell, 325n87
Height, Dorothy, 85, 86
Helms, Jesse, 177
Help America Vote Act (HAVA), 188, 190
Henderson, Wade, 138, 248
Heritage Foundation, 154t, 198t, 233, 259t
Highway Improvement Act of 1982, 120
Hills v. Gautreaux (1976), 323n56
Hispanic National Bar Association, 343n112
Hispanics. *See* Latinos
Hoar, George F., 25, 55, 63. *See also* Radical Republicans
Hochschild, Jennifer, 11–12, 213, 285
HOLC (Home Owners' Loan Corporation), 145t, 146
Holder v. Hall (1994), 186
Hollinger, David, 207–8

Holmes Jr., Oliver Wendell, 60, 63
Home Owners' Loan Corporation (HOLC),
  145t, 146
Hoover, Herbert, 146
HOPE VI, 323n67
Horton, Willie, 230
House of Representatives. *See* U.S. House of
  Representatives
housing: and alliance, color-blind, 138, 154t,
  163, 165, 166–67; and alliances, modern,
  11, 137–50, 153–59, 164t, 258, 259t, 261t;
  and alliance, race-conscious, 138–39, 142,
  151, 153, 155t, 156, 158, 159, 165, 166,
  167; and alliances, segregation era, 65–66,
  143–51; and conservatives, 154t, 156, 159,
  160, 162; and Democrats, 137–43, 147–53
  passim, 154–55t, 158–59, 160–62 *passim*,
  163–67, 258, 325n86; economic alignments, 156, 157, 167; and education,
  324n77; federal funding, 144–45t, 146–48,
  153, 156, 158, 160, 163, 289–90, 319n1;
  inequalities, 13, 75, 138–39, 143–50, 157,
  295n35; and Latino groups, 258; and A.
  Mitchell, 26; and Republicans, 86, 150–53,
  159–63; restrictive covenants, 77; and
  Social Security Act of 1935, 74, 75; and
  U.S. Supreme Court, 307n14, 322nn39,56,
  324n71. *See also* mortgages; *specific*
  legislation
Housing Act of 1961, 145t
Housing Advocates, Inc., 155t, 261t
Housing and Community Development Act
  of 1974, 146t, 151–52
Housing and Urban Development, U.S. De-
  partment of (HUD). *See* U.S. Department
  of Housing and Urban Development
  (HUD)
Housing and Urban Development Act of
  1968, 145t
Houston, Charles, 78
Howard University, 103
HSBC Holdings subsidiaries, 139
HUD. *See* U.S. Department of Housing and
  Urban Development
Huddleston, Walter, 325n87
Hughes, Charles Evans, 15–16, 27
Humphrey, Hubert, 102

Husock, Howard, 138
Hussey, Zuch v. (1975), 322n56

ideas, 21, 192, 298n60
identity categories: and alliance, color-blind,
  208–9, 211–12, 213–14, 337n78; and alliances, modern, 207–8, 337n78; and alliance, race-conscious, 102, 108, 204, 206,
  208–14, 337n78; and alliances, racial policy, 20–22; and alliances, segregation era,
  21, 205, 308n32; and alliances, slavery era,
  21; and economic classes, 142, 153; and
  education, 192, 237; and egalitarianism,
  67; and federal funding, 105; mixed race
  (multiracialism), 134, 204–5, 207, 209t,
  211–14, 337n78; and U.S. Supreme Court,
  131. *See also* census; mixed race (multiracialism); *specific categories*
"I have a dream" speech (King), 9
IIRIRA (Illegal Immigration Reform and
  Immigrant Responsibility Act of 1996),
  246–47, 344n127
Illegal Immigration Reform and Immigrant
  Responsibility Act of 1996 (IIRIRA),
  246–47, 344n127
Illinois: and crime, 216; employment policies,
  100; and housing, 139, 148, 152, 323n56,
  324n71; and majority-minority districts,
  168, 181, 183t, 185, 290, 330n46; riots, 69;
  and segregation, 27. *See also individual*
  Illinoisians
immigration: and alliance, color-blind,
  235–38, 240, 241t, 243t, 260t, 291; and
  alliances, modern, 30, 127, 234–49, 257,
  342n112; and alliance, race-conscious, 127,
  237, 240, 242t, 246, 262t, 291; and alliances, segregation era, 25, 64–67, 70, 76,
  82, 84, 238; and alliance, segregation era,
  238–39; and alliances, slavery era, 38; antebellum period, 47, 237–38; and anti-black
  votes, 39; and census, 206; Chinese, 25, 51,
  54–57, 76, 238, 307n14; and conservatism,
  70, 235, 236, 239, 240, 241–43t, 242, 244,
  245–47; and crime, 234–36, 284; and
  Democrats, 64, 70, 82, 238–48; and economic alignments, 237, 238, 239, 240,
  242t, 246, 247; and identity categories,

immigration (*cont.*)
  256–57; and integration, 280–81; and
  Obama, 234–36; and polarization, 291; and
  political parties, 88; and quotas, 66, 70, 86,
  127, 238, 239; and Republicans, 64, 70, 84,
  86; and World War II, 82
immigration acts, 238, 239, 241, 243
Immigration and Customs Enforcement
  (ICE), 247
Immigration and Naturalization Service
  (INS), 247
Immigration Reform and Control Act of 1986
  (IRCA), 241, 243
income, 13, 246, 272, 275–76. *See also* economic classes
Independent Insurance Agents of America,
  154t, 259t
Indiana, 148
individualism, 23, 111–13, 122, 125, 281, 288
industrialists/manufacturers, 39t, 40, 41t, 72,
  97, 254t. *See also* business
inequalities: and alliances, modern, 258, 283;
  basics, 6, 277, 280; contemporary data,
  269–80; and crime, 234; and Darwin, 56;
  employment, 95, 96–98, 101, 269, 278t;
  housing, 13, 138–39, 143–50, 157, 295n35;
  and Latinos, 13; and New Deal consequences, 75; and Obama, 31, 132, 133,
  135–36; and polarization, 12–13, 284. *See
  also* equality; segregation; *specific areas of
  inequality*
INS (Immigration and Naturalization Service), 247
Institute for Justice, 114, 188, 198t
institutions: and alliances, 16–19, 24, 26, 119,
  296n50; and Democrats, 26; and foundational structures, 22–23; and housing,
  299n67; and ideas, 21; and white supremacy, 63. *See also specific institutions*
integration: and alliances, segregation era, 68;
  basics, 257; and crime, 220; and housing,
  148, 158, 165–66; and identity categories,
  207–8; and political parties, 115–16, 146t,
  280–81. *See also* affirmative action; armed
  services and leadership; busing, forced;
  desegregation; education; housing
International Labor Defense organization, 77

international treaties, 48, 55
International Union of Operating Engineers,
  124
interstate commerce, 15–16, 22, 36, 42, 47,
  48, 87, 296n51. *See also Mitchell v. United
  States et al.* (1941); *Morgan v. Virginia*
  (1946)
inverse (reverse) discrimination (racism), 8,
  88, 102, 110, 125, 286. *See also* alliance,
  race-conscious
IRCA (Immigration Reform and Control Act
  of 1986), 241, 243
IRS, 195, 333n15
Islamic immigrants, 245
Islamic radicals, 122

Jackson, Andrew, 48
Jackson, Jesse, 166, 189, 212–13
Jackson, Robert, 15, 81
Jackson Board of Education, Wygant v. (1986),
  311n5
Jacksonian Democrats, 10, 46, 253t
J.A. Croson Co., Richmond v. (1989), 126
Japanese Americans, 76, 81, 82, 212
Jarvis, Howard, 116
Javits, Jacob, 85
Jefferson, Thomas, 3, 35, 49
Jeffersonian Republicans, 10, 39t, 253t
Jeffords, Jim, 201
Jews, European, 71
Jim Crow. *See* alliances, segregation (Jim
  Crow) era and transitions (1865–1978)
Johnson, Albert, 70
Johnson, Andrew, 25, 50, 51–52, 53
Johnson, James, 70
Johnson, James E., 138
Johnson, J. Bennett, 325n87
Johnson, Kimberley, 71, 73
Johnson, Lyndon Baines: and crime, 221;
  employment policies, 96, 99, 100, 101,
  103–7, 120; and immigration, 238; and
  segregation, 25, 86–88, 87; and voting
  rights, 171
Johnson, Miller v. (1995), 184, 186, 187
Johnson-Reed Immigration Act of 1924, 70,
  238
Johnston, Richard, 256, 263–65, 266, 268

Joint Center for Political and Economic Studies, 199
Joints Chiefs of Staff, 127
Jones, Albert, 14–15
Jones v. Alfred Mayer Co. (1968), 149–50
Jordan, Barbara, 174–75
judges. *See* courts and judges; *individual judges*
Julius Rosenwald Fund, 68t, 255t
juries, 66–67, 76–77, 307n14, 309n50
"just compensation," 37
Justice Department. *See* U.S. Justice Department

Kaiser Aluminum, 120
Kaiser Report, 145t, 149
Kansas-Nebraska Act of 1852, 46, 303n37
Karol, David, 298n61
Katzenbach, Nicholas, 120
Katzenbach, South Carolina v. (1966), 172
Katzenbach v. Morgan (1966), 172
Katznelson, Ira, 73, 75
"Keeping the Promise: Ending Racial Discrimination and Segregation in Federally Financed Housing" (Roisman), 323n67
Kemp, McCleskey v. (1987), 230, 233
Kendrick, Kim, 157–58
Kennedy, Anthony, 94, 185, 187
Kennedy, Edward, 129, 160, 189
Kennedy, John F., 85–86, 100, 145t, 171, 238
Kentucky, 77, 230, 296n51, 311n94, 325n86, 325n87
Kerner Commission Report, 149
Kerr, Peter, 217
Key, V.O., 264
Kinder, Donald R., 298n56
King, Desmond S., 305n78, 346n9
King Jr., Martin Luther: and alliance, color-blind, 9, 114, 123; assasination of, 149; background, 20, 84, 86; and employment, 95; and housing, 148; and morality, 11; Selma march, 171; and Wright, 4, 6
Kirwan Institute for the Study of Race and Ethnicity, 165
KKK (Ku Klux Klan), 52, 65, 66, 255t
Kleinberg, Otto, 75
Knights of Labor, 56

Korematsu v. U.S. (1944), 81
Kramer, Shelley v. (1948), 81, 147, 321n39
Krauthammer, Charles, 117t, 154t, 259t
Ku Klux Klan (KKK), 52, 65, 66, 255t
Ku Klux Klan Act (Civil Rights bill of 1871), 52
Kultznick, Fullilove v. (1980), 121–22
Kurzman, Lemon v. (1971), 334n16

labor: and alliances, segregation era, 73, 74–75, 80; and alliances, slavery era, 11; forced, 50, 51; immigrant, 39; and U.S. Supreme Court, 77, 80; and World Wars, 72, 79. *See also* employment; labor unions; U.S. Department of Labor
labor unions: African American, 72; and alliances, modern, 106, 116, 121–22, 127, 257, 259t, 261t; and alliances, segregation era, 56, 65, 68t, 105, 148, 254t; and crime, 224t, 260t; and employment, 98, 99, 104, 107, 117t, 118t, 120–21, 311n6; and federal government, 66, 107; and housing, 148, 155t; and identity categories, 208; and immigration, 236, 239, 246, 257, 260t; and voting rights, 178t. *See also specific unions*
Latin American Management Association, 131
Latino groups and leaders: and alliances, modern, 258; and alliance, race-conscious, 127; and employment, 120–21, 258; and housing, 139, 148, 258; and identity categories, 21, 208, 212; and immigration, 244, 248; and majority-minority districts, 169, 181, 182, 258; office holders, 170, 270t (*see also individual office holders*); and prison populations, 228; and Republicans, 181, 182; and U.S. Supreme Court, 76, 125; and voting rights, 174–75, 176, 190; and vouchers, 196–97, 199, 201, 202, 206. *See also individual leaders; specific groups*
Latinos (Hispanics): and alliance, color-blind, 269; and alliances, modern, 257; and census, 207; and crime, 235; and education, 12–13, 130, 269, 270–72t, 273t, 274t; and employment, 96–97, 98, 119, 125, 269, 270, 278t; and health, 13, 276–77; and housing/mortgages, 13, 137, 138–39,

Latinos (Hispanics) (*cont.*)
141–42, 143–44; housing/mortgage statistics, 144, 163, 276, 327n119; and identity categories, 210–11; and immigration, 237, 239, 245; income, 13, 272, 275–76; and majority-minority districts, 180, 181–82, 185, 186, 191, 257, 330n46; and minority businesses, 104, 115; prison populations, 277, 279t; and U.S. Supreme Court, 28–29, 125. *See also* Latino groups and leaders; Latino voters

Latino voters, 199, 201. *See also* voting rights

Laufman v. Oakley Building and Loan (1976), 323n56

Law Enforcement Assistance Administration (LEAA), 221

Lawyers' Committee for Civil Rights Under Law, 120, 122, 126, 129, 131, 175, 180, 186, 323n56

LBMC (Long Beach Mortgage Company), 327n119

LEAA (Law Enforcement Assistance Administration), 221

Leadership Conference on Civil Rights, 129, 138, 155t, 161, 248, 261t

League of United Latin American Citizens (LULAC), 190, 201–2, 242t

League of United Latin American Citizens (LULAC) v. Perry (2006), 190

League of Women Voters, 155t, 159

Lear, Tobias, 37

Lee, Chungmei, 333n9

Lemon v. Kurzman (1971), 334n16

Lewis, John, 85, 189

Lewis-Beck, Michael S., 318n147

liberalism: and African American voters, 82, 92; and alliances, modern, 14, 104, 109, 121, 236, 286; and alliance, race-conscious, 118t, 155t, 178t, 200t, 210t, 225t, 242t, 244t, 256, 260–62t; and alliances, segregation era, 25, 68t, 71, 73–74, 254t, 255t, 266; and alliances, slavery era, 36; and crime, 221, 225t, 226, 291; and Democrats, 82, 85, 109, 173, 248 (see also *specific issues and* U.S. Congress *this entry*); and employment, 73, 98, 99, 102, 103, 108, 120, 188t; and housing, 140, 141, 148, 150, 155t, 158,

160, 161; and identity categories, 208, 210t; and immigration, 70–71, 235, 238, 242, 244t; and majority-minority districts, 178t, 180, 182, 187; and morality, 122; and Republicans, 53, 85, 118t, 155t, 161, 179, 187, 200t, 201, 225t, 254t, 255t, 263 (see *also* U.S. Congress *this entry*); and U.S. Congress, 264, 265, 268; and U.S. Supreme Court, 80, 108, 150, 173, 180, 297n55; and voting rights, 173, 179, 180, 187; and vouchers, 199–200t

Libertarian Party, 212, 242t, 262t

Liberty Party, 41t, 253t

Lieberman, Joseph, 201

Lieberman, Robert, 74

Limbaugh, Rush, 117t, 259t

Lincoln, Abraham, 3, 11, 47, 49–51, 52, 304n55

"Lincoln Birthday Call" (Villard), 69

Lincoln Republicans, 255

Linmark Associates v. Township of Willingboro (1977), 324n71

literacy tests, 77

The Litigation State: Public Regulation and Private Lawsuits in the U.S. (Farhang), 311n91

Lodge, Henry Cabot, 70

Lodge, Rogers v. (1982), 179–80

Long, Russell B., 220, 325n87

Long Beach Mortgage Company (LBMC), 327n119

Louisiana, 166, 172, 183t, 184–85, 296n51, 304n55, 325nn86,87, 330n46

Louisville, New Orleans, and Texas Railway Co. v. Mississippi (1890), 296n51

Lowndes, Joseph L., 346n31

Lublin, David, 181, 184

LULAC (League of United Latin American Citizens), 190, 201–2, 242t

lynching: and alliances, segregation era, 67, 71; anti-lynching legislation, 14, 26, 64, 69–72, 80, 81; and political parties, 64, 80, 81, 83

Madison, James, 36

majority-minority districts: and alliance, color-blind, 187, 190, 191, 262; and alliances, modern, 30, 168–69, 186–88, 191, 257, 258, 262; and alliance, race-conscious, 11, 186–88, 190, 191, 261t, 283; and alliances, segregation era, 169; and conservatives, 177, 179, 184, 188, 189; and Democrats, 258; and Latino groups, 258; and Latinos, 180, 181–82, 185, 186, 191, 257, 330n46; and nonwhites, 283, 290; state data, 330n46; and U.S. Supreme Court, 173, 177t, 179–89, 191, 290; and Voting Rights Acts (1965, 1975, 2006), 170–79, 189–90

MALDEF (Mexican American Legal Defense and Educational Fund), 127, 129, 178t, 200, 201, 210t, 212–13, 233, 235, 242t, 343n112

Manhattan Institute, 138, 154t, 209t

manifest destiny, 38

manufacturers/industrialists, 39t, 40, 41t, 72, 97, 254t. See also business

March on Washington (1963), 86, 96, 98, 114

Marshall, Thurgood, 78, 124, 324n71

Martin, James G., 180

Martin v. Texas (1906), 309n50

Maryland, 139, 148, 183t, 185, 330n46. See also individual Marylanders

Maryland Legislative Black Caucus, 126

Massachusetts, 36, 55, 63, 216. See also individual Bay Staters

Massey, Douglas, 97, 143, 150, 312n14

Mathias, Charles, 179

MBEs (50 percent minority ownership), 119–20

McCain, John, 132–33, 134, 166

McCarty, Nolan, 256, 260, 265–68

McCleskey v. Kemp (1987), 230, 233

McGovern, George, 109, 114

media: and alliances, modern, 259t, 261t; and crime, 225t; and employment, 117t, 118t; and housing, 154t, 155t; and identity categories, 210t; and voting rights, 178t, 189; and vouchers, 200t

Medicaid, 246, 344n127

Meese III, Edwin, 123, 316n101

Memphis, Tenessee, 139

Mendelberg, Tali, 298n60

merchants, 41t

Metro Broadcasting, Inc. v. FCC (1990), 131

Metropolitan Housing Development Corporation, Arlington Heights v. (1977), 152, 158

Metropolitan Life Insurance Park Merced Apartments, Trafficante v. (1972), 322n56

Mexican American/Hispanic Contractors, 122

Mexican American Legal Defense and Educational Fund (MALDEF), 127, 129, 178t, 200, 201, 210t, 212–13, 233, 235, 242t, 343n112

Mexican Americans, 187–88, 270

Mexican-American War, 44, 47

Mexicans, 66

Mexico, 38, 239, 245, 302n29

Michigan, 130, 147, 148, 201, 311n5

Midwestern Indemnity, Dunn v. (1980), 323n56

midwestern states, 303n31

migrations to north, 72

military. See armed services and leadership

Military Reconstruction Act of 1867, 51

Miller, Clarence, 220

Miller, William, 239

Miller v. Johnson (1995), 184, 186, 187

minorities, 207, 212. See also specific minorities

Minority Business Enterprise LDF, 126, 131

Minority Contractors Assistance Project, 122

Minority Media and Telecommunications Council, 131

minority-owned small businesses: and alliance, race-conscious, 107, 261t; amicus briefs, 122; federal funding of, 114–15, 119–20; and Latinos, 104, 115; and modern political parties, 120; and Obama, 165; and Republicans, 110, 114; and vouchers, 200t

Miranda decision, 221–22

Mississippi, 48, 51, 52–53, 57–58, 59, 172, 296n51, 325n86, 330n46, 333n15

Mississippi, Louisville, New Orleans, and Texas Railway Co. v. (1890), 296n51

Missouri, 49, 82, 148

Missouri controversy (1820), 41, 42, 43–44, 301n25, 302n28

Mitchell, Arthur W., 75, 296n39. See also Mitchell v. United States et al.

Mitchell, Clarence, 106, 119

Mitchell, Parren, 119–20

Mitchell v. United States et al. (1941), 14–16, 18, 20, 22, 24, 26–28, 78, 81. *See also* Mitchell, Arthur W.

mixed race (multiracialism), 134, 204–5, 207, 209t, 211–14, 337n78. *See also* identity categories

Mobile v. Bolden (1980), 175, 176

moderates, 73, 76, 84

modern era. *See* alliances, modern (race-conscious) era (1978–2008)

Moe, Terry, 196, 197

Mongolians, 54. *See also* Chinese immigration

morality: and alliances, modern, 11–12, 112, 158, 218, 283, 284; and alliances, slavery era, 40–41; and Civil Rights Act of 1964, 87–88, 101; and consequences, 281, 283, 285, 288; and conservatism, 23, 221, 248, 267, 269, 283, 284; and Reagan, 122–23, 267

"A More Perfect Union" (Obama), 6–7

Morgan, John F., 54

Morgan, Katzenbach v. (1966), 172

Morgan, Robert, 325n87

Morgan v. Virginia (1946), 81

mortgages: and alliances, modern, 159; and alliances, segregation era, 144, 146, 147; and conservatism, 140–41, 165; and Democrats, 161–62, 166; and discrimination, 158; federal funding, 74, 160 (see *also* Fannie Mae; Freddie Mac); and NAACP, 320n14; and Republicans, 164–65; sub-prime, 138–41, 144, 162, 163, 165, 167, 276, 283, 327n119. *See also specific legislation*

Mott Foundation, 155t

Mountain States Legal Foundation, 126

Mullainathan, Sendhiil, 312n14

multilingual ballots, 189, 190

multiracialism (mixed race), 134, 204–5, 207–8, 209t, 211–14, 337n78. *See also* identity categories

Murakawa, Naomi, 219–20, 228–29

Murphy, Frank, 80–81

NAACP (National Association for the Advancement of Colored People): and alliance, race-conscious, 129, 261t; and alliances, segregation era, 24, 68, 69, 76, 77, 81, 148, 255t; and anti-lynching bills, 14; and census categories, 210t; and crime, 225t, 232, 233; and education, 78; and employment, 75, 85, 99, 103, 118t, 120, 122, 125, 126, 129, 131; and housing/mortgages, 139, 148, 155t, 159, 320n14, 324n71, 327n119; and immigration, 70, 238, 242t, 343n112; and majority-minority districts, 185, 186; and P. Mitchell, 119; and political parties, 24, 82, 106; and voting rights, 171, 178t, 180; and vouchers, 196, 200t, 201–2

Nadeau, Richard, 318n147

NAFTA (North American Free Trade Agreement), 245

NAM (National Association of Manufacturers), 124, 232, 242t, 260t, 262t

National Alliance of Businessmen, 104

National Association of Insurance Commissioners, 154t, 259t

National Association of Manufacturers (NAM), 124, 232, 242t, 260t, 262t

National Association of Mortgage Brokers, 166

National Association of Realtors, 154t, 159, 259t

National Bar Association, 122, 131

National Black Caucus of State Legislators, 189

National Black Police Association, 232

National Catholic Conference for Interracial Justice, 155t

"National Civil Rights Mobilization" (conference), 99

National Coalition of Latino Clergy, 235

National Coalition of Minority Businesses, 131

National Committee Against Discrimination in Housing, 148, 150, 323n56

National Coordinating Committee for Trade Union Action and Democracy, 121

National Council for a Permanent FEPC, 99

National Council of Catholic Women, 178t

National Council of Churches, 118t, 178t, 225t

National Council of La Raza, 118t, 155t, 202, 210t, 212, 225t, 242t, 261t, 327n119, 343n112

National Council of Negro Women, 85

National Education Association (NEA), 155t, 193, 261t, 323n56

National Election bills of 1870 and 1872, 52

National Elections Act of 1890, 59

National Fair Housing Alliance, 155t, 157, 261t, 324n77

National Funeral Directors and Morticians Association, 178t

National Hispanic Caucus of State Legislators, 189

National Housing Act (1934), 145t, 146

National Immigration Forum, 242t, 262t, 343n112

National Labor Relations Act, 108

National Labor Relations Board, 101

National Latino Officers Association, 232

National League of Cities, 126

National Negro Congress, 72

National Organization for Women, 233

National Puerto Rican Coalition, 120

national security, 28, 88, 128, 240, 246, 247

National Union of Hospital and Health Care Employees, 120

National Urban League, 72, 75, 129, 233

National Women's Law Center, 129, 232

National Women's Rights Convention, 56

National Youth Administration, 73

Native American groups and leaders, 127, 209, 212, 254t

Native Americans (American Indians): and alliances, modern, 104, 115, 119; and alliances, segregation era, 51, 55, 57–58, 66; and alliances, slavery era, 35, 38, 39t; housing statistics, 157; office holders, 170; and U.S. Supreme Court, 66; and voting rights, 175. *See also individual Native Americans*

naturalization, 49, 66, 190, 238, 246–47

natural racial order, 38

natural rights, 40

Nazism, 78, 79

NEA (National Education Association), 155t, 193, 261t, 323n56

Negro Fellowship League, 68t, 69, 255t

"Negro Question," 73

neighborhoods, 157

Nevada, 130

New Century Foundation, 224t, 241t, 259t

New Deal, 64, 73–76, 80, 147, 219, 246, 285. *See also specific legislation*

New Dealers, 63, 73, 146, 255

New England, 55, 69. *See also specific states*

New Jersey, 183t, 185, 217, 324n71, 330n46

New Right, 346n31

"new slavery," 77

New York: and crime, 217; and employment, 99; employment policies, 125; and housing, 137–42, 148, 165–66, 167, 288, 289–90; and majority-minority districts, 183t, 185, 330n46; and voting rights, 172

New York Times: and alliance, race-conscious, 261t; and census, 210t; and crime, 217, 225t; and housing, 155t; and immigration, 55, 242t; and voting rights, 178t; and vouchers, 200t, 297n54

Niagara Movement, 69

9/11, 5–6, 248

Nixon, Richard: and alliance, race-conscious, 285; basics, 86; and employment, 102, 105, 106–7; and housing, 146t, 150–53; and quotas, 109; and voting rights, 173

Noel, Hans, 298n61

NOMINATE (data set), 265

nonwhites: and alliances, modern, 21, 191, 200t, 210t, 248, 261t, 290; and alliances, segregation era, 56–57, 63, 66, 68t, 76, 78, 255t; and anti-tax uprisings, 20; and crime, 217, 219, 220, 223, 225t, 227, 233, 277, 284; and Democratic Party, 179, 182, 185; and economic factors, 38–39; and education, 196, 198t, 199, 200–203, 205, 270, 274t, 343n9; and employment, 107, 118, 119, 126; and foundational systems, 40; and health, 276; and housing/ mortgages, 141–42, 144, 148, 155t, 156–58 *passim*, 161–62, 167, 283, 322n56, 327n119; and immigration, 66, 127, 237, 240, 246; and majority/minority districts, 168, 169, 173, 178t, 191, 283, 330n46; office holders, 269, 283; and Republican Party, 181; and results, 281, 282, 284, 289; and science,

nonwhites (*cont.*)
56–57; and U.S. Supreme Court, 76, 78, 126, 185–89; voters, 127, 185, 203. *See also* identity categories; *specific nonwhite identities*
Noonan, Peggy, 122
the North. *See* northern states
North American Free Trade Agreement (NAFTA), 245
North American Review (1878), 54
North Carolina, 180, 182, 183t, 184, 186, 230, 325n86, 330n46
northern states: and African Americans, 38, 72, 78, 263; and alliances, segregation era, 67, 254t; and alliances, slavery era, 39t, 40, 41t, 42, 43, 49, 253t, 254t, 303n31; and Democrats, 72, 266; and employment, 74; and housing, 77, 144; and immigration, 55, 70–71. *See also* free states; New England; *specific states*
Northwest Territories, 35, 41–42
Norton, Eleanor Holmes, 202
Nott, Josiah, 20
Novkov, Julie, 256–57
NumbersUSA, 241t, 260t
Nunn, Sam, 325n87

Oakley Building and Loan, Laufman v. (1976), 323n56
Obama, Barack: and alliances, modern, 7–8, 10, 31, 284, 285, 286; and alliance, race-conscious, 29, 132–36; and crime, 217, 234–36; and education, 332n4, 348n59; and employment, 94, 132–36; and favoritism toward blacks, 318n147; and housing, 137–43, 163–67; and identity categories, 203–4, 207, 213, 214; and immigration, 248; and majority-minority districts, 168; and polarization, 344n1; and vouchers, 193, 194; and Wright, 5–7, 134, 288. *See also specific books by Obama*
"Obama's Missed Landslide" (Lewis-Beck, Tien and Nadeau), 318n147
Obama's Race: The 2008 Election and the Dream of a Post-Racial America (Tesler and Sears), 344n1
O'Connor, Sandra Day, 131, 185, 186, 282

OFCC (U.S. Office of Federal Contract Compliance), 96, 101, 102–3, 105, 107, 111, 124, 205, 213
Office of . . . *See entries beginning U.S. Office of . . .*
Ohio, 105, 148, 202, 296n51. *See also individual Ohioans*
Ohio State chapter of the Federalist Society, 131
Oklahoma, 77, 325n87
OMB (U.S. Office of Management and Budget), 205–7, 211, 212
Omi, Michael, 298n56
Omnibus Anti-Drug Abuse Act of 1988, 229–30
omnibus crime bills, 221–22, 227
omnibus housing bills, 145t, 147–48
opportunity *versus* past discrimination, 105
Option One Mortgage of Irvine, 320n14
Oregon, 38–39
Orfield, Gary, 333n9
Orren, Karen, 296n50

Pacific Islanders, 66, 76, 115, 144, 157, 170, 206, 207, 209
Pacific Legal Foundation, 121–22, 126, 131, 315n93
Pager, Devah, 312n14
Painter, Sweatt v. (1950), 83
Palin, Sarah, 134
Parents Involved in Community Schools v. Seattle (2007), 194
Parents of Murdered Children, 224t
Parks, Rosa, 84
parochial schools, 195, 196, 202
The Party Decides: Presidential Nominations Before and After Reform (Cohen, Karol, Noel and Zaller), 298n61
The Passing of the Great Race (M. Grant), 66
Pataki, Haden v. (2006), 232
Paul, Rand, 311n94
Pena, Adarand Constructors v. (1995), 131
Pennsylvania, 4, 36–37, 48, 124, 148, 181, 183, 185, 330n46. *See also individual Pennsylvanians*
Pennsylvania, General Building Contractors Association v. (1982), 124

Pennsylvania, Prigg v. (1842), 48

People for the American Way, 129, 196, 200t, 201–2, 232, 242t, 261t

people of color. *See* nonwives; *specific identities*

Perez, Thomas, 166

Perry, League of United Latin American Citizens (LULAC) v. (2006), 190

"personal liberty" laws, 43, 48

Personal Responsibility and Work Opportunity Reconciliation Act (PRWORA), 246, 344n127

Petri, Thomas, 211

Phelps-Stokes Foundation, 68t, 255t

Phi Delta Kappa/Gallup pools, 199

Philadelphia Plan, 105, 106–8, 111

physical security, 83. *See also* violence

Pillsbury, Albert, 69

Pinckney, Charles Cotesworth, 36

Pioneer Fund, 65, 241t, 255t

Pittsburgh Courier (newspaper), 74

A Place for Us (APFU), 206

Plessy v. Ferguson (1896), 20–21, 60

Plyler v. Doe (1982), 245

polarization: and alliances, modern (race-conscious) era, 11–14, 31, 111–16, 142, 262, 291–92; background (1856–1876), 11, 49, 50, 256; breaking out of, 284–87; consequences of, 280–84; and crime, 291; and economic alignments, 266–67; and employment, 106, 112–16; and housing, 156–57, 158; and majority-minority districts, 169; and morality, 12; and Obama, 344n1; and political parties, 267, 280; and racism, 268; and U.S. Congress, 260; and voting rights, 178–79; and vouchers, 196

Polarized America (McCarty, Poole, and Rosenthal), 265–68

police forces, 6, 47, 64, 65, 125, 216, 221, 223, 227, 231, 234–35

policies, 7, 13–14, 284. *See also* alliances, racial policy; *specific policy areas and eras*

policies, results of, 13–14, 111, 177, 269–70, 281–84, 288–91

policy alliances. *See* alliances, racial policy

Polish American Congress, 121

political parties: and alliances, modern, 10–12, 223, 260–66, 298n61; and alliances, segregation era, 27, 50, 53, 80; and alliances, slavery era, 46, 47; and crime, 220, 227–28; and economic/racial alignments, 263; and employment, 110–11, 114; and enfranchisement, 55; and equality, 50, 55; and immigration, 248–49; and institutions, 17, 18; platforms, 63–64, 297n54 (see also Democratic Party platforms;Republican Party platforms); and polarization, 267, 280. *See also specific parties*

Politics, Markets, and America's Schools (Chubb and Moe), 196

poll taxes, 76, 79–80, 81, 83

Poole, Keith, 256, 260, 265–68

Posner, Mark, 182

"post-ethnic America," 207–8

poverty, 221, 247. *See also* classes, economic

Powell, Colin, 11, 127

Powell, John, 165

Powell, Lewis, 152, 282, 311n5

preference, racial. *See* alliance, race-conscious

presidents. *See* U.S. presidents

President's Commission on Law Enforcement and Administration of Justice (Johnson), 221

President's Committee on Civil Rights (Truman), 82

President's Committee on Equal Employment Opportunity (Kennedy), 100

President's Committee on Equal Opportunity Housing, 145t

President's Committee on Government Employment Policy (Eisenhower), 100

Prigg v. Pennsylvania (1842), 48

principles, 289

prison populations, 227, 228, 231, 233, 277, 279t, 284, 291, 339n36

"private actors," 57–58

private schools, 193

Proctor, Samuel DeWitt, 4

profiling, racial, 216–17, 232, 234, 235, 291

Progressive era, 76, 77

Progressive Party, 64, 75–76

Index

Project Race (Reclassify All Children Equally), 206, 260t
property rights, 37, 49
Proposition 13 (California), 116
protests, 85, 86, 88, 234. *See also* riots
PRWORA (Personal Responsibility and Work Opportunity Reconciliation Act), 246, 344n127
public housing, 145t, 147–48
public lands, 66
public opinion, alliances *versus*, 19–20
Public Works Administration, 73
Public Works Employment Act of 1977, 119–20, 121
Puerto Rican Legal Defense Fund, 232
Puerto Ricans, 66, 120, 188

Quakers, 35, 37, 41t, 254t
quotas: and alliances, modern, 106, 110, 156; and Democrats, 10, 88, 102, 106, 109–10, 114–16, 120, 129, 131, 159, 220; and education, 84, 152, 282; and employment, 103, 111, 283; and housing, 137, 152, 153, 156, 159, 161, 162–63; and immigration, 66, 70, 86, 127, 238, 239; and Republicans, 10, 52, 102, 105–6, 109–10, 114–30 *passim*, 164, 177, 223, 285; results of, 111, 177; and U.S. Supreme Court, 94, 120–22, 126, 131, 282; and voting rights, 127, 177. *See also* busing, forced; "disparate impact"; set-aside employment

"*Race at Work: Realities of Race and Criminal Record in the New York City Jobs Market*" (Pager and Western), 312n14
The Race Card (Mendelberg), 298n60
race hierarchy. *See* racism
racial categories. *See* identity categories; *specific categories*
Racial Formation (Omi and Winant), 298n56
Racial Justice Act, 230, 231
"racial order/state," 17, 297n52, 298n57, 308n32
racial policy alliances. *See* alliances, racial policy
racial preference. *See* alliance, race-conscious
racial profiling, 216–17, 232, 234, 235, 291

racial steering, 157, 324nn71,77
racism, 12, 66, 75, 112, 256, 265–68, 284. *See also* alliance, segregation (Jim Crow), pro-; alliance, slavery, pro-; discrimination; reverse (inverse) discrimination (racism); slavery; white supremacy
Racketeer Influenced and Corrupt Organizations Act (1996), 246
Radical Republicans, 51, 52, 53, 71
Raft-Ellender-Wagner Housing Act (1949), 145t
Rainbow Coalition/PUSH Coalition, 166
Raines, Franklin, 212
Randolph, A. Philip, 72, 75, 79, 86
Rangel, Charles, 217–18, 229
Ray, Joseph, 147
Reagan, Ronald: and alliance, color-blind, 23, 116, 123; and alliance, race-conscious, 285; and crime, 223–28, 229; and diversity, 280; effect of, 122–27; and housing/mortgages, 141, 157, 159–61; Obama on, 6; and polarization, 267; and U.S. Supreme Court, 185; and voting rights, 176, 179, 180; and vouchers, 195
real estate transactions, 81, 83
"Rebuilding the Reagan Coalition" (Meese), 316n101
recommendations for the future, 13–14, 29, 31, 284–92
Reconstruction, 25, 51–53, 57, 59, 67, 76, 87, 88–89, 256, 304nn55,84
Rector, Ricky Ray, 231
redlining, community, 140, 146, 159, 162, 323n56
Reed, David, 70
Reed, Thomas, 59
"Reed Rules" of 1890, 59
referenda, 20
Regester, White v. (1973), 174, 175, 176
Rehnquist, William, 124
religion: and alliances, segregation era, 65t, 68t, 69; and alliances, slavery era, 39t; and employment, 118t; and moral character, 122; and political parties, 80, 82, 84, 287–88; and voting rights, 178t; and vouchers, 200t. *See also* religious groups and leaders; *specific religions*

religious groups and leaders: and alliances, modern, 259t, 261t; and alliances, segregation era, 254t, 255t; and alliances, slavery era, 254t; and crime, 225t; and housing, 150, 155t; and immigration, 242t, 244–45, 246; and multiracialism, 208; and vouchers, 259t. *See also* Christians; *specific groups*

Reno, Shaw v. (1993), 186, 187

Reno v. Bossier Parish School Board (2000), 186

Republican Party (GOP): and African American voters, 101–2; and alliance, color-blind, 10, 114, 115, 127, 130, 255, 259t; and alliances, modern (race-conscious) era, 260–266, 257, 261t; and alliances, segregation era, 65, 68t, 72, 146, 254t; and alliances, slavery era, 41t, 46–47, 49, 51, 253t; and anti-lynching bill, 70; and armed forces, 83; and citizenship, 343n121; and Civil Rights Acts (1957, 1991), 85, 129; and conservatism, 319n7; and crime, 220, 222–23, 224t, 225t, 226, 227, 229, 231, 233, 239; and diversity, 280–81; and education, 53, 83, 84, 86, 114–15, 130; egalitarianism, 19th century, 50, 52, 53–54, 55, 58; and employment, 52, 98, 100, 101, 103–4, 109–10, 117t, 118t, 122–27, 125–26, 223; and housing, 146, 147, 151, 153, 154t, 155t, 159–62, 164–65; and identity categories, 208, 209t, 211, 212; and immigration, 55, 238, 239, 240, 241t, 242t, 244, 245, 247–48; and majority-minority districts, 169, 178–79, 181–85, 186, 188, 189, 190, 191, 257, 261t, 262; and Reconstruction, 52; and southern states, 72, 256, 263–64, 266; and voting rights, 59, 79, 171, 174, 175, 178t, 179, 180; and vouchers, 195, 197, 198t, 201, 202, 203. *See also* political parties; Republican Party platforms; U.S. Congress; *individual Republicans especially Presidents*

Republican Party platforms: 1850s, 303n37; 1900–1930 platforms, 64; 'forties, 79, 80, 81; 'fifties, 83, 84; 'sixties, 86, 87–88, 102, 195, 222, 239; 'seventies, 114, 115–16, 120, 151, 153, 174, 175, 195, 239; 'eighties, 115, 153, 195, 196, 240, 281; 'nineties,

162, 226, 245; 2000–2008 platforms, 190, 202, 247

restrictive covenants, 77

results of policies, 13–14, 111, 177, 269–70, 281–84, 288–91

reverse (inverse) discrimination (racism), 8, 88, 102, 110, 125, 286. *See also* alliance, race-conscious

reverse redlining, 166

Reynolds, William Bradford, 176

Rhode Island, 36–37

Ricci, Frank, 93–94, 288, 289

Ricci v. DeStefano (2009), 93–94, 130, 132, 135, 136

Richmond v. J.A. Croson Co. (1989), 126

rights. *See* citizenship; civil rights; *specific rights*

riots, 67, 69, 101. *See also* protests

Rogers v. Alabama (1904), 307n14, 309n50

Rogers v. Lodge (1982), 179–80

Roisman, Florence Wagman, 323n67

Romney, George, 150

Roosevelt (Fair Employment Practices Committee (FEPC)), 73, 79–80, 82, 86, 96, 98–99

Roosevelt, Franklin D. (FDR): and alliances, segregation era, 25, 73–74, 75–76, 80; and anti-lynching bills, 71; and economic classes, 63–64; and employment discrimination, 79, 96, 98–99; and immigration, 76; and A. Mitchell, 27; and U.S. Supreme Court, 80–81, 83, 297n55

Rosenthal, Howard, 256, 260, 265–68

Russell, Charles Edward, 69

Russell, Jim, 138, 319n7

Russell, Richard, 220

Rustin, Bayard, 84–85, 86

Samuels, Howard, 104–5

Sander, Richard, 294n30

Sanders, Lynn M., 298n56

Sandoval, Alexander v. (2001), 232

San Francisco, California, 105, 139

Sargent, Aaron, 54

SBA (Small Business Administration), 96, 104–5, 107, 115, 119

Scalia, Antonin, 185, 186, 190, 194, 232

scholars and academic institutions, 65, 68t, 73, 78, 255t, 292. *See also* science

schools. *See* education

school vouchers. *See* vouchers, school

Schooner Amistad, U.S. v. (1841), 48

Schuck, Peter, 108, 111, 207–8

Schuck, Peter H., 343n121

Schultz, George, 105, 106

Schumer, Charles, 229

Schwartzkopf, Norman, 128

science, 56, 65–67, 75–76, 157

Scottsboro cases, 77–78

Sears, David O., 344n1

Seattle, Parents Involved in Community Schools v. (2007), 194

Second Reconstruction, 4

Section 8 Housing Assistance Payments program, 146t, 151–52, 163, 323n67

To Secure These Rights (President's Committee on Civil Rights) (1947), 82

segregation: contemporary statistics, 270, 272; and crime, 221; and Democrats, 66, 266; and housing, 137, 143–50, 156, 157–58; and schools, 194, 195; and U.S. Supreme Court, 296nn42,51. *See also* alliances, segregation (Jim Crow) era and transitions (1865–1978); desegregation; "separate but equal"

SEIU, 261t

Senate. *See* U.S. Senate

sentences, prison, 228, 229

"separate but equal," 16, 50, 60, 78, 83, 107, 144, 147, 270

separatists, 72

set-aside employment, 119–22

Shafer, Byron, 256, 263–65, 266, 268

Shalikashvili, John, 128

sharecroppers, 52

Shaw, Lemuel, 60

Shaw v. Reno (1993), 186, 187

Shelley v. Kramer (1948), 81, 147, 321n39

Shreveport Times (newspaper), 100

Simmons-Harris, Zelman v. (2002), 202

Sims, Ronald, 137–38

Skowronek, Stephen, 296n50

Skrentny, John David, 102, 104

Slaughter, Groves v. (1841), 48

slavery, 35–37, 41, 43–44, 46, 47, 49, 150, 237–38. *See also* alliances, slavery era (1787–1865); slaves, fugitive

"Slavery and the Origins of the Fifth Amendment's Taking Clause" (Stohler), 299n8

slaves, fugitive, 36, 41, 43–44, 46, 48–49, 301nn25,28

slum clearance, 145t, 147–48

Small Business Administration (SBA), 96, 104–5, 107, 115, 119

Smith, Ed, 168

Smith, Rogers M., 343n121, 346n9

Smith v. Allwright (1944), 81

social groups, institutions *versus*, 17, 18

Social Security Act of 1935, 73, 74–75. *See also* SSI (Supplemental Security Income)

social structures, 22

Society for Promoting the Abolition of Slavery, 37

Society for Real Estate Appraisers, 159

Soros Foundation, 261t

Sotomayor, Sonia, 28–29, 93, 94, 135, 232, 291

Souter, David, 185–86, 282

the South. *See* southern states

South Africa, 299n1

South Carolina, 51, 172, 183t, 184, 309n50, 325n87, 330n46

South Carolina, Brownfield v. (1903), 309n50

South Carolina, Franklin v. (1910), 309n50

South Carolina v. Katzenbach (1966), 172

Southeastern Legal Foundation, 121, 126

Southern Christian Leadership Conference (SCLC), 84, 171

Southern Conference for Human Welfare, 68t, 255t

Southern Electoral Reform League, 68t, 255t

"Southern Manifesto" (1956), 83–84

southern states: African American office holders, 170; and alliances, modern, 264–65; and alliances, segregation era, 18, 65, 67, 73–76, 78–79, 220, 254t, 255t; and alliances, slavery era, 35–36, 37, 39t–40, 253t; and anti-lynching bills, 70, 71; and Civil Rights Acts (1957, 1964), 85; and courts, 48; and crime, 220; and Democrats, 72, 77, 81, 82, 106, 263, 266; and economics, 256,

264, 268; and education, 84, 195; and employment, 98, 99, 101; and housing, 159, 160; and immigration, 55, 244, 245, 247 (*see also* labor unions); and majority-minority districts, 173, 181, 182; and Republicans, 72, 87, 102, 106, 263–64, 266; secession of, 49; and U.S. House, 42, 45–46; and U.S. Supreme Court, 24, 80; and voting rights, 59, 171, 179, 189 (*see also* poll taxes); western states alliance, 54, 55; and white supremacy, 47, 303n31. *See also* Civil War; Confederate States of America; *individual southerners; specific states*
Spanish-American War, 76
Specter, Arlen, 179, 189, 201
square deal, 79
SSI (Supplemental Security Income), 246
Stanton, Elizabeth Cady, 56
State Board of Elections, Allen v. (1969), 173
states: and alliance, color-blind, 260t; and alliances, modern, 263; and alliances, segregation era, 60, 75, 81; and alliances, slavery era, 36, 37, 39t, 41t, 43, 47; and black Latino office holders, 270t; and census, 262t; and employment, 99–100; and identity categories, 209t, 210t; and immigration, 343n112, 344n127; and prison populations, 227. *See also* northern states; southern states; states' rights; *specific states*
states' rights, 53, 64, 70, 80, 83, 86, 111–12
States' Rights Democratic Party, 82
Steelworkers v. Weber (1972), 120
Stephens, Alexander, 39t, 49, 253t
Steward, Potter, 150
Stohler, Stephan, 299n8
Storey, Moorfield, 69, 77
Story, Joseph, 48
Stowe, Harriet Beecher, 41t, 254t
Strader v. Graham (1851), 48–49
"strange bedfellows," 30, 180, 182, 188, 235–36, 240–41
Strickland, Bartlett v. (2009), 186, 187
"strict scrutiny," 131
strikes, right to, 51
"strong basis in evidence" test, 94, 311n5
Student Nonviolent Coordinating Committee (SNCC), 85, 171

subprime mortgages. *See* mortgages: subprime
subsidized housing, 158
suffrage. *See* enfranchisement
Sugrue, Thomas, 147
Sumner, Charles, 53, 63, 69. *See also* Radical Republicans
Supplemental Security Income (SSI), 246
Support Our Law Enforcement and Safe Neighborhoods Act (2010), 234
Supreme Court. *See* U.S. Supreme Court
Swain, Carol, 181
Sweatt v. Painter (1950), 83

Talmadge, Herman, 220
Taney, Roger, 48–49
TANF (Temporary Assistance for Needy Families), 75, 246, 344n127
Tarrance v. Florida (1903), 309n50
taxes: anti-tax movement, 116; and housing, 158, 161, 162, 164t; poll, 76, 79–80, 81, 83; property, 116; and Republicans, 123, 281; and vouchers, 199
teacher's unions, 193, 194, 199, 200t. *See also specific unions*
Tea Party, 311n94
Teasley, Giles v. (1904), 60, 61
Teles, Stephen, 114
Temporary Assistance for Needy Families (TANF), 75, 246, 344n127
Tennessee, 59, 139, 172
Tesler, Michael, 344n1
Texas, 77, 172, 174, 183t, 190, 309n50, 325n86, 330n46. *See also individual Texans*
Texas, Carter v. (1900), 309n50
Texas, Martin v. (1906), 309n50
"They Gave Your Mortgage to a Less Qualified Minority" (Coulter), 141
think tanks, 117t, 154t, 155t, 198t, 209t, 224t, 241t, 242t, 259t, 261t, 262t
Thomas, Clarence, 123, 129, 186, 190, 194
Thornburg, Lacy, 180
Thornburg v. Gingles (1986), 180, 181, 182, 190
three-fifths clause, 36
"three strikes you're out," 231

Thurmond, Strom, 82, 85, 159–60, 161, 171–72, 219–20, 230, 234
Tidwell, Billy, 211
Tien, Charles, 318n147
"Tiger Woods" bill, 211
"'Tis Sixty Years Hence" (C. Adams, Jr.), 62
Title VII, 103–6, 108, 115, 121, 124, 126, 129, 145t, 149, 311n94, 325n84
To Secure These Rights (1947), 219
Townsend, Grovey v. (1935), 77
Township of Willingboro, Linmark Associates v. (1977), 324n71
Trafficante v. Metropolitan Life Insurance Park Merced Apartments (1972), 322n56
Transition, Era of, 50–61
transportation, interstate, 81, 86
Treaty of Guadalupe Hidalgo, 302n29
tribal lands, 66
Trinity United Church of Christ (Chicago), 4–5
Trotter, William Monroe, 69
Truckers Association, 122
Truman, Harry, 25, 81–83, 99, 219
Tucker, Thomas, 37
Tuskegee Institute, 14

UCC (United Church of Christ), 3, 4, 5, 200t
unemployment insurance, 73, 74–75
"unholy alliances," 181–82, 184
unions, labor. See labor unions
Union Theological Seminary, 4, 5
United Church of Christ (UCC), 3, 4, 5, 200t
United Electrical Workers, 121
United for a Fair Economy, 139
United States. See entries starting U.S. . . .; Federal government
United States, Bob Jones University v. (1983), 333n15
United States, Korematsu v. (1944), 81
United States et al., Mitchell v. (1941), 14–15, 18, 20, 22, 24, 26–28, 78, 81
United States v. Booker (2005), 233
United States v. Cruikshank (1876), 57
United States v. Schooner Amistad (1841), 48

United States v. Wong Kim Ark (1898), 76, 307n14
United Steelworkers of America, 108, 120, 121
unity, 3–4, 7, 10, 14, 22, 36, 37, 50, 292. See also diversity
Universal Negro Improvement Association, 72
University of California Board of Regents v. Bakke (1978), 10, 282
University of Michigan, 109, 128, 282
University of Texas Law School, 83
urban infrastructure, 23, 145t, 281
Urban Institute, 155t
Urban League, 85, 210t, 211, 255t
Urban Renewal Administration, 147–48
U.S. Chamber of Commerce, 108, 124, 126, 242t, 260t, 262t
U.S. Civil Rights Commission, 85, 86, 107, 145t, 163, 210
U.S. Civil Service Commission, 100
U.S. Commission on Interracial Cooperation, 68t, 71, 255t
U.S. Commission on Urban Housing, 145t, 149
U.S. Conference of Catholic Bishops, 202
U.S. Congress: and alliances, modern, 258, 260–68; and alliances, segregation era, 50, 57, 59, 65, 68t, 254t; and alliances, slavery era, 37, 41, 42–45, 48; background, 19th century, 51–55; and crime, 217, 221, 229–30; and economic alignments, 268; and employment, 120; and housing, 149; and identity categories, 209; and immigration, 54, 241, 243, 245, 246, 343n121; and lynching, 69; and polarization, 265–66; and southern states, 263, 264; and vouchers, 198t. See also individual office holders; individual representatives and senators; specific acts and branches; specific caucuses; specific legislation
U.S. Constitution: and alliances, modern, 256; and alliances, slavery era, 36, 46–47, 48; Article I, 36; Article IV, 41, 47; Fourth Amendment, 221; Tenth Amendment, 172; Thirteenth Amendment, 53, 57–58, 77, 150; Fourteenth Amendment, 51, 53, 56, 57–58, 76–77, 84, 175, 307n14 (see also

equal protection); Fifteenth Amendment, 52, 53, 56, 57, 59, 175; and voting rights, 175. *See also* U.S. Supreme Court

U.S. Department of Agriculture, 207

U.S. Department of Commerce, 207

U.S. Department of Defense, 207

U.S. Department of Education, 336n58

U.S. Department of Health and Human Services, 207

U.S. Department of Homeland Security, 247

U.S. Department of Housing and Urban Development (HUD): and alliance, race-conscious, 155t; and alliances, segregation era, 145t; failure of, 323n67; and housing/ mortgages, 137, 141, 157–58, 159, 327n119; and political parties, 150, 160, 161, 162; regulations, 322n50

U.S. Department of Justice (DOJ): alliances, modern, 163, 164t, 168, 175; and alliances, segregation era, 80–81, 82, 83, 85; and census, 205; and crime, 232, 233, 235; and Democrats, 83; and employment, 94, 124, 125, 126; and housing, 137, 149, 159, 160, 163–64; and identity categories, 207; and majority-minority districts, 173, 174, 181, 182, 184, 186, 187; Obama's, 96, 135, 142, 166; and Republicans, 150–51, 180; and voting rights, 175, 180

U.S. Department of Labor, 101, 105–6, 124, 207. *See also* U.S. Office of Federal Contract Compliance (OFCC); *individual Secretaries*

U.S. English (organization), 232

U.S. executive agencies, 118t. *See also specific agencies*

U.S. Government Accountability Office (GAO), 163

U.S. House of Representatives: African American office holders, 170; and alliances, modern, 265; and alliances, slavery era, 36, 42–45, 42f, 44f, 45f, 53, 301nn25,28, 302n29; and crime, 217, 229, 230, 231–32; and employment, 99, 119–20, 127; and housing, 159, 160–61, 325n84; and immigration, 55, 239, 243, 245, 247; and Reconstruction, 52; rules, 59, 303n31; and southern states, 263; voting behavior mea-

sures, 302n30; and voting rights, 171–72, 178, 179, 189; and vouchers, 201, 202. *See also individual representatives; specific legislation*

U.S. Office of Federal Contract Compliance (OFCC), 96, 101, 102–3, 105, 107, 111, 124, 205, 213

U.S. Office of Management and Budget (OMB), 205–7, 211, 212

U.S. Office of Minority Business Enterprise, 107, 109

U.S. presidents: and alliances, modern, 259t, 261t; and alliances, segregation era, 65, 254t; and alliances, slavery era, 37; and crime, 225t; and employment, 117t, 118t; and housing, 154t; and vouchers, 198t. *See also entries beginning* President's . . .; *individual presidents*

U.S. Senate: 1980s, 127; African American office holders, 170; and alliances, modern, 265; and alliances, segregation era, 82–83, 254t; and alliances, slavery era, 36; and Civil Rights Acts (1957, 1964), 85, 87; and crime, 217, 229, 230, 231–32; and housing, 149, 159–60, 161; and immigration, 55, 239, 243, 247, 248; and modern employment legislation, 120; policy disputes, 23; and slavery era, 43f, 301n28, 302n29; and three-fifths clauses, 36; and voting rights, 171–72, 178; and vouchers, 201, 202. *See also individual office holders; individual senators; specific legislation*

U.S. Supreme Court: and alliance, colorblind, 124, 126–27, 131, 166, 194, 258, 259t, 282, 290, 291–92; and alliances, modern, 19 (*see also specific issues this entry*); and alliance, race-conscious, 121, 282; and alliances, segregation era, 27, 65, 68t, 77, 78, 254t, 296n42, 296n51; and alliances, slavery era, 39t, 48, 253t; and crime, 224t, 230, 232, 233; and education, 78, 83–84, 195, 282, 333n15, 334n16; egalitarianism, 19th century, 54, 58; and employment, 107–10, 117t, 120–22, 126, 130–32, 289, 311n6; FDR's, 80–81, 83, 297n55; and housing, 145t, 147, 149–50, 152–53, 154t, 166, 324n71; and identity

U.S. Supreme Court (*cont.*)
  categories, 20–21; immigration cases, 343n112; and Interstate Commerce Act, 15, 18; and majority-minority districts, 173, 177t, 179–89, 184, 185–89, 191, 290; and quotas, 94, 120–22, 126, 131, 282; and Reagan, 124; and Scottsboro cases, 77–78; and voting rights, 60, 172, 174, 175, 190; and vouchers, 198t, 202; and wiretaps, 221. *See also* U.S. Constitution; *individual justices; specific cases*
The U.S. Supreme Court, State Action, and Civil Rights (Brandwein), 305n84
U.S. v. . . . See entries beginning United States v. . . .
Utah, 201

vagrancy, 51, 66
Valelly, Richard, 304n55
Vera, Bush v. (1996), 186, 187
Vermont, 35, 36
veterans, 146, 148
victims' rights, 224t, 226, 227, 230, 231, 260t
Village of Bellwood, Gladstone, Realtors, v. (1979), 324n71
Villard, Oswald Garrison, 69
Vincent, Roland, 116
violence, 52–53, 57–58; 1960s, 101; and alliances, segregation era, 76; and civil rights, 220; and housing, 144; *and Miranda*, 221. *See also* lynching; physical security
Violent Crime Control and Law Enforcement Act of 1994, 231
Virginia, 126, 172, 183t, 184, 195, 196, 330n46. *See also individual Virginians*
Virginia, Morgan v. (1946), 81
Voter Education Project, 171
voters, 20. *See also* African American voters; Latino voters; white voters
voting rights: and alliances, modern, 175, 176, 178t, 179, 180, 189–90; and alliances, segregation era, 169; and Civil Rights Act of 1964, 170–71; and conservatism, 170, 171, 173, 175, 176; and Democrats, 59, 84, 175, 178t, 181–85, 190; and identity categories, 205; and polarization, 178–79; and Republicans, 59, 79, 84, 86, 163, 174–81 *passim*,

190; and U.S. Congress, 171–72, 178; and U.S. Supreme Court, 60, 172, 174, 175, 179–81, 190. *See also* enfranchisement; majority-minority districts; *specific legislation*
Voting Rights Acts (1870, 1965), 9, 59, 85, 169, 170–79, 189–90, 232. *See also* majority-minority districts
vouchers, housing, 323n67. *See also* Section 8 Housing Assistance Payments program
vouchers, school: and alliance, color-blind, 197, 198, 203, 259t; and alliances, modern, 23, 196, 197–203, 207–14, 258; and alliance, race-conscious, 194, 197, 199, 200t, 203, 206, 262t; basics, 23, 31, 192–97, 284; and conservatives, 197, 198t, 201–2; and identity categories, 203–5, 213–14; and OMB, 205–7

Wade-Davis bill, 304n55
Wagner-Steagall/National Housing Act (1937), 145t, 147
Walker, Francis, 56–57
Wallace, George, 84, 102, 116
Walling, William English, 69
Walton Family Foundation, 201
Wards Cobe Packing Co. v. Atonio (1989), 126
Warley, Buchanan v. (1917), 77, 144, 307n14
War on Drugs, 223–24
Warren, Earl, 83, 173
Washington, Booker T., 14, 25, 26, 60–61, 72, 296n39
Washington, George, 37, 48
Washington Legal Foundation, 121, 125, 126, 131, 186, 188, 232, 233, 343n112
Washington Mutual, 327n119
Washington state, 130
Watergate scandal, 120
weapons, 221, 223, 230, 231
Weaver, Vesla, 213
Webb, James, 11
Weber, Steelworkers v. (1972), 120
welfare, social, 1, 16, 22, 122, 243, 245–46, 247, 263, 264
Welke, Barbara Y., 296n42
Wells, Ida B. (Wells-Barnett), 69
Wells Fargo, 139

Western, Bruce, 312n14

western states: and alliances, segregation era, 65, 67; and alliances, slavery era, 303n31; and housing segregation, 144; and immigration, 55, 56, 70, 245, 247; migrations to, 38, 72; southern states alliance, 54, 55. *See also specific states*

westward expansion, 38

Whigs, 10, 37, 39t, 41t, 46, 253t. *See also individual Whigs*

White Citizen Councils, 65, 255t

whites: and alliances, modern, 107; and alliances segregation era, 254t; and anger, 6–7; and census, 207; and drugs, 228, 233; and education, 272t, 273t; and employment, 117t, 120–21, 127; employment statistics, 96–98, 278t; and health, 276–77; and housing/mortages, 139, 142, 144, 154t, 295n35, 324n77, 327n119; and identity categories, 206, 212; income, 275t; poor, 66; prison populations, 279t. *See also* reverse (inverse) discrimination (racism); white supremacy; white voters; *individual whites*; *specific white groups*

white supremacy: and alliance, color-blind, 259t; and alliances, segregation era, 25, 38, 73, 75, 255t; and alliances, slavery era, 303n31; background, 9, 63; background, 19th century, 62; and businessmen, 56; and census, 205; and crime, 224t; and Democrats, 63; and egalitarianism, 40–41, 47, 50; and employment, 98, 117t; factors other than slavery era, 40; and immigration, 54, 237, 241t; and Andrew Johnson, 51, 52; and southern states, 47, 303n31; and U.S. Supreme Court, 77; and West-South alliance, 55, 56. *See also* alliance, segregation (Jim Crow), pro-; *individual white supremacists*; *specific groups*

white voters: and alliance, race-conscious, 114; and education, 130; and employment, 132; and housing, public, 148; and Obama, 133, 135–36; and Republicans, 102; southern, 263, 268; and taxes, property, 116; and voting rights, 66; and vouchers, 194, 197, 198, 199–200, 201, 203

White v. Regester (1973), 174, 175, 176

Wilkins, Roy, 85

Williams, Anthony, 196, 202

Williams, Kim, 206

Wilmot, David, 41t, 47, 253t

Wilson, Pete, 245

Wilson, Woodrow, 11, 66

Winant, Howard, 298n56

wiretaps, 221

Wisconsin, 196, 201

women, 56, 64, 96, 121, 224t, 230–31, 260t, 275t. *See also specific groups*

Women's Caucus of the United Steelworkers of America, 120

Women's Legal Defense Fund, 129

Wong Kim Ark, U.S. v. (1898), 76, 307n14

Woods, Tiger, 213

work ethic, 122. *See also* morality

working-class European immigrants, 39t

World's Fairs, 56

World Trade Center bombing (1993), 245

World War I, 26, 72

World War II, 77, 78–79, 82, 96, 97, 98

Wright Jr., Jerry (Jeremiah), 4–8, 107, 134, 288, 293n18

Wygant v. Jackson Board of Education (1986), 311n5

Young, Andrew, 189

Young, Whitney, 85

Zaller, John, 298n61

Zelman v. Simmons-Harris (2002), 202

Zinni, Anthony, 128

zoning, 152, 158, 322n56

Zuch v. Hussey (1975), 322n56

Princeton Studies in American Politics: Historical, International, and Comparative Perspectives

Still a House Divided: Race and Politics in Obama's America by Desmond S. King and Rogers M. Smith

The Litigation State: Public Regulations and Private Lawsuits in the United States by Sean Farhang

Reputation and Power: Organizational Image and Pharmaceutical Regulation at the FDA by Daniel Carpenter

Presidential Party Building: Dwight D. Eisenhower to George W. Bush by Daniel J. Galvin

Fighting for Democracy: Black Veterans and the Struggle against White Supremacy in the Postwar South by Christopher S. Parker

The Fifth Freedom: Jobs, Politics, and Civil Rights in the United States, 1941–1972 by Anthony Chen

Reforms at Risk: What Happens after Major Policy Changes Are Enacted by Eric Patashnik

The Rise of the Conservative Legal Movement: The Long Battle for Control of the Law by Steven M. Teles

Why Is There No Labor Party in the United States? by Robin Archer

Black and Blue: African Americans, the Labor Movement, and the Decline of the Democratic Party by Paul Frymer

Political Foundations of Judicial Supremacy: The Presidency, the Supreme Court, and Constitutional Leadership in U. S. History by Keith E. Whittington

The Transformation of American Politics: Activist Government and the Rise of Conservatism edited by Paul Pierson and Theda Skocpol

Disarmed: The Missing Movement for Gun Control in America by Kristin A. Goss

Filibuster: Obstruction and Lawmaking in the U.S. Senate by Gregory Wawro and Eric Schickler

Governing the American State: Congress and the New Federalism by Kimberley S. Johnson

What a Mighty Power We Can Be: African-American Fraternal Groups and the Struggle for Racial Equality by Theda Skocpol, Ariane Liazos, and Marshall Ganz

When Movements Matter: The Townsend Plan and the Rise of Social Security by Edwin Amenta

Shaping Race Policy: The United States in Comparative Perspective by Robert C. Lieberman